M Cole

OEDIPUS
MYTH AND COMPLEX

To
Janet MacKenzie Rioch

OEDIPUS
MYTH AND COMPLEX

A Review of Psychoanalytic Theory

By
PATRICK MULLAHY

Introduction
ERICH FROMM

HERMITAGE PRESS, INC.

NEW YORK

1948

COPYRIGHT 1948 BY PATRICK MULLAHY

FIRST EDITION

MANUFACTURED IN THE UNITED STATES OF AMERICA

INTRODUCTION

In this volume Patrick Mullahy approaches the familiar problem of the Oedipus complex in an unfamiliar way. For the first time, Sophocles' *Oedipus* trilogy is published together with the various psychoanalytic interpretations of the Oedipus myth in one volume.

That such an approach is new may seem surprising, since a thorough knowledge of the myth should be the premise for all interpretations. The reasons for the peculiar dissociation between the myth and the complex can be found in our general attitude toward myths.

In the last century knowledge of Greek mythology was essential to being an educated person. People studied it and admired it. They interpreted it in a variety of ways— historically, philosophically or esthetically but hardly anyone thought of the possibility that the myth could have any connection with oneself and one's life here and now. With an increasing tendency not to bother with things which were not "practical," the Greek myth was relegated to a marginal area of superfluous and useless information. Then came a revival of just one Greek myth—that of Oedipus—because of the use one could make of it in psychotherapy. Oedipus returned through a back door, as it were.

Freud, in studying the relationship of the child to his parents and observing intense attachment to the parents of the opposite sex and antagonism against the parent of the same sex, believed he had found the explanation for this puzzling phenomenon in the secret incestuous wishes of the child. The myth of the Greek hero who killed his father and married his mother without any awareness that he had committed patricide and was living in an incestuous relationship seemed to prove Freud's thesis that incestuous strivings are found in every child in a veiled and distorted manner; in such a way the secret code of the myth could be deciphered by a psychologist. Thus, he named the complex blended of incestuous attraction and hostile rivalry after the hero of the myth—Oedipus complex.

"Oedipus" became a household word familiar to everyone interested in psychology. But the familiarity of Oedipus' name did not necessarily include thorough knowledge of the Oedipus myth, and only a few take the trouble to read the trilogy of plays which is published in this volume.

This book is thoroughly functional in its approach by combining the text of the myth with a discussion of its meaning. It tempts the reader to venture into Greek mythology and thus enables him to arrive at a deeper—and perhaps different—understanding of the "Oedipus complex." By arousing the reader's interest in *one* myth the book may accomplish the even more important task of awakening the interest in symbolic language in general, which is the language both myth and dream have in common. This language is one of man's basic modes of expression and we must understand it if we want to understand ourselves.

In the nineteenth century myths were supposed to be at best artistically valuable fiction. The few men who proposed that myths contained philosophical and even historical truth were discounted as romantic dreamers. Quite in contrast to most cultures in the past, modern man believed myths and dreams to be meaningless products of man's imagination, which made no sense and did not deserve to be taken seriously. The reason for the contempt in which myths and dreams were held is the difficulty of understanding their language, the symbolic language in which sensory experiences are used to express inner experiences, in which the world of things becomes a symbol of the world of the mind. Symbolic language is the only common language of the human race, because all men share certain basic experiences and are capable of expressing them in a pictorial language which is not confined within the boundaries of any culture or tongue.

All great cultures of the past regarded symbolic language and hence myths and dreams as highly significant and as expressions of universal and individual experiences; the understanding of symbols became an art which had an important cultural function. But while we all continued to speak the language in our dreams, we forgot its meaning, much to the detriment of our insight into the past of the human race and into the depth of our own experiences.

But the intention and accomplishment of this volume goes far beyond the task outlined above. This volume will prove to be a real help to one who is interested in psychoanalysis. The student seeking enlightenment in the field of interpersonal relations is confronted with a bewildering picture. He finds Freudians, Jungians, Adlerians, Rankians and a number of other schools, each of whom claims to have the true gospel and who frequently denies that the rival schools have anything important to offer. Thus, the newcomer in the field either loses interest and respect for the science of man or wanders from one lecture to another remaining puzzled; or he becomes an addict to a cult and rationalizes his emotional satisfaction at having found a shrine as intellectual satisfaction at having found the truth. Many psychologists foster the public's quest for certainty and become the prisoners of their own creation. Rival intellectual bureaucracies are formed, each of them claiming to know all the answers. Their ambition has unfortunate results. If the leaders and their adherents want to form a school of their own, they must have a theory of their own. Hence, they must deny the validity of the rival's viewpoint, over-emphasize the originality of their own contribution, and cut out from their own system all points which can be traced back to the rival. In order to do this, they find it convenient to ignore other theories since real knowledge would stand in the way of quick dismissal. That they don't encourage their followers to study the rival theories except enough to reject the words specific of each system is only another consequence of this attitude.

Thus, theories become flags around which one rallies and emotes. Productive research is replaced by intellectual propaganda, and the very people who pride themselves on having freed themselves from religion and dogmatism have unwittingly landed in just another denomination. Undoubtedly the orthodox Freudian school has its share in this cultification of psychoanalysis. But this weakness is hardly an excuse for the self-appointed "successors," who exploit Freud's prestige and try to minimize the achievement of Freud and maximize the newness and importance of their own system. The credulous public oftens fails to distinguish between a genius, whose name will be remembered centuries from now as one of the pathfinders in the development of human insight, and those who add to, revise and correct his basic findings. Indeed, to stand on a giant's shoulders makes some people think they are taller than the giant and that they have reason for looking down on him.

However, these claims and counter-claims made by the various schools are not only detrimental to the development of a science of man; they are also ridiculous. What we know about man, his motivations and the laws which govern his behavior is pitifully little. Most of what we ought to know, we are ignorant of. We know much about the atom, we know less about the living cell, and we know even a great deal less about the mind. In fact, the preoccupation with the mastery of nature which has obsessed the Western World in the last centuries has made us forget the considerable knowledge of man's soul which, for instance, the Egyptians, the Indians, the Chinese had thousands of years back. It sometimes looks as if we had forgotten more than we discovered in the field of the science of man.

By emphasizing the necessity of knowledge of the various psychoanalytic theories, I do not intend to recommend eclecticism. The eclectic prides himself on selecting and uniting "the best features of every system." But the various pieces thus gathered have lost their real value; they were meaningful in a structure of thought; they are meaningless when removed from their context and brought together with other equally isolated pieces. While the scientist must confront his own thinking with that of others and permit himself to be impressed by it and to weigh the evidence for and against his own and others' theories, he must not confuse objectivity with eclecticism.

Patrick Mullahy presents the various systems in a spirit of objectivity, avoiding both eclecticism and cultism. This book is written with a thorough knowledge and a real respect for the specific contributions of various theories in the field of psychoanalysis. It does not and should not want to be a substitute for the original writings, which must be read by any serious student. But it is an excellent guide and commentary in a difficult field, which will greatly facilitate the understanding of psychoanalysis, counteract the spirit of partisanship and enhance the respect for the serious work that has been done by the various authors represented in this volume.

Mullahy reasons that in order to understand the interpretation of the Oedipus myth given by each psychoanalytic author, one has to know his whole system—of which the Oedipus interpretation is only a part. His book proves that he is right since he shows that the interpretation of the Oedipus myth is an integral part of the psychoanalytic systems he presents. Indeed, there is hardly any problem in psychoanalysis which is as characteristic of the whole system as the interpretation of myths.

The myth, like the dream, is the "regal road" to the understanding of unconscious processes, as Freud put it; psychoanalysis is "the" method of understanding these creations of man's unconscious. The test of any psychologist's understanding of unconscious processes lies in his ability to understand symbolic language. And the test of the validity of any psychoanalytic system is its ability to make sense of symbolic productions. For these reasons it seems to be a most fortunate idea to center the discussion of various psychoanalytic systems around the interpretation of one myth, because myth interpretation is the most strategic point from which the differences in psychoanalytic thinking can be made transparent.

The psychoanalytic treatment of myth was frequently handicapped by lack of sufficient knowledge of mythology, theology and philosophy. Many psychoanalysts have attempted to analyze myths and were convinced that their own science was so all-embracing that they need not have more than a superficial knowledge of myth, theology or philosophy in order to be able to interpret them. Quite in contrast to the laborious task of knowing the most intimate details of a patient's life history, they thought that a smattering knowledge of the cultural phenomena would do. Thus, their analysis generally lead them only to "prove" what they had expected to find anyway. But the specialists in the field of culture who raised this very objection to the psychoanalyst's work often did not do any better as far as their use of psychoanalytic theory was concerned. A few convenient concepts like Super-Ego, Ego and Id, libido, guilt feeling, etc., often serve to convey the impression of profound erudition in psychoanalytic theory. The innocent bystander is impressed in both instances. He admires the analyst's knowledge of mythology and the social scientist's knowledge of psychoanalysis. He fails to recognize, however, the amount of serious work and care which are necessary to understand either one of these fields.

The present volume is distinguished by the fact that its author is a man who is solidly grounded both in the knowledge of psychoanalysis and in the field of philosophy. It may be due to this training that he has acquired the remarkable objectivity towards various schools of psychoanalysis which he exhibits in this volume. For all these reasons it is to be hoped that his book may stimulate and deepen the interest in psychoanalysis and in symbolism and that it may further the real cooperation between representatives of both these fields.

—Erich Fromm

TABLE OF CONTENTS

2. THE THEORIES OF SIGMUND FREUD: LATER ADDITIONS AND MODIFICATIONS

3. THE THEORIES OF SIGMUND FREUD AND HIS DISCIPLES: ADDITIONAL FREUDIAN CONCEPTS

4. THE THEORIES OF SIGMUND FREUD AND HIS DISCIPLES: SYMBOLISM

5. THE THEORIES OF ALFRED ADLER

6. THE THEORIES OF C. G. JUNG

8. THE THEORIES OF KAREN HORNEY

9. THE THEORIES OF ERICH FROMM

PREFACE

Originally Dr. Erich Fromm and I planned to do a book entirely on the theme of the Oedipus myth and complex. Unfortunately, before he was able to do any work on the book, Dr. Fromm, due to pressure of other business, was obliged to withdraw. The publishers agreed that I should complete it. However, as the work progressed I discovered that a discussion confined solely to the theme of the Oedipus myth and complex would be too limited and would scarcely convey an adequate idea of the significance attached to it. Hence, I found myself including a good deal of other though related theory and explanatory matter. But a partial, somewhat fragmentary account of psychoanalytic theory seemed quite unsatisfactory. To the best of my knowledge there is no coherent, straightforward account of psychoanalysis, although there are dozens of expository works on the subject. Therefore, I decided to combine an exposition of the Oedipus complex and myth with a fairly comprehensive exposition of psychoanalytic theory. I have not attempted to build a systematic, logical structure out of psychoanalysis, if that is possible. But my hope is that a reader unfamiliar with the field will gain a general theoretical view of the subject as it has developed from the work of Freud to contemporary "neo-Freudians."

The question may arise as to why I include Adler, Jung, and Rank, who are no longer considered to belong to psychoanalysis, and who have rejected a good deal of it—most or all of it, some people would say. There are several reasons. The theories of Adler, Jung and Rank have in some sense developed out of psychoanalysis. All of these were originally "orthodox" psychoanalysts or at least were so considered. Their own work, especially that of Jung and Rank, is profoundly influenced and permeated with psychoanalytic concepts, even though many would consider their use of these concepts as an inferior distortion of real psychoanalysis.

While I hold no brief for any of these men, I do believe that they have made genuine and important contributions to the understanding of psychology, and in the last chapter I try to indicate why. Furthermore, it is instructive to compare the theories of the strict Freudians, "deviants," and "neo-Freudians." A comparison of the various writers included in this book should furnish a better basis for appraising the work of all of them.

I do not wish to give the impression that I believe the psychoanalysts included here are the only ones who have made, or are making, important contributions to psychoanalytic and psychological theory. Practical considerations of time and energy have played a part in limiting the number of writers included. But I do believe that they are the most important ones.

It is a pleasure to express my gratitude to Dr. Erich Fromm for writing the introduction to this book, for giving me access to his, as I write, yet unpublished manuscript on the Oedipus myth and complex, for reading the manuscript of this book and for making helpful suggestions concerning the inclusion of material in Chapter Four.

Dr. Harry Stack Sullivan's generosity in allowing me freely to use the material outlined in his lectures which has never been published, and in giving me liberty to avail myself of the material in his forthcoming paper, *Towards a Psychiatry of Peoples*, has rarely been equalled. I wish to express my thanks to Dr. Sullivan also for reading Chapter Ten and

making several helpful criticisms and suggestions. Finally
I am indebted to him as well as to the William Alanson White
Psychiatric Foundation, for permission to quote from *Conceptions of Modern Psychiatry* by Dr. Sullivan and from
articles appearing in *Psychiatry*.

I take pleasure, too, in expressing acknowledgment and
thanks to the following for permission to quote excerpts:

George Allen & Unwin, Ltd., London, from *The Interpreta-
by Alfred Adler.
tion of Dreams* by Sigmund Freud, and *The Education of Children*

Balliere, Tindall and Cox, London, from *Collected Papers
on Analytical Psychology* by C. G. Jung.

Cosmopolitan Book Corporation, New York, from *Problems
of Neurosis* by Alfred Adler.

Doubleday & Company, Inc., New York, from *Stendhal* by
Matthew Josephson.

Faber & Faber, Ltd., London, from *Social Interest: A Challenge To Mankind* by Alfred Adler.

Greenberg: Publisher, New York, from *Understanding Human
Nature* by Alfred Adler.

Grosset & Dunlap, New York, and the executors of Alfred
Adler, from *What Life Should Mean To You* by Alfred Adler.

Harcourt, Brace and Company, New York, and Routledge and
Kegan Paul, Ltd., London, from *Contributions to Analytical
Psychology, Psychological Types* and *Modern Man In Search Of
A Soul,* all by C. G. Jung, and *The Trauma of Birth* by Otto Rank.

Harper & Brothers, New York, and Dr. Ruth Nanda Anshen,
Editor of The Science Of Culture Series, from Volume V, *The
Family: Its Function And Its Destiny,* Monograph by Erich
Fromm: "The Oedipus Complex And The Oedipus Myth," to be
published in the autumn of 1948.

The Hogarth Press, Ltd. and The Institute of Psycho-
Analysis, London, and the executors of Sigmund Freud, from
Beyond The Pleasure Principle, Civilization And Its Discontents,
and *Collected Papers,* all by Sigmund Freud, and *Selected Papers
on Psychoanalysis* by Karl Abraham.

Alfred A. Knopf, Inc., New York, from *Moses And Monotheism* by Sigmund Freud, *Will Therapy and Truth and Reality, Modern Education* and *Art And Artist,* all by Otto Rank, and *The Structure And Meaning Of Psychoanalysis* by William Healy, Augusta F. Bronner and Anna Mae Bowers.

Macmillan & Company, Ltd., London, from *Three Essays On Sex And Marriage* by Edward Westermarck.

W. W. Norton & Company, Inc., New York, from *The Neurotic Personality Of Our Time, New Ways In Psychoanalysis,* and *Our Inner Conflicts* by Karen Horney, and *New Introductory Lectures On Psychoanalysis* by Sigmund Freud.

Oxford University Press, Inc., New York, from *The Republic Of Plato,* translated with notes by Francis MacDonald Cornford.

Rinehart & Company, Inc., New York, from *Escape From Freedom* and *Man For Himself* by Erich Fromm.

The Ronald Press Company, New York, from *Contemporary Schools Of Psychology* by Robert S. Woodworth.

Yale University Press, New Haven, from *Psychology And Religion* by C. G. Jung.

Mrs. A. A. Brill and Edmund Brill, executors of Dr. A. A. Brill, from *Totem And Taboo* by Sigmund Freud, translated by A. A. Brill.

Mme. Estelle Simon, widow of Otto Rank, from *Beyond Psychology* by Otto Rank.

The American Journal of Psychology, from "The Origin And Development Of Psychoanalysis" by Sigmund Freud, and "The Association Method" by C. G. Jung.

The Journal of Abnormal and Social Psychology, from "On Psychological Understanding" by C. G. Jung.

The Psychoanalytic Review, from "A Study In Symbolism" by David B. Barron.

Mrs. Carolyn Wilson Link, for the use of her poem, "To A Very Young War Widow," published in The Saturday Evening Post, March 11, 1944.

Mr. Nathan Halper of New York, from a forthcoming work on James Joyce's *Finnegans Wake.*

The Macmillan Company, New York and Cambridge University Press, London, for permission to reprint the complete and unabridged text of the three plays by Sophocles: *Oedipus Rex, Oedipus at Colonus* and *Antigone* in the Sir Richard Jebb translations.

Finally, I wish to express my gratitude to Mr. Arthur Ceppos, president of Hermitage Press, Inc., at whose suggestion this book was written, for his unfailing enthusiasm at every stage of the work. Likewise, Mr. Milton Goodman, vice president of Hermitage Press, has given freely of his time and energy in helping me with various matters concerning the production of this book. Mrs. Nancy Roodenburg, who read the entire manuscript and made several excellent suggestions, and Miss Marcia Manson of the staff of Hermitage Press have been of superb assistance concerning various practical details connected with the book. Dr. Harry Bone and Mr. Benjamin Wolstein also each read several chapters and contributed excellent criticisms.

—*Patrick Mullahy*

New York, N. Y.
July, 1948

A Review of Psychoanalytic Theory

"If the OEDIPUS REX *is capable of moving a modern reader or playgoer no less powerfully than it moved the contemporary Greeks, the only possible explanation is that the effect of the Greek tragedy does not depend upon the conflict between fate and human will, but upon the peculiar nature of the material by which this conflict is revealed. There must be a voice within us which is prepared to acknowledge the compelling power of fate in the Oedipus . . . And there actually is a motive in the story of King Oedipus which explains the verdict of this inner voice. His fate moves us only because it might have been our own, because the oracle laid upon us before our birth the very curse which rested upon him. It may be that we were all destined to direct our first sexual impulses toward our mothers, and our first impulses of hatred and resistance toward our fathers; our dreams convince us that we were. King Oedipus, who slew his father Laius and wedded his mother Jocasta, is nothing more or less than a wish-fulfillment—the fulfillment of the wish of our childhood. But we, more fortunate than he, in so far as we have not become psychoneurotics, have since our childhood succeeded in withdrawing our sexual impulses from our mothers, and in forgetting our jealousy of our fathers. We recoil from the person for whom this primitive wish of our childhood has been fulfilled with all the force of the repression which these wishes have undergone in our minds since childhood. As the poet brings the guilt of Oedipus to light by his investigation, he forces us to become aware of our own inner selves, in which the same impulses are still extant, even though they are suppressed . . . Like Oedipus, we live in ignorance of the desires that offend morality, the desires that nature has forced upon us and after their unveiling we may well prefer to avert our gaze from the scenes of our childhood."*[1]

—Freud

I. THE THEORIES OF SIGMUND FREUD
PRIMARY CONCEPTS

Freudian theory, like most theories which aim at some comprehensiveness, is an interrelated network of hypotheses and ideas. To be sure, one may find stray strands running through this network and others loosely woven. But this is mainly because Freudian theory, again quite like other theories, has a history; it has a beginning and a development.[2] It is not our purpose here to tell the story of that development. Nevertheless, we may observe that, as he continued his investigations through the years, Freud was obliged, as one might expect, to modify some of his theories, to add others, and to alter the significance of some of the parts in the light of the whole. Whatever may be the merits of Freudian theory in detail, this is in keeping with the history of science.

Any particular idea of Freud's, such as the Oedipus complex, cannot be properly understood when taken alone. It has to be understood in the light of his other ideas about human development. While it is not our intent to give a comprehensive, systematic account of all of Freudian theory, we think it is desirable first to introduce the reader who may be unfamiliar with Freud to his basic ideas. In order to do this we begin with the so-called pleasure principle.

1

THE PLEASURE PRINCIPLE

A basic assumption about human behavior underlies Freud's earlier writings, namely, that there is a fundamental purpose recognizable in the workings of the human psychological "apparatus." This purpose is the pursuit of pleasurable excitement and the avoidance of pain. Hence, according to Freud, the human organism is automatically regulated by a "pleasure-principle." Furthermore, pleasurable excitement causes or involves a decrease or obliteration of the amount of stimuli present in the psychic apparatus. Pain, on the other hand, increases the amount of stimuli. Freud admits he does not know in detail how pleasure is connected with the lowering of stimulation and pain with the heightening of it.[3] In general, pleasure and pain processes are related to "economic" or quantitative alterations of energy. Sexual activity, which, according to Freud, is the most intense experience of pleasurable excitement, leaves little doubt on this point. He expresses the pleasure principle in another way by saying that "any given process originates in an unpleasant state of tension and thereupon determines for itself such a path that its ultimate issue coincides with a relaxation of this tension."[4]

A state of tension beyond a certain point is painful, while the process of releasing tension carries with it a sense of pleasure, which in the case of sexual orgasm is poignantly intense. Thus, there is an attempt by the "psychic apparatus" to keep the quantity of excitement as low as possible or at least constant.[5]

Freud later modified his notion that pleasure and pain can be explained solely by a quantitative alteration of stimulus-tension, admitting a "qualitative peculiarity" which he could not explain.[6]

Pleasure and pain may be pictured as opposite poles of one of several polarities or contrasting relationships or paired opposites which are said to govern mental life.[7] These polarities include:

> Pleasure - Pain
> Subject (Ego) - Object (External World)
> Active - Passive

THE THEORY OF INSTINCTS

For Freud a theory of instincts plays a fundamental role. It is, he says, a basal concept, admittedly obscure and conventional. The concept of instinct may be ascertained partly from the side of physiology. Physiology "has given us the concept of *stimuli* and the scheme of the reflex arc, according to which a stimulus applied *from the outer world* to living tissue (nervous substance) is discharged by action *towards the outer world*. The action answers the purpose of withdrawing the substance affected from the operation of the stimulus, removing it out of range of the stimulus."[8] Thus, a light striking upon the eye acts as such a stimulus effecting in a moment a characteristic response. This is an external stimulus. But there are other stimuli which come from within the organism. The internal stimulus is in several vital respects quite different. For one thing it never acts as a momentary impact but as a *constant force*. And it is *inescapable*. One can flee from the light but one cannot flee, for example, from the internal stimulus known to the mind as the pangs of hunger. The internal stimulus is said to be instinctual. An instinct is pictured as a certain sum or quantity of energy forcing its way in a certain direction. From a biological point of view an "instinct" appears to Freud "as a borderland concept between the mental and the physical, being both the mental representative of the stimuli emanating from within the organism and penetrating to the mind, and at the same time a measure of the demand made upon the energy of the latter in consequence of its connection with the body."[9] Thus the sex instinct's mental representative in an adult appears in the form of a certain quality of feeling, recognized as sexual excitement, emanating from the genital zone. At the same time the intensity of the feeling or excitement may be said to be an indication ("a measure") of the effort required by the mind (the psyche) to relieve the excitement by appropriate sexual activity, apparently on the principle that the greater the instinctual stimulus, as manifested in feeling, the greater will be the energy required to relieve it.

The task of the nervous system, Freud suggests, is to master stimuli. Reflex mechanisms can take care of external stimuli such as light. But internal stimuli cannot, he says, be taken care of in this way. For "higher" demands are made upon the nervous system, compelling it to perform complicated and interdependent activities which effect such changes in the outer world as enable it to offer satisfactions to the internal source of stimulation. Consider, for example, the enormously complicated activities involved in procuring, preparing, and consuming food in order to satisfy the demands of hunger. Above all, internal stimuli oblige the nervous system to renounce its "ideal intention" of warding off stimuli. Internal stimulation is incessant.

A stimulus of internal orgin defines *need*. The pangs of hunger, under ordinary circumstances, manifest the need for food. That which does away with the need is *satisfaction*. A glass of water usually satisfies thirst.

We can say that an instinct is characterized by having (1) a *source* of excitation within the body, (2) an *aim*, the removal of that excitation, and (3) an *object*, the means by which the achievement of satisfaction of the aim is accomplished.

Satisfaction of the aim can often be achieved in the subject's own body by some kind of somatic modification, but usually an external object is introduced in which and by which the instinct achieves its (external) aim.[10] The sexual aims of childhood, for instance, particularly at a certain period, can be achieved "in their own body." In adult life, of course, an external object, to use Freud's language, is normally introduced. Hence, the object of a (sexual) instinct is the most variable thing about it, and this object is originally not connected with it.

An instinct becomes related to an object when the latter is peculiarly fitted to provide satisfaction. A very close attachment of the instinct to its object is called a *fixation*. Fixations occur in the experiences of infantile sexuality, in the "component-tendencies" (like sadism and masochism), at one of the somatic zones, and the objects of childhood. One sometimes learns of a boy who is so attached to his mother that he cannot bear to be separated from her for any length of time. In popular language he is a "mamma's boy." In Freudian language, his sexual instinct has been fixated on the mother. But the object may be changed any number of times, and when this happens *displacement* is said to occur.

An instinct may be inhibited *in respect to the aim*. A certain advance toward satisfaction occurs and then an inhibition or deflection of the aim occurs. The instinct is partially satisfied but "aim-inhibited." Freud thinks that affection is of such a kind. The source of affection lies in sexual needs but full satisfaction is renounced.

In love (and many other) relationships one partner often assumes an active role while the other remains passive. Such behavior of the partners manifests a contrast or antithesis. In other words, the sexual aim of the partners is contrasted in the activity of the one and the passivity of the other. Instinctual aims are said to be *active* or *passive*. The antithesis lies in loving - being loved. Another form which active-passive aims take occurs in gazing - exhibiting. Some people ("voyeurs") are said to derive sexual satisfaction from gazing or looking at the body of another, particularly the genitals. Others ("exhibitionists") gain pleasure from being gazed at.

In general when one makes another person or his body the object of an action calculated to satisfy a sexual aim, one's aim is said to be active. And when oneself or one's body becomes the object of the action of another (the active subject), one's aim is said to be passive. Active and passive roles can of course be exchanged.

An instinct may, among other things, undergo *sublimation* and *repression*. Sublimation is a process in which the aim of direct sexual gratification is abandoned. A new aim (nevertheless related to the original one) is substituted, and the object is changed. Energy is diverted from its sexual goal and directed to other, usually social, ends. Thus, the energy that might be exerted in direct sexual gratification may be diverted to the struggle for the realization of social aims and ideals.

(The subject of repression will be discussed in connection with the theory of the unconscious.)

As we shall see, Freud does not deny that society plays a most important role in moulding human behavior, but he assigns to it a *primarily suppressive* function.[11]

Curiously enough, he says that instincts are "mythological"; yet throughout he tends to ignore the fact. For explanatory purposes he seems to find such concepts necessary.

THE EGO

At this stage in our discussion we shall mention two kinds of instincts which Freud in the course of his investigations came to distinguish: *ego instincts* and *sexual instincts*. That part of the personality which is primarily concerned with self-preservation is represented by the ego. Impulses toward self-preservation are expressions of ego instincts. The ego refers to that aspect of the personality which objects to or struggles against any behavior which would threaten its existence. For that reason it interposes objections to the satisfaction of sexual desire when such a process of satisfaction threatens or seems to threaten self-preservation. Otherwise it tries to remain in harmony with and accommodate itself to our sexual organization. The ego controls consciousness. It also controls motor innervation and therefore the actualization of psychic impulses. Thus, if a person has an impulse to engage in sexual activity, the ego, if threatened or if it feels threatened, will disapprove and, by preventing the necessary motor innervation, inhibit the impulse.[12] In certain circumstances conflict "within" the personality may arise. On some occasions, or in certain other circumstances, sublimation, the process of diverting sexual energy to non-sexual or social achievement, occurs.

The ego appears as a gradual development both in the history of the individual and the race. At first the infant is not able to make any distinction between himself and the rest of the world. "Originally the ego includes everything, later it detaches from itself the external world. The ego-feeling we are aware of now [as adults] is thus only a shrunken vestige of a far more extensive feeling—a feeling which embraced the universe and expressed an inseparable connection of the ego with the external world."[13] Gradually, because of various exigencies, the infant does learn the distinction. A discrepancy between various kinds of experience is felt. Certain sources of excitation which he will later recognize as coming from his own body can be experienced at any time; others, such as the mother's breast, as he will eventually learn, become temporarily cut off and reappear after he cries. Thus, the distinction between "object" and ego is gradually, very gradually, borne upon him. The unqualified drive of the pleasure-seeking infant becomes rebuffed.

Pain and unpleasant sensation by degrees force recognition of an "outside," of an external world, split off from the ego. The infant gradually learns methods of discrimination, perception, and manipulation so as to protect himself from painful sensation or its threat. In this way the "reality-principle," which normally controls further development, in addition to the pleasure principle, forces its recognition on the developing ego.

THE LIBIDO

The *libido*, which is analogous to hunger, as Freud once defined it, is a force of variable quantity which measures processes and transformations in the sexual life.[14] Libido, as Freud at one time used the term, is synonymous with sexuality or, as he put it, properly reserved for the instinctual forces of the sexual life.[15] Sexuality, however, does not mean only adult genital sexuality—the desire for and the pleasure in "normal" sexual intercourse. Sexuality includes that, but, as we shall see, it includes much more. In general, the libido is a pleasure-striving force of a certain qualitative character.

THE EVOLUTION OF THE EGO

Both the ego and libido are heritages from a long past, that is, from the evolution of the human race. Necessity, the struggle for existence, has to some extent forced mankind to be reasonable, to exert self-denial on its impulses for the sake of self-preservation. Thoughtless, impulsive action can be fatal; or lack of foresight may bring irretrievable loss.

But the sexual instincts and the instincts of self-preservation, the ego instincts, do not behave similarly when confronted with the necessities of actuality. The ego instincts learn to adapt themselves to the requirements of necessity, and to arrange their development as the imperatives of existence, of fact, demand. The sex instincts are less tractable and educable. At the outset they do not suffer from the need of an object. They gratify themselves autoerotically by way of one's own body. Hence, they tend to lack the discipline which comes, sometimes, from denial. In most people, Freud says, the sex instincts remain throughout life obstinate and inaccessible to the influence of reason.

THE EVOLUTION OF THE REALITY PRINCIPLE

The ego instincts also at first strive for pleasure, but necessity soon teaches them to qualify the pleasure principle. The task of avoiding pain becomes almost as important as that of gaining pleasure. The ego learns that direct gratification is unavoidably withheld, that pleasure must be postponed, and that always some pain must be borne and certain sources of pleasure entirely abandoned. While the ego still remains fundamentally addicted to the pursuit of pleasure, it learns to postpone pleasure and to take the facts of life, the requirements of existence, into account. (Work is said to be of the utmost importance in binding a person more securely to reality.)[16] In order to help protect itself, the ego denies the existence of unconscious strivings and represses them.

THE THEORY OF REPRESSION

According to Freud, repression is the foundation on which the whole structure of psychoanalysis rests. The essence of repression, he says, "lies simply in the function of rejecting and keeping something out of consciousness."[17] By and large its purpose is the avoidance of pain. Repression is a continuous, unremitting process, unless and until it is "abrogated" or abandoned by the self. Hence, repression involves a constant expenditure of energy, and there is a great saving of such energy, under certain circumstances, if it can be abandoned. Repression has to be a continuous process because there is something striving, pressing toward, conscious awareness and/or overt realization. Its function is to exclude painful and unpleasant material from consciousness and from motor expression. One may picture repression as a state of dynamic equilibrium, which may not infrequently be upset.[18]

Repression arises from a conflict of opposing wishes and desires. Certain experiences are of such a character that they contain such conflicting desires. Repression eventuates from the conflict. Conflict occurs when certain wishes and desires, notably sexual ones, or their implications for conduct, are in sharp opposition to the ethical, aesthetic and personal values ("pretensions," in Freud's language) of the personality and cannot be reconciled. In such situations, as in the case of a hysterical patient, there "had been a short conflict, and the end of this inner struggle was the repression of the idea which presented itself to consciousness as the bearer of this irreconcilable wish. This was, then, repressed from consciousness and forgotten. The incompatibility of the idea in question with the 'ego' of the patient was the motive of the repression, the ethical and other pretensions of the individual were the repressing forces. The presence of the incompatible wish, or the duration of the conflict, has given rise to a high degree of mental pain; this pain was avoided by the repression. This latter process is evidently in such a case a desire for the protection of the personality."

The following example gives a vivid idea of the process of repression and of the possible consequences. "It is that of a young lady, who was deeply attached to her father, who had died a short time before, and in whose care she had shared . . . When her older sister married, the girl grew to feel a peculiar sympathy for her new brother-in-law, which easily passed with her for family tenderness. This sister soon fell ill and died, while the patient and her mother were away. The absent ones were hastily recalled, without being told fully of the painful situation. As the girl stood by the bedside of her dead sister, for one short moment there surged up in her mind an idea, which might be framed in these words: 'Now he is free and can marry me.' We may be sure that this idea, which betrayed to her consciousness her intense love for her brother-in-law, of which she had not been conscious, was the next moment consigned to repression by her revolted feelings. The girl fell ill with severe hysterical symptoms, and, when I came to treat the case, it appeared that she had entirely forgotten that scene at her sister's bedside and the unnatural, egoistic desire which had arisen in her. She remembered it during the treatment, reproduced the pathogenic moment with every sign of intense emotional excitement, and was cured by this treatment."[19]

The detailed explanation of repression is complicated and has not been clearly worked out.[20] Statements concerning repression are often conflicting. Although instincts are sometimes said to be repressed, this is a loose manner of speaking. Instincts are not objects of consciousness; only the ideas and feelings which represent the instincts are. Hence, it is an "instinct-presentation" that gets repressed. An instinct-presentation is composed of two elements, the one ideational, the other affective. In other words, an instinct presentation is composed of an idea or group of ideas which are "cathected" (charged) with a definite amount of energy. Thus, in consciousness a libidinal instinct-presentation seems to consist of certain feelings, feeling tones, and ideas associated with them.

Repression consists essentially in preventing the ideational presentation of an instinct from becoming conscious and in suppressing the development of affects. In other words, it is the idea or group of ideas of an instinct which gets repressed. Only by a looseness of expression can instinctual impulses be said to be repressed, or affects be said to be unconscious. Strictly speaking, there are no unconscious affects in the sense in which there are said to be unconscious ideas. Although the concept of affect is obscure, it seems to correspond with processes of discharge of energy which are perceived as feeling. In the unconscious, affects exist as "affect-

formations," "potential dispositions," configurations of instinctual energy which at least often press toward discharge in
some fashion.[21]

Repression can (sometimes, not always) inhibit or prevent
the transformation of an instinctual impulse into direct affective expression. Ordinarily the ego has much better control
over motility than affectivity. A person can, for example,
much more easily control overt forms or expressions of anger;
when repressed, it may take the form of increased muscular
tension, increase of blood pressure, intense perspiring, etc.

Now affects (or charges of affect) can be "detached"
from the ideas with which they are normally connected.
Under repression a "severance" may be said to take place
between the affect and the idea to which it belongs. Actually
the affect does not usually succeed in reaching or penetrating
consciousness until it can "attach" itself to some new substitutive idea ("displacement"). One may repress one's anger
against a superior but later raise Cain with a fellow-worker.

The true aim of repression is sometimes said to be the
complete hindering of the development and expression of
affect. In many cases when an instinct-presentation is
repressed, the "libidinal cathexis" (energy charges or invest-
ments of the libido) undergoes complete "destruction" (for the
present we may say in the unconscious) and is diverted into
other channels. In normal circumstances the true aim of the
repression of the Oedipus complex is the latter.[22]

Two phases of repression are to be observed: a primal
repression and, secondly, a repression proper. In primal repression the ideational element of an instinct-presentation is in
the first place denied entry into consciousness. This is said
to be accomplished by a fixation, in which the affective energy
remains attached to the ideational element. The preconscious
system sets up a "counter-charge" or "anticathexis" which
blocks the instinct presentation from any progress toward
consciousness. This anti-cathexis is the sole "mechanism" of

primal repression. In repression proper trains of thought or "mental derivatives" (such as phantasies), distorted expressions of the repressed idea or associated ideas which have come into connection with the repressed idea, are said to undergo the same fate as the instinct-presentation in primal repression.[23] Repression proper is therefore an "after-expulsion." But in addition there is a withdrawal of the preconscious cathexis which the original (primal repressed) idea never attained. Furthermore, what was originally repressed is said to exercise an "attraction" upon those ideas with which it can establish some connection.

We are told also that repression does not necessarily hinder the instinct presentation from continuing to exist in the unconscious, from further organization, and from putting forth derivatives and instituting connections. In addition an instinct-presentation withdrawn from consciousness sometimes develops "in a more unchecked and luxuriant fashion," finally taking an extreme and sometimes terrifying form of expression.[24]

THE THEORY OF THE UNCONSCIOUS

In striving to communicate his notion of the complicated processes of mental life, especially the concepts of repression and the unconscious, Freud resorts to the following imagery: The unconscious system is compared to a large ante-room which is occupied by the various mental excitations. These crowded excitations are pushing forward to gain admittance into a second, smaller room, like a reception room, which is occupied by consciousness. Between the two rooms there stands a doorman, the "censor," who scrutinizes the excitations seeking to gain admittance. Those which the doorkeeper disapproves of he turns back at the threshold or, if they slipped by him, drives out again. Consciousness, however, cannot see the mental excitations in the ante-room, so those which remain there are at the outset unconscious. The mental excitations which have been turned back by the doorkeeper are *repressed*. But even those which the censor permits to cross the threshold need not necessarily become conscious. They become conscious only if they attract the eye of consciousness. Hence, Freud calls the second chamber the preconscious system. What is here called the doorkeeper is otherwise known in analysis as resistance.

Anyone who has attempted to follow Freud's theory of the unconscious and repression in detail will observe that the psyche needs larger, perhaps duplex, apartments and at least one more door-keeper. As we shall see, a mental act may have to undergo a "scrutiny" between two "censors" or "door-keepers"; the one between the unconscious and the preconscious, another between the preconscious and the conscious.

The differentiation of mental life into what is conscious and what is unconscious is a fundamental premise of Freudian psychology. It holds that powerful mental processes exist outside conscious awareness which can produce in the mind all the effects which ordinary ideas can, including the effects which then become conscious as ideas, without those processes themselves becoming conscious.

Any mental element is not usually permanently conscious. Ideas, so to speak, come and go in consciousness, so that it is said to be a transitory state. But many of our ideas can again easily become an object of consciousness under certain circumstances. In the meantime, it is assumed, they have been latent, a condition in which they can become conscious at any time. Such mental elements are said to be *preconscious;* they are, as a rule only temporarily unconscious, awaiting the recognition of consciousness. Strictly speaking, they do not belong to the unconscious, forming instead a kind of inter-vening and intermediate state between consciousness and the unconscious.

However, other mental processes are also in some sense latent, but they do not, except in extraordinary circumstances, ever become objects of conscious awareness; and it is these which are properly said to be unconscious.

To be sure, philosophers have often raised objections against the conception of an unconscious mind, primarily on the ground that it is a contradiction in terms, that to speak of an unconscious mind is in effect to speak of an unconscious consciousness. Freud was aware of such objections, and in several places he discusses and then rejects them. We do not intend to take up such objections here, for they would involve so much discussion that we would be led far from our main theme.

One of the most characteristic features of unconscious mental life is that of being *dynamic*. Unconscious impulses are forever pressing toward expression instead of being passive, static and inert. The unconscious mental life manifests tendencies striving towards a goal. Thus, sexual impulses when repressed still press toward some kind of fulfillment and are said to manifest themselves often in devious forms such as in the symptoms of mental illness.

There is another feature of mental processes which we need to mention only in passing since we make various indirect references to it, namely, the *economic* or quantitative. This property is derived from the theory that mental processes involve a distribution of the quantity of mental excitation and energy. In the course of its operation the mental apparatus has to master (control) or discharge quantities of energy in order to keep the quantity of excitation as low as possible or at least constant. As we have already observed, pleasure and pain are bound up with the distribution of mental stimuli.

Conscious and unconscious are used in both a descriptive and a "systematic" sense.[25] In a descriptive sense, a mental process is characterized mainly by having or manifesting a certain quality, that of being conscious, of being consciously

perceived, or the analogous quality of existing outside discriminated awareness, of being unconscious.[26]

In the systematic sense of the term, a "topographical"
feature is ascribed to the mind. Here the unconscious, for
example, is said to be a mental region or province separate
from the conscious, which also has a topographical aspect;
the two are mediated by the preconscious.

A mental act usually goes through two phases, mediated
by a testing process or censorship (between the unconscious
and the preconscious and/or between the preconscious and
the conscious). Originally the mental act is unconscious both
descriptively and systematically. To get to the second phase it
must pass the censorship existing between the unconscious and
the preconscious. If it can successfully pass this "scrutiny,"
it enters upon the second phase; otherwise it remains repressed.
In the former case it reaches the preconscious, where it again
sometimes undergoes "scrutiny" before it can become conscious. Here again many preconscious "formations" do not
become conscious. (So we must qualify our earlier statement
that all the ideas of the preconscious can become conscious at
any time. As we shall see, Freud was eventually obliged to
revise this scheme.) "Unconsciousness is a regular and inevitable phase in the processes constituting our mental activity;
every mental act begins as an unconscious one, and it may
either remain so or go on developing into consciousness,
according as it meets with resistance or not."[27]

THE THEORY OF INFANTILE SEXUALITY

Freud was the first one to call attention to infantile
sexuality and point to its great significance. Failure to
observe this phenomenon and give it its proper due was
accounted for on two grounds. Since writers on the sexual
impulses (instinct) were conditioned by the prevailing cultural
conventions and taboos, they were unable clearly to notice

and study the phenomenon. The other factor, he says, is a peculiar psychic phenomenon called amnesia, a kind of forgetting, which veils from the conscious recollection of most people the first six or eight years of their lives. The memory of childhood sexual experience becomes repressed.

Freud forcefully expressed it in the following words: It "is not at all true that the sexual impulse enters into the child at puberty, as the devils in the gospel entered into the swine. The child has his sexual impulses and activities from the beginning, he brings them with him into the world, and from these so-called normal sexuality of adults emerges by a significant development through manifold stages."[28]

Oral Eroticism

Sexual or libidinal experience, then, occurs in infancy and not merely at adolescence, as one might assume, particularly if one is forgetful of one's own early life experience. The mother's breast is the original *object* of the sexual desire of the infant. During the suckling of the infant there is revealed the first expression of the sexual instinct. Of course, suckling also involves the ingestion of food, which satisfies another instinct, hunger. But the infant "wishes" to repeat the act of taking in food without actually demanding more food. The act of sucking itself gives him pleasure. And this satisfaction, it is said, is libidinal or sexual. The gratification derived from sucking is a prototype of subsequent libidinal satisfaction. At first the gratification is experienced during the taking in of nourishment, but the infant quickly learns that sucking *per se* is pleasure-giving. The pleasure in sucking is attributed to the excitation of the mouth and lips. Thus, the mouth and lips, among other parts of the body, form one of the *erogenous zones*, areas of the body which afford sexual pleasure.

Auto-Eroticism

Soon the infant[29] replaces the breast of the mother as
a source of gratification by a part of his own body, his
thumb or his tongue or, what is more exciting, his genitals.[30]
When the infant seeks and finds objects of sexual interest
in his own body, he is said to behave *auto-erotically*. Another
source of gratification which the child quickly learns is connected with excretion. He experiences pleasure during the
excretion of urine and feces. The mucous membrane of the
bowels is said to be a source of pleasure, an erogenous zone,
an organ of pleasure with a passive sexual aim. At first an
infant discharges his waste products more or less automatically. Gradually the child is "educated." He is induced to
renounce the satisfaction in excretion. Everything relating to
the functions of excretion, he is told by word, gesture, facial
expression, etc., is indecent, dirty, and must be concealed.
Until this time he experiences no disgust toward his excre-
tions; he regards them as part of his own body. After a time
he learns to look with shame and disgust on excretory activities. Excretion becomes regulated in accordance with the
demands of the mother or nurse and of the society they
represent.[31]

Reaction Formations of the Psyche

But education does not tell the whole story in the
development of shame, loathing, disgust, moral and aesthetic
ideals. According to Freud before puberty "psychic forces"
develop which later act as inhibitions on the sexual life and
narrow its direction. These psychic forces are said to develop
more or less spontaneously; they are organically determined.
The function of education is to follow and strengthen the
organic development. These psychic forces awaken as contrary
forces, or feelings of reaction against the impulses toward
childhood sexual gratification.

Component Impulses of the Libido

The sexual life of the child is said to be loosely organized before the "primacy" of the genital zone is effected. Although the sexual life is mainly under the control of the erogenous zones, it also comprises various partial impulses which afford sexual gratification and which later are integrated into the adult forms of sexuality. These partial impulses include, for example, gazing, exhibiting, and the cruelty impulses (sadism). Thus, the young child is "shameless" and manifests pleasure in exhibiting his body and sexual organs. In other words, sexuality in childhood is pictured as comprising various libidinal streams, which gradually as the child matures unite into one main current or a "network of communicating canals" —adult genital sexuality.

Oral Stage of Development

We return now to the first period of infant development in order to add some other ideas of Freud on the subject. This first phase is usually referred to as the *oral* or cannibalistic stage. Since there is no clear differentiation yet between the taking of food and sexual activity, the object of one activity is also said to be that of the other. "When the object becomes a source of pleasurable feelings, a motor tendency is set up which strives to bring the object near to and incorporate it into the ego . . . "[32] Hence, the sexual aim seeks to take the object into one's own body; this is later transferred to the important psychic role of *identification*. During the latter part of this stage biting activities become manifest, and so the oral stage is subdivided into an earlier phase of oral incorporation and a later, oral-sadism.[33] During the oral-sadistic period, for the first time a kind of contradictory attitude toward objects, such as later appears as a mixture of love and hate, *ambivalence*, appears.

Anal-Sadistic Stage of Development

The next stage is called *anal-sadistic*. During this time an instinct to mastery bordering on cruelty is manifested. Sadistic and anal impulses are marked when the cutting of the teeth, strengthening of the musculature, and control of the sphincters occur. Two phases are also distinguished here. In the earlier phase destructive tendencies are predominant. Intermediate to the two phases a consideration for the object is manifested, which is said to be a forerunner of the later relation of love towards the object. In the latter phase tendencies which are friendly to the object appear predominant. The child also expresses tendencies to possess things and to hold them fast.

Before outlining the next period of development, the *phallic*, we want to mention some other facts which Freud observed and certain theories he proposed.

Sexual Activity in Children

The curiosity of children is a celebrated fact. For children the world is a strange and often mystifying place, and they normally show an unflagging eagerness to find out about it, to observe what is going on, to manipulate objects, to ask questions.[34] This curiosity certainly extends to sexual matters, including the origin of babies. According to Freud, sexual curiosity begins very early, sometimes before the third year.

At this stage the curiosity is not related to differences of sex, which do not mean anything as yet to the child. The boy ascribes the male genital to both sexes.[35] When he discovers the "primary sexual structure" of the female, he at first tries to deny the evidence of his senses. To the little boy, according to Freud, it is inconceivable that a human being should lack that part of the body which is so important to the boy himself.[36] His discovery horrifies him and its implications, too.

The castration complex takes hold of him. And this is said to be very significant for the development of his character, whether he is healthy or sick.[37] The little boy develops a castration complex—an intense fear of losing such a precious possession.

Castration Complex of the Boy

From about the third year on the genitals are said to become active. Psychic and social expressions of the sexual life appear. Freud thinks there is perhaps regularly a period of infantile masturbation around this time. Often parents or nurses who discover this infantile masturbation threaten the child that his little penis or his hand will be cut off.[38] Or the child himself, without any direct threat, may concoct one on the basis of hints and allusions about his "auto-erotic" satisfactions, especially if he gets the impression that the clitoris of the little girl is a stunted or castrated penis.[39] But Freud, as we shall see in some detail later, has further ideas on this subject. He thinks that the little boy's phantasy of castration was in prehistoric periods of the human family a genuine reality when, according to his theory, boys' penises were often cut off. The phantasy is reminiscent of this prehistoric occurence.

Penis Envy of the Girl

What about the little girl? She has her troubles, too. She wants to have an imposing penis and is greatly disturbed by her lack of such an impressive organ, and she wishes she were a man. She feels injured because of her lack of a large visible penis, envies the boy his possession of it and, primarily from this motive, desires to be a man. Later on, in womanhood, this wish may, in certain circumstances, manifest itself in neurosis. However, the little girl's clitoris, an especially excitable zone, enables her to achieve auto-erotic satisfaction.

Her clitoris is said to be equivalent, in childhood, to the little boy's penis.

Phallic Stage of Development of the Boy

At the height of the development of childhood sexuality, the functioning of the genitals and the interest in them achieves predominant significance, falling little short of that of maturity. The difference is that only one kind of genital for both sexes, it is said, is taken into account, that of the male. And so at this time the primacy of the *phallus* occurs. In regard to this phase in the little girl, Freud admits insufficiency of knowledge. For the boy, the penis "so easily excitable and changeable, and so rich in sensation, occupies the boy's interest to a high degree, and never ceases to provide new problems for his epistemophilic impulse. He wants to see the same thing in other people, so as to compare it with his own . . ."[40] He finally comes to the conclusion that the little girl's penis, in certain cases, was taken away, and this stimulates the thought of castration in relation to himself. In the next period, that of the Oedipus complex, the thought of castration will play an important role.

Up to and including the anal-sadistic level of sexual organization, the dominant "antithesis" is not between male and female but between *active* and *passive*. Then the antithesis becomes: "a male genital organ or a castrated condition."[41] Only at the completion of development at puberty does the polarity of sexuality coincide with male and female.

The Mystery of Birth

The Oedipus complex of the boy is contemporaneous with the phallic stage of development. The interest and pleasure in the penis become related to an external object. In order to discuss the Oedipal phase, we must, once more, make some preliminary remarks about infantile curiosity. The sexual interest of children of both sexes is very early directed to the mystery of birth. This curiosity, Freud thinks, is in the main aroused by the selfish dread of a new child, who would be a potential rival.[42] At first children are not able to solve the problem of birth alone. If they consult their parents or nurse, they may be told the story of the stork, which they by no means always accept. However, the child's immature sexual constitution restricts his ability to understand. So he makes all sorts of assumptions and speculations of his own, based on his very limited knowledge and experience.

The Child's Interpretation of Parental Intercourse

The growing child quickly observes that the father plays some role in reproduction, but he cannot make out what this role is. If he happens to observe a sexual act of his parents, he is not able to relate it to reproduction. Instead, he interprets the act as a struggle or fight between the two partners. Should he find traces of blood on the sheets or on the clothing of his mother, he interprets it as proof that his father injured his mother in the presumed scuffle. In a sensitive child such an experience may tend to arouse disgust or fright, possibly with resentment toward the father or contempt for the mother. During later childhood he probably catches on to the fact that the male organ plays an important role in the procreation of children.

The Role of the Mother

We have already observed that the first "object" for the oral component of the sexual instinct is the mother. This is succeeded by a phase in which the oral impulse becomes auto-erotic. Normally the child follows this phase by renouncing or at least subordinating his auto-eroticism in favor of an external object and by combining the several objects of

the separate impulses and substituting for them a single one.
For Freud love is simply the "psychic" side, the mental
representation, of sex impulses. But the suckling at the
mother's breast, he says, becomes a model for every love relation. The mother or her surrogate, the nurse, cares for the
infant in every vital respect. She kisses, fondles, pets him,
may even stimulate his genitals, all of which adds to his
pleasure. By her tenderness she further awakens his sexual
interest and prepares its future intensity. She thus teaches
the child to love.

According to Freud, the child loves itself first and afterwards learns to love others, to "sacrifice" something of its
ego for another. As a matter of fact, in the beginning of life
there is no distinction between self and "object." If the infant
seems from the outset to love others, this is simply a manifestation of the infant's needs. He cannot do without others.
Severance of the umbilical cord at birth effected physical
separation, but he is still in every other way attached to the
mother or the nurse for all his needs. His further development
requires that he abandon or rather subordinate auto-erotic
satisfactions, to substitute a "foreign" object for his own
body. When this occurs he may, in Freudian theory, be properly said to love an object.[43] Because normally the mother
has been the one to care for him since birth, she quite
naturally becomes the first object of the child's love.

The Boy's Erotic Love for His Mother

As the infant grows, he develops an "erotic attachment"
to the mother. He may want to sleep with her at night, be
present while she is dressing, caress her. It may seem to the
child that it is to his advantage that the mother trouble
herself about no one else, pay no attention to others. But
this is not the crux of the matter. Freud appears to assume
that an erotic attachment is by its nature exclusive and
jealous of any rival.[44]

Sibling Rivalry

If there are brothers and sisters, not only do they get some of the attention and loving care which he would otherwise receive, but they become rivals. Frequently, if not always, he hates them for this very reason. The little boy may even attempt to do the new arrival bodily harm. The nursery becomes a scene of violent conflict, actuated by rivalry for love of the parents. Sometimes, of course, there are circumstances which mitigate this intense rivalry. But the hostility to the rivals is said often to persist, if only unconsciously.

Beginning of Repression

In regard to his erotic attachment to the mother, Freud does not mean that the child has a clear conscious awareness of what is happening. About the time when the mother becomes the object of love for the little boy, repression has already begun in him and blots out of conscious awareness the knowledge of a part of his sexual aims.

The Oedipus Complex

The father is, of course, the great and formidable rival. The "little man" would like to have the mother all to himself. The father's presence is disturbing. When the latter shows tenderness toward the little boy's mother, the little boy is irritated, and he expresses satisfaction when the father is away or on a journey. Frequently the boy expresses his feelings in words and promises to marry the mother. He regards her as his own property. This may seem, says Freud, to be not much in comparison with the deeds of Oedipus, but it is indeed enough, for it is essentially the same.

The Boy's Sexual Rivalry with the Mother for the Father

But the little boy, according to Freud, may also want to have an "incestuous" relation to the father. The Oedipus complex offers the child two "possibilities," one active, the other passive. Besides his wish to put himself in the father's place and have intercourse with the mother (although his idea of sexual intercourse may be quite vague except that he knows it involves a penis), he may want to supplant the mother and be loved by the father.[45] This idea of Freud's may at first sight seem to contradict a good deal of what he has said, but it is in harmony with another theory of his which we shall discuss below, namely, his theory of *bisexuality*. According to this theory, every human being has male and female elements, or more accurately, active and passive tendencies. In the normal male active tendencies will predominate; in the female, passive ones.

Ambivalence

Thus, on other occasions the little boy evinces great tenderness for the father. Partly for this reason, he is said to manifest an attitude of *ambivalence*, in which both tender and hostile, aggressive tendencies appear, which will later exist permanently in his unconscious. However, ambivalence appears early, making its appearance in the oral-sadistic stage and is markedly in evidence by the next or anal-sadistic stage.[46]

Parental Preference

The parents likewise are said frequently to show a sex preference when there are several children. The mother usually manifests most affection and preference for her son, while the father is unmistakably partial to the daughter.

The new-born female infant is, of course, just as dependent on the mother as the male. But as she develops she begins to manifest an interest in the father, and she forms an erotic attachment to him. She lavishes affectionate devotion on the father and manifests a desire to set aside the mother as superfluous and to take her place.

The Family Complex

When there are several children in the family, the Oedipus complex expands and becomes a family complex. As the children grow up, a little boy may take his sister as his love object, who then replaces his "faithless" mother; a little girl may take an older brother as a substitute for the father, whose affection may wane with the passing of the years. Or she may take a younger sister as a substitute for the child she vainly wished to have by the father.

The Death Wish and Hate

By and large, with the qualifications noted above, the father is, at this time, at any rate, anathema to the son. The father embodies all the social restrictions and requirements to which the son with great unwillingness submits. He likewise thwarts the son's will, his early sexual pleasures, and the enjoyment of any family property there may be. If such a prize as a throne is involved, the death of the father is longed for with enormous impatience.

Nor is the daughter overburdened with love for the mother. The mother is in certain cases a rival who does not want to be superseded. At the same time she represents the authority who thwarts the daughter's sexual freedom and imposes social restrictions and other limits upon her.

The Passing of the Oedipus Complex

In order to account for the passing of the Oedipus complex in normal or relatively normal people, Freud considers two views on the subject. The first is that painful experiences bring it about. In the case of the boy, he discovers that his mother transfers her love and care to a new arrival. The little girl has to endure a gradual cooling of affection and interest from the father. Even when such possibilities do not occur, the situation itself is inherently frustrating, if only because little boys and girls are biologically immature in regard to the sexual equipment.

Another view has it that children having to go through hereditarily preordained stages of development inevitably cast

aside or dissolve the Oedipus relationship when they reach a
certain point in their progress toward adult maturity just as
they lose their milk-teeth.

Freud finds both views compatible. Each contains an
element of the truth. The one expresses the ontogenetic aspect;
the other, the phylogenetic.

When the boy sees the female genitals, he becomes finally
convinced that the threat of castration is real,[47] that possession of the mother would involve his losing the penis. This
idea precipitates a conflict which normally ends in the child's
turning away from the Oedipus complex, from his erotic
attachment to his mother. This attachment is abandoned with
the help of repression, sublimation and *identification,* a process
we shall discuss below. "The whole process, on the one hand,
preserves the genital organ and wards off the danger of losing
it; on the other hand, it paralyzes it, takes away its function
from it."

The Latency Period.

With the passing of the Oedipus complex, there is introduced the latency period, which ends at puberty. Most of the
mental experiences and excitations occurring before this time
are said to be veiled by amnesias. From the end of the fourth
year, "reaction-formations," such as shame, disgust, morality,
arise, which tend to act as barriers against later sexual activity.[48] There is a slowing up, if not a regression, of sexual
development. While education contributes much to the appearance of these "psychic forces," this development is organically
determined and may occasionally be produced without education.

Sexual energy is partially deflected from direct gratification and conducted to other aims; it is partially sublimated.

Before coming to the last great stage in the evolution of
sexuality, we may summarize the origins of infantile sexual
excitement as follows: "(a) as an imitation of a gratification

which has been experienced in conjunction with other organic processes; (b) through the appropriate peripheral stimulation of erogenous zones; (c) and as an expression of some 'impulse' like the looking and cruelty impulses . . . "[49] Mechanical excitation, muscular activity, affective processes like fear, even intellectual work, all contribute toward sexual excitement.

The normal completion of the development of the sexual instinct is reached when it serves the function of procreation. When the various component instincts, such as looking, exhibiting, masochism, sadism, are organized together and synthesized with the erotogenic zones under the primacy of the genital zone, adult genital sexuality supervenes.[50]

The Adolescent's Struggle for Freedom

At puberty the importance of the Oedipus complex has by no means vanished. When at this time the sexual instinct asserts its demands with all the strength and intensity of adolescent lust, the original objects of sexual desire, the parents, become once more the objects of the libido. The individual must now free himself from his parents and discover a "foreign object" whom he can love. Only then can he, in Pauline language, put away childish things and take his place as an adult member of society. The son must now become reconciled with his father, or, if by his infantile opposition he becomes subject to the father's domination, he must now free himself from this domination. The son must also, of course, release his sexual desires from his mother; the daughter, from her father. Failure in either case means a crippling of personality. People who are "neurotic" have never been able to free themselves from the parents or their surrogates and remain more or less "attached" to them.[51]

2. THE THEORIES OF SIGMUND FREUD
LATER ADDITIONS AND MODIFICATIONS

Thus far we have introduced the reader to what is, on the whole, an earlier tentative stage of Freud's thought. We shall now go on to give some of the later modifications and additions which represent his matured ideas.

ASSUMPTIONS IN THERAPY

Lack of knowledge on the part of a mentally sick person regarding his childhood and its relation to his present life experiences, etc., cannot be said to have of itself precipitated his illness. Nor does enlightenment *per se* concerning the causative relation of such experiences to his illness effect cure. The necessity for this ignorance, originally caused by inner resistances and still maintained by them, is the pathogenic motive.[1] Successful therapy will combat and overcome these resistances of the ego. Part of the therapeutic art lies in uncovering these resistances, calling the patient's attention to them, and teaching him to abandon them.

For example, suppose a patient has attempted to repress a fierce hatred of the father which has never been resolved and which still manifests itself in devious forms through failure of repression. In analysis by means of certain techniques such as "free association" and interpretation, the resistances will, according to theory, gradually be conquered or resolved and "forgotten" situations and connections remembered. In this way, the patient's ego "fuses into one all the instinctual trends which before had been split off and barred away from it."[2]

THE REPETITION COMPULSION

But what not infrequently happens? The patient, it turns out, is unable to recollect the repressed fragments of the infantile sex life. Instead, having invested the doctor with, say, the qualities and role of his father, he manifests an intense and blind hatred toward the physician. The patient is unable to recall his "forgotten" experiences in spite of all the skill of his physician. Instead, he displays a tenacious and unremitting tendency to repeat as a current experience what was repressed, as if the experience of hatred were justified by his present relationship to the doctor. He acts out, in a manner of speaking, instead of recollecting, his past experiences. And furthermore, to complicate matters, he may know how to arouse the resentment of the physician, to force the latter to become brusque and to adopt a chilling manner towards him, thus re-creating the feeling of being disdained, rejected. In this way recollection of the past becomes doubly difficult. The patient is unable to become aware that his hatred is a carry-over from the past. When this occurs, the treatment reaches an *impasse* and he may find some pretext to break it off.

For some reason he is compelled to repeat an earlier experience, a phenomenon called a "repetition-compulsion." But the striking fact is that the original experience never brought any pleasure, nor does its reenactment. The expression of the repetition-compulsion is said to manifest an "instinctual" character and sometimes, a "daemonic" character.

BEYOND THE PLEASURE PRINCIPLE

Without going into further details of psychoanalytic treatment, we shall simply give Freud's view in this connection.[3]

"The new and remarkable fact . . . we have now to describe is that the repetition compulsion also revives experiences of the past that contain no potentiality of pleasure, and which could at no time have been satisfactions, even of impulses since repressed."[4] Furthermore, even "normal" people show a tendency to repeat old experiences in a manner analogous to that of the "neurotics." These observations led Freud to the conclusion that the repetition-compulsion is a manifestation of something "more primitive, more elementary, more instinctive than the pleasure principle which is displaced by it."

THE IMPACT OF WORLD WAR I ON FREUDIAN THEORY

Another factor contributing toward the modification of Freud's views appears to have been World War I and the "traumatic neuroses" of wartime. A mind as sensitive and brilliant as Freud's could hardly fail to be impressed by the enormous and staggering destructiveness and hate let loose in such a war. He speaks of it with sad disillusionment: "We are constrained to believe that never has any event been destructive of so much that is valuable in the common wealth of humanity, nor so misleading to many of the clearest intelligences, nor so debasing, to the highest that we know. Science herself has lost her passionless impartiality; in their deep embitterment her servants seek for weapons from her with which to contribute towards the defeat of the enemy. The anthropologist is driven to declare the opponent inferior and degenerate; the psychiatrist to publish his diagnosis of the enemy's disease of mind or spirit."[5]

TRAUMATIC NEUROSES

In regard to the traumatic neuroses, soldiers who had undergone severe psychic traumas seemed to relive the experience of the traumatic situation in their dreams. This, of course, played havoc with Freud's theory that dreams are usually if not always the disguised expression, in the case of adults, of unfulfilled wishes—that they are "wish-fulfillments."[6] Freud seems to express an initial bewilderment in his question: "What conative impulse could possibly be satisfied by this reinstatement of a most painful traumatic experience?"[7]

DEATH INSTINCT

Since the compulsion to repeat such experiences ignores the pleasure-principle, in what way, he asks, is the instinctive connected with the compulsion to repetition. His answer is that there is a characteristic of instinct, perhaps of all organic life, not hitherto clearly recognised. "According to this, *an instinct would be a tendency innate in living organic matter impelling it toward the reinstatement of an earlier condition*, one which it had to abandon under the influence of external disturbing forces — a kind of organic elasticity, or, to put it another way, the manifestation of inertia in organic life."[8] There would then be, if this hypothesis is correct, a conservative, regressive tendency in living things. This regressive tendency may be expressed by saying the goal of all life is death.[9] Without repeating all of Freud's speculations and observations, we state summarily that he finally postulated a "death-instinct" as characteristic of all living matter. In other words, he assumed that in all living matter there is a tendency to return to its original (and primeval) inorganic state.

THEORY OF EROS

But this idea presents Freud with a dilemma, and of course he was much too keen not to be well aware of it. If there is an inherent tendency in living things to die, to return to a simpler and earlier state, how is one to explain the occurrence of reproductive cells the operation of which seems almost to guarantee the immortality of the species? How is one to explain the presence of a sexual instinct? How, in fact, is one to explain the persistence of life at all or even its existence? In order to reconcile the theory of the death instinct with his theory of sexuality, Freud resorted, in part, to complicated dialectical maneuvers, which we shall not go into here,[10] and to the acceptance of instincts which have the function of sustaining and enhancing life processes.[11]

MODIFICATION OF THE THEORY OF LIBIDO

Before the theory of the death instinct Freud had already modified some of his ideas in regard to the ego and the libido. The reader will recall that at first they were sharply distinguished.

However, on the basis of certain clinical observations, it was later assumed that under certain circumstances libidinal energy directed toward (or invested in) objects is withdrawn and redirected toward the ego itself, a process called secondary narcissism. Thus the distinction arose of "ego-libido" and "object-libido." The more that is taken up by the one, the more impoverished does the other become. In fact, originally in the infant the libido is concentrated on himself — primary narcissism. Narcissism is the probable original universal condition from which object-love develops. Egoism and narcissism are one and the same thing.[12] Since, then, ego-libido can be converted into object-libido, and conversely, the distinction between the ego-instincts and the libidinal instincts becomes vague. The self-preservative instincts are themselves libidinous or possess a libidinous quality.[13]

EROS AND THE DEATH INSTINCT

At any rate the theory of narcissism made easier the transition to Freud's final dualistic theory of life, namely, that there are "two fundamentally different kinds of instincts, the sexual instincts, in the widest sense of the word (Eros . . .), and the aggressive instincts, whose aim is destruction."[14] The association and opposition of these two forces create the phenomena of life. These two kinds of instincts are inherent in every particle of living substance. Eros and the death instinct are "fused, blended, and mingled with each other . . . "[15] Through the combination of unicellular organisms into multicellular organisms, the death instinct of the single cell is said to be neutralized,[16] and the destructive impulses diverted towards the external world through the instrumentality of a special organ, the musculature.[17] Thus, in part, the death instinct expresses itself as an instinct of destruction directed against the external world and other living organisms. As we shall see, it may also be directed against oneself. In fact, in Freudian theory human nature is burdened with an insoluble and terrible dilemma: one must either divert his aggressive, destructive instincts against others or turn them against oneself.[18] Thus, Freud finally worked out a theoretical explanation for his almost unmitigated conviction of the inherent evilness of man.

BASIS OF SADISM AND MASOCHISM

For the purpose of discharge the death instinct is habitually enlisted in the service of Eros.[19] In this way Freud finally arrives at a theoretical explanation of sadism and masochism. When he had abandoned his original theory of the libido, or rather modified and expanded it, he was willing to admit that the earlier formulation could hardly account for sadism and masochism.[20] Indeed, it is difficult to see how they can be derived, logically speaking, from the pleasure principle — at least without considerable dialectical manipulations of that principle. Sadism and masochism, in Freud's final formulation, are fusions of Eros and the destructive instincts. Sadism represents a fusion of the erotic instincts and the destructive instincts directed outwards, in which the destructiveness has the character of aggressiveness. Masochism represents the fusion of the erotic instincts and the destructive instincts turned against oneself, the aim of the latter being self-destruction.[21]

While the theory of Eros and the death instinct purport to inform us as to the nature of the fundamental drives governing human behavior, they do not tell us how these driving "forces" are organized in the personality. This is done in Freud's final formulation of personality organization and development. This formulation embraces the theory of the *id*, the *ego*, with which we are somewhat familiar, and the *super-ego*.

CHARACTERISTICS OF THE EGO

The ego is a coherent organization of mental processes. As we know, it controls consciousness. Even when it "goes to sleep" at night, it exercises a censorship on dreams. The ego is responsible for repression, cutting off certain mental processes from consciousness as well as from other forms of manifestation and activity. A part of the ego is, however, itself unconscious, so that normally one is not aware (in the sense of being conscious) of all the processes which one's ego controls and directs.[22]

It represents reason and sanity, in contrast to another aspect of the personality to be discussed below, which "contains" the passions. Normally it controls motility; it is somewhat like a man on horseback who must control and guide his steed (the id) but sometimes the horse can get out of hand or run away with the rider.[23]

REVISION OF THE THEORY OF MENTAL TOPOGRAPHY

As we know, the earlier formulation of personality held that three aspects of mental processes could be distinguished:

the conscious (over which reigned the ego), the preconscious, and the unconscious. But the ego was discovered to be not synonymous with consciousness, and the preconscious was found to have elements characteristic of the unconscious. It will also be remembered that these aspects of the mind were assigned a "topographical" feature, in which they were pictured as regions or "psychic localities." Now if these three "regions" have certain traits in common, the distinction between them tends to become vague. Furthermore, certain other traits of the ego which originally were not clearly perceived had to be taken into account. The result was apparently that the original classification became too inexact and awkward. The *quality* of being either conscious, preconscious, or unconscious was retained, but they no longer designated "regions" or "mental provinces." This feature, the topographical, was now designated as ego, id, and super-ego. And there was no one-to-one correlation between the properties of being conscious, preconscious or unconscious and the "topography" of the mind.

CHARACTERISTICS OF THE ID

The region of the mind or element of the personality designated as the *id* (originally the unconscious as a system having topographical and other features) expresses that character of the personality which is said to be foreign to the ego. The id is by far the most obscure and inaccessible part of the personality, for it is entirely unconscious, entirely outside the field of conscious awareness. Figuratively speaking, it is a "cauldron of seething excitement."[24] It is the "great reservoir" of the libido — and of the destructive instincts. Somehow it is in connection with somatic processes and thus takes over instinctual needs, to which it gives psychical expression. The id is by its very nature, according to Freud, blind, impulsive, irrational. Moral and ethical values are

unknown to it. This part of the personality has no organization or unified will. Contradictory impulses exist side by side
without neutralizing one another or drawing apart; at most
they are said to combine in compromise formations under
the overpowering pressure towards discharging their energy.
Finally, the id is immune to time, in the sense that it makes
no "recognition" of the passage of time. The conative impulses
of the id are therefore uninfluenced by time and are virtually
"immortal."

THE EGO'S RELATION TO THE ID

The ego is the agent of the id. In fact, it is part of the
id, the part which has been moulded and modified by its
more direct relation to the external world. The ego is thus
the seat of intelligence and reason, and by checking, and to
some extent controlling, the blind impulsions of the id, it saves
the latter from annihilation. Nevertheless, the ego. Freud says,
is weak, having to draw its energy from the id itself.

THE SUPER-EGO

The ego can subject itself to study and observation. It
"can take itself as object, it can treat itself like any other
object, observe itself, criticize itself, and do Heaven knows
what besides with itself."[25] A part of the ego stands off, as
it were, and surveys the rest. Thus the ego can be "split,"
at least temporarily, when it assumes a self-observing or
self-critical function. A "separating off," of an observing
function is, according to Freud, a normal function of the ego
structure. One can investigate the characteristics and relations
of this separate function. To do this Freud thought it advis-
able to give it a name, the *super-ego*. While he pictures it as
a mental realm, it is also a function of the ego.[26]

The super-ego has a kind of independence and pursues its own ends, with energy at its disposal free from the ego. It dominates the ego and operates with severity and cruelty. In fact it has the ego at its mercy and controls it with the most severe moral standards. The super-ego represents the demands of morality and of society. Our moral "sense of guilt" has its origin in a tension between the ego and the super-ego. Conscience is an expression of the super-ego, though the latter has other characteristics too. Small children, at first, do not manifest any internal inhibitions or compunctions against pleasure-seeking. But the parents, or their surrogates, gradually instill in them such inhibitions. The parents represent the external power which first plays the role later taken over by the super-ego. By giving affection, which of course the child needs, or by threats of punishment, with all that this action implies, including the loss of love, the parents thus exert enormous power and control over the psychological development of the child. The latter thus develops an anxiety as to the vicissitudes of the parental behavior. Freud calls this anxiety objective anxiety. This objective anxiety is a forerunner of a later phenomenon called moral anxiety. But the super-ego is not constituted by objective anxiety. Only when the child adopts the restrictions, moral sanctions, and moral code of his parents or their surrogates as his own or "introjects" them, can he be said to develop a super-ego.

The development of the super-ego is fundamentally a process of *identification*. Identification goes through two phases, a primary and a later phase. The child learns and adopts the behavior and attitudes of the parents, strives to become like them, imitates them. This process occurs, at least in a rudimentary way, before the child forms any "object cathexes." This identification is said to be direct and immediate, but we are not told anything more about it.[27]

The further development of identification is complicated, and Freud appears to be not too clear in his own mind about

it. Very early in life when the boy begins to take his mother
as a love-object (an object-cathexis of the libido) he then
normally identifies himself with the father, and in various
ways, often subtle, has the personality of the father as his
model. In this way the child's ego tends to become like the ego
of the father, or what the child takes to be the ego of his
father; and his character is formed and moulded in such a
fashion. But when the father is perceived as an obstacle in
the fulfillment of the boy's sexual wishes regarding the mother,
the identification takes on a hostile coloring and changes into
a wish to remove the father. In this way the relation to the
father becomes ambivalent, while that to the mother remains
affectionate. Such a relationship is by Freud referred to as
"the simple positive Oedipus complex in the boy."[28]

But according to the theory of bisexuality (which we
discuss below), everyone has both masculine and feminine
elements in his make-up. Hence, the relative strength of the
masculine and feminine dispositions in both sexes determines
whether the outcome of the Oedipus complex will be an
identification with the father or the mother.[29]

The little boy is not only ambivalent toward the father,
while manifesting an affectionate object-relation to the mother,
he also behaves like a girl towards the father, manifests an
affectionate attitude toward him and accompanying hostility
and jealousy toward the mother.[30] And here he forms an
identification with the mother.

Freud warns us not to confuse identification with "object-
choice." In the first case, the boy wants to be *like* his father.
But "when he makes him the object of his choice, he wants to
have him, to possess him" as his sexual object.[31]

Another observation of Freud's throws some light on his
theory of identification:

"When it happens that a person has to give up a sexual
object, there quite often ensues a modification in his ego
which can only be described as a reinstatement of the object

within the ego . . . "[32] Such a process is compared with or analogous to the original wishes toward oral incorporation of the object.

The result of the two identifications is that they form a "precipitate" in the ego, which retains the special characteristics known as the ego-ideal or super-ego. The growth of the super-ego may be described as a successful process of identification of the child with the parental function. When the Oedipus complex passes away, the child must abandon his intense emotional attachments to his parents, and he must find a compensation for this loss. Human beings are so constituted that they cannot abandon an intense emotional attachment without finding some compensation or substitute for it. The loss of a love object may, however, be compensated for by identification with it. One may regain a spurious possession by taking the ego of the lost one or part of it and adopting it as one's own. In the case of the child, the process of identification with the parents, which has long been continuing, is greatly intensified so as to compensate for the abandonment of the object-cathexes. If the Oedipus complex is not completely overcome, the development of the super-ego will be retarded and incomplete. One may think of the super-ego undergoing a gradual development as the child grows up and his knowledge of the parents increases. Others who take the place of the parents, such as teachers, governesses, tutors, also influence the super-ego development. They become, at least sometimes, ideal models whom the child adopts.[33]

FURTHER DEVELOPMENT OF THE SUPER-EGO

But the super-ego is not merely the precipitate left by the earliest object-choices; it also represents an energetic "reaction-formation" against the father and mother as love objects, who ordinarily are the first object-choices. This reaction-formation contains a prohibition against doing all that the father does, certain things being his prerogative.[34] The differentiation of the super-ego is due not only to the development of the individual; it is due also to the development of the race, as we shall see.

The child values the parents differently at different periods of his life. Early in life when he is abandoning the Oedipus situation, he regards his parents as splendid figures, but later he usually learns to form a more accurate appraisal of them. In identifying himself with the parents, he naturally adopts this exalted image of them, thus setting up within himself an ideal by which the ego measures itself, towards which it strives, and forever struggles to fulfill the demands which it implies for an ever-increasing perfection. But this is reinforced by the attitude of the parents. Parents and other authorities are governed by the commands of their own super-egos in bringing up children. The former are severe and exacting in the education of the children. Obedience brings approval and "love," which to the child means relief and satisfaction. In an analogous manner the appreciation of the introjected authority consequent on the fulfillment of its demands entails good feeling, pride and satisfaction. Failure to obey the demands of the introjected authority, as in the original prototype, entails punishment, reproaches and disapproval, which are felt as pangs of conscience and feelings of guilt. The most feared punishment appears originally to be the dread of castration, and this is the kernel around which the subsequent fear of conscience gathers. "The result is that the super-ego of the child is not really built up on the model of the parents, but on that of the parents' 'super-ego,' it takes over the same content, it becomes the vehicle of tradition and of all the age-long values which have been handed down in this way from generation to generation."[35]

In this way the super-ego comes to dominate the ego in the form of conscience or perhaps of an unconscious sense of guilt.

(While we do not intend to discuss group psychology, we may observe that, in Freudian theory, the person acquires an ego-ideal in common with others; that is, a number of individuals substitute the same object, a leader, for their ego ideal and consequently identify themselves with one another in their ego.)[36]

THE EGO'S THREE HARSH MASTERS

The ego, then, has to serve three harsh masters: the external world, the super-ego, and the id. In order to live, one must not only acquire a certain amount of knowledge of the external world, but also take account of its requirements and necessities. This function is carried on by the ego. But it also is in the service of the id and hence tries as best it can to satisfy the latter. In other words, man tries to satisfy or somehow come to terms with his passions. Finally, the ego is under the close scrutiny of the super-ego, which makes uncompromising demands on behalf of society, tradition, etc. Failure to obey the sanctions of the super-ego is punished by feelings of tension, inferiority and guilt.

Before coming to the theory of the Oedipus complex as it relates to women, we wish briefly to discuss the theory of *bisexuality*.

The Theory of Bisexuality

Ordinarily one thinks of people as being in an unequivocal manner sexually differentiated into male and female. But Freud advances the view—more accurately, emphasizes the view — that there is no sharp, unequivocal differentiation of male and female. Without going into the evidence which Freud marshalled for the theory of bisexuality, we may mention the following views:

Freud claims that the notion of what is masculine and feminine is extraordinarily confused. The designations are

used in at least three different senses. It may mean activity
and passivity. It may also be used in the biological sense,
where masculine and feminine denote the presence of semen
or ovum and the functions derived from them. In the sociological sense, the meaning is obtained from the observation of
actual male and female persons.

The result of all this, according to Freud, is that biologically and psychologically, there is no pure masculinity or
femininity. Everyone, he says, is a mixture of the two.

In regard to biological masculinity, activity and its
secondary manifestations (such as aggression, a stronger
intensity of libido, more developed muscles) are said to be as
a rule "soldered" to it. Yet there is no necessary connection
since species of animals are found where the female reputedly
has these qualities, which are usually attributed to the human
male.

The first meaning of the conception of masculinity and
femininity designating activity and passivity is, for Freud,
the essential one and the one which he says has significance
for psychoanalysis. And it agrees with his conception of the
libido as "lawfully" and regularly of a masculine nature,
whether in man or woman, whose object may also be either the
man or the woman. Even when the libido is diverted to a
passive aim it is always active, always masculine.[37]

The "Riddle" of Femininity

However, Freud does not, in the end, think that active
and passive can be said to be the ultimate differential traits of
mankind. The fact that little girls can have plenty of aggressiveness was soon observed. And men for various reasons often
manifest passive characteristics. For these and other reasons,
Freud was never able to find, in any unequivocal fashion, any
psychological characteristic which would clearly differentiate
masculine and feminine. But his conclusion that women are a
"riddle" is, even from a logical point of view, very curious.

In any case, psychology, he says, cannot solve the riddle of femininity.

And so he contented himself with studying those "who are characterized as manifestly or preponderantly female by the possession of female genitals."

PASSIVITY AND MASOCHISM IN WOMEN

Nevertheless, Freud does, by and large, characterize femininity by a tendency to passive behavior and passive aims and also by masochism. Both their constitutions and society compel women to repress their aggressiveness, favoring the turning inward of their destructive tendencies and thus furthering the development of strong masochistic impulses.[38] Therefore, masochism in men is said to display or imply obvious feminine traits of character.

The task left for psychoanalysis is to describe the way in which women (who may or may not manifest preponderant feminine traits as illustrated above) develop from children with their bisexual disposition.

Masochism is said to be observed in three forms: as a condition under which sexual excitement may be aroused, as an expression of feminine nature, and as a norm of behavior. Freud distinguishes three types of masochism: erotogenic, feminine, and moral.

Erotogenic masochism is characterized by the "lust for pain," although the lust for pain is also found in the other two.

"The erotogenic type of masochism passes through all the developmental stages of the libido, and from them it takes the changing shapes it wears in the life of the mind. The fear of being devoured by the totem-animal (father) is derived from the primitive oral stage of libido-organization; the desire to be beaten by the father from the next-following sadistic-oral stage; castration, although it is subsequently denied, enters into the content of masochistic phantasies as a residue from the phallic stage; and from the genital stage are derived of course the situations characteristic of womanhood, namely, the passive part in coitus, and the act of giving birth."[39]

Feminine masochism is said to be based entirely on the "primary" type, the lust for pain. (Yet Freud's material for this classification is derived primarily from men.) Phantasies of people of this type serve for sexual gratification or terminate in onanism. The manifest content of the phantasies "is of being pinioned, bound, beaten painfully, whipped, in some way mishandled, forced to obey unconditionally, defiled, degraded." Mutilations may occasionally, though far more rarely, appear in the manifest content, but only in a very restricted way. Freud's interpretation is that the masochist wants to be treated like a little, helpless, dependent child, especially like a naughty child. From a study of richly elaborated phantasies of this sort, one discovers that the subject is put "in a situation characteristic of womanhood, *i.e.*, they mean that he is being castrated, is playing the passive part in coitus, or is giving birth. For this reason, I have called this form of masochism *a potiori* feminine, although so many of its features point to childish life."[40] Feelings of guilt are expressed in the manifest content of the phantasies, the subject feeling he has committed some crime which he is to expiate by pain and torture. Behind this idea, Freud finds a relation to infantile masturbation.

In moral masochism, the connection with sexuality is "loosened." It is suffering itself which matters. While all other types of masochism retain the condition of suffering at the hands of the loved one, in moral masochism, this limitation is dropped. Who the person is who administers the "sentence" is of no importance, even impersonal circumstances may be the "cause" of the suffering. The "true masochist always holds out his cheek wherever he sees a chance of receiving a blow."[41]

The ego seeks punishment "whether" (either?) from the super-ego or from parental authority. Such a person is unconscious of his need for punishment. Freud claims that the need for some punishment by the parental authority is a "repressive distortion" of a wish to have some passive, that is, feminine sexual relations with him. This is presumed to imply or to be connected with moral masochism. "Conscience and morality arose through overcoming, desexualizing the Oedipus-complex; in moral masochism, morality becomes sexualized afresh, the Oedipus-complex is reactivated, a regression from morality back to the Oedipus-complex is under way."[42] A temptation to perform sinful acts arises, which must be expiated by the reproaches of the sadistic conscience or by chastisement from the parent-substitute — fate. To provoke punishment by fate, the masochist must do something inexpedient, act against his interests, ruin his real prospects in life, and possibly destroy his own existence in the world of reality.

The development of the little girl, for Freud, is more difficult and more complicated than that of the little boy. Besides the difference in the formation of the genitals and other accompanying bodily differences, there are said to be differences of instinctual disposition as well. Generally, the girl is less aggressive, less defiant, and less self-sufficient. And she seems to have a greater need of affection shown her, thus being more dependent and docile. Freud has the impression, also, that the girl is more intelligent and lively. She is said to be more inclined to meet the world half-way and to make stronger "object-cathexes," that is, in ordinary language, to form more intense emotional attachments to people.

For the female infant, like the male, the first object of instinctual interest is the mother, since of course, she too feeds at the mother's breast and is cared for by the mother. Often she remains attached to the mother beyond the fourth year. Her libidinal relations are said to be manifold. Since she goes through the oral, anal-sadistic, and phallic phases also, her wishes find expression in these varying phases. She manifests both active and passive libidinal wishes, hence both masculine and feminine wishes.[43] Ambivalence, as in the case of the boy, will manifest itself. In the phallic phase the little girl "is a little man."[44] There will be both a desire to impregnate the mother and to have a child by the mother. Phantasies of being seduced by the mother are aroused, and later such phantasies about the father will occur.

Eventually, for a variety of reasons, the little girl turns away from the mother in an atmosphere of hate. Complaints about the mother's care reflect—so it seems to Freud—an insatiable need for the first form of nourishment, and she seems never to get over the pain of losing the mother's breast. The appearance of another child arouses an intense feeling of jealous hatred against the new arrival and resentment against the faithless mother. The little girl becomes "naughty" and intractable. Even when there is no rival, and she remains the affectionate favorite of the mother, her demands for affection are boundless. She requires exclusive attention and tolerates no sharing whatever.[45] When, during the phallic phase, the mother forbids and disapproves any suggestion of masturbation, the greatest frustration of her libidinal wishes and desires occurs.

Still, all of these disappointments and deprivations, Freud remarks, occur in the case of the boy without alienating him from her. The specific factor which turns the little girl away from the mother lies in the castration complex. For some obscure reason the female child holds her mother responsible for her lack of a penis and never forgives her. The little girl does not lightly get over her "penis-envy." For a long time she clings to the possibility of getting something like it. And even when she, under the pressure of reality, does consciously abandon the wish for a penis of her own, it persists unconsciously.[46]

The girl's discovery of her "castration" gradually leads her to turn away from the mother. She accepts castration as an established fact, while the little boy, in the course of his development, dreads its future possibility. Since the castration-dread in the boy is said to be a most powerful factor towards repressing and, in most cases, destroying the Oedipus complex and forming the super-ego, the little girl cannot develop a strong super-ego. Education and threats of loss of love must serve the function of the castration-dread in boys.

Her unfavorable comparison with the boy wounds her self-love, causes her to repudiate her love toward the mother, to repress a good deal of her sexuality, and to abandon masturbation. She had loved the phallic mother, the mother whom children endow with a penis, and her discovery that her mother too is "castrated" enables her to abandon her love for such an inferior object and to turn to the father. Now she is more free to give rein to her pent-up and long-accumulating hostility to the mother.

The Oedipus Complex of the Girl

By abandoning her clitoric masturbation, the little girl surrenders part of her active strivings. The passive side of her nature becomes dominant. In turning to the father, her passive instinctual impulses preponderate and assist her in this turning to the new love-object. This tends to smooth the path toward femininity. She still possesses the wish for a penis, and she expects it from the father.[47] Only when she substitutes a wish for a child, at first by the father, for a penis can she be said to establish a feminine orientation.[48] Later if she marries, this wish will perhaps be fulfilled, and if the offspring is a boy with the "longed for" penis, her happiness is said to be great indeed.

The transference of the child-penis wish on to the father marks the little girl's entry into the Oedipus complex situation, which she regards as a haven of refuge. Now the mother becomes the rival, who gets all that she herself desires from the father, and the girl's hostility is greatly reenforced. For an indefinite period she remains more or less transfixed in the Oedipus situation. She only abandons it late in life, and then incompletely. Since there is no fear of castration, the primary motive for abandonment of her Oedipus complex relationship does not exist.

AVOIDANCE OF FEMININITY

But there is a further complication. The discovery of her castration may be an unpalatable fact which she cannot accept, and she may refuse to recognize her deficiency. This may exaggerate the active masculine side of her nature which hitherto was in evidence, and if by constitution the active side is, for a girl, unusually strong, she will take refuge in an identification with the phallic mother or the father. In such a way femininity is said to be avoided.

Or, again, the little girl may temporarily abandon this infantile masculinity, enter the Oedipus situation, but, because of the inevitable disappointments experienced from the father, revert to the pre-Oedipal situation. Female "homosexuals" are said to manifest an alternation reminiscent of the two phases.[49]

Freud lays great stress on the vicissitudes of the girl's development in explaining the complications arising in married life and the mental attitudes and traits of women as he knew them.

3. THE THEORIES OF SIGMUND FREUD AND HIS DISCIPLES

ADDITIONAL FREUDIAN CONCEPTS

THE THEORY OF NEUROSIS

Libidinal Development

As we have seen, the libido is conceived as normally developing through various stages until it reaches and becomes finally canalized and structured under the primacy of the genital zone. But not all the preparatory phases are passed through and completely outgrown. Apparently "single portions" of every separate sexual impulse may remain at an early phase of development, while "other portions" may reach their final goal. An arrestation in a component impulse is called a fixation. There may also be a libido-fixation on an earlier type of object choice. Another possibility is that portions which progressed further may, under certain circumstances, regress to an earlier phase.

The two possibilities are not independent of each other. Freud believes that a constitutional predisposing tendency may make fixation more likely in some cases; in others, an accidental occurrence in childhood can induce a fixation. In such instances resistance to external difficulties will be less

51

powerful; the libido will regress more easily. But a constitutional or acquired predisposing tendency to regression is not so necessary in all cases. When external difficulties create undue pressure, or, in other words, when frustration is very great, regression apparently may take place in spite of a more "normal" sexual constitution and development. Cases of neurotic illness then fall in a "series," in such a manner that either sexual constitution or events experienced predominate, while the other is said to be proportionately less.

The tendency of the libido to hold to particular channels and objects is sometimes referred to as its "adhesiveness." This adhesiveness is very important in understanding "neurotics" and "perverts," though it is also found in "normal" people under numerous conditions.

The Role of Conflict

There is no neurosis without a conflict. This conflict, evoked by frustration, is of opposing and contradictory wishes. When one is frustrated, the libido is driven to find other paths and objects, which may then arouse the disapproval of a part of the personality. According to the earlier formulation, there is a conflict between the ego and sexuality. In other words, impulses consistent or in harmony with the ego collide, so to speak, with impulses which threaten or seem to threaten the ego. Three conditions are necessary in the etiology of neurosis: privation, fixation, and a susceptibility to conflict produced by the ego.

As Freud points out, conflict is of itself not unusual. The special conditions we mentioned are necessary for the conflict to be pathogenic. In other words, external libidinal frustration must be supplemented by internal frustration. While some people do not fall ill from frustration, this is because, at least to a considerable degree, they can abandon aims previously gratifying and adopt new, though related, aims (sublimation).

Certain people whose libido has undergone a powerful fixation at an earlier point in development do not, however, become neurotic. These are the "perverts." This is because their ego "countenances" the fixation. They do not have to repress the arrested impulses. To be perverse is the same as to be infantile. Because among other things they feel no great anxiety about their activities, such people do not become neurotic.

Suppose, however, a person cannot find external, real, gratification of the libido because of the moral and other requirements of part of the ego (in the latter formulation the part that is split off—the super-ego, which the ego must obey as it can). The libidinal impulses then may, in a loose manner of speaking, become repressed, the experience of them erased from conscious awareness.[1] (Actually the temporal sequence is not as simple as this, as we shall note below.) A damming up of the libido occurs. But here too fixations in childhood make frustration more probable.

Hence, a conflict arises between the sexual drives and the repressing power of the ego, due to the demands of the super-ego. In striving to find an outlet, that is, gratification, the blocked libido streams backward to positions earlier abandoned (and repressed) and "re-cathects" them. In this process the libido is withdrawn from control by the ego and its laws and all the training acquired under the influence of the ego. The earlier positions to which the person regresses are found in the component tendencies, the activities, and objects of childhood. The process of regression occurs, by and large, unconsciously.

Symptom Formation and Phantasy

As this process occurs, the ideas to which the libido becomes attached or rather re-cathects are subject to the special processes characteristic of the unconscious (of the id), namely, condensation and displacement. In other words, the cathected ideas or libido-representatives have still to contend

with the (preconscious) ego. If the conscious part of the ego
knew what was going on, the whole process could not occur.
Hence, a form of expression is adopted by which the opposing
forces find an outlet.

The modes of outlet of the libido take the form of
phantasy and sometimes neurotic symptoms.[2] The symptom is
a derivative, a distorted expression of an unconscious libidinal
wish-fulfillment, cleverly ambiguous with two completely contradictory meanings. Symptoms are compromise-formations,
being in some ways similar to dreams.

Fixation and Regression

We said above that the temporal sequence is not as
simple as we had expressed it. The fact is, according to
Freud, when a neurosis occurs in an adult, there is always
revealed that the person had experienced an infantile neurosis,
although perhaps only in a veiled and incipient form. Hence,
to some degree because of the infantile neurosis, a fixation of
libido at some pre-genital stage had already occurred, sometimes exaggerated by a constitutional tendency. The fixation
exerts an attraction on the libido. In ordinary language, we
may say that due to pathogenic experiences in childhood the
person grew up with an immature psychological equipment,
an immature personality, and being unable to meet the usual
requirements and possibilities of adult living, regressed to a
phase of development which he never really and fully outgrew
and which at one time provided some satisfaction. The neurotic
is said to be tied to his past, especially to his early relations
to mother and father. There are, in fact, two kinds of regression: a return to the first objects invested with libido, which
are incestuous in character, and a return of the whole sexual
organization to earlier phases of development.

Psychic Reality and Neurosis

The symptoms yield a satisfaction lacking in reality,
although the person is not conscious of it. Consciously he

suffers and complains. The symptom is a disguised repetition of an infantile sexual experience although complicated by the incorporation of factors drawn from subsequent experience.[3] There is a rejection of the reality principle and a return to the pleasure principle. As in a dream, also, the symptom by means of condensation and displacement, can compress satisfaction into a single sensation. There is a neglect of the difference between phantasy and reality. Living to a large extent in a phantasy world, the person tends to take his phantasies as real. In other words, the phantasies of the neurotic have "psychical reality." And in the world of neurosis psychical reality is said to be the determining factor.

The Role of Primal Phantasies

Neurotics, according to Freud, continually recount certain experiences: observation of parental intercourse, seduction by an adult, and the threat of castration. These experiences, however, for the most part, represent phantasies of childhood, not actual experiences. Hence, Freud believes that such phantasied experiences are "required" by the neurosis. He calls them primal phantasies, and they are a phylogenetic possession. The child, partly from hints and allusions perhaps concerning such matters, "fills out the gaps" in his own individual experiences with true prehistoric experiences of the same kind stored up and inherited.

The Role of Phantasy in Life

Phantasies in general serve as a substitute for the pleasure (sexual and other) which reality compels one to renounce — temporarily or permanently. The phantasy life of people serves as a substitute gratification, a wish fulfillment. The meagre satisfaction which man can extract from reality leaves him starving. The objects and modes of satisfaction in childhood abandoned by the libido have not been entirely relinquished. They or their derivatives persist via phantasy.

These phantasies, such as day-dreams, enable one to find the way back to the repressed fixations. Under frustration the libido "withdraws on to the phantasies." Previously they were tolerated. With the return of the libido stream on to the phantasies, a quantitative factor is introduced, which serves as an intermediate step to symptom formation. The augmented phantasies then become assertive, press for realization and have to be repressed by the ego, while at the same time they are subject to the attraction of the unconscious (of the id). The libido travels back to its fixation points, to the sources of the phantasies in the unconscious.[4]

The Economic Factor in Neurosis

The quantitative factor is therefore very important in neurosis. Conflict does not break out until a certain degree of intensity of the energy of opposing forces is attained. Hence, whether a person becomes neurotic or not also depends upon the amount of undischarged libido that a person can "hold freely suspended" and how much he can sublimate. In general a person falls ill of a neurosis only when his ego cannot somehow come to terms with the libido.

Secondary Advantage in Neurosis

Freud points out that a person pays heavily for his neurosis. The suffering is as severe as the conflict it replaces, often much worse. Still he will try to get all of the "secondary advantage" from it that he can, that is, he will try to use it for various purposes, such as for getting attention, and especially as a *modus vivendi*, wherein the neurosis appears useful and expedient. The neurosis comes to represent a way of life.

The Role of Anxiety or Dread

Since a neurosis occurs only with repression, a further word about this process is necessary. Originally Freud

believed that repression caused neurotic anxiety. He believed
the repressed impulses became converted into anxiety or discharged in the form of anxiety. Later he tended to believe
that anxiety caused the repression and not conversely. The
anxiety is caused by a danger; it is a fear of danger. Every
stage of development is said to have its own conditions for
anxiety, its own dangers, mental helplessness at the stage of
early immaturity of the ego, loss of object or of love during
the early years of childhood, castration at the phallic phase,
fear of the super-ego during the latency period. Neurotic
persons are those who remain infantile in their attitude toward
danger. They combine any and all of these anxieties.[5]

An Explanation

In order to avoid confusion, we must point out that we
have discussed only one of the conditions, although perhaps
the most important one, for the development of neurosis,
namely, the moral demands of a part of the ego or what is
latterly called the super-ego. In general, the ego may be
unable to stand the strain of serving its three harsh masters,
the id, the super-ego, and the external world; hence, the person
develops a neurosis or in extreme cases a psychosis.

The Death Instinct and Neurosis

The death instinct theory further complicates matters,
and Freud does not seem able to assimilate it clearly to his
general theory of neurosis. The need for punishment, the
masochistic wishes of neurotics are to be recalled in this
connection as a fusion of Eros and the death instinct turned
inward. Freud is not clear whether all of the aggressiveness
that is turned inward is "bound" or controlled by the super-
ego and used against the ego, or whether part of it works
directly and destructively in the ego and the id. In any case
the super-ego is said to make the dangerous aggressive
impulses its own, thus limiting the degree of aggressiveness

that is directed against society, while the person himself in
this way, to the same degree, is sacrificed to it.

THE THEORY OF CHARACTER

Many people believe that Freud's contributions to charac-
terology are among his most lasting and valuable achievements.
Some of the following exposition is derived from the work of
Karl Abraham, who developed Freud's ideas on character and
who also made superlative contributions of his own. Abraham
defined character as the sum of a person's reactions towards
his social environment.[6] This definition, unfortunately, is too
vague or too inclusive to be very enlightening, so we shall
approach Freud's concept of character from a developmental
standpoint.

At each stage of libidinal development the person's reactions are determined or at least circumscribed primarily by
the way the libido is organized and structured at that stage,
at least when there is a normal progress toward maturity.
For example, at the early oral stage impulses to suck predominate, and sucking, aside from the taking of nourishment,
gives pleasure because of the excitation of mouth and lips.
As Abraham points out, the pleasure in the sucking of this
period is largely a pleasure in taking, in being given something.[7] Later the pleasure in sucking may be replaced or
rather subordinated to the pleasure in biting. As the child
grows, under normal circumstances the pleasures of sucking
and biting are to a large extent renounced or subordinated to
other forms of pleasure.

But renunciation of pleasure occurs only on the basis of
exchange for other pleasures.[8] Under certain conditions, the
libido or part of it, as we have observed above, may be fixated
at, say, the oral stage. When this happens a person will manifest characteristics throughout life which are related to this
stage. The sucking impulses and biting impulses remain pre-

dominant, or characteristics due to "reaction-formations" against them develop, or they become sublimated.[9]

The Oral Character

In some cases the person's entire character is under "oral influence." For such people sucking was undisturbed and highly pleasurable. And they retain from this happy period a deep conviction that everything will always be well with them, an imperturbable optimism which often helps them to reach their goals in life. In other cases, one meets with the type who believes that there will always be a kind person, a mother-substitute, who will care for them and give them everything they need. "Their whole attitude towards life shows that they expect the mother's breast to flow for them eternally."[10] Such people make no kind of effort. They also often have an intense appetite for food.

An ungratified sucking period has quite other consequences. Socially, they always seem to be asking for something, whether modestly or aggressively. They plead and insist. They dislike being alone for even a short time. In certain cases, when there has been a regression from the anal stage, an element of cruelty appears. Their longing to receive gratification by way of the mouth changes into a need to give something orally. Besides a craving to obtain everything, they show a constant need to communicate orally to others. Hence, there is a great verbal flow from them. In certain neurotics the expression of hostility by speech is striking. In fact, in certain neurotics whose libido was not fully gratified during the oral-sadistic stage, speaking is used to express all of their instinctual trends.

In general, desires derived from the oral stage do not have the tendency to destroy the object, a feature which is characteristic of the anal stage. But important differences still exist in oral character formation between the earlier and later phases of the oral stage, between the phase marked by sucking and that by biting. In the biting phase, ambivalence—hostile and friendly tendencies—is marked, while ambivalence seems to be lacking in the character-traits derived from the sucking phase.

We shall end our discussion of the oral stage by mentioning a few more character-traits derived from it. In general, phenomena of very intense craving and effort are traced back to the first stage. Generosity, sociability, open-mindedness, restlessness, curiosity, an inclination toward scientific investigation, ambition are all marked in the oral character.

Abraham points out that when the problems of character formation are considered from one large unifying view, from the standpoint of infantile sexuality, everything forms a whole in the characterological sphere. Infantile sexuality covers not only the entire unconscious instinctual life of the mature human being; it also includes the very important mental experiences of the earliest years, as well as prenatal influences.

The Anal Character

In 1908 Freud published a paper that has become famous among psychoanalysts, *Character and Anal Eroticism.*[11] Freud, in this paper, describes a regular combination of certain peculiarities which he found in people of a certain sort. These peculiarities or traits are orderliness, parsimony, and obstinacy. Each term really refers to a group or interrelated series of traits. Orderliness for instance, includes cleanliness, reliability and conscientiousness concerning petty duties. From the childhood history of certain people having this combination of traits Freud learned that they derived an "incidental" pleasure from defecation and manifested various other striking characteristics in regard to the bowel movement, including unseemly performances with the stool. From this he inferred that the erotogenic significance of the anal zone was intensified in the innate constitution of such persons.

But since none of these striking characteristics in regard to bowel movement persisted, Freud concluded that the anal zone in the course of development lost its erotogenic significance, and that the triad of orderliness, parsimony, and obstinacy had a definite relation to the disappearance of the anal eroticism.

Without going into all the details, we shall give one or two examples of how Freud linked up the various phenomena. Cleanliness, orderliness, and reliability constitute a reaction-formation against an interest in things that are unclean, intrusive and which ought not to be on the body. Obstinacy is directly connected with the infantile defiance about parting with the stool and also the fact that, as Freud puts it, "painful stimuli to the skin of the buttocks" serve as a means in the child's education "designed to break his will and make him submissive."

And so Freud gave a "formula" for understanding the formation of character: "the permanent character-traits are either unchanged perpetuations of the original impulses, sublimation of them, or reaction-formations against them."[12]

Abraham, among others, elaborated Freud's ideas on the anal character. Pleasure in the act of excretion is differentiated from pleasure in the products of excretion. The pleasure includes psychical gratification.

The strict regularity and cleanliness demanded of the child exposes his narcissism to a severe test. Although the majority of children adapt themselves sooner or later to the demands of the mother, some manifest an "obstinate holding fast to the primitive right of self-determination," hidden behind an "over-compensation" of politeness and obedience. When the child succeeds in making a virtue out of necessity, he is said to identify himself with the requirements of his educators and is proud of his attainment. Thus, the primary injury to his narcissism is compensated, and the original feeling of self-satisfaction gives way to a feeling of self-satisfaction in being "good."

Early injuries to the child's narcissism, however, may result if a habit is prematurely forced upon him. When cleanliness is required too soon, the child will acquire the habit through fear. An inner resistance will remain, the libido continuing in a tenacious narcissistic fixation, with a permanent disturbance in the capacity to love.

In the child's pride in evacuation there is to be recognized a primitive feeling of power. And this persists unconsciously in adults. Persons with an anal character are very sensitive to an encroachment on what they regard as their field of power, taking the questionings and probings of psychoanalysis as an unheard-of interference with their way of life. They cling obstinately to their way of doing things, and they expect compliance from others.

If full genital organization of the libido is not attained, or if there is a regression to the sadistic-anal stage, the person loses not only his productive power in the generative sense, but he also loses productivity and initiative in other respects. But the effects are still more pervasive.

"Together with the man's genital activity there goes a positive feeling-attitude towards his love-object, and this attitude extends to his behavior towards other objects and is expressed in his capacity for social adaptation, his devotion to certain interests and ideas, etc. In all these respects the character-formation of the sadistic-anal stage is inferior to that of the genital phase. The sadistic element, which in a normal man's emotional life is of great importance, once it has undergone appropriate transformation through sublimation, appears with particular strength in the obsessional [anal] character, but becomes more or less crippled in consequence of the ambivalence in the instinctual life of such persons. It also contains destructive tendencies hostile to the object, and on account of this cannot become sublimated to a real capacity for devotion to a love-object. For the reaction-formation of too great yieldingness and gentleness which is frequently observed in such people must not be confused with a real transference love. Those cases in which object-love and genital libido-organization have been attained to a fair extent are more favorable. If the character-trait of over-kindness mentioned above is combined with a partial object-love of this kind, a socially useful 'variety' is produced, which in essential respects is, nevertheless, inferior to full object-love."[13]

People with an anal character or who have marked anal character traits make an unconscious identification of feces with money (something to hold on to, to keep, to possess). Hence, they are often famous for their avarice. In general, the more male productivity and activity is thwarted in neurotics, the more pronounced does their interest in possession become. For marked cases of anal character formation almost all relationships in life are proprietary. Envy is another outstanding trait of theirs. Not only do they covet others' possessions, they manifest spiteful impulses against those who have possessions. They have difficulty in separating themselves from any possession and hence they love to hoard.

Those who have become fixated at the anal-sadistic stage are in general hostile, cruel, and malicious, morose, jealous, inaccessible, and reticent, with a conservative behavior and attitude toward life.

These two character types we have just discussed are called archaic character types, because they are recapitulations of primitive states of development through which the human race has passed. A retrograde development of character in the main comes to a stop at the anal-sadistic stage.

The Genital Character

According to Abraham, the individual is able to fill his place and exercise his powers fully and satisfactorily in his social environment only if his libido has attained the genital stage. The genital stage, however, everywhere shows traces of the previous stages from which it evolved: enterprise and energy from the oral stage; endurance, perseverance and various other characteristics from the anal stage; the necessary power to carry on the struggle for existence from "sadistic sources" (of both stages). The final stage of character development is said to be relatively unnarcissistic. Ambivalence is overcome, which implies an absence of internal conflict. If a person is to succeed in reaching the genital stage, he must also possess a sufficient quantity of affectionate and friendly feeling.

Here, too, the Oedipus complex is of decisive importance. In normal development the boy's sexual feelings for the mother become aim-inhibited; feelings of fondness, devotion and so on predominate during the latency period. Under favorable circumstances these positive feelings are carried over to the father. "They gradually extend their field and the child adopts a friendly and well-wishing attitude, first to persons of his near environment, and then to the community at large." Hence, the definitive character of everyone "is dependent upon the history of the Oedipus complex, and particularly on the capacity he has developed for transferring his friendly feelings on to other people or on to his whole environment."

A marked disturbance of character results from failure to develop social feelings, due to certain circumstances in early childhood. The sexual impulses of such people are unaccompanied by any desire for affectionate relations. And in their daily life they have difficulties in making proper contact with others. Illegitimate children furnish a good example, having from the beginning of their lives suffered from a want of sympathy and affection. And if "a child has no examples of love before it, it will have difficulty in entertaining any such feelings itself, and it will besides be incapable of discarding those primitive impulses which are originally directed *against* the external world."[14] The same sort of thing is said to happen to the neurotic who, born in ordinary circumstances, grows up feeling that he is the Cinderella of the family, that he is not loved.[15]

Concluding Remarks On Character

We shall conclude the discussion of character with a few brief observations. The evolution of character results from the early childhood experiences and from the struggle of the ego to come to terms with the id, the super-ego, and reality. "The incorporation of the early parental function in the shape of the super-ego is no doubt the most important and decisive element; next come identifications with the parents of a later date and with other persons in authority, and the same identifications as precipitates of abandoned object-relations."[16] Finally, Freud mentions reaction-formations as another important factor.

THE INDIVIDUAL'S ARCHAIC HERITAGE

We have already had occasion to mention in passing Freud's theory that the individual brings with him at birth fragments of phylogenetic orgin, an archaic heritage. This archaic heritage of mankind "includes not only dispositions, but also ideational contents, memory traces of the experiences of former generations."[17] Furthermore, the individual undergoes in his development, in an abbreviated form, a repetition of the most important events of a process which occurred long before the dawn of history. In the following pages we give a summary account of this notion.

The Scientific Myth of the Primal Father

Freud, in *Totem and Taboo*, borrowing from Darwin and others, propounded the theory of a primal horde, existing perhaps in a small community at a remote period of time, led by a violent and jealous father, who kept all the females for

himself and drove away the growing sons.[18] Then one day the
expelled sons, who naturally did not take kindly to this
arrangement, banded together, slew, and ate the father.[19] By
this action they ended the father-dominated primal horde. By
devouring the envied and feared model, the primal father,
each brother realized his wish for *identification* with him and
partook of a portion of his strength. But here too we find
the same contradictory feelings towards the father which we
know as ambivalence. While they hated the powerful father,
who stood in the way of their sexual demands and desire for
power, they also loved and admired him. After the death of
the primal father and the subsequent identification of the
brothers, their repressed tender impulses asserted themselves.
The expression of these tender feelings took the form of
remorse, a sense of guilt. And what the father prevented, they
now themselves prevented by erecting a psychic prohibition in
themselves, a subsequent obedience to the wishes of the dead
father.

According to Freud, sexual needs, instead of uniting
men, separate them. With the death and cannibalistic incorporation of the father, each brother was now the rival for
possession of all the women. The boys would have liked to
emulate the "old man," but none of them was strong enough
to subdue or expel the rest. A fight of each against every
other would have destroyed the new organization of the
brothers. Hence, in order to survive, they erected an incest
prohibition, by which they renounced the women whom they
desired.[20] In this way they saved the social organization which
they had formed, and which, says Freud, could have been
based upon "homo-sexual" feelings and activities which probably manifested themselves during their banishment.

The Origin of Totemism

But they still had to find a way to assuage their burning
sense of guilt and to bring about a reconciliation, if only

symbolically, with their father. They erected a totemic system by which they found a substitute for the father in an animal, whose life was to be protected, treated as sacred, in relation to whom certain taboos were developed, and so on. In this way the father may be said to live on, although in a symbolical sense, while the original event is glossed over and forgotten. By establishing certain restrictions in regard to the animal and performing sacrificial rites under the proper circumstances, the enduring sense of guilt is allayed.

The totemic system is said to be a kind of agreement with the father in which he (through the magic powers of the totem) exercises protection, care and forbearance in exchange for the pledge to honor his life (by proscribing the killing of the totem animal). Totemism also acts as an attempt at justification, presumably by showing that the brothers know how to respect the father when he adopts the proper behavior toward them.

Deification of the Father Ideal

With the passage of time an extraordinary increase of longing for the father occurred. The father's perfection of power and his untrammelled freedom grew into an ideal capturing the minds of men, with a willingness to submit themselves to him. The bitter feelings against him declined. Certain individuals who had distinguished themselves above all others came to be invested with the qualities of the father ideal. They bcame paternal gods.[21] The animal loses its sacredness and becomes a fitting subject for sacrifice to the tribal god, a simple offering to the deity, who is now so exalted that only a priest can act as intermediary.

The Triumph of Authority

Hence, the deposed and reinstated father exacts a cruel revenge: the totemic system culminates in the dominance of authority.

In the course of time, the fatherless society gradually evolved into a patriarchal one. In another work Freud tells us that the brothers eventually revived the old situation on a new level. Man assumed the role of head of a family, usurping the prerogatives of the gynecocracy, set up during the fatherless period. Compensatorily, he may then have acknowledged the mother deities, whose priests were castrated for the mother's protection, following the example given by the father of the primal horde. The new family was only a shadow of the old one; there were many fathers, each one limiting the rights of the others.[22] (The example of the primal father refers, of course, to castration. Among his other activities, the jealous and cruel primal father castrated the growing boy. Only the youngest son, the mother's favorite, whom she protected, escaped, and he in the era of the primal horde became the father's successor.) As the social order further evolved, godlike kings arose, who transferred the patriarchal system to the state.[23]

The Perpetuation of Ambivalence

The ambivalence attached to the father complex has not been resolved and continues in totemism and in religions in general. Freud thinks that all later religions express attempts to solve the same problem of palliating guilt and conciliating the father through obedience. But religion also in its ceremonies commemorates the triumph over the father. In the further development of religion, the son's sense of guilt and his defiance were never obliterated. Due to ambivalence, the son's wishes against the father are expressed by his becoming a god himself beside or in place of the father. But according to the law of retaliation, deeply rooted in human feeling, a murder can be atoned only by the sacrifice of another life. By the sacrificial death of the son, there is effected a reconciliation with the father, especially since woman is renounced, for whom the sons killed the father. The Christian concept of man's original sin expresses an offense against God the Father, and mankind is redeemed only by the sacrifice of Christ, God the Son. The Christian sacrament of the Eucharist is said to express the after-effects of the original deed.

In Greek tragedy, the hero suffers from "tragic guilt," and is doomed to die. The hero has to suffer, in the Freudian interpretation, because he represents the primal father.

Social Significance of Totemism

We may conclude this part of the discussion by observing that Freud finds that the original deed, its symbolical representation, and the symbolical "mechanisms" to which they gave rise, have had the greatest influence upon the development of society. Certain feelings find expression in the sanctification of common blood, ensuring the solidarity of life within the clan.[24] A prohibition against fratricide arises. Social and fraternal feelings are born.

The Significance of the Original Oedipus Complex

According to Freud, society is founded on the complicity in the common criminal deed, while religion develops from the ensuing feelings of guilt and subsequent remorse. Morality, likewise, while founded partly on the exigencies of social life, is also based on the necessity of expiating the common sense of guilt.[25] The beginnings of religion, ethics, society and art, are said to meet in the Oedipus complex.[26]

Theory of the Mass Psyche

Freud expresses one of his most interesting speculations in his assumption of a psyche of the mass, in which psychic processes occur just as in the psychic life of the individual. In accordance with this assumption, the sense of guilt of the brothers is said to survive for thousands of years and still to remain effective in generations which could not have known anything about the original deed. By the assumption of a mass psyche, he attempts to explain the continuity in the emotional life of mankind. But how does this occur? He hazards the following explanation: The individual inherits certain psychic dispositions which, however, usually need incentives in his own life to become effective. Furthermore, every person, in his unconscious psychic activity has "an apparatus" which enables him to interpret the reactions of others.[27] This unconscious understanding of all customs, ceremonies and laws left behind from the initial relation to the primal father, Freud surmises, may also have enabled later generations to acquire the legacy of feelings of past generations.[28]

THE GREAT MAN THEORY

A very suggestive theory of Freud's, as we shall see later in detail, is the one of the Great Man, to whom he assigns an enormous historical significance. It is not so much his nature, says Freud, which interests us, but the qualities by which he influences his contemporaries.

The great man influences his contemporaries in two ways, through his personality and through the idea for which he stands. There are several ways by which an idea may effect its influence on the masses. It may lay stress on an old group of wishes in the people, or it may direct their wishes toward a new aim. Still again, the great man may lure the masses by other means (unspecified).

The more effective way, however, is through his personality, that is, by force of personality, the idea being subordinated to a minor role. Why? The masses have a strong need for an authority which they can admire, to which they can submit, and which sometimes dominates and abuses them. But one may wonder why the masses have such (an alleged) need. Freud's answer is that the need springs from a longing for the father, the father who lives in each of us from childhood. It is the same father, he says, whom the hero of legend boasts of having overcome.

So we know that the traits with which the masses endow the great man are traits of the father. "The decisiveness of thought, the strength of will, the forcefulness of his deeds, belong to the picture of the father; above all other things, however, the self-reliance and independence of the great man, his divine conviction of doing the right thing, which may pass into ruthlessness. He must be admired, he may be trusted, but one cannot help also being afraid of him."[29]

There are two things to be observed here. One is, we suspect, that Freud believes that the alleged need of the masses to submit is innate. The other point is that the description of the great man is really a description of the authoritarian ruler. Very few civilized people can live without the support of others. One can hardly be too extreme in describing the mania for authority and the inner instability of humanity.[30] "One might say," Freud remarks, "that the great man is the authority for whose sake the effort is made, and since the great man achieves this because he is a father substitute we need not be surprised if he is allotted the role of Super-ego in mass psychology."[31] The effort to which Freud refers is instinctual renunciation for the sake of gaining love and approval of the father substitute, which is analogous to the childhood form of renunciation.

4. THE THEORIES OF SIGMUND FREUD AND HIS DISCIPLES

SYMBOLISM

In this chapter we present a synopsis of Freudian concepts of symbolical interpretation as applied in dream, myth, religion and art. These samples serve to illustrate concretely, not to exhaust, the manifold fields which psychoanalysis has penetrated. We begin with Freud's interpretation of dreams and then show how the principles of dream interpretation and symbolism are applied in those other fields. It is scarcely necessary for us to add that these notions of Freud which we expound in the following pages are today extremely influential in various fields of thought and endeavor. They add a new perspective and serve as a powerful tool in comprehending some of the most complex phenomena of human experience.

FREUD'S INTERPRETATION OF DREAMS

There is perhaps no sector of human experience which seems so irrational or nonsensical as dreams. At first blush, it looks as though dreams do not make any sense. They seem to be completely unreal, illogical, contradictory and "childish." Dreams seem to ignore fact and everything that sound common sense demands. In dreaming we seem to be transported into a shadowy and crazy world where the mind takes a long holiday and goes off to an amusement park or on a visit to a chamber of horrors.

Of course, not a few people do believe that dreams have significance, although they may often be rather shamefaced in admitting it. In many places all over the world dreams were and are frequently regarded as having considerable significance. In the Bible, for example, as Joseph's interpretation of the Pharaoh's dream testifies, considerable significance is attached to dreams.

Perhaps the most famous statement about dreams before Freud is that of Plato. He tells us that certain pleasures and desires not disciplined by law and by the higher desires with the aid of reason "bestir themselves in dreams, when the gentler part of the soul slumbers and the control of reason is withdrawn; then the wild beast in us, full-fed with meat or drink, becomes rampant and shakes off sleep to go in quest of what will gratify its own instincts. As you know, it will cast away all shame and prudence at such moments and stick at nothing. In phantasy it will not shrink from intercourse with a mother or anyone else, man, god, or brute, or from forbidden food or any deed of blood. In a word, it will go to any length of shamelessness and folly."[1]

Not only did Freud claim that dreams are meaningful and have a specific place in the psychic activities of the waking state. He also claimed that every dream has a psychological structure, which is full of significance and which can be understood according to certain principles of interpretation. It is unnecessary for our purposes to review the history of Freud's *Interpretation of Dreams* and to tell how he arrived at his theory, interesting as that may be. We need only observe that his principles of interpretation are closely related to his other theories of psychic phenomena and that dreams came to be regarded as "symptoms" with a meaning analogous to that of the symptoms of the mentally ill.

For Freud, what we call dreams are usually a facade behind which lie certain hidden, latent thoughts and unconscious impulses striving for fulfillment. The hidden, latent thoughts are, as Freud would say, at least in part, residues of waking life, a continuation of some preconscious mental activity of the day before. The impulses are instinctual in nature, internal stimuli caused by the pressure of the instincts. In other words, the impulses provide the energy for the dream and make use of the day's mental residues in which to clothe themselves. But these impulses in the form of wishes, according to Freud, are often opposed by the moral demands of the ego (that is, the super-ego), whose repressive function is reduced but not abolished in sleep. The repressive function of the ego appears as a censorship of dreams, which forbids the unconscious impulses to be expressed in the form which they would otherwise assume. The latent dream thoughts embodying the wishes of the dream have to be altered and softened so that the meaning of the dream will be unrecognizable to the conscious mind. Hence, a dream is usually the disguised fulfillment of a repressed wish, at least in adults.

In other words, dreams are the reaction to a stimulus (usually and on the whole) of internal origin disturbing sleep. Their function, according to Freud, is to maintain sleep.[2] They effect a discharge of excitation so that the stimulus is removed and sleep can continue. Since they are a mental phenomenon, they have a meaning, known to the dreamer unconsciously although not to his conscious mind. This meaning can usually be revealed by the process of free association.

That which we ordinarily call the dream is known as the manifest dream. Its meaning is contained in the latent dream thoughts. The manifest dream is, usually, a disguised substitute or expression of the latent dream thoughts. In dream interpretation one starts with the substitute, the elements of the dream which are remembered, and by a train of associations one arrives at their hidden meaning. "Free" associations are determined. That is to say, the associations which the dreamer later has with a word, an idea, or a feeling are determined by a certain mental background or complex. This background or complex is constituted by "circles of ideas," thoughts and emotional interests which are unknown to the dreamer consciously. In other words, the remembered elements of the dream are associatively connected with this complex, which reveals their meaning, and to which one is led along the path of association.

In sleep there is said to be a withdrawal of psychical energy from the interests of life. Furthermore, since all "the paths to motility" are blocked, less energy is needed for repression. Therefore, since there is ordinarily no possibility for the unconscious drives to manifest themselves overtly, directly in action, the ego may relax somewhat and give them enough free play to be expressed in a phantasy-like way. In other words, the dreamer knows unconsciously that this form of expression is far less dangerous or morally reprehensible than overt expression in action. He can, as it were, more easily indulge his repressed wishes and desires in this relatively passive and secret form of expression.

Just what are the tendencies and desires which express themselves in sleep? They are the evil, primitive and infantile impulses and desires which remain in the unconscious (or in the id) of every adult. In fact, the unconscious (or rather the id, according to the later formulation) for Freud is the infantile in mental life. In dreams we regress to the infantile level of development. Since incestuous desires and wishes to destroy rivals are said to be so prominent in early life, they will be markedly in evidence in our dreams.

Hate is said to rage unrestrainedly. Wishes for revenge and death wishes against parents, brothers and sisters, husband or wife, one's own children are not rare. Aesthetic and moral considerations are discarded, and the libido is shorn of all inhibition.[3]

The manifest dream content and the (latent) dream thoughts may be considered to be two different languages expressing the same things. The "dream-content appears to us as a translation of the dream-thoughts into another mode of expression, whose symbols and laws of composition we must learn by comparing the origin with the translation."[4]

The language of the manifest dream is obscure, "presented in hieroglyphics," symbols of which must be translated into the language of the dream-thoughts. Because of the moral, aesthetic and other requirements of a certain part of the ego, the meaning of the dream as embodied in the dream thoughts cannot be presented directly. They must first undergo, as a rule, a process of disguise and distortion. This process is known as the dream work.

The manifest dream, which is usually expressed in pictorial imagery, although it may contain speeches or even involved processes of mental calculation, is meagre, paltry and laconic in comparison with the range and copiousness of the deciphered dream thoughts. A dream may be told in half a page or less, while its interpretation (which conveys the dream thoughts) may require a half-dozen pages.

Since there are several ways by which the dream work may distort or disguise the latent dream thoughts, several kinds of relation may be said to exist between the manifest dream and the latent dream thoughts. Among them are condensation, displacement, plastic representation and fixed symbolism.

In condensation, (1) some latent elements are left out, (2) only a fragment of the several constituents of the latent dream emerges in the manifest dream, and (3) latent elements possessing a common trait are fused into a unified whole.[5] An example of (3) would be the formation of a composite image of a person which combines the actual features or other characteristics of two or more people. A composite image of a person may resemble A in superficial appearance, wear clothes like B, pursue a profession which reminds one of C; yet this composite image represents someone else, D. Places and situations may be represented in analogous fashion. In any actual dream, condensation is much more complicated.[6]

In displacement, a latent dream element is replaced by something more remote, like an allusion. There is also a transference of "accent" or emphasis from some element which is important to something unimportant. The result is that the manifest content is centered around or focused on inessential elements. A young woman, married for several years, has the following dream after she learns that an acquaintance of about the same age, Elise L., has just become engaged: *"She is sitting in the theatre with her husband, and one side of the stalls is quite empty. Her husband tells her that Elise L. and her fiance had also wished to come to the theatre, but that they only could have obtained poor seats; three for one florin 50 kreuzer, and of course they could not take those. She thinks they didn't lose much, either."*

The dream is the reaction to the news of Elise L.'s engagement. Furthermore, other incidents of the day before are incorporated in the dream. The one florin 50 kreuzer is a reference to the news that her sister-in-law had received 150 florins, which is 100 times greater, as a present from her husband and rushed off to buy jewelry with the money. The detail of the empty stalls is an allusion to an occurrence of a week before when she booked tickets for a play so early that she had to pay extra for them, and when she and her husband got to the theatre they found that one side of the house was almost empty. Concerning this her husband teased her about being in too great a hurry.

The meaning of the dream according to Freud is as follows: " 'It surely was nonsense to marry so early; there was *no need* for my being in such a hurry. From Elise L.'s example I see that I should have got a husband just the same—and one a *hundred times* better—if I had only waited (antithesis to the *haste* of her sister-in-law). I could have bought *three* such men for the money (the dowry).' "[7]

Going to the theatre is a symbol for getting married. Her rushing off to buy tickets signifies her haste and impatience in getting married. Likewise, the sister-in-law's rushing off to buy jewelry refers to the dreamer's haste and impatience. The empty stalls also refer to her childlessness (an empty womb)[?]. The fact that two persons are expected to take three seats manifests another-characteristic of dreams, their apparent absurdity. But the absurd may serve to signify the most strongly emphasized element of the dream thoughts— it was *nonsense* to marry so early.

Freud arrived at the meaning of the dream with the help of the dreamer's free associations. This statement does not imply, however, that the meaning of this dream has been exhaustively worked out.[8] Dreams have various "levels" of meaning.

Another relation between the dream and the dream thoughts is manifested in representation—"a plastic, concrete piece of imagery, originating in the sound of a word."[9] The manifest dream represents the latent elements by a certain kind of imagery. Thus, a man dreams he is climbing a mountain from which he has a remarkably fine view. Free association reveals that an acquaintance of the dreamer is publishing a Review on the subject of the most distant foreign relations.[10] The dreamer in the latent thought of the dream identifies himself with the "reviewer," that is, one who takes a survey. Presumably the dreamer is himself making a survey of his own life in analysis.

Another kind of relation is that of constant symbolism which we discuss below.

By and large, the dream work cannot directly express the logical and syntactical relations of the dream thoughts in the manifest content. Temporal relations may be expressed in terms of space. Thus a person figuring in the past may appear small and far away. Relations expressed by such terms as "because," "therefore," "but," "if . . . then," "either . . . or" cannot be put in the pictorial form of the manifest dream. Opposites can be represented by the same element in the manifest dream. In general, the dream transforms the connection existing between the elements of the dream thoughts into a unified situation, or into a unity of some sort. Similarity of persons appears as identification. Agreement between things other than persons is often expressed by composition of some aspects of the various things into a unified whole. But composition of diverse aspects can also be made of persons. Localities can be represented by persons. In identification the one person, A, appearing in the dream enters into all the relations and situations which pertain to B, with whom he possesses some feature in common, or other persons whom A "screens." In composition of persons, features characteristic of but not common to two or more people are combined to form a composite image. To put this simply, the visual features, or some of them, of A and B may be combined to form a new image. In this way the characteristic in which they agree as far as the dreamer is concerned need not appear. Thus, for example, hostility toward the dreamer may be the common characteristic of the two, although not appearing directly. In other words, the dreamer is saying in pictorial language. "A and B are hostile to me." Such an interpretation will be revealed by free association.

But actually, according to Freud, when a strange person appears in the dream-content, the dreamer's ego is concealed behind that person. Every dream treats of oneself. "In cases where not my ego but only a strange person occurs in the dream-content, I may safely assume that by means of identification my ego is concealed behind that person. I am permitted to supplement my ego. On other occasions, when my ego appears in the dream, the situation in which it is placed tells me that another person is concealing himself, by means of identification, behind the ego. In this case I must be prepared to find that in the interpretation I should transfer something which is connected with this person—the hidden common feature—to myself. There are also dreams in which my ego appears together with other persons who, when the identification is resolved, once more show themselves to be my ego. Through these identifications I shall then have to connect with my ego certain ideas to which the censorship has objected. I may also give my ego multiple representation in my dream, either directly or by means of identification with other people."[11]

Opposites, contrasts, contraries, are treated as similarities in the manifest dream. An element may stand for its usual meaning or its contrary, or for both together. A blossoming bough may stand for sexual innocence or sexual sophistication or both. The manifest dream content may also contain a number of "transformations into the opposite" or "multiple inversions." A patient dreams that his father scolds him because he comes home late. The context reveals that the *dreamer* is angry with his father because the latter came home *early*.

Another striking feature of dreams is that a short preliminary dream may serve as an introductory or causal relation to a subsequent main dream. All dreams during one night are said to deal with one whole, one main theme. Different dreams may represent a different treatment or solution (the adequate expression of a wish) of the same subject.

Before coming to a discussion of symbolism, there is a final point to mention called secondary elaboration. Not only does the dream work distort and disguise the dream thoughts but at the same time it attempts to give the manifest content a semblance of coherence and an intelligible pattern. It tries to give the dream content something of the appearance of a day-dream. But it does not always succeed.

As we have already indicated, the dream work transforms the latent thoughts, as expressed in words, into perceptual forms, usually visual images. But, according to Freud,
it is from such perceptual forms that our thoughts originated,
their first developmental phases likewise consisting of memory-
pictures of such sense-impressions. Subsequently, words were
united with the pictures and connected in a manner so as to
form thoughts and ideas.[12] Hence, the dream work subjects
our thoughts to a regressive process, to a form of expression
characteristic of the childhood of the individual and the race.
Furthermore, the dream life "knows the way back" to latent
infantile experiences consciously forgotten and repressed. (But
they are not entirely forgotten; certain clear recollections
are retained mostly in the form of plastic imagery.)

Symbolism, according to Freud, is a mode of expression
which has never been individually acquired; it is a racial
heritage going back to long past ages. We have already
discussed this point in another connection, but it will be
taken up again, especially in connection with Jung.

According to Freud, certain elements in dreams retain a
constant meaning. Concerning such elements, associations do
not arise no matter how persistently the doctor or interpreter
may press for them. The same situation holds in the case of
the dreams of healthy people. These elements are construed
as constant symbols—symbols having a fixed meaning.[13]
Furthermore, these symbols are not confined to dreams. They
are found in mythology, folklore, religion, art and in a great
number of other fields.

A constant relation between a dream element and its
"translation" is called symbolic, and the dream element itself
is called a symbol of the unconscious dream thought. According to Freud, the overwhelming majority of symbols in dreams
are sexual symbols. However, other things are also represented
symbolically in dreams, for example, the human body as a
whole, parents, children, brothers and sisters, birth, death,

nakedness. The human body as a whole is represented by a
house. When the walls are smooth it means a man; when
there are ledges and balconies to be caught hold of, a woman.
Parents are represented as *emperor* and *empress*, *king* and
queen or similar exalted personages. Children are symbolized
as *little animals* or *vermin*. Birth is symbolized by a reference
to *water*, falling into water, or climbing out, saving someone
from it or being saved. Dying is referred to by situations of
going on a journey, or *traveling* by train. Nakedness is symbolized by *clothes* and *uniforms*.

The sexual life, Freud finds, has a rich symbolism. The
entire male genitalia are symbolized by the number *three*.
The penis has a variety of symbols: *sticks*, *umbrellas*, *poles*,
trees and similar objects. Objects which, like the penis, have
the property of penetrating, and therefore injuring, symbolize the penis: *knives*, *daggers*, *lances*, *sabres*, and, because of
their shape, *guns*. The penis is also symbolized by objects
from which water flows: *taps*, *watering cans*, *springs*. Objects
capable of elongation represent the penis: *pulleys*, *lamps*,
pencils with a sheath. Still other symbols are *penholders*, *nail
files*, *hammers* and other *implements*. Things which have the
property of raising themselves up are to be included as
phallic symbols: *balloons*, *aeroplanes*, *zeppelins*. When the
sexual organ is made into the essential attribute of the person,
the *dreamer himself flies* in order to symbolize the phenomenon
of erection. Finally, there are somewhat obscure sexual symbols: *reptiles*, *fishes*, *hats* and *cloaks*.

The female genitals are often symbolically represented by
objects which have the property of enclosing a space or of
acting as receptacles: *pits*, *hollows*, and *caves*, *jars*, *bottles*,
boxes, *chests*, *pockets*, *ships*. The uterus is symbolized by
cupboards, *stones*, and especially *rooms*. *Doors* and *gates*
represent the genital opening. A noteworthy symbol of the
female genital organ is a *jewel case*, *jewel* and *treasure* representing the beloved one. Other symbols of the female sexual

organs are *landscapes, gardens, blossoms* and *flowers*. A part of the body, the *mouth*, may also represent the genital opening. *Snails* and *mussels* are said to be unmistakable female symbols.

Material of different kinds symbolizes woman: *wood, paper;* objects made of the raw materials, *tables* and *books.* Buildings like *churches* and *chapels, castles* and *fortresses* symbolize woman. The female breasts are symbolized by *apples, peaches* and *fruit in general.* The pubic hair of both sexes is represented by *woods* and *thickets*, while *rocks* and *mountains* are symbols of the male organ.

Sexual pleasure may be symbolized by *sweetmeats*. Rhythmical activities such as *dancing, riding, climbing,* and an experience of violence like *being run over* often represent sexual intercourse. Onanism may be symbolized by any form of play, such as playing the piano. Other such symbols are *sliding, gliding, pulling off a branch.* The *falling out* or *extraction* of teeth represents castration as a punishment for onanism. Evil impulses or passions may be symbolized by *wild animals*.

However, the symbols for male and female sexual organs are sometimes not as sharply distinct as might appear. Thus, a woman may dream of flying, symbolizing her wish to be a man.

Symbolism is not the work of the "censor" or the result of the process of distortion effected by the "dream work." But the censorship makes use of this archaic language lying ready at hand, so to speak, for the purpose of rendering the dream strange and incomprehensible. Freud attempts to explain symbolism at least in part on the basis of a view put forth by a philologist, H. Sperber. According to Sperber's theory, sexual needs had the largest share in the origin and development of language. The first sounds uttered were for communication and for summoning the sexual partner. Later the elements of speech were used as an accompaniment to the work carried on by primitive man. By working to the accompaniment of rhythmically repeated utterances, primitive man transferred a "sexual interest" to his work. According to the theory, primitive man thus made work more agreeable. Hence, words came to have two meanings, one pertaining to the sexual act, another to the work with which such words were uttered. Gradually the word was disassociated from its original sexual significance. In this way a number of "root-words" arose, all of sexual origin, but having lost their sexual meaning. If the theory is correct, Freud suggests that the sexual symbolic relations of dreams are survivals of the old identity in words. What once had the same name as the genitals or the sexual act would now appear in dreams as symbolizing them.

Rank and others have elaborated this notion of Freud and we shall take it up again in the discussion of mythology.

This outline of Freud's theory of dream interpretation is only a skeleton. For a comprehensive understanding, one must devote considerable study to the *Interpretation of Dreams*.

Since Freud, other writers, notably Jung and Fromm, have claimed that dreams may sometimes be an expression of genuine knowledge of and insight into the dreamer's own life or that of others. However, the content of their interpretation differs in conformity with their own theories.

MYTHOLOGY

The notion of a conflict of psychic processes in the personality resulting in a certain psychic tension or anxiety was regarded as fundamental early in the history of psychoanalysis. In Freudian theory, certain ideas heavily charged or invested with "affect" or emotion are forever pressing toward conscious recognition and awareness, and certain impulses are always pressing toward overt satisfaction and fulfillment. As we have seen, these emotionally charged ideas and impulses have been repressed and inhibited. The reasons for this have already been discussed.

But unconscious desires remain active. In other words, repressed instinctive impulses and unconscious wishes still influence the thoughts and actions of men. They make their appearance in a disguised and distorted fashion. The distortion varies, depending on the personality of the individual, the stage of repression, and the degree of civilization attained by the human race.[14] To accomplish this distortion, the mind uses various techniques or mechanisms: projection, disassociation, representation by the opposite, displacement, inversion, and so on.

But certain formal and logical demands of consciousness are said to require further modification of the unconscious material. This modification occurs, for example, in the secondary elaboration of the dream, a process which we discussed above. Another formal factor which the unconscious material must conform to in becoming conscious is the tendency toward dramatic form, as manifested in artistic performances and in dreams.

Finally, there is, because of its especial suitability for disguise and its adaptability to the new contents of consciousness, the symbol. According to Rank and Sachs, the symbol represents an ideal union of many means of expression, such as simile, metaphor, allegory, allusion and other forms of pictorial representation of thought material (after the manner of the rebus). It is a pictorial substitute for something covert. It is a condensation of two or more meanings, an amalgamation.

Symbol formation is not arbitrary and capricious; it follows definite laws. As we have indicated above, Freud and his followers have attached primary significance to sexual symbols.

Psychologically, the symbol formation is regarded as a regressive phenomenon, a reversion to pictorial thinking more characteristic of the childhood of the individual and of the early history of humanity. Symbolism is regarded by Freudians as a survival of primitive forms of adaptation, now super-fluous and inadequate. In times of stress or reduced capability adults regress to this earlier form of adaptation. But what is now regarded as a symbol at one time had full "real" meaning and value.[15]

The study of the history of civilization is said to show that, for example, ploughing and the creation of fire, which in dreams sometimes appear as completely unconscious sym-bols of the sexual act, originally in the early history of humanity represented the sexual act, that is, they were invested with the same energy and ideas as in sexual inter-course. Symbol formation is in our present civilization met with especially in religion and artistic experiences, in dreams, phantasies, and in mental disturbances.

The conditions for the comprehension of the symbol stand in a "contrasting correlation" to the tendencies of the symbol formation. In other words, the more fully a symbol expresses a profoundly repressed, an anxiety-provoking tendency, the more carefully is its significance, in terms of unconscious wish and desire, hidden and uncomprehended. The symbol varies from transparent ambiguity, as in jokes and witticisms, to utter incomprehensibility, as in dreams and neuroses.

How does one interpret the hidden meaning of a symbol? Rank and Sachs, following a certain Wilhelm Müller, offer a kind of coherence theory of interpretation. The explanation of the symbol is considered correct if such an explanation fits in every context where the symbol occurs or in a very large number of instances and agrees with the "connection" of the myth. Interpreting a symbol is somewhat analogous to the process of finding the meaning of unknown words in a text. The place they occur (their context) contributes toward their understanding and at the same time, once a meaning is found suitable to the recurring use, it helps to clarify the entire text.[16]

In order to explain how the origin of myth is envisaged, psychoanalysts have assumed the existence of a remote period of time when "heedless sexual and primitive egoistic motives" controlled the conscious action and thought of man. During this time people are said to have had neither the necessity nor the ability to create myths. But with the progress of humanity, these heedless sexual and primitive egoistic motives had to be gradually renounced, at least to a considerable degree, in action and conscious thought. Gradually such motives became repressed—but not abolished. Hence, "substitutive gratifications" via phantasy gradually arose as overt, unqualified satisfaction slowly ceased. These substitutive gratifications, in turn, rendered it possible for men progressively and successfully to suppress their more socially destructive impulses to a certain degree.

From this time on, the vicissitudes of phantasy-making become complicated. In the myth the primitive impulses are expressed in a disguised form. Nor are they told of the human race, which could still be too shocking. Instead, these impulses are imputed to super-human beings, to mysterious heavenly bodies, to gods who govern them, or to heroes raised to gods. This is perhaps the reason that the myth consciously represents a crude form of knowledge about nature, and at the same time incongruously embodies certain human qualities which complete the form of the myth. However, it is the damming up of human affects which furnishes the instinctive force for the formation of myth.

There is a further and related point to be observed in this connection. It is thought that the everyday world of practical activity designed to prolong life and raise the standard of living was not held in high esteem by man in dim past ages. Men of an earlier age found it necessary to carry on their work with the aid of symbolic phantastic acts.

These phantastic acts furnished a hallucinatory gratification for repressed sexual wishes. Thus, agriculture or the administration of justice were at one time carried on with such symbolic gratifications. In such a way a powerful stimulus was provided for performing the uncomfortable and tiresome, though necessary, tasks of life. Hunger, on the other hand, is not subject to any substitute form of gratification because its direct satisfaction is necessary for survival.

"Phantasy gifted" man of ancient times attributed ("projected") various affective qualities of his own to natural processes. He wove them into his own mental experience in a manner somewhat analogous to that of a "neurotic" who projects his own feelings of hostility on to others and at least consciously believes that they, instead, are hostile to him. Natural processes furnished him with the materials, not the motive of myth. At the same time, he anthropomorphized natural processes, which in the myth came to represent the will of the gods.

The "mechanisms" of unconscious phantasy formation and those of myth creation serve generally not only to retain and gain pleasure from actions, wishes and thoughts destined for inhibition and repression, but also the denial or nullification of the unpleasant and painful experiences which are demanded of man by reality.

While dream and myth have many traits in common, they are not identical. The myth occupies a middle position between dream and waking life, in a fashion that is close to the day dream.

We can now begin to indicate the relation of the Oedipus complex to myth.

As in dreams there is a "splitting" of the personality into several figures, all of whom represent its characteristics. In the hero myth, for example, the rebellious son expresses the hostility which really belongs against the father against a tyrant who represents the hated aspect of the father-image.

At the same time the cultural requirements of propriety and piety are met by a "superlative acknowledgment" of a dearly revered, defended, or avenged father-image. Complicated myths which portray a variety of persons in complicated situations may, it is said, be traced back to the relationships of parents and child. In the final analysis they have their origin, however disguised in a justifying fashion, in the egocentric attitude of the child.

Another phenomenon of myth is what is called duplication or multiplication. All the participants in the myth represent in various situations and with changing nuances of significance the personalities of the parents and child. Since the experiences, wish tendencies and fears of an individual are so complex, and since likewise human situations in which he finds himself are so involved, a series of episodes in the myth in which apparently different participants appear is required in order to fulfill the function of the myth.

Different mythological figures are "duplicates" or "multiplicates" of the one representation, say, of the mother. Each figure plays one or more of the many roles which the mother plays in the family until her various significant roles are played through.

To take another example from the side of duplication of the male partner: In many legends a king consciously desires to marry his own daughter, who flees and escapes. After many adventures she marries a king who is easily recognized as a double of the original father. The Lohengrin saga is said to be a classical example of duplication of the female partner in order to accomplish incest. In the first part the son saves the mother from the violence of the father. But marriage with the rescued one is brought about in the second part when the saving episode occurs again with a strange lady who turns out to be a double of the mother.[17]

Thus, not only do we find duplication or multiplication

of individual mythical figures but duplication or multiplication of saga episodes or situations.

Still another phenomenon occurring in myths, as in dreams, is displacement, in which the "affective accent" is transferred from the important to the unimportant, even to "full inversion" of affect or content of ideas. For example, in a myth or legend, instead of a cruel father pushing his sons out of the parental home against their wishes, a kindly father is compelled by his sons to grant his permission for their departure into the world, more or less against his will when they refuse to accept food and drink until he acquiesces.

While we have discussed only a few of the numerous "mechanisms" employed in myth and dream, we want to emphasize the fact that the myth has a history and cannot rightly be understood otherwise. It is fluid, never completed, adapted by successive generations to their religious, cultural and ethical standards, that is, in psychoanalytical language, geared to the current stage of psychic repression of the population. Isolated and gifted persons, on whom the progress of repression manifested itself most plainly and "probably also earlier," are credited with an important role in the evolution of myth. Over generations the narrative appears to have been worked on, altered, embroidered, by such people, so that it keeps pace with cultural standards and patterns, while it also exercises an influence on the culture.

For reasons of space we cannot enter deeply into actual myth interpretation, but we may give an abbreviated example of such a procedure. There is an old Egyptian legend of the brothers Anup and Bata. The elder brother, Anup, was married, and the younger brother, Bata, lived with Anup in the latter's house, like a son. But trouble finally arose when one day the wife of the elder brother tried to seduce Bata. However, Bata did not succumb to her charms. Instead he indignantly rebuked her, though he did not reveal the incident to his brother. The wife, however, told Anup that Bata had done violence to her. Enraged, Anup sharpened his knife in order to kill Bata when the latter was to arrive home in the evening. But the animals of his herd warned Bata, who fled. Anup pursued him, knife in hand. Then the younger brother supplicated the god, Re. Re heard him and raised a flood between the brothers, who spent the night separately on its shores. Next morning, when the sun appeared, the younger brother defended himself before it, informed Anup of his wife's treachery, and swore his innocence. Then Bata castrated himself to signify his purity. The phallus which he cast into the flood was swallowed by a fish. Anup, on hearing Bata's story, was remorseful and wept, whereupon Bata told him he would take his heart and place it in the flower of the cedar tree. Should someone give Anup a glass of beer which foamed, the latter, as a favor to Bata, on the signal of the foaming beer, was to come and seek Bata's heart. When he returned home, the elder brother killed his wife and cast her to the dogs. This done, he sat down and, putting dust on his head, sorrowed for Bata.

The younger brother, who in the meantime had been living in a cedar valley, received the praise of the gods for his chastity and was granted a wish. He wished for a maiden, and the gods created and presented one to him. Unfortunately, the maiden had certain traits and whimsicalities traditionally accorded to the Biblical Eve. She disobeyed the one prohibition her husband Bata imposed upon her, namely, not to go near the sea. As she neared the sea, a curl of her hair was snatched away by the waves and was carried to the laundry of the king of Egypt. This king caused her to be discovered and married her. At her wish, the king had the cedar containing Bata's heart cut down in order to escape Bata's revenge.

Thereupon Bata dropped dead. When this happened, Anup observed the signal of the foaming beer and went hastily to the cedar valley. After a long search, in the fourth year he discovered Bata's heart, revived him with a drink, and was embraced by his brother.

Bata, who had changed into an Apis bull, was taken to the Egyptian king's court by his brother. There Bata permitted himself to be recognized by his former wife, the queen. She was frightened and persuaded the king to have the bull killed. At the palace gate two drops of blood fell to the ground, from which sprang up two giant sycamore trees in one night. Once more Bata let the queen recognize him, and she then had the sycamores cut down. As the trees were being cut, a splinter went into her mouth, and she was impregnated, and Bata was born as her son. But this time the king died and Bata succeeded him as king and caused the queen to be executed. Bata ruled for thirty years and when he died he left the crown to Anup.

What is the hidden meaning of the legend, the real theme, so to speak, of the narrative? It is of the bitter rivalry of the brothers for the same irreplacable incestuous object, and, when the forbidden wish is gratified, of the resulting punishment, castration. The different episodes of the legend are duplications of the one fundamental situation, that of the son who seeks for sexual possession of the mother against the elder brother, who really represents the father. The king is the socially elevated double of the elder brother, while the wicked queen is the double of Anup's wicked wife. It is not difficult to see, according to psychoanalytical notions of interpretation, that the queen, who is the wicked wife's double, is actually the mother, in view of Bata's rebirth in the second part of the tale. That the elder brother and his double, the king, represent the father's place is suggested from the fact that the king as husband of the queen becomes his nominal father.

From the beginning, Bata strives to seduce the "mother," whom he later pursues in symbolical disguise. The "slander" of her as Anup's wife at the beginning of the tale is to be considered as a projection of Bata's incestuous wish. His self-castration in the first part is another piece of not very opaque embroidery.

The castration originally occurred by the hand of a jealous rival, a brother or father. The myth itself is said to furnish internal evidence of this. Thus the head of the bull, which is a symbol of masculine potency, is cut off at the king's order. The drops of blood from which two trees spring up, whose splinters have the masculine power of impregnation, only to be again cut down, suggest the same idea. Individual psychological experiences and mythological parallels are said to indicate that Bata's castration in the first part of the legend occurred not by his own hand but by a jealous rival.[18]

Religious myths, in particular, seem to have had a fascinating history, as the Greek, Vedic and Eddaic traditions testify. In the course of time they often undergo a social and psychological depreciation, reappearing as legend and relegated to the nursery, where, "in a deep sense," they belong and where only can they be "really understood." But to the child with a gift for phantasy and endowed with primitive affects, they must appear real since he is still close to the time when he must believe in the mental reality of his own primitive impulses.

In fact, the hero of myth is said to be analogous to the ego of the child, and the vicissitudes of childhood experience are contrasted with the situation of the myth. In early years the child regards the parents as splendid figures, but as he grows he discovers that they are more ordinary people with various imperfections and shortcomings. Dissatisfaction with them may lead to the idea that other parents are preferable. At the same time intense emotions of sexual rivalry exist. Neglect, or feelings of regret at having to share the love of the parents with other siblings, may lead to the conviction that one's own inclinations are not recognized. This feeling may lead to the idea that one is a stepchild or an adopted child. So the "neurotic" child's imagination becomes busily engaged in the task of getting rid of the parents, who are now, via phantasy, dispossessed for persons of high rank. An accidental meeting of the child with a noble or in some way distinguished personage will arouse his envy and is expressed in "fancy fabrics," which replace the parents by other persons of higher rank. The child creates a romantic picture in phantasy of another "real" parentage of exalted station.

With increasing knowledge of parental sexual relations, the family romance which the child envisions undergoes a restriction. He has come to realize that the father is always uncertain, while the mother never is. The child then is content to ennoble the father while he accepts descent from the mother as unquestionable. With knowledge of sexual relations, he tends to erotic phantasy, to which he is impelled by the pleasure of picturing the mother, or whoever stimulates the greatest sexual curiosity, as secretly unfaithful and engaging in clandestine love.

Revenge and retaliation motivate the child once more. Having been punished by the parents, as a rule, in order to be broken of "bad" sexual habits, such "neurotic" children avenge themselves in phantasy.

Younger children are especially likely to deprive their predecessors of their legitimacy. The mother may be credited with as many love affairs as the younger child has older rivals. While the other children may all be deprived of their legitimacy, the "plotting hero" may find a way to restore his own. The youthful romancer may also have some special interest to stimulate his creations. If, for example, he has a sister who attracts him sexually, he will deprive her of kinship.[19]

The endeavor to replace the real father by a more distinguished one is an expression of the vanished happy time when the parents were splendid figures in the child's eyes. Not only in phantasy does this longing appear for the time when the father seemed to be the strongest and greatest man and the mother, the dearest and most beautiful woman; it appears in the dreams of normal adults.

The significance of myth can be summed up as follows: The child's psychological conflicts, his ambivalent feelings toward the parents and other members of the family, his many and complex relations and experiences in the family furnish the principal motive of myth and form the essence of the mythical tradition. The development of myths portrays the social relations of the individual in the family, and the relation of the family in the tribe.[20]

RELIGION

Since religion and myth are said to be closely allied, we wish to elaborate certain characteristics of the early history of myth as outlined by psychoanalysts which we passed over in previous discussion. The latter, as well as others, have posited a "prereligious" stage called the animistic in the history of humanity, in which "primitive races" peopled the world with beings to whom they ascribed life and soul like themselves.[21] They did not recognize inanimate objects as such, not having learned to distinguish clearly and precisely between external natural processes and inner "endopsychic" perceptions and experiences. The difference between the internal and external world, ego and non-ego, had not yet been fully elaborated and fixed in their minds. Hence, there was no carefully discriminated and fixed awareness of the difference between psychic experience and objective reality. The subjective and objective were more or less confused. But as in the analogous case of the infant, the independent, autonomous existence of the external world, both theoretically and practically, gradually came to be recognized, along with the necessity of controlling it with real means. And this had significant consequences for the psychic life. Progressive

adaptation to reality forced the feeling of omnipotence derived
from the confusion of objective and mental reality to be
largely abandoned. This feeling, however, was preserved for
"endopsychic" gratification in phantasy.

Here, it is said, is the starting point of all those things
which are calculated to ‾ensure the pleasures sacrificed to
culture within a psychically self-contained realm apart from
reality. At first the phantasy gratification has no sharply
differentiated forms. These gradually evolve.

The immediate precursors of religion are said to be
totemism and taboo. These institutions, however, do not represent a higher being, a god, from whom they would derive their
efficacy and power; the commands and prohibitions associated
with them are taken for granted as self-evident. The rules
which they enjoin are in the service of the community. The
opportunity for realizing certain wishes is removed because
they have to be renounced for the sake of the community's
welfare. Certain modes of pleasure are entirely prohibited
and are then deeply repressed, but they manifest themselves
again in various disguises in phantasy and myth. One of
the most important functions of totemism is the prohibition
of incest. Taboo of the ruler is clearly designed especially
to make the use of force against the chief impossible, who
originally was head of the family.[22]

The prohibitions set up against powerful, compelling
drives always pressing toward satisfaction produce a psychic
tension felt as anxiety. To relieve this tension, the phenomenon
of projection is utilized, whereby the most painful aspects of
the conflict are ascribed to external, non-human beings, called
demons, who have the will and the power to do harm. This
is said to mark the first stage of religion. Magic and witch-
craft appear as techniques for influencing the demons so
that they may be frightened away or can be submitted to
or put in good humor.

We have already mentioned that ancient man attributed

certain of his own experiences to the awe-compelling but in-comprehensible inanimate processes of nature. In such a way the impressive processes of nature, including the heavenly bodies, are associated with the demonic spirits. Demons and natural processes probably in a rather vague way are assumed to be connected.

Then the creation of mythology, it is said, began, while magic continued in cult and rite. The need of humanizing or incarnating the processes of nature and the need of solving inner emotional conflicts by projecting them onto nature unite in the process of myth formation. The demons who originally were conceived in a vague fashion take on traits of natural phenomena and are then conceived as having rela-tions with one another. These are modeled on human qualities while they also represent the contrasting influences of natural processes on one another.[23] One after another the demons are raised to gods. But since repressed wishes are dynamic, forever striving toward fulfillment, they spur phantasy toward new creations. New figures and stories are always ascribed to natural occurrences, as long as the formation of myth remains adaptable to new influences. This explains the exis-tence of the numerous supernatural figures in all ancient religions.

In order to understand fully the significance which psycho-analysts attach to mythology and religion, one must remem-ber that many believe that man by nature has certain instincts which inherently are socially destructive and, for the sake of social welfare, must be repressed.[24]

Mythology performs the social function, at least to some degree and as well as it can, of diverting the powerful repressed instincts toward gratification in phantasy only. However, the original form of gratification in reality, which has been repressed, returns in some degree for satisfaction as of yore. This is known as the principle of the return of the repressed. A part of the imperious instinctual drives newly revived for gratification in reality utilizes the very institutions which originated to prevent their gratification in reality. While one part of religion provided an outlet by means of substitute gratifications, in accordance with human aspirations, other parts "redirected" instinctual impulses by cult and rite. Religion is a compromise between the unconscious and the processes of repression. It opens a way to civilization; yet at times in some circumstances permits the things most hostile to civilization. This characteristic is said to be typical of the whole history of religion. When at times the compromise wholly fails, fanaticism runs riot and becomes a means of destruction of everything which makes human society possible.[25]

In very early times, the killing of the totem animal, ordinarily strictly forbidden is enjoined on certain feast days as a religious duty. Here, it is said, is the origin of sacrifice, by which man offers up to god what he had to give up in order that later, on festal days, he may be allowed it as representative and servant of the god. Hence, sacrifice presupposes an identification with the god. On festal occasions incest could recur as holy orgy.

Gradually festal celebrations and religious ceremonial undergo a development which may often disguise or dissolve their original meaning. Yet religious ceremonies still retain various purification measures for sins and penitential acts, which reveal the hidden feeling of guilt pervading every religion.

Primitive humanity assumed as self-evident that everything which was forbidden to itself was permitted to the god and his chosen servants, kings and priests, as their essential prerogative.

While in the stage of the demons, only the hostility which the son feels toward the father and the wish to oust him are evident, in the stage of the gods the influence of the love and reverence which the son feels toward the father appears. The gods are not merely hostile like the demons, who are angry and punish; they are also gracious beings who can protect and reward.

In the case of the mother, the incest barrier between mother and son becomes so fixed that not only libidinous but the "inseparably united" impulses of affection are prohibited. This thwarted affection finds gratification in religious phantasy, giving rise to the figures of maternal godhead, Istar, Isis, Rhea, Mary. Thus, in the course of time the austere traits of the paternal gods are lessened.

Individual legends become united in a religious system adapted to the ethical and intellectual level of the period. Certain commands and prohibitions disappear or live on as hygienic rules. Cult and ceremonial undergo a radical evolutionary change. The religious system ignores difference of age, sex, etc., and imposes its entire content on all believers. The elaboration of religion, among other things, results in dogmatism, from which certain gifted religious natures revolt —Christ, Mohammed, Luther—and avoid the "cooling circumlocution" of dogma to seek anew a direct personal expression and release of emotion. In this way a founder or reformer of religion may arise, when he has the gift to act suggestively on his contemporaries. These gifted religious natures are said to reproduce for themselves some of the old content of religion.

Even when a new sect is not founded, a "mythical emotional stream" flows constantly into religion. There is, for example, mysticism. Mysticism, fundamentally, contains the idea of the restoration of the ancient notion of identification with the godhead, already realized in the idea of sacrifice. The highest and most intimate expression of mysticism is characterized as immediate union of the soul with its creator. But even here the repressed material in the form of a desire for sexual union in the role of the passive female with the godhead is said to appear (Christ as bridegroom).[26]

The incestuous union between mother-goddess and husband-
son, psychoanalysts claim, is characteristic of one of the most
important and most frequent cultistic traditions. It is to be
found in the Babylonian Istar and Tammuz, to whom Astarte
and Adonis are said to correspond, in Isis, Osiris and Horus
in the Egyptian, Kybele and Attis in the Greek, Moja and
Agni, Tanit and Mithra in the Indian, Izanami and Izanagi
in the Japanese, as well as several others. It is pointed out
that in the apocalypse of John the queen of heaven is called
the mother of the victor and that in other contexts she is
celebrated as his bride. Robertson, it is said, has surmised
that Christ's relation to Mary probably goes back to an old
myth in which a Palestinian god, possibly called Joshua, has
the alternating roles of lover and son toward a mythical
Mary.[27] And the practice of incest, partly undisguised, partly
symbolical, is said to have invested such cults with manifold
mysterious halos.

One of the vicissitudes of the incest motive in myth and
cult is thought to have especial importance for the formation
of religion, namely, that the youthful son, who ordinarily is
brought into sexual relation with the mother goddess, with
the appearance of masculine maturity, dies an early death.
His death after castration either by sexual rivals or by his
own hand is punishment for the tabooed incest, as, for example,
in the story of Uranus.

This notion of the early demise of the strong young god
became associated with certain striking processes of nature,
such as the setting of the sun and the disappearance of
vegetation, thereby adding a motive or theme for the need
for regular repetition of cultistic acts. Thus, although in
symbolic fashion, a comparison between individual fate and
cosmic processes is effected.

Hence, another universal wish impulse comes into account:
the tendency to deny the fact of death and avoid recognition
of it. The god who is sacrificed in the service of fructification

gains the possibility of resurrection, which is accounted to be an essential aspect of various traditions. There is also another phantasy to be considered here which, fundamentally, embodies the symbolism of the earth as mother of living beings, giving a broader basis and new meaning to the incest phantasy. The husband-son's excised and creative phallus is carefully preserved by the mother-wife, and from it rises the new vegetation. Likewise from mother-earth where he or his essential attribute, the phallus, has been buried, the sacrificed god arises to new life. His resurrection is connected to the incest wish by an old and typical idea of dying as a return to the mother's womb, death being considered as a continuation of the state before birth. Before resurrection the god-savior lives in a hole, often surrounded by water, symbolic of the mother's womb. Beneath the elaborate symbolism of the religious phantasy, therefore, is to be found the phantasy of the incestuous rebirth from the mother.

With increasing knowledge of the necessity of death, the incestuous significance of the mother godhead recedes, the wish for immortality comes to the fore, and ideas of a future life are elaborated. In this way a consolation for the brute fact of death, which originally manifested itself in unconscious identification with the god hero, is preserved.

The belief in immortality and resurrection on analysis is said to show the most complete denial of the father, who is replaced by the son. The denial ultimately springs from the infantile rivalry and hostility to the father, which persisted in the unconscious, as is evidenced by guilt feelings "in every religion." The later dualism of many religions (god-devil), expressed by a bifurcation of creator-destroyer figures originally united in one, is said to be an expression of the early childhood ambivalence. The individual's attitude toward the father furnishes the model for his attitude toward the creator of the world and the Father in heaven. Although at puberty he may have been forced to emancipate himself from

his father or he may have rebelled against the father's authority, the individual can unconsciously retain and express in
religion his infantile feelings of love and dependence on the
father.[28] One who has felt intense sexual rivalry with the
father may find the Virgin Mary as the focus of his own
childish wishes especially appealing and adorable.

Hence, those aspects of a religion which are in harmony
with the individual's instinctive tendencies and experiences
will have especial appeal, even though he accepts the religion
in toto. In this way a personal variation behind apparent
uniformity of belief occurs, which eventuates in a kind of
private religion of the individual.[29]

AESTHETICS

The Artist

Like the neurotic, the artist is said by Freud to have an
introverted disposition and, in fact, to have not far to go
to becoming a neurotic. He is impelled by his too clamorous
instincts. He yearns for honor, power, wealth, fame and the
love of women. But he does not have the necessary means
toward achieving these goals.[30] Therefore, he turns his back
on reality, transfers his interests and his libido to the creation
and expression of his wishes in phantasy.[31] However, he
eventually finds his way back to reality.

Every "hungry soul," everyone whom reality frustrates
and in whom it creates deep and abiding yearnings, looks to
the world of phantasy for comfort and consolation. However,
most people's power of phantasy is meagre. The artist has
more resources. He knows how to develop the material of
his day-dreams so that they cease to have any irritating or
unpleasant personal flavor and instead become enjoyable to
people in general. With his artistic cunning he transforms
them so that their origin in prohibited sources is disguised.
And at the same time his skill is such that by his art he can

faithfully express the ideas of his phantasy. Then, too, he knows how to invest his creation with such intensely pleasurable feeling that it temporarily outweighs the force of repression and negates it.[32] In this way he opens a way to others to return to their own unconscious sources of pleasure. For this he gains their gratitude and admiration—and honor, power, and the love of women.

Poetry and Literature

We shall briefly consider the traditional psychoanalytical theories of aesthetics as they apply to poetry and literature.[33] In this connection two questions may be asked: what kind of enjoyment does a poem create, and secondly, how does it achieve the creation of this enjoyment? As to the first question, poetry is said to arouse and transform painful emotions or rather their effects, which we avoid in real life, into pleasurable ones. In tragedy painful affects and experiences like sorrow and calamity, the suffering and downfall of noble men are the only themes. They are also the most frequent ones in the epic, the novel, and the romance. Cheerfulness can be evoked only when misunderstandings and accidents cause people to be brought together temporarily in unpleasant and difficult situations. When a work of art nearly takes our breath away and makes our hair stand on end, evoking the deepest suffering and sympathy, the height of artistic pleasure is said to be achieved. We flee from such affects in life only to seek them in art.[34]

In regard to the second question, the listener is put into a suggestible condition by means of the poetic art. He is compelled to experience vicariously things which are told about someone else, to transpose them into "subjective reality," although he never completely loses the knowledge of the true state of affairs.

According to psychoanalytic theory, a good deal of emotion may be or even must be unconscious, while its pleasant

or painful effect is consciously believed to be associated with
something else. As we have had occasion to point out previously, repressed ideas and emotions become manifest in
consciousness in a disguised, distorted manner as "servants
and substitute formations" of what is repressed. Between
what is repressed and what is overtly manifest a close associative connection is established and maintained.

A work of art arouses not only conscious ideas and
emotions but also unconscious ones of much greater intensity
and often of the opposite pleasure phase. To accomplish this
certain suitable ideas must be chosen so that they establish
the necessary associative connections with the unconscious
"constellation of affect." Furthermore, the work of art must
be so constituted that it achieves the discharge and gratification of unconscious wishes and emotions by means of
phantasy for both artist and listener.

Because of the "censor" and of resistance, poetry must—
and does—make extensive use of various representations and
disguises: transposition of motive, inversion to the opposite,
weakening of the connection (as in an allusion), splitting of
one figure into several, duplication, condensation, and especially fixed symbolism. From a few typical repressed wish
phantasies, it is said, arises the endless, inexhaustible variety
of the work of art. Individual variation and changing cultural
pressures as they are brought to bear on the individual
assure this variety.

The work of art relieves, at least temporarily, emotional
conflicts and effects a purification of the soul. Imperious
emotion and desire find a satisfying outlet and fulfillment.
There is a break-through of the unconscious (the id) without
a direct attack on the barriers of the censor, which are cir-
cumvented. However, the conflict is not entirely done away
with. The disguised phantasies in consciousness carry "in-
verted signs of pleasure." The longed-for situations which

are portrayed, even though disguised, still have certain painful qualities.

The consciously experienced unpleasant affects are put in the service of artistic form, and at the same time forbidden, unconscious pleasures are enjoyed in the disguise of the consciously experienced painful affect.

But even the affects perceived in consciousness as painful may be made to serve "a primary gain of pleasure," a direct pleasure, by gratifying the infantile sado-masochistic tendencies which have been repressed and now find an outlet in phantasy woven into the work of art.

For the work of art to achieve its fullest effect, the hearer must identify himself unhesitatingly with any feeling or figure portrayed in the work. The world of reality as ordinarily perceived and expressed must be set aside. He who will enjoy a work of art to the fullest for the time being must lose himself in it, so to speak, ignoring ordinary concerns and aims.

The greater intensity of feeling aroused by a work of art than in, say, a day-dream is to be explained by its structure, which conserves the feeling and enhances its intensity in gradual stages until the highest pitch is reached when it is as quickly as possible discharged ("abreacted"). Of course, different materials require different forms and modes of expression in order to achieve the maximum of intensity. Thus, the artist must know how to achieve "an economy of affect."

He must likewise know how to effect an economy of thought by which all the events are made to occur in a logical, reasonable fashion. Everything—unlike events in everyday life—must have a visible motive. In a poem, for example, the thread of action must never break "unaided," that is, the cause of everything which occurs must appear evident according to strict rules. The world of art has to be a harmonious, clearly understood world, one which leaves no room for incompatible trains of thought or incongruous facts. Thus, it is said to require a minimum of energy for its "reception" in the mind, and consequently the conserved energy leads to an increase in pleasure. Still other technical devices of art may aid the economy of thought and therefore also increase pleasure all the more.

As to the external means of achieving effects in poetry, they are said to be chiefly rhyme and rhythm. In rhyme there is a saving of attention in understanding because, for example, of the repetition of the same syllable. The energy of the effort thus saved is transformed into pleasure by the repeated recognition of the same meaning. In addition, the verbal play by means of which associative connections are established furnishes a source of childish pleasure, evoked by the rhyme, for the purpose of art.[35]

Rhythm facilitates labor and hence achieves an economy of energy like rhyme. Furthermore, the most important forms of sexual activity, especially the pleasure sucking of the child, as well as the sexual act itself, are rhythmical. The introduction of rhythm during a definite action, it is claimed, "sexualizes" such an action. Therefore, the pleasure derived from the rhythm of poetry, aside from the motive of economy of work, probably has a sexual root.

In fact, the artistic forms and devices mentioned are analogous to the preliminary phases of the sexual act in that they serve as "forepleasure." In Freudian terminology the pleasure derived from the preparatory love play is called forepleasure, which stimulates and entices the lovers to sexual orgasm, the intense sentience of which is called the "end-pleasure." Artistic forms and aids, as in poetry, by furnishing a certain amount of easily obtained pleasure, create the hearer's initial interest. A series of such "pleasure premiums" causes a psychic tension which is gradually increased so that the listener is enticed to the proper imaginative effort and frame of mind to conquer his resistances. In this way the hearer gradually reaches an emotional peak at which there is a discharge of affect, a release of tension, and the end-pleasure is attained.

However, the means which call forth the forepleasure are only a "facade," behind which the "real pleasure" derived from unconscious sources (from the id) is hidden.

Is the chief theme of poetry, as some have claimed, "whether Hans will get his Gretel?" Not precisely—but almost. Strictly speaking, it is the instinctive forces of the unconscious (of the id) which determine not only the material but also the creative force in art. And these are to a great extent, though not entirely, sexual. And here we again encounter the Oedipus complex, to which, in a sublimated form, according to Rank and Sachs, we owe the masterpieces of every age and people.[36]

The Oedipus situation is portrayed in various ways, sometimes directly but more often in a disguised form. Sometimes, as in the case of Oedipus, the deed occurs directly. At other times the incestuous desire is consciously sought but expiated by the relationship's being "false," as in the case of the family romance. The most frequent occurrence portrays a situation where not the mother but another figure such as a stepmother, the wife of the ruler, or some other figure appears. Only the subtle details of the work reveal the fact that the mother, so to speak, is hiding behind them. The role of the hostile father is similarly disguised.[37]

Analysis of a Poem

We shall now illustrate some of the principles of symbolism and symbolical interpretation which we discussed above as they are applied to literature. In the following pages we present a psychoanalytical interpretation of a poem in the classic Freudian style.

To A Very Young War Widow[38]

Having been made for love, you will love again,
And happily, although against your will.
The lacerated plain, the gutted hill
Accept the natural cure of sun and rain;
The meadow is made whole at last, by birth,
And wears the scattered gaiety of flowers.
It cannot be that you will harbor scars
Deeper, more stubborn than the wounds of earth.

Take love again and find it specially blest,
For you will harvest, when the crop is grown,
A safety and a strength you have not guessed.
A richness that you never would have known
Had not a boy, half stranger, at your side
Learned valorous life and valorously died.

One meaning of the poem according to Barron is :—

"You have been made for love and will love again, and
just as the sun and rain heal the countryside causing life to
spring up and flowers to bloom, so will your new love heal
the scars of the old. Therefore you should take love again
for it will bring a new safety, strength, and richness to your
life made possible by the boy you loved who dared to live
valorously and died."

This interpretation, according to Barron is all right,
only it does not go far enough. He then offers an interpretation which follows a frequent pattern in Freudian literature.

"The plain and meadow represent the area of the vulva;
the hill represents the mons veneris; the sun by its life-giving
powers and its elevation represents the penis in erection; the
flowers represent organs of reproduction, in this case the
male genitalia, which scatter their semen ('gaiety') about
the field . . .

"It is clear that the girl addressed in the poem had previously been loved by a soldier, and therefore the 'lacerated' plain and the 'gutted' hill refer to the trauma to the girl's genitalia produced by the physical act of love by that soldier. If the sun symbolizes the penis in erection, then the rain in association with it symbolizes the ejaculation; this would account for the meadow being made 'whole' at last by birth, as a result of intercourse with the succeeding lover. The 'scars' refer again to the trauma produced by the love act . . . The 'crop' that the girl will 'harvest' as a consequence of 'taking love again' most probably refers to the birth of a child, especially since in the first stanza she speaks of the 'meadow' previously identified as the female genitalia, being 'made whole at last by *birth*.' Literally the poem says that she will harvest 'safety' and 'strength' *when* the crop is grown, so that the safety and strength refer to benefits derived from the consciousness of motherhood which will make her safe from the dangers and strong to withstand the pain at the time of childbirth, which the author promises will be followed by the 'richness' derived from the consciousness of motherhood. The 'boy, half stranger,' is the soldier who 'at her side' conquered her in intercourse ('learned valorous life') and underwent detumescence ('died'); 'valorous' is used to indicate that the idealized lover is the fearless and dominant type rather than the weak and hesitating, and 'life' is used in the sense that a person who has 'seen a lot of life' is a person who has had many strong experiences, often of a sexual nature, while 'died' is used in the sense that excitement or activity 'dies down.' "

Hence a second meaning based on this interpretation may be found. "You who have been made for love will happily accept love again, and the injuries the soldier wrought on your genitalia will be cured by the second lover's ejaculations till finally your genitalia will be made whole by birth and wear the semen sprinkled by the male organs; for as surely as the earth's scars are thus cured, so will your own wounds be cured. Therefore, take love again and you, protected by the consciousness of motherhood from the dangers and pains of childbirth, shall have the rich experience of bearing a child which you would not have experienced had not this soldier, half-stranger, conquered you in intercourse and undergone detumescence."

However, Barron is not entirely satisfied with this interpretation because it involves certain difficulties. Why, for example, should the second lover have an opposite effect to that of the soldier? Why should he serve to cure the wounds wrought by the first? Why should the girl's genitalia at birth be scattered with semen? Barron offers another interpretation which will, he says, clear up the difficulties.

The whole poem, he says, expresses an analogy of procreation to agriculture. The symbols are not mere individual substitutions for sexual objects and acts but express an analogous relation of sexual objects and acts to sun, rain, flowers, earth, etc. "The girl in the poem is to take love again and to have her wounds cured in the same manner as the lacerations of the earth are cured by sun and rain."

Many of the words in the poem are related quite directly to the agricultural sphere. But the question arises, if the poem is an expression of the analogy of agriculture to procreation, what "concepts" in agriculture correspond to the laceration of the girl? Why was the idea of laceration necessary in order that the girl might bear a child?

The answers to both questions are not difficult. To the lacerated genitalia there correspond the lacerated plain, the gutted hill, which refer to fields which had been ploughed and sowed. In relation to the girl, the soldier carried out this side of the analogy.

In regard to the objection about the girl's genitalia at birth wearing semen, actually in the poem it is not the girl's genitalia that wear semen, it is the agricultural products of the field which are covered by the pollen of the flowers. This probably means that, as the agricultural products are now ripe and ready for re-sowing to bring forth new crops, so are the decorative flowers which scatter the pollen from the reproductive organs about the field, "as if to celebrate their own maturity as well as the ripening of the harvest rites of puberty."

Barron offers internal evidence for his interpretations, evidence which satisfies him that the author of the poem either consciously or unconsciously had the agricultural analogy in mind. Thus she has transposed predicates, indicating how closely she holds birth and harvesting to be: The *meadow* is made whole at last by *birth, you* will harvest when the *crop* is grown.

The third interpretation of the poem following this last idea is: "You who have been made for love will happily accept love again; for as the fields which have been ploughed respond to sun and rain, till the crop ripens and the flowers sprinkle their pollen to celebrate the maturity of the grain, so will your wounds be cured, since they are no deeper or more stubborn that the wounds of earth."[39] The last interpretation does not change the meaning of the second stanza.

The reader will recall how Freud held the theory that there came to be a close association of sexuality and agriculture in primitive society.[40] Barron holds that the close parallelism between procreation and agriculture in the poem is a phylogenetic inheritance, a hypertrophied vestige of a primitive specific adjustive mechanism. He considers the author of the poem "as a genius of the archaic who was able to expound and articulate the traces of our ancestors' conceptions of procreation and agriculture which persist to some degree in all of us but to a heightened degree in her, though she had only slight contact with such primitive conceptions."[41]

Symbolism in "Finnegans Wake"

The psychoanalytic journals contain a considerable number of papers which offer psychoanalytic symbolic interpretations of literature.[42] However, instead of reproducing some of these works, we give an excerpt from a work on James Joyce's *Finnegans Wake* by a writer who applies symbolical methods of interpretation.[43] However, we must remind the reader that Joyce's last work is as obscure as it is famous and that a brief excerpt cannot be expected immediately to reveal the secret of *Finnegans Wake* in a transparent glow. But we do suspect that a careful study of this small fragment will be enlightening. Here is the excerpt on Joyce:

"In *Finnegans Wake*, the archetypical Man, the archetypical Father, is shown as having twin sons. These sons, Shaun and Shem, are the polar faces of the Father himself.

The Father bears the face of Shaun. Shaun is what he wants to be. Shem is what he conceals, what he tries to suppress, to censor, to inhibit.

When he looks at himself, he sees the face of Shaun. Yet he knows that Shem is present. In himself, Shaun is marred by Shem.

And, when he looks at Shaun, the Father sees himself. He sees himself — unmarred by time, by guilt, by defeat. He sees himself — unshamed by Shem.

In the Future, Shaun — unshamed by Shem — he will do all the things that the Father did not do.

In him he will live again.

And yet — he himself replaced his own Father. Knowing this, the Father knows that his Son will replace him.

He knows that this son will wear the face of Shaun.

Shaun is object of his love. Embodiment of his hopes. And — a source of fear.

The Father looks at himself. He sees himself as Potiphar. *Pot-au-feu!*

He, who was Tristan once, sees himself as Mark.

Shaun is Tristan now.

Shaun is Edipus. He will be king.

He is the Edipus who will take the Father's wife. Who will take the Father's life.

And yet — the Father knows he himself was Edipus. He himself was Tristan once.

His anxieties mingle with a sense of guilt.

The Daughter — the Female Child.

As the Child, she is the object of the Father's love. The embodiment of his hopes.

She is like Shaun. But — unlike Shaun — she won't take the Father's wife, won't take the Father's life.

While, as the female, she bears the Mother's face. She is the Father's wife.

But — as yet — unmarred by Time. Unmarred by Defeat. Unmarred by Shame and Guilt.

She is his nostalgia.

For his past. For his youth. The youth of his wife.

She purifies his past.

She purifies himself.

He knows that this love, the purity of this love, is a sign of the weakening of his powers. Is a sign of his age. His defeat.

He does not escape his guilt!

This love is not pure.

His daughter bears the face that his wife used to wear. His yearning takes the colors of that former yearning.

Trying to escape his guilt, he finds a new guilt.

The Father seeks the Daughter.

The Son seeks the Mother.

To the Son — the Edipus — the Mother is the symbol of conquest, the symbol of Success and Power.[44]

Son-yearning-for-the-Mother. That is the Demiurge of the Outer World.

Father-yearning-for-the-Daughter. That is the dynamics, the Demiurge, of the Inner."[45]

5. THE THEORIES OF ALFRED ADLER

According to Alfred Adler, another early disciple of Freud, the formula or imaginary goal, "I wish to be a complete man" is the "guiding fiction" or "guiding principle" of every neurosis.[1] The sexual drives and the tendencies toward "sexual perversions" are said to subordinate themselves according to this guiding principle. The preponderance of sexual phantasy and even of sexual feeling is a "jargon" in the life of the neurotic, a *modus dicendi*, expressing a compulsion in the direction of the "masculine goal." This drive toward a masculine goal springs from profound and all-pervasive feelings of inferiority and a compelling, insatiable need to neutralize these tortured feelings of inadequacy and inferiority. The drive toward a masculine goal is designed to fulfill this need. Only by positing such a goal can the "neurotic" find life bearable.

Adler ascribes the origin of the difficulties of the "neurotic individual" in many cases to a "constitutional inferiority," an inferiority of some organ or "systems of organs." The inferiority of an organ manifests itself in a pervasive influence on the psyche in action, in thought, in dreams, in the choice of a vocation and in artistic inclinations and capabilities.

ORGAN INFERIORITY

What is organ inferiority? Adler distinguishes two forms or groups, both of which, he says, are present at the same time in the majority of cases: the morphological and the func-tional.[2]

Functional inferiority, he believes, is perhaps the chief group since through some functional defect the morphologic anomaly is discovered. The characteristic trait of functional inferiority is a quantitative or qualitative insufficiency of work, which is determined by a standard criterion of required effi-ciency. Since there is an inherent tendency in the organism to counteract a defect, a "compensation" occurs. Among other ways, a compensation may occur by the use of another organ instead of the inferior or weaker one, or by an intensified training of the inferior organ itself.[3]

Adler places no small emphasis on compensation. Even genius is construed as a result of over-compensation in an inferior brain.

Full normality of an organ, he says, is not at all the same thing as health. An organ may be inferior and yet func-tion in a fashion called normal. Certain conditions may conceal such a deficiency. Scrupulous hygiene, for example, may enable one to escape dangers to the organism. Or again compensation may so relieve the burden of an inferior organ that it can function in a way which appears healthy.

Organs of slight inferiority may develop greater func-tional capacity than normal organs. The stuttering boy, Demosthenes, Adler observes, became the greatest orator of Greece. The greater functional capacity results from a con-tinual exercise and adaptation of the inferior organs under varying conditions as well as from the development of related nervous and psychological structures stimulated by watchful attention and concentration on the vicissitudes of the inferior organ.

This is the brighter side of the picture. But there is another side, too. According to Adler, the psychical structure accompanying organ inferiority furnishes a basis for neuroses and psychoses.[4]

Observation of children and the anamnesis of adults reveal that the possession of definitely inferior organs results in a lowered self-esteem and an increased psychological uncertainty. From the lowered self-esteem an intense struggle for self-assertion eventuates.[5] The child with an inferior organ thus develops various stratagems calculated to increase his sense of personal worth and value. Those stratagems sometimes then take on the character of neurosis or psychosis.

ENVIRONMENTAL FACTORS IN INFERIORITY

But organic inferiority is not the only factor which disposes a child toward mental illness. Adler is not unaware that a "foolish" environment of the child can create difficulties in living and form a character which will develop various traits labeled "neurotic" or "psychotic." If the parents, for example, have little or no tenderness for their child, he will not be able to recognize love nor "make the proper use of it."[6] To take another example, the parents may ridicule the child's expressions of tenderness, thus causing him to believe that love is ridiculous. Or still again, the child may be exposed to gross neglect. Such experiences tend to isolate the child from others and to impress him with the inordinate difficulty of life and its tasks.

THE HUMAN SITUATION AND INFERIORITY FEELINGS

For Adler, inferiority feelings are inherent in the human situation. To *"be a human being means the possession of a feeling of inferiority that is constantly pressing on towards its own conquest."*[7] The struggle for self-preservation and for bodily and mental equipoise, bodily and mental growth, the striving for perfection, support the view that the fundamental law of life is that of overcoming deficiencies and inadequacies. The life process is to be regarded as a struggle aiming always at a goal of adaptation to the demands of the world. Since there is a discrepancy between the demands and problems raised by the external world and man's equipment and powers, mistakes and at least partial defeats are inevitable. Furthermore, man's envisioned end is death. Hence, the difference between the mentally healthy and the sick is one of degree and not of kind.[8] When a feeling of inferiority, due either to organic defect or environmental inadequacies, is stronger than the normal, all sorts of physical, emotional and mental disturbances and changes may arise which manifest themselves in the symptoms of neuroses and psychoses.

Yet Adler's attitude is, in general, optimistic in regard to the human situation. "Who can seriously doubt," he says, "that the human individual treated by nature in such a stepmotherly fashion has been provided with the blessing of a strong feeling of inferiority that urges him towards a plus situation, towards security and conquest? And this tremendous enforced rebellion against a tenacious feeling of inferiority is awakened afresh and repeated in every infant and little child as the fundamental fact of human development."[9]

DIFFICULTIES OF THE CHILD SITUATION

He puts enormous stress on the difficulties of the infant- and child-situation. Every child's instincts, he says, "are baffled in their fulfillment by obstacles whose conquest gives him pain. He realizes at an early age that there are other human beings who are able to satisfy their urges more completely, and are better prepared to live. His soul is born, one might say, in these situations of childhood which demand an organ of integration, whose function is to make a normal life possible. This the soul accomplishes by evaluating each situation and directing the organism to the next one, with the maximum satisfaction of instincts and the least possible friction. In this way he learns to over-value the size and stature which enables one to open a door, or the ability to move heavy objects, or the right of others to give commands and claim obedience to them. A desire to grow, to become as strong or even stronger than all others, arises in his soul. To dominate those who are gathered about him, becomes his chief purpose in life, since his elders, though they act as if he were inferior, are obligated to him because of his very weakness. Two possibilities of action lie open to him. On the one hand, to continue activities and methods which he realizes the adults use, and on the other hand to demonstrate his weakness, which is felt by these same adults as an inexorable demand for their help. We shall continually find this branching of psychic tendencies in children."[10]

Some children will emulate the adults directly for the purpose of gaining power and recognition; others will dwell on their own weakness and attempt to demonstrate it in various ways. In any case, out of the feeling of inferiority, inadequacy, insecurity, there arises a drive to overcome the difficulties of the environment in order to gain peace, security, social "equilibrium." In order to accomplish this, a human being can, depending on circumstances, resort to countless stratagems and techniques.

The child who is constitutionally handicapped, or who meets with extraordinary difficulties in his economic, social, racial or family relations will be predisposed toward an exaggerated sense of inferiority. He will picture the world as hostile and threatening, and he will have a hostile attitude toward it. In such cases, the intensified feelings of inadequacy and inferiority are not so likely to be resolved, because a conviction of personal worth cannot arise from an orientation of hostility toward mankind. There will be developed a striving for power by conquest rather than by cooperation — a goal of dominance over one's fellows. Human relations will be understood in terms of struggle, not in terms of cooperation with one's fellow men or in genuine love. Such an "inferiority complex" drives the individual to overcompensate for his weakness by creating for himself an exaggerated and unrealizable ideal of personal importance, embodying all the powers and natural gifts of which the child believes himself deprived.

As a rule, people do not change their attitude toward life after infancy, Adler observes, although the expressions of their attitude are in later life quite different.

Development of Compensatory Techniques

The feeling of inferiority, incompetency and the "realization" of his smallness, weakness, and uncertainty demand a compensation in the form of a "maximation of ego-consciousness." The child, burdened as he is by a profound feeling of inferiority, especially the "constitutionally inferior" child, aims to be great, to be strong, to be "above."[11] These aims come to be symbolized in the person of a powerful figure of the child's immediate environment: father, mother, teacher, and so on. The father, especially, is the all-powerful figure with whom the child endeavors to raise himself on a level or even to surpass him.

Schemes of Orientation in Life

Every child likewise in order to reduce what is chaotic, fluid and intangible in life to "measurable entities," that is to make sense out of the world and his relation to it, avails himself of "guiding fictions," schemes of understanding and orientation, reference-frames, modes of organizing experience. This is analogous to the device of dividing the globe into meridional and parallel lines, by which we can preserve fixed points which we can place in relation to one another. In this respect, however, the difference between a healthy and a mentally ill person is that the former chooses an orientation, a scheme of guiding principles, which enables him, in varying degrees, to realize the goals he strives for, to solve difficulties in life, to arrange the cosmic picture and his own place in it, in some fairly satisfying way. The healthy person likewise regards his guiding principles as devices for making workable distinctions, which, however, he does not take to be fixed and infallible in the process of living. But the individual who is mentally ill chooses an unworkable and unrealistic scheme, one which is inapplicable to the world but which, nevertheless, is rigidly maintained. The "neurotic" chains himself to his "guiding principles" or "fictions" so strongly that he is unable to reject or properly modify them. People who are profoundly uncertain about themselves and the world will usually cling doggedly to anything that has seemed or does seem sufficient to enable them to live and to provide a kind of security, however specious, rather than face the horrors of the new and strange.

Development of Life Goals

The organism, says Adler, has to adapt itself and respond to the environment; and the demands of life compel the child to respond in a unified manner. Hence, human behavior is purposive. The psyche is determined by movements toward a goal. "No human being," he avers, "can think, feel, will, dream, without all these activities being determined, continued, modified and directed, toward an ever-present objective."[12] In the widest meaning of the term goal, it is a striving by various means for security and adaptation to life. All subordinate and particular strivings are orientated to this all-comprehensive goal.[13] This unified manner of meeting situations constitutes the individual character. Because of a constitutional inadequacy or because of unfortunate toxic elements in the social environment (especially in early life) in many people this striving for security becomes thwarted and distorted so that they grow up with an insatiable need to dominate, to gain power over everything and everyone. This striving for power takes the form of a "masculine goal," power, superiority, and masculinity being regarded as practically synonymous, while femininity is looked upon as an expression of weakness, of inadequacy. Adler traces this phenomenon, in a general way, to certain characteristics of our society.

MALE DOMINANCE

In Western culture, he points out, [14] men occupy and control the dominant social positions, hold great social power and advantage, and often lord it over women. Not only our institutions but our traditional attitudes, morals, and customs testify to the dominance of the male sex. Hence, men are usually assumed to belong to a superior sex; they become a symbol of power and greatness and privilege, whom people in a weaker position (children, women, "neurotics") envy and strive to emulate or surpass.

In the (European) family, it is usually the father who is the symbol of power. The child notes and is impressed by his mysterious comings and goings, his role of leader in the family who gives commands and makes arrangements, and to whom the mother looks for advice. It is therefore not surprising that there are children who determine the rightness of their views simply on the ground that their father "said so."

Adler also observes that male domination is by no means an eternal and fixed rule. Men nowadays help perpetuate their power by various legal and institutional devices. But there were epochs when women, especially mothers, played the most important role in life. This was in the days of the matriarchate. Over a long period of time men have wrested power and control from women and subjugated them.

Nevertheless, in contemporary Western civilization every human being, Adler claims, is measured according to the standard of the privileged male, so that every boy and many girls grow up with a "masculine ideal." Women are said to have an almost universal dissatisfaction with the feminine role. Their psychic life is pervaded by a strong feeling of inferiority because of their situation in a man's world. An additional and aggravating burden is added by the prejudice about feminine inferiority. Consequently, many women, put up a battle against the feminine role. Some become extraordinarily energetic, ambitious, aggressive, and, wherever possible, strive to outdo the male. Others adopt an attitude of resignation, obedience, humbleness, and helplessness; such women may develop nervous symptoms, and in general manifest a need for consideration and solicitude. Still others accept the dogma of male superiority, approve the privileged position of men — for a price; they demand a special position and they shift their responsibilities to the men. Thus there results a definite division and separation between the sexes.

RELATION OF SEX TO THE LIFE GOAL

For Adler, the pleasure striving of the Freudian libido, the impulses toward sexual activity, the influence of the infantile wishes concerning sexual activity with the parents, are all subordinate to and in the service of the imaginary masculine goal in the life of the mentally ill. The Freudian theory that the neuroses have a sexual etiology is erroneous. The unremitting struggle for the imaginary masculine goal, not sex, is the key concept for understanding neuroses. For the "neurotic" the enjoyment of sexual pleasure or any form of sexual expression is secondary. In fact, the "whole picture of the sexual neurosis is nothing more than a portrait depicting the distance which the patient is removed from the imaginary masculine goal and the manner in which he seeks to bridge it." The "neurotic" person uses sex, like everything else, as a means toward the one all-inclusive end.

The sexual components cannot be properly estimated

except in relation to the person's orientation toward life, to his "style of life." The erotic phases are functions of the life style and are to be understood in this way because all feelings adapt themselves to the life style. The nuclear form of an individual's adaptation to life, the "prototype," is established by the age of four; it is the essential form of one's orientation to life, which includes the "idea" one has of oneself. The expression and enjoyment of sexuality is determined according to the particular pattern of the original form of orientation. "If the prototype is sociable and interested in others, the personality into whom it develops will solve all love-problems with loyalty to the partner and responsibility to society. If the prototype is strugging to attract notice and to suppress others, its later manifestations will include the use of sexuality towards the same ends: that person will establish sexual relations in order to rule. A prototype formed by attaining superiority in a limited sphere of activity which excludes the opposite sex will tend later to produce homo-sexuality or other perversions. The main outlines of the erotic life are thus strictly pre-conditioned."[15]

THE THREE GREAT LIFE PROBLEMS

In his later work, Adler seems to put more emphasis on the person's relation to society rather than on organ inferiority or lack of it, although there is, of course, no contradiction between the two. There is only one single standard by which one can form an estimate of a human being, he says: "his movement when confronted with the unavoidable problems of humanity."[16] These problems are the attitude adopted toward fellow men, one's vocation or profession, and love. The three problems, he maintains, can only be solved by persons who have an adequate amount of social feeling. The attitude adopted toward one's fellow men is central, for the other two depend in some sense on it. These three problems arise from the relationship of man to society, to the cosmic factors, and to the other sex. Man is part of the whole, and his value is said to depend on his solution of these three great problems.

IMPORTANCE OF SOCIAL FEELING

In the last analysis, Adler traces much of human failure to a lack of social feeling. "All failures — neurotics, psychotics, criminals, drunkards, problem children, suicides, perverts and prostitutes — are failures because they are lacking in fellow-feeling and social interest. They approach the problems of occupation, friendship and sex without the confidence that they can be solved by cooperation. The meaning they give to life is a private meaning: no one else is benefited by the achievement of their aims and their interest stops short at their own persons. Their goal of success is a goal of mere fictitious personal superiority and their triumphs have meaning only to themselves."[17]

The mother, through the evolutionary development of mother-love, is by nature best suited to give the child the experience of living with one's fellow beings. From her, "standing as the first fellow creature at the gateway that opens on the development of social feeling, come the earliest impulses urging the child to make his appearance in life as a part of the whole and to seek the right contact with other persons in his world."[18] But the mother may be, says Adler, tactless, clumsy, ignorant in her "handling" of the child, or she may take her role too lightly or carelessly. Again, she may pamper and "over-protect" the child, thus crippling his development by hindering the need to exercise his powers or to learn to cooperate with others. In the latter case the child develops his goal of superiority by opposing the development of his powers and functions. He demands an excessive degree of attention and affection, with the result that he alienates others and believes they are essentially hostile.[19] His "style of life" is oriented toward a feeling of helplessness and an unremitting desire for what he conceives to be affection and attention. In this way he may obtain a considerable degree of power and control over members of the family, since his helplessness constitutes a weapon against those who are obligated to take care of him. According to Adler, such phenomena as bed-wetting or retention of feces are to be understood as demands for excessive attention and not as derivable from the sexual libido or sadistic urges.

Since feelings of inferiority are extremely painful and are usually regarded as signs of weakness and as shameful, there will be a strong effort to conceal the experience. The child as he grows may cease to be aware of his inferiority *per se*, becoming preoccupied with the consequences of the feeling and with all the stratagems which help to conceal it. Compensatory ideas and phantasies of greatness, of superiority, develop. Impossible goals of achievement are elaborated ("fictions"). One may say that in these cases the formula, "I wish to be a complete man" amounts to "I wish to be a superman." But these unrealistic constructions, of course, serve to make the person's difficulties all the greater. Lacking social feeling, consideration for others, and at the same time making impossible demands for attention and recognition, he finds that his ability to get along with people progressively diminishes.[20]

The Pampered Child

Adler places great importance on the pampering of the child in understanding the phenomena of the Oedipus complex. He thinks that the normal attitude of the child is an *almost equal* interest in father and mother, especially after the very early period of infancy. But certain external circumstances may direct the interest of the child to either one of the parents. For instance, certain traits of the father's personality, a pampering mother, illness or difficulties in organic development requiring the prolonged care of the mother may tend to create a distance between child and father. This eventuality is unfortunate if for no other reason than that the expansion of social feeling is hindered. Should the father intervene in order to prevent the mother's coddling of the child, he increases the distance. Or a mother's tendency to induce the child to side with her against the father may have the same effect.

When pampering on the part of the father predominates, the child turns away from the mother to him. If the child, because of pampering and over-indulgence, remains tied to the mother, he becomes more or less of a parasite and looks to her for the satisfaction of all his wants, including his awakening sexual wants. If there is otherwise any attraction of the boy to the mother or the girl to the father, Adler believes it is mainly a non-sexual, preparatory sort of play in anticipation of a later stage of development. The "spoiled" child, however, is sexually precocious because he has learned to deny himself nothing.

Hence, the Oedipus complex "is nothing else than *one of the many forms that appear in the life of the pampered child,* who is the helpless sport of his excited phantasies."[21]

THE OEDIPUS COMPLEX

A child who has been pampered has a "hesitant attitude" toward the world. He fears to move out from the circle of the family. A boy who is pampered by the mother attaches his sole interest to her, perhaps permanently after encountering defeat in his tentative and ineffective struggles with the outside world. Since he has been accustomed to gratify all his wishes, he will indulge in erotic phantasy and in masturbation beyond the normal degree, thus over-stimulating his developing sexuality. In this respect the excessive kissing and caressing of the pampering mother may be another factor disposing toward sexual excitation. Since he is sexually precocious, his sexual phantasies, on which he dwells, will be directed at the mother. Because he rejects all others, she is expected to gratify all his desires. But here, too, his sexual phantasies and wishes are subordinated to and in the service of his life-goal: domination and exclusive control by possession of the mother. The sexual pleasure is incidental to the lust for power over the mother, whom he has discovered he can dominate.

The following well illustrates Adler's conception of the nature of the Oedipus complex. A "barrister of thirty-six has lost all interest in his work. He is unsuccessful and attributes this to the fact that he does not make a good impression on the few clients who come to consult him. He always found great difficulty as well in mixing with other people, and, especially in the company of girls, he was always extremely shy. A marriage into which he entered with great reluctance, indeed with aversion, ended a year later in divorce. He now lives quite withdrawn from the world in the house of his parents, who have for the most part to provide for him.

"He is an only child and he was spoiled by his mother to an incredible extent. She succeeded in convincing both the child and his father that he would one day become a very outstanding man. The boy grew up with this expectation, and his brilliant success at school seemed to confirm it. As commonly happens with most spoiled children, who can deny themselves nothing, childish masturbation gained a harmful mastery over him and soon made him the laughing-stock of the girls in the school, who had discovered his secret misdemeanor. He withdrew from them entirely. In his isolation he abandoned himself to the imagination of achieving the most glorious triumphs in love and marriage; but he felt himself attracted only to his mother, whom he completely dominated, and with whom for a considerable time he connected his sexual fantasies. It is also obvious enough from this case that this so-called Oedipus complex is not a 'fundamental fact,' but is simply a vicious unnatural result of maternal over-indulgence. This comes more clearly into view when the boy or the youth in his inordinate vanity sees himself betrayed by girls and has not developed sufficient social interest to be able to mix with other people."[22]

6. THE THEORIES OF C. G. JUNG

Jung, who also was one of Freud's early pupils, appears never to have wholeheartedly accepted his teacher's views *in toto*.[1] Of course, the possibility that Jung always had reservations as to Freudian theory may be mainly of historical interest, but it is often enlightening to trace the development of a man's ideas. In any case, while we do not intend to go into Jung's early theories in any detail, we can probably make our exposition clearer by noting his point of departure from strict Freudian orthodoxy.

EARLY DOUBTS OF SOME FREUDIAN IDEAS AND METHODS

In 1906, while acknowledging very great indebtedness to Freud, he refused to accept the exclusive importance which he thought the founder of psychoanalysis attached to the infantile sexual trauma, the preponderance of sexuality, or the universality of its psychological implications. Furthermore, he expressed uncertainty as to the complete adequacy of Freudian methods.[2]

PSYCHOLOGICAL EFFECTS OF PARENTS ON CHILDREN

A few years later, in 1909, having journeyed to the United States with Freud, Ferenczi, and Jones to lecture at

129

the celebration of the twentieth anniversary of the opening
of Clark University, Jung put forth a view which, *in its
emphasis*, differs considerably from Freud's orientation. In
discussing childhood experiences and their subsequent effects,
he says: "It is not the good and pious precepts, nor is it
any other inculcation of pedagogic truths that have a
moulding influence upon the character of the developing child,
but what most influences him is the peculiarly affective state
which is totally unknown to his parents and educators. The
concealed discord between the parents, the secret worry, the
repressed hidden wishes, all these produce in the individual
a certain affective state with its objective signs which slowly
but surely, though unconsciously, works its way into the
child's mind, producing therein the same conditions and
hence the same reactions to external stimuli. We know that
association with mournful and melancholic persons will depress
us, too. A restless and nervous individual infects his surroundings with unrest and dissatisfaction, a grumbler, with
his discontent, etc. If grown-up persons are so sensitive to
such surrounding influences we certainly ought to expect
more of this in the child whose mind is as soft and plastic
as wax. The father and mother impress deeply into the child's
mind the seal of their personality, the more sensitive and
mouldable the child the deeper is the impression. Thus even
things that are never spoken about are reflected in the child.
The child imitates the gesture, and just as the gesture of
the parent is the expression of an emotional state, so in
turn the gesture gradually produces in the child a similar
feeling, as it feels itself, so to speak, into the gesture. Just
as the parents adapt themselves to the world, so does the
child. At the age of puberty when it begins to free itself
from the spell of the family, it enters into life with so to
say a surface of fracture [an adaptation] entirely in keeping
with that of the father and mother. The frequent and often
very deep *depressions of puberty* emanate from this; they

are symptoms which are rooted in the difficulty of new adjustment. The youthful person at first tries to separate himself as much as possible from his family, he may even estrange himself from it, but inwardly this only ties him the more firmly to the parental image."[3]

One is struck by the fact that there is here no explicit reference to the sexual, while in Freud's writings probably no important event in childhood is discussed without such explicit reference. The emphasis is on the emotional interplay between the child and the adults rather than on the development or suppression of instincts.[4] To be sure, in discussing the analysis of a little girl, Jung closely follows Freud, a fact which gives the remarks quoted above a rather ambiguous status. Furthermore, Freud's definition of the term "sexual" is sufficiently wide that it can include an extensive range of "affects." Yet in view of the subsequent development of his views, it seems safe to say that Jung is here thinking primarily of *non-sexual*, emotional relationships between the child and the parents. In any case, he very soon abandoned or rather widened the designation which Freud gave to the libido.

REVISION OF LIBIDO THEORY

In *The Psychology of the Unconscious*, originally appearing in 1912, Jung advocates a thorough revision of the concept of libido. A "descriptive" (Freudian) view of libido is contrasted with a "genetic" (Jungian) interpretation. According to the descriptive standpoint, the sexual instinct is only one of a multiplicity of instincts, but having its own special character. In this sense, the libido can be "displaced" and, when dammed up, may overflow into other channels. The non-sexual instincts may receive "affluxes" of libido.

The genetic standpoint regards the multiplicity of instincts, including the sexual, as arising from a relative unity, a "primal" libido. The history of evolution is alleged to show that countless complicated functions now lacking any sexual character were originally derivations from the general impulse to propagation. In the ascent through the animal kingdom an important displacement of the energy of the procreative instinct occurred. Thus, for example, some of the energy expended in the production of eggs and sperma has been "transposed" into the creation of mechanisms for allurement and for protection of the young. Such mechanisms are maintained by a special differentiated libido. This displaced, "desexualized" energy can no more be classified as sexual than can the cathedral of Cologne be classified as mineralogy because it is built of stones. The diversion of sexual libido into other associated functions is still occurring. The altered mode of reproduction marks a heightened adaptation to reality.

The history of evolution, it is said, shows that there are really few things in human life which cannot in the last analysis be reduced to the instinct of procreation. In nature, however, the artificial distinction between libido and hunger (the instinct of the preservation of the species and the instinct for self-preservation) does not exist. The libido manifests itself as a continuous life impulse which maintains both the preservation of the individual and, through it, the creation and continuation of the whole species.[5] The libido has to be related to every desire. It is "will." Hence, the libido cannot rightly be characterized by the traits of any given instinct. Instead, it underlies them all.

Although there are further ideas on the subject of libido in this book, we now turn to a work published shortly after, in which Jung has elaborated his ideas with far greater clarity. In *The Theory of Psychoanalysis* the concept of libido is altered so that it is made synonymous with undifferentiated energy. In this sense, the meaning of libidinal or psychical energy is analogous to the meaning of energy in physics, which may be considered as manifesting itself in various forms: potential, kinetic, etc. Due to evolutionary change, the libido, which was originally to a large extent of a primarily sexual character, became desexualized. So the libido is considered to be manifested in various activities and forms, in nutrition, play, sexual feeling and love, etc.[6] For Jung, the real value of the libido theory lies not in its sexual definition, as he puts it, but in the "energic" conception of it. "We owe to the energic conception," says Jung, "the possibility of dynamic ideas and relationships, which are of inestimable value for us in the chaos of the psychic life."[7] In other words, psychical "energy-processes" are life-processes.[8]

Having arrived at such a concept of libido, Jung categorically rejects the idea that such activities as the sucking of the infant are in any way of a sexual nature. Instead, he claims that at the age of sucking only the function of nutrition occurs, which carries with it both pleasure and satisfaction. Since sucking first gives satisfaction and pleasure, it is a *petitio principii* to maintain that sucking therefore has a sexual character. The experience of any kind of pleasure is not synonymous with sexuality or sexual pleasure. If we assume that both sex and hunger exist side by side, we project the psychology of adults into the mental life and experience of the child. If the sex instinct exists at all at this age, it is quite embryonic. To say that the drive for pleasure has a sexual character is in effect to say that hunger is also a sexual striving since hunger "seeks" pleasure by obtaining satisfaction.[9]

THE THREE PHASES OF DEVELOPMENT

Along with the abandonment of Freud's theory of *libido sexualis*, his idea of the multiplicity of sexual components is also given up. This of course involves a considerable modification of the theory of child development and the evolution of personality. In formulating his own ideas on these matters, Jung divides the life of the individual into three phases. The first phase, called the pre-sexual, comprises the first three to five years of life. Nutrition and growth, he says, almost exclusively characterize this period. During this time the helplessness of the baby is gradually overcome, and a series of important psychological functions have taken firm hold. By the end of this first phase a considerable step has been made in the emancipation and the formation of a new and independent personality.

The second phase takes in the later years of childhood to puberty and is called the pre-pubertal stage.

Finally, the third phase extends from puberty onwards, and might be called the time of maturity.[10]

THE BEGINNING OF SEXUALITY

Jung does not deny that infantile sexuality exists, but he gives it a much narrower meaning. The first signs of interest and activity which may "fairly" be called sexual appear around the end of the "pre-sexual" phase, although such indications are said to manifest characteristics of harmlessness and naïveté. There is a gradual development of sexuality. With the gradual maturation and development of the individual, the libido gives rise to new ways of desire, new activities and satisfactions. The original model rhythmic activity in the act of sucking which gave rise to satisfaction and pleasure is carried over into other functions whose final end is sexuality.

For Jung, what Freud calls the latent sexual period, occurring around the sixth year, when overt sexual behavior often disappears, is the *real beginning* of sexuality. Everything preceding this, he says, is but the fore-stage, which lacks any real sexual character.

Very slowly and with great difficulty can the libido, or

rather part of it, "detach" itself from the characteristics of the nutritive function in order gradually to pass over into the characteristics of the sexual function. Two epochs are distinguished during this transition, the epoch of sucking and that of displaced rhythmic activity. Originally food is taken in the act of sucking with certain rhythmic movements associated with it. The act gives every sign of satisfaction. Gradually the sucking "passes beyond" nutrition to gaining pleasure and satisfaction in rhythmic activity *per se* without the taking of nourishment. As the child develops, the hand comes into play, especially during the epoch of rhythmical activity. Gradually the mouth ceases to give this kind of pleasure or at least full satisfaction. The gaining of pleasure spreads to other bodily regions. As a rule, the other orifices of the body become the first objects of interest; then the skin, or special parts of it. Certain actions performed on the body, like rubbing, piercing, tugging, picking, accompanied by a certain rhythm, bring pleasure. Sooner or later the child discovers some of the possibilities of pleasure in the genital zone; the libido "arrives" at the sexual zone, where onanistic attempts may follow.

The "progress" of the libido from the function of nutrition to the sexual zone carries with it traits of the former, which explain the many close associations between the function of nutrition and the sexual function.

In regard to childhood experiences, their profound importance for determining the future life course is affirmed but with a non-Freudian twist. The first impressions of childhood accompany us throughout life, and certain educational influences may confine people within certain limits all their lives. Frequently, a conflict has to break out, as one might expect, between the personality formed by educational and other influences and that which may be described as the real individual line of life. All people who are called upon to live an independent and productive life must meet this conflict.

Those who are "neurotic" to a greater degree than others unconsciously retain certain childish pretensions, expectations and illusions which are unsuited to the world of reality.

THE EVOLUTION OF THE OEDIPUS AND ELECTRA COMPLEX

Regardless of its sex, the first love of the child belongs to the mother. When at this early stage the love for the mother is intense, the father is jealously regarded as a rival. But at this time the mother has no sexual significance of any importance for the child. The mother is still the protecting, enveloping, food-providing being who, for these reasons, is a source of delight. The desire for food is said to have much to do with the first feelings of jealousy; however, a relatively germinating eroticism is also connected with it. As the years pass, the germinating eroticism grows so that the Oedipus complex gradually assumes the classical form. The typical affection of the girl for her father with corresponding jealousy toward the mother is, by Jung, called the Electra complex.

Both the Oedipus complex phantasy of the boy and the Electra complex phantasy of the girl reach a new stage after puberty, when the emancipation from the parents is more or less attained.

The so-called castration complex is a symbol, a symbol of self-sacrifice, and the latter is preeminent at this time, for the phantasy of self-sacrifice means sacrificing infantile wishes. The more sexuality matures, the more the person is forced to leave the family and acquire independence and autonomy. In his individual history the child is closely connected with the family, especially with his parents; and, therefore, often only with the greatest difficulty can he free himself from his infantile surroundings, where his personal history has been enfolded and developed. If adults are not able to free them-

selves spiritually, the Oedipus or Electra complex gives rise
to conflict. From this conflict comes the possibility of neurotic
disturbance.[11] The sexually developed libido assumes a form
engendered by the complex, creating feelings and phantasies
which clearly reveal the existence of the hitherto unconscious
complex. There follow intense resistances against the "im-
moral inner impulses" which have sprung from the now active
complexes. In the case of the son, strong resistances against
the father and a "typical" affectionate and dependent attitude
toward the mother may arise. Or, there may be an indirect
outcome, that is, a "typical" submissiveness toward the
father with an irritated, antagonistic attitude toward the
mother. In regard to the daughter, analogous consequences
may take place.

From these statements it might appear that in essential
respects Jung is still close to the orthodox Freudian standpoint. But, as we shall see, the Oedipus and Electra complexes
for Jung have both a "semiotic" and a "symbolical" meaning.
In explaining this distinction we must introduce some other
ideas of Jung.

Two Modes of Analysis

In order to point out certain methodological and theoretical differences between himself and Freud, he distinguishes
between a *causal* and a *functional* analysis. In a causal
analysis, everything is explained in terms of generally known
principles of a simple nature. Such a method, he says, is
reductive. It claims that any given phenomenon is "nothing
but" a relatively few ultimate elements mechanically combined
in a certain way. In a functional analysis, a thing is explained
in terms of what it does or is striving to do, that is, what
function it serves.

One example he gives is that of a commentator of
Goethe's "Faust." The commentator may explain the manifold
figures and scenes of the second part by reference to their

historical origins. The meaning of the poem is explained in terms of, and is "reduced to" its historical origins. Or, if he gives a psychological analysis, he shows that the conflict in the drama corresponds to a conflict within the poet himself, a conflict which is based upon certain ultimate elements of human nature familiar to all of us. In this case he may explain the meaning of the poem by reference to certain humanly characteristic psychological factors or elements operating in the poet.

But one has to ask, what is the poet's real purpose in his symbolic creation? The poem was not written in order to convey historical information or merely for the sake of expressing an inner conflict of the poet. These are not the "real" purposes of the poem.

To take another example which Jung states, one may learn the kinds of steel of which the various parts of a locomotive are made and from what ironworks and mines they come. But this does not tell us anything about the locomotive's *function*, which, he says, is its *meaning*.

So a causal analysis gives us a *retrospective* understanding, while a functional analysis gives us a *prospective* understanding. The one looks to the past in order to discover what elements have gone into the making of an occurrence or a thing; the other looks to the present and the future in order to discover what function something serves, to its *end* or goal.

The two kinds of analysis and thinking, Jung points out, are not opposed. They supplement each other. Taken alone, either one is inadequate.

Retrospective and Prospective Understanding of the Psyche

But what bearing has all this on the human psyche? The answer is that the psyche has to be understood both retrospectively and prospectively.

"Psyche is transition, hence necessarily to be defined under two aspects. On the one hand the psyche gives a picture of the remnants and traces of the entire past, and, on the other, but expressed in the same picture, the outlines of the future, inasmuch as the psyche creates its own future.

"The psyche at any given moment is at one and the same time result and summit of the past and a symbolic formula of the future. The future is only *similar* to the past, but in its essence always new and unique; thus the actual formula is incomplete, germlike, as it were, as regards the future."[12]

Role of Symbols in the Psychic Life

Since Jung attaches great importance to symbols, that is, as indications of what is to come, rather than what has occurred, we must note that he regards those actions as symbols whose meaning and aim are not directly evident as such. The symbol is the psychological machine which transforms energy. Any psychological phenomenon is a symbol if we assume that it signifies something different and greater than itself, something yet unknown. Just as the living body is itself a machine which transforms energy, so culture provides a "mental machine," the symbol, for transforming instinctive energies. The transformation of the libido by means of the symbol is not new; it is "a process that has been taking place since the beginning of time and its effectiveness continues." But as in the physical world only a small part of energy can be transformed into practically useful energy, into the energy of the living body, or into work, so in the psychical realm, only a small part of "psychical energy" can be drawn away from the "natural" (biological) flow and transformed. An incomparably greater part goes to sustain the regular course of life. There is, so to speak, a division of labor of the libido. It is apportioned among the various

"function-systems" of the organism, from which it cannot
be wholly withdrawn. But the history of man, of human
culture, has shown that mankind possesses a superfluity of
energy not required for the essential activities of the organism,
which is capable of application over and above "the natural
flow." By means of the symbol the excess libido can be
deflected. From this excess libido certain psychical processes
result, manifested and expressed in symbols. Often symbols
in the form of "representations" are religious ideas; in the
form of action, they are rites and ceremonies. "At the same
time, they are transitions to new activities, which must be
specifically characterized as cultural activities in contrast
to the instinctive functions that run their course according
to natural law."[13] The symbol is "a libido analogue," a mental
representation, a myth, rite, phantasy, dream image, etc.,
by virtue of which the excess libido finds a new form and
path of outlet.

For many centuries the tendency of mental development
has been to suppress individual symbol-making. In this suppression Christianity has played an outstanding role.[14] In
fact, through various institutions, as well as through "reason,"
the psyche has been regimented. However, in mentally ill patients one comes upon symbol-formations at every step. In
such people the "libido is not converted into effective work,
but flows away unconsciously along the old channel, that is,
into archaic sexual phantasies and phantastic activities." But
these symbol-formations are not to be explained reductively,
for their significance lies in the fact that they represent an
endeavor to elucidate by analogy what is as yet completely
unknown and only in process of formation. And if symbols
are explained reductively, people will still search for a more
favorable outlet than the "merely natural one," for man can
never rest satisfied with the "natural course of things" since
he has an excess of libido.

A symbol is never thought out consciously; it is always

produced unconsciously "in the way of so-called revelation or intuition."[15]

Freud Versus Jung

We now can permit Jung to state the difference between himself and Freud in his own words:

"The Viennese School takes the standpoint of an exclusive sexualistic conception, while that of the Zurich School is symbolistic. The Viennese School interprets the psychological symbol semiotically, as a sign or token of certain primitive psychosexual processes. Its method is analytical and causal.

"The Zurich School recognizes the scientific feasibility of such a conception, but denies its exclusive validity, for it does not interpret the psychological symbol semiotically only, but also symbolistically, that is, it attributes a positive value to the symbol.

"The value does not depend merely on historical causes; its chief importance lies in the fact that it has a meaning for the actual present and for the future, in their psychological aspects. For to the Zurich School the symbol is not merely a sign of something repressed and concealed, but is at the same time an attempt to comprehend and to point out the way of the further psychological development of the individual. Thus we add a prospective import to the retrospective value of the symbol."[16]

Hence the Zurich School regards the fundamental thoughts and impulses of the unconscious as symbols, indicative of a definite line of future development.

Take the case of a young married woman who begins to have terror attacks. She awakes at night from a nightmare, uttering a piercing cry. Calming herself with difficulty, she clings to her husband, imploring him not to leave her. She makes him repeat again and again that he loves her, and so on. A nervous asthma gradually develops.

In such a case a Freudian psychiatrist at once looks for the inner causality of the illness. He wants to know what the initial anxiety-dreams contained. The patient recalls wild bulls, lions, tigers, bad men. The doctor will also want to know what she associates with them. In answer she tells the following story. One time, a few years before she married, she was staying at a summer resort in the mountains . . . While she was there, she met a young Italian who played the guitar very well, "and who also knew how to play the guitar in the evenings." With the young man our patient developed a harmless flirtation, which led at once to a walk in the moonlight. During the walk, "the Italian temperament" asserted itself, causing the girl great terror. He "looked at her with such a look" that she never forgot it. In her dreams she sees this look; the wild animals have it.

But the skilled Freudian analyst does not rest here. Does this look originally come from the young man? Another reminiscence traces it further back. Once the patient's father, who died when she was about fourteen, took her, not long before his death, to Paris where, among other places, they visited the Folies Bergères. As they were leaving the Folies Bergères, a "rouged female" suddenly pressed close to the father "in an impertinent way." The patient, who became frightened, at that moment happened to look at the father to see what he would do—and she saw "that look," "that animal glare" in his eyes.

From this time, her attitude toward her father changed. An "inexplicable something" clung to her constantly. In overt behavior she oscillated between irritability and venomous moods, on the one hand, and, on the other, extravagant love. Then "causeless" fits of crying suddenly began. A terrible choking at table for a time overtook her when the father was at home, accompanied by apparent attacks of suffocation, usually followed by voicelessness for one to two days. On receiving the news of her father's death, she was overcome by uncontrolled grief, which ended in hysterical laughter. But her condition improved quickly and she became almost entirely well apparently.

However, the experience with the Italian had aroused something which frightened her, and she dropped him completely. A few years later she married. Her present trouble (the "neurosis") began only after her second child was born— at a moment when she discovered that her husband had a "tender interest" in another woman.

Further analysis reveals that the mother of the patient was herself nervous, manifested certain symptoms, had tried many sanitoria and systems of cure. The patient believed that the mother did not understand her father; that she herself understood him better. Furthermore, the daughter was her father's declared favorite. Toward the mother she was inwardly cool.

Three Possible Interpretations of the Electra Complex

Omitting many additional details, we repeat Jung's observation—that the symptoms can easily be comprehended as the expression of disappointed love for the father. "Sexual psychology," he continues, "finds the cause of the neurosis in the fact that the patient is not at bottom free from her father. This forces her to resuscitate her former experience at the moment when she discovered in the Italian the very same disturbing something that had made such a deep impression upon her when perceived in her father. These recollections were naturally revived by the analogous experience with another man, and formed the starting-point of the neurosis. It might therefore be said that the content and cause of the neurosis lay in the conflict between the phantastic infantile-erotic relation to the father on the one hand, and her love for the husband on the other."

But one can interpret the same illness, Jung observes, from the standpoint of another "instinct," that of the will to power, enunciated by Alfred Adler. Since we discussed Adler above, we need not repeat Jung's interpretation according to the Adlerian system here. Instead we give Jung's views and criticisms of both the former "Schools."

Both theories, he says, "explain to the patient that his symptoms come from here or there, and are 'nothing but' this or that. It would be very unjust to wish to maintain that this reductive theory is wrong in a given case, but when exalted into a general explanation of the nature of the soul— whether sick or healthy—a *reductive theory becomes impossible*. For the human soul, whether it be sick or healthy, cannot be reductively explained. Sexuality, it is true, is always and everywhere present; the instinct for power certainly does penetrate the heights and the depths of the soul; but the soul itself is not solely either the one or the other, or even both together, it is also that which it has made and will make out of them both. A person is only half understood when one knows how everything in him came about. Only a dead man can be explained in terms of the past; a living one must be otherwise explained. Life is not made up of yesterdays only, nor is it understood nor explained by reducing today to yesterday. Life has also a tomorrow, and today is only understood if we are able to add the indications of tomorrow to our knowledge of what was yesterday. This holds good for all expressions of psychological life, even for symptoms of disease. Symptoms of neurosis are not merely consequences of causes that once have been, whether they were 'infantile sexuality' or 'infantile instinct for power.' They are endeavors toward a new synthesis of life. It must immediately be added here that they are attempts that have miscarried. None the less they are attempts; they represent the germinal striving which has both meaning and value. They are embryos that failed to achieve life, owing to unpropitious conditions of an internal and external nature."[17]

Jung does not give us his own interpretation of the

case of the young woman. But from his general position, we can surmise that what might be called the reactivation of the Electra complex would be interpreted symbolically as a representation of her failure to achieve moral autonomy and a tendency toward a return to the relative security obtained from her father's protection and love. For Jung, the "neurosis" does *not* spring from a conflict between an unresolved craving for sexual union with the father and the demands of her ethical ideals and her love for her husband. It represents the miscarriage of her endeavors toward a new synthesis of life experience.[18]

Sexuality as a Symbol

He insists that the sexuality of the unconscious is only a symbol. Its reference is prospective, not retrospective. It is a form of expression typical of an earlier mode of adaptation to life, but it signifies something about the future, a decision or a step forward on the road to every purpose in life.

MAN'S ARCHAIC HERITAGE

Like Freud, Jung believes that the human mind contains archaic remnants, residues of the long history and evolution of mankind.[19] In the unconscious, primordial "universally-human images" lie dormant. Those primordial images are the most ancient, universal and "deep thoughts" of mankind. Since they embody feeling as much as thought, they are properly "thought feelings." Where Freud postulates a mass psyche, Jung postulates a collective psyche.[20] The collective psyche represents a certain part of the mental function which is fixed and automatic in its action. It is inherited and, being present everywhere in man, is universal and therefore "super-personal" or "impersonal."

The Collective Psyche

The collective psyche[21] is to a large extent unconscious;

hence, Jung distinguishes a personal or individual unconscious and an "impersonal" or "collective" unconscious.[22]

Jung explains his conception of a collective psyche and a collective unconscious as follows. "In the same way as the individual is not only an isolated and separate, but also a social being, so also the human mind is not only something isolated and absolutely individual, but also a collective function. And just as certain social functions or impulses are, so to speak, opposed to the egocentric interests of the individual, so also the human mind has certain functions or tendencies which, on account of their collective nature, are to some extent opposed to the personal mental functions. This is due to the fact that every human being is born with a highly differentiated brain, which gives him the possibility of attaining a rich mental function that he has neither acquired ontogenetically nor developed. In proportion as human beings are similarly differentiated, the corresponding mental functions are collective and universal. This circumstance explains the fact that the unconscious of far-separated peoples and races possess a remarkable number of points of agreement."[23] The "extraordinary" unanimity of indigenous forms and themes of myths seems to Jung to bear out his contention that there exists a collective mental function.[24]

But the contents of the collective unconscious consist not only of the residue of archaic human functions, but also of the residue of the functions of the longer animal ancestry of man. When these archaic residues become active, they are likely to divert the libido temporarily into regressive channels.[25]

Hence, every individual has not only memories of his own personal, unique history, but also the "primordial images" by virtue of his membership in the human family, inherited potentialities of the human imagination, lying latent in the structure of the brain.

". . . The unconscious, regarded as the historical background of the psyche, contains in a concentrated form the entire succession of engrams (imprints) which from time immemorial have determined the psychic structure as it now exists. These engrams may be regarded as function-traces which typify, on the average, the most frequently and intensely used functions of the human soul. These function-engrams present themselves in the form of mythological themes and images, appearing often in identical form and always with striking similarity among all races; they can also be easily verified in the unconscious material of modern man. It is intelligible, therefore, that avowedly animal traits or elements should also appear among the unconscious contents by the side of those sublime figures which from oldest times have accompanied man on the road of life."[26]

Psyche refers to the totality of all mental processes, both conscious and unconscious. These processes include thought, feeling, intuition and sensation. The psyche has three "levels": (1) consciousness, which is partly collective, (2) the personal unconscious, and (3) the collective unconscious. The contents of the psyche are fundamentally "images." Every psychic image has two sides, the one directed to the object being as faithful a "likeness" of it as possible, the other directed to the inner life, the soul, and the laws peculiar to it. Consequently, images indicate or refer to objects and the world generally, on the one hand, and, on the other, to "psychic function," roughly in the sense of "subjective" mental function which obeys inner laws irrespective of the world. Since the psyche must take account of the environment "in the most intimate fashion," it manifests reactions and adaptations relating to the present and recent past. This is the function of consciousness; it contains recent "object-images." The object-images of one's individual past are contained in one's personal unconsciousness in so far as they have either been forgotten or repressed. What Jung calls inherited world images, generally under the form of primordial images or mythical themes, are contained in the collective unconscious.[27] Thus, the daily course of the sun and the change from day to night have become recorded in the collective mind by way of the following myth: "Every morning a god-hero is born from the sea; he mounts the chariot of the sun. In the west a great mother awaits him and he is devoured by her in the evening. In the belly of a dragon he traverses the depths of the midnight sea. After a frightful combat with the serpent of night he is born again in the morning."[28]

Primordial images are archetypes, universal categories of intuition and apprehension. Wherever we meet with uniformly and regularly occurring ways of apprehension and intuition, they are referable to archetypes. The primordial image or archetype is always collective, always common to entire nations or epochs. Its constant and universal distribution corresponds with the universal and continuous influence of the environment on living matter and therefore has the character of a natural law. The archetype represents the chthonic part of the mind, by which man's relatedness to earth and universe seems most comprehensible. But it is not merely the effect of surrounding conditions; it is also just as much an effect of the peculiar and autonomous quality of living matter. It is therefore related to inner determinants of the mental life and to life in general. It expresses the unique and unconditioned creative power of mind. The archetype is an inherited organization of psychic energy. "Archetypes are systems of preparedness that are at the same time images and emotions. They are inherited with the structure of the brain of which they represent the psychic aspect."[29] Whenever there are no ideas present to consciousness, or whenever those present are "impossible" on either extrinsic or intrinsic grounds, the archetype begins to function.

"The theory of archetypes or primordial ideas is not to be confused with the long abandoned theory of innate ideas.

The collective unconscious does not contain ideas exactly—. nothing so clean-cut as that. But it contains natural ways of thinking, lines of least resistance, tendencies to gravitate in our ideas toward primitive modes of thought. In dreams, in the night terrors of children, in the hallucinations and delusions of the insane, and even in waking life when we are caught off guard by something for which we are totally unprepared, such as an earthquake, our recently won scientific conceptions of natural processes drop away from us, and we think animistically or have vague primitive notions of sympathetic magic and of spirits, fairies, witches, dragons, and devils. Father, mother, and child, male and female, generation, growth and decay, are primitive facts which have so impressed themselves on racial thought that they constantly reappear as symbols in the thought of today. We gravitate toward them as easy and explanatory ideas, and speak of the 'birth of a nation' or the 'decay of an institution,' scarcely noticing the figure of speech. Some archetypes, such as that of energy, have been appropriated by scientific thought; and it may often be of advantage to an individual's mental health to become aware of some of his racial archetypes, as of some of his instincts, and to integrate them with his conscious thought and action. The study of mythology and of primitive customs is valuable to analytical psychology for the light it throws on the collective unconscious."[30]

The Mother Archetype

Like Freud, Jung believes that childhood "rehearses" reminiscences of the pre-history of the race and of mankind in general. "Phylogenetically as well as ontogenetically we have grown up out of the dark confines of the earth." The mother is the most immediate primordial image or "archetypal experience." Since the child is not yet an individual in the sense of being aware of himself as a unique, differentiated personality, he remains for some time a psychological appendage of his parents. His mother is not known as a definite, feminine, and unique personality, but as *the mother*, a warming, protecting, nourishing entity. She is an "archetype," a composite image of all pre-existing mothers, a model or pattern of all the protecting, warming, nourishing influences which man has experienced or the child will experience. The protecting mother is also associated with the nourishing earth, the provident field, the warming hearth, the protecting cave, the surrounding vegetation, the milk-giving cow and the herd. The symbol of the mother refers to a place of origin such as nature, to that which passively creates, to matter, to the unconscious, natural and instinctive life. As traces of the experience of mankind lie dormant, in a potential form, in the brain of the child, they become activated and blend with the nearest and most powerful experience, the child's mother, producing the archetypal experience of the mother.

Jung believes that a child can be afraid of the mother even when there is no rational cause for it. In such a case, the situation of fear is said to be an archetypal one. The childish terror is a re-enacting of primitive psychology, a phylogenetic relic.

An excessive degree of fear, however, is derived from the psychological behavior of the actual parents. And this has a direct bearing on the Oedipus complex.

"We should make the archetype responsible only for a definite, small, normal degree of fear; on the other hand, a pronounced increase, felt to be abnormal, must have special causes. Freud, as we know, explains this terror as the collision of the child's incestuous tendency with the incest prohibition. He explains it from the angle of the child. I have no doubt that children can have 'incestuous' tendencies in the extended sense used by Freud. But I am very doubtful as to whether these tendencies can be ascribed without more ado to child-psychology *sui generis* . . .

"I am therefore inclined to explain possible incestuous tendencies of the child from the psychology of the parents, just as every childish neurosis should be considered first and foremost in the light of the parental psychology. A frequent cause of increased infantile terrors is an especial 'liability to complexes' on the part of the parents, that is, a repression and disregard of certain vital problems. Whatever goes into the unconscious takes on a more or less archaic form. If, for example, the mother represses a painful and terrifying complex, she will feel it as an evil spirit following her—a 'skeleton in the cupboard,' as the English say. This formulation shows that the complex has already assumed an archetypal force. It weighs upon her like a mountain, a nightmare torments her. Whether she tells 'night-stories,' *i.e.*, terror stories, to the child or not, she none the less infects the child and awakens in its mind archetypal terror images from her own psychology. Perhaps she has erotic phantasies about a man other than her husband; and the child is the visible sign of their marriage tie. Her resistance to the tie is unconsciously directed against the child, who has to be repudiated. On the archaic level this corresponds to child-murder. In this way, the mother becomes a wicked witch who devours children."

The Father Archetype

As the child develops, the father comes into the picture and activates an archetype which is said to be in many ways opposed to that of the mother. The archetype of the father signifies such things as strength, power, authority, the creative breath (*"pneuma," "spiritus"*) and all that is moving and "dynamic" in the world. The father image is associated with rivers, winds, storms, lightning and thunder, battle and weapons, raging animals, like wild bulls, the violent and changeful phenomena of the world, as well as the cause of all change.

EFFECTS OF PARENTAL IMAGE

While the primordial image of the mother always remains, subtly, unconsciously, determining our relation to woman, society, and to the world of feeling and fact, the father archetype determines our relation to man, spirit, law and the state, and the *dynamis* of nature. "As the growing consciousness becomes more capable of understanding, the importance of the parental personality diminishes. But in the place of the father there comes the society of men, and in place of the mother, family and clan. Finally, instead of the father, the image of God appears, and in the mother's place, the mysterious abyss of all-being."[31]

With the widening and growth of consciousness which the advance of the child toward maturity carries with it, the unconscious union with the parents is severed. But the archetypal images remain, though now driven into the background, that is, into the unconscious. But in dreams and phantasies they will reappear.

With most men, however, the process of differentiation and of individual development does not proceed far. They go to their graves as children.[32] In place of the parents they substitute a "participation mystique" with the life of the group. In other words, the mass of men live within the bounds of tradition, which provides convenient substitutes, such as organized religions, for their unconscious submission to the parental psyche. Unconsciously they identify themselves with the tribe, society, the church, the nation. "The mechanism of convention keeps people *unconscious*, and then, like wild game, they can follow their customary runways without the necessity of conscious choice."[33] Their relationships with people remain predominantly determined, unconsciously, of course, by the parental image. They identify themselves with the collective psyche—thus drowning themselves in the vast sea of the collective mind and soul and sacrificing their individuality. For the most part, they live "instinctively." Collective thought and feeling and action are relatively easy. Most people are prone to take the easier, in a sense less demanding way of life, although such a way of life is disastrous to personal development. There is no coming to individual consciousness, says Jung, without pain. "The critical survey of himself and his fate, permits a man to recognize his individuality, but this knowledge does not come to him easily. It is gained only through the severest shocks."[34] Hence, most men avoid this critical survey as they would Satan himself.[35]

ROLE OF THE UNCONSCIOUS

Yet Jung believes man "is never helped in his suffering by what he thinks for himself but only by revelations of a wisdom greater than his own."[36] This help comes from the hidden depths of the unconscious. The collective psyche is the "mother foundation," or matrix upon which all personal differentiation rests. The greater the harmony and coordination—not identity—of the unconscious with consciousness, the more healthy one is.[37]

Hence, Jung believes that the unconscious (individual and especially the collective) has possibilities of wisdom that are denied to consciousness. The former contains not only the psychic contents acquired in the individual's life history which have been forgotten or "overlooked" but also the wisdom of untold ages lying dormant and potential in the human brain. Continually active, the unconscious creates combinations of its materials which serve to indicate the future path of the individual.[38] These unconscious combinations are said to be superior both in refinement and extent to the conscious ones. Therefore, the unconscious may be "an unparalleled guide" for human beings.[39]

Jung, as we have seen, does not attach much significance

to incest as such. Cohabitation "with an old woman" originally could hardly be preferred to intercourse with a young woman. The mother seems to have acquired incestuous significance only *psychologically*.[40] The fundamental basis of incestuous desire is the thought or impulse of becoming a child again, or turning back to the parents' protection, of coming into the mother once more to be born again.

SYMBOL AND INCEST

According to Jung, if one "takes away" the libido from a real object without "real" compensation, that is, without some other equally valuable and "real" interest to take its place—a process which Jung calls introversion—one suffers serious and inevitable consequences. The introverted libido reactivates earlier forms of adaptation to life. An adult need not encounter much difficulty in life before the unequalled and imperishable memories of the first and foremost relationship he ever sustained, the relationship to the parents, are reawakened. Organized religion is said to offer a systematized regressive reanimation of the parental image. The protection and peace of religion have their origin in the experience with the parents. The mystic feelings of religion represent unconscious memories of the tender experiences and emotions of earliest childhood.[41]

Jung maintains that we have not really abandoned our "incest wish." In religion and through religious symbols we unconsciously commit incest. Religion no longer represents an ethical ideal; its symbols, rites and ceremonies embody an unconscious transformation of the incest wish. Heaven and earth become father and mother. The people upon the earth appear as children, as brothers and sisters. And so we remain children and satisfy our incest wish unwittingly.

Mankind does not take kindly to being deprived of the hopeful certainty of childhood when people live as an appendage of the parents, unconsciously and instinctively, without awareness of self. Man also has reacted with deep animosity to the brutal separation from the harmony of animal existence when there existed no moral prohibitions. This separation is marked by, among other things, the incest prohibition and laws of marriage.[42]

THE THEORY OF TYPES

Jung's concept of types has been one of the best known and influential of all his theories. We shall now attempt to outline this concept. In most general terms, our relation to the world, in harmony with traditional philosophical ideas, is conceived in terms of subject and object, of person and external world. Given this way of understanding things, experience is also interpreted dualistically, though the two modes of experience are not, in Jung's theory, fundamentally opposed. In one form of experience, there is said to be an outward movement of interest toward the object (the other fellow, or the world in general) and in the second form of experience, a movement of interest away from the object, toward the self or subject and his psychological processes. In the first form of experience, the person is drawn to the object like a magnet, while in the second, the self is and remains the center of every interest.

The first mode of experience or relation to the world is called extraverted, the second, introverted. The extraverted standpoint sets the subject below the object in interest and value, while to the introverted view, the subject has a higher value than the object.

Everyone is said to possess both tendencies or dispositions. Normally or ideally a rhythmically alternating procession of both forms of relationship and psychic activity may occur. But this seldom occurs in fact. Complicated external conditions of life and even more complicated inner processes and dispositions seldom permit this diastolic-systolic rhythm. Hence, one side of this ideally rhythmical activity is predominant, and when this occurs a *type* is produced. One or the other mode of experience is uppermost.

But this is too general. The various basic psychological functions which make up the entire personality must be similarly differentiated. These basic psychological functions, as we mentioned above, are thinking, feeling, sensation and intuition. A psychological function is said to be a certain form of psychic activity which theoretically remains the same in varying circumstances. Thinking and feeling are called rational, sensation and intuition, irrational (non-rational) functions.

But these functions refer to the whole personality, not only to consciousness. Hence, the unconscious attitude must also be considered.

The Extraverted Attitude

First we shall mention some general characteristics of the extraverted general attitude type. This type lives according to external necessity. Although he has "subjective" values, they have less determining power in his life. He is oriented toward objective relations. His interest and attention go to objective happenings, especially those of his immediate, local environment. Persons and things seize and rivet his interest. His moral laws are those of the community. If objective conditions are abnormal, then he accepts an abnormal position. He is adjusted but not adapted, because adaptation is more than a frictionless participation in his local milieu; it implies adjustment to the universally valid laws of life. Although he easily fits in with external conditions, mere local adjustment is his limitation. Hence, his soul especially suffers for he "tries to do or to make just what his milieu momentarily needs and expects from him, and abstains from every innovation that is not entirely obvious, or that in any way exceeds the expectation of those around him."[43] His tendency is to neglect subjective needs and requirements; even his body may receive inadequate consideration with resulting suffering. In general, he tends to lose himself in objects, to spend and propagate in every way.

The relation of the unconscious to the conscious is compensatory. A consciously extraverted person is unconsciously introverted. Since man bears his age-long history with him, complete assimilation to the object is impossible. Such an assimilation encounters the resistance of the suppressed minority, the elements from the past. Unconscious tendencies deprived of their energy by a lack of conscious recognition, at least to a considerable degree still possess enough potency to become destructive and cease to be compensatory. When these tendencies reach a stratum of the unconscious which corresponds with a level of culture "absolutely incompatible with our own," they form a block which opposes consciousness, and open conflict ensues. The repressed tendencies take on a regressive character, becoming more infantile and archaic. The unconscious attitude of the extraverted orientation often verges on the cruel and brutal. Unconscious infantilism, egoism, and archaism, having lost their original compensatory quality, develop in opposition to consciousness. The unconscious counter-influence may result in a neurosis, a cleavage between consciousness and the unconscious. Either the person no longer knows what he really wants and has no interests, or he desires too much at once and has too much interest, but in the impossible.

The Introverted Attitude

The introvert, on the other hand, does not give the object the importance which is said to belong to it. He is defensive against external claims and tries to conserve himself. For him subjective determinants, the inner laws of the psyche, are decisive. There tends to be an artificial "subjectification" of consciousness. He likewise tends to equate the ego with the whole personality. The neurotic introvert makes an unconsciousness identity of ego and personality, while in actuality the personality includes much more.

When the ego usurps the claims of the subject, of the whole personality, there is an unconscious reenforcement of the object, a compensatory development which is felt consciously as an unconditional and irrepressible tie to the object. The object becomes terrifying in spite of its depreciation by consciousness. The ego strives to control the object and to detach itself from it. Nevertheless, the ego tends to become the slave of objective, brute facts which cannot be ignored. The moral superiority of the introvert gets swamped in inferior relationships. He becomes enmeshed in practical difficulties. His desire to dominate and control ends in a pitiful craving to be loved. His ego builds a system of safeguards to preserve an illusion of superiority, but objects frustrate him.

In time the introvert develops an abundance of phantasies coupled with fear of the "animated" object. He shrinks from making himself or his opinion effective, dreading an intensified "influence" from it. He is terrified at the "impressive affects" of others and is hardly ever free of fear of hostility. Objects come to possess terrifying qualities which, through his unconscious perception, he must believe in. His consciousness becomes loaded with qualities of the unconscious, qualities that are primarily infantile and archaic. It seems to him as though objects have strange and magical powers.

FUNCTION TYPES

Experience has shown, according to Jung, that individuals can be differentiated or typed not only by their general attitude of extraversion or introversion, but also by their particular predominant psychological function, thinking, feeling, sensation, or intuition, each of which again is either extraverted or introverted. It seems that it is always only one of the four by which man relates, at least when he has developed beyond the primitive. The particular predominant function is called the superior function, because it is always the expression of the conscious personality, its aim and its will, while the inferior functions happen to one, so to speak, against one's conscious will.

Towards middle age an opposition between the functions and attitudes often becomes intensified and psychological conflict results.

THE ROLE OF RELIGION

Jung regards religion or rather a religious attitude as an element in psychic life the importance of which can hardly be overestimated. He claims that all the patients over thirty-five who consulted him during the last thirty years had the same problem, that of finding a religious outlook on life. Religion for Jung does not mean a dogma or creed. The truly religious person has a kind of deep respect for facts and events and for the person who suffers from them; hence, a respect for the "secret of such a human life." Healing or psychotherapy can also be called a religious problem. The patient needs faith, hope, love, and insight.

His attitude toward religion, he says, is one of the points of difference between himself and Freud. "I do not, however, hold myself responsible for the fact that man has, everywhere and always, spontaneously developed religious forms of expression, and that the human psyche from time immemorial has been shot through with religious feelings and ideas. Whoever cannot see this aspect of the human psyche is blind, and whoever chooses to explain it away, or to 'enlighten' it away, has no sense of reality."[44]

THE PERSONA AND INDIVIDUALITY

A very suggestive concept of Jung is that of the "persona." The persona is a certain kind of image one has of oneself and presents to the world as the essential personality. Persona, of course, originally referred to the mask worn by an actor to signify his role. The persona for Jung is a role that one plays in life; it is not authentic since it does not portray what one essentially is. Hence, it is not really individual, unique to the person; it is a substitute for individuality. The persona is actually a "slice" of the collective psyche. It is what a man appears to be. Thus one acquires a title or an office and adopts the role which he thinks or society thinks a person in such a position actually is. He becomes more or less the role which he plays.[45]

It is instructive to compare the concept of persona with what is individual:

"1. What is individual appears partly as the principle that decides the selection and limitation of the contents that are accepted as personal.

"2. What is individual is the principle by which an increasing differentiation from the collective psyche is made possible and enforced.

"3. What is individual manifests itself partly as an impediment to collective accomplishment, and as a resistance against collective thinking and feeling.

"4. What is individual is the uniqueness of the combination of universal (collective) psychological elements."[46]

We shall conclude our discussion of Jung with a statement of his unflattering view of the spiritual life of modern Western man:

"Whether from the intellectual, the moral or the aesthetic viewpoint, the undercurrents of the psychic life of the West present an uninviting picture. We have built a monumental world round about us, and have slaved for it with unequalled energy. But it is so imposing only because we have spent upon the outside all that is imposing in our natures — and what we find when we look within must necessarily be as it is, shabby and insufficient."[47]

7. THE THEORIES OF OTTO RANK

THE BIRTH TRAUMA

Like many other early disciples of Freud, Otto Rank eventually broke decisively with the master. Rank's deviation was gradual, and we shall see something of the evolution of his ideas. *The Trauma of Birth* marks a significant departure from traditional Freudianism and serves as a convenient starting-point for the exposition of his ideas.

It was Freud who first arrived at a theory of the trauma of birth. Nevertheless, it does not play a vital role in his psychology, and he categorically rejects the "extreme deductions" which Rank drew from it with regard to theory and therapy.

As a matter of fact, there is an important difference in the two theories of the birth trauma itself, aside from its consequences. While Freud emphasizes the physical hazards and physiological difficulties of the birth process as a cause of anxiety, Rank stresses the *separation* of the organism from or deprivation of the "pleasurable primal situation in the womb" as of primary significance, although the difference is one of degree of emphasis. For Rank, so blissful is the intrauterine situation that man yearns for the original intrauterine life and in some fashion or other strives to restore it. With the exception of death, which, it is said, is unconsciously felt as a return to the womb, physical birth is the most painfully anxious experience man undergoes. The earliest place of abode, namely, the mother's body, where everything is given without even the asking, is paradise. To be born is to be cast out of the Garden of Eden. And the rest of life is taken up with efforts to replace this lost paradise as best one can and by various means.

The experience of being born causes a profound shock to the helpless organism, involving not only physical separation from the mother but also physiological hazards and changes of state. This painful experience sets up or carries with it the first and most fundamental feeling of anxiety one ever has, which Rank calls the "primal anxiety." This primal anxiety somehow "blots out the memory of the former pleasurable state" before birth. A mental "barrier" to recall of the earliest state is established, instituting an initial "primal" repression. Whenever there is a tendency to regress to a condition which attempts to restore the "primal pleasure," anxiety appears and effaces the "memory" of it and at the same time by reason of the pain involved effectually discourages such an enterprise.[1]

For Rank the psychical or mental has its origin in the experienced anxiety of the birth trauma. The change from a highly pleasurable situation to a highly painful one acquires a psychical quality of feeling. Furthermore, "not only all socially valuable, even over-valued, creations of man but even the fact of becoming man, arise from a specific reaction to the birth trauma."

He believes that every human being needs the whole period of childhood to overcome the birth trauma in an approximately normal way. The "neurotics" are people who have not succeeded in this task. The child's proneness to anxiety originates in the birth trauma, and the original anxiety is transferable to almost anything. Every childhood fear and anxiety is used again and again for the "abreaction" (discharge) of the undisposed-of primal anxiety-affect. In this way the birth anxiety is gradually got rid of or at least assuaged. There is, so to speak, a gradual catharsis of the primal anxiety.

Weaning, consciously experienced and painful, though later repressed, represents a second trauma, but it derives a great part of its traumatic effect from the first one.

The castration threat "hits" not only the primal trauma but also the second, which more clearly explains why it causes such a "stupendous and lasting" effect on the child. This genital fear of castration is said to be predisposed to take up the greatest part of the natal anxiety as guilt feeling. Yet in "comparison with the painfully experienced actual traumata of birth and weaning, a real threat of castration seems even to make easier the normal discharge of the primal anxiety as genital guilt feeling, insofar and just as soon as the child has discovered the insincerity of the castration threat, as of all other untruths of adults."

However, according to Rank, the "deepest Unconscious" (Freud's "id") knows only the universal primal anxiety of birth.

Just as the primal anxiety forms the basis for every subsequent anxiety or fear, every pleasure aims to reestablish the primal pleasure of the intrauterine situation. The child's normal functions, such as the assimilation of nourishment (sucking) and excretion of waste products, are said to evince the tendency to continue the unlimited freedom of the pre-natal state as long as possible. Likewise, a too persistent clinging to other infantile forms of pleasure is said to be an expression of the wish to restore the original state.

For Rank, at this time, the whole problem of infantile sexuality is located in the question as to where babies come from. The child is said to seek in himself the lost memory of his earlier place of abode which, because of the primal repression, he cannot find. Usually the child needs an outside stimulus, such as the birth of a brother or sister, in order to be able to formulate the question. But even when the parents give a truthful answer, the child cannot understand it properly or at least accept it because of unconscious inner resistances and repressions. However, the real interest of the child is said to be in the problem of *"how to get inside,"* to return to the place where he came from.

Freud held the theory that the boy at first believes that every human being has a phallus, and that he clings to this notion as long as possible. For Rank, however, the boy clings to such an idea not merely because of "narcissistic self-over-estimation" but because he wants to deny the existence of the female genitals. They tend to remind him of the "horror" of his birth, the memory of which he wishes to avoid at all costs since it would reproduce the primal anxiety. Likewise, the "penis envy" of the girl is based primarily on a reaction formation against the existence of the female sex organs from which she, like the boy, was painfully cast out.

It will be recalled that Freud held that the "perversions" and the "neuroses" have their roots in infantile sexuality, that, in fact, they represent a psychological lag in development or, owing to insuperable obstacles in living, a regression to infantile forms of sexual pleasure.

According to Rank, abhorrence of the female genitals accounts for "homosexuality." For the male homosexual, a woman is only the maternal organ of birth, and he does not acknowledge her or her sex organs as a means of giving pleasure. Furthermore, homosexuals of both sexes unconsciously, or in the case of women, consciously play the part of mother and child, which is said to be "a direct continuance of the asexual but libidinal binding of the primal situation." In other words, homosexuals by playing the role of mother and child manifest a special kind of love relationship, one based on the sexually undifferentiated embryonal condition where there is a complete physical identity of mother and child.

In masochism it is a question of the conversion of

the pains caused by parturition into pleasurable sensations, ("phantasy of being beaten"). The masochistic phantasy of being bound, for example, expresses the tendency to a partial reinstatement of the primal state of immobility.

The "typical sadist," the murderer of children and women, "who wallows in blood and in bowels, seems completely to play the part of infantile curiosity, and seeks to discover the nature of the inside of the body. Whilst the masochist seeks to reestablish the original pleasurable condition by means of affective revaluation of the birth trauma; the sadist personifies the unquenchable hatred of one who has been expelled; he really attempts with his full grown body to go back into the place whence he came as a child, without considering that he thereby tears his sacrifice to pieces — this being by no means his main intention."

The exhibitionist wants to return to the original "paradisiacal primal state of nakedness" before birth. The condition of nakedness, as it is somehow associated with the primal state, is on that account especially loved by the child. At the heterosexual level of development, a representative part, the penis in the case of men, serves as a substitute for the whole body.

The sexual act, according to Rank, is the final and sublimest substitution for the reunion with the mother. But more than that, and, aside from its most intense sensation of pleasure, it signifies a partial gratification of the primal wish, to return to the womb, or is a symbolic realization of it. The "man, penetrating into the vaginal opening, undoubtedly signifies a partial return to the womb, which by identification with the penis known as a symbol for a child (Tom Thumb, German *Däumling*) becomes not only a complete but also an infantile return. But in the case of the woman, the attitude is quite similar, as analytic material has shown. By means of the clitoris libido, experienced so intensely in masturbation, the woman is able — often only too able — to identify herself with the penis or the man and so indirectly to approach the return into the womb. The tendency to apparent masculinity revealed in it rests on the unconscious identification with the father and finally aims at becoming at least a participator in the inestimable advantage which the man has over the woman, and which consists in his being able partially to go back into the mother, by means of the penis itself, representing the child. For the woman there results a still more far-reaching and normal gratification of this primal wish manifesting itself as mother love in the identification with the fruit of the body."

The male can gratify his primal wish at least partially by remaining attached to the "same" object, who represents for him mother, lover, and wife. In other words his female partner becomes a surrogate of the mother as well as lover and wife. But with a woman it is different. She has had to transfer a part "of the original mother libido" to the father concurrently with her resigning herself to a more passive role. "It is a matter, then, for the girl to give up all idea of an active return to the mother, a penetration which is recognized or imagined to be the masculine privilege, and in the supreme joy of motherhood, to be content with the wish to regain the blessed primal state by means of passive reproduction — that is, by means of pregnancy and the birth of her own child."

Those who cannot reconcile themselves to the form of sexual gratification "designed" for them when they wish to gratify the primal libido for the mother as a compensation for the birth trauma become "neurotic." The best means of avoiding a reactivation of the birth trauma is to be found in normal sexual love. Those who strive for the original form of gratification, sometimes by "identification" with the mother, stumble upon the "anxiety-borders" of the birth trauma and develop a neurosis. Healthy people find satisfaction in the partial, substitutive and symbolical modes of gratification of the primal wish, which we mentioned above, while the neurotics, who remain "infantile," desire to go back *"completely"* into the mother.[2]

The Oedipus Complex

The Oedipus complex represents the first clear expression of the sexual instinct. It marks the first effective attempt to overcome the anxiety connected with the mother's genitals by being able to accept them in a pleasurable way as "libido-object." In other words, it marks an attempt to transfer the intrauterine pleasure of the primal libido to the anxiety-invested genitals, "and there to reopen a former source of pleasure buried by repression." But this effort is doomed to failure not merely because of the child's immature sexual apparatus but because it is made upon the source of the primal trauma with which intense anxiety is connected. Now this thwarted attempt represents once more a repetition of the birth trauma at the first stage of the child's sexual development as a sexual trauma, a severance from the mother on the sexual level. But it is said to be a necessary condition for the success of the later normal transference in the love-choice. This transference, which Rank does not make intelligible in any clear fashion, is somehow accomplished at puberty, "when the primal and painful experience connected with the genitals has successfully been changed back into the nearest possible approach to the pleasure experienced inside the mother as one's original abode."[3]

The Oedipus Myth

While we shall return to Rank's discussion of the Oedipus myth, we should like to record his general interpretation here: "At the back of the Oedipus saga there really stands the mysterious question of the origin and destiny of man, which Oedipus desires to solve, not intellectually, but by actually returning into the mother's womb. This happens entirely in a symbolic form, for his blindness in the deepest sense represents a return into the darkness of the mother's womb, and his final disappearance through a cleft rock into the Underworld expresses once again the same wish tendency to return into the mother earth."

Sleep is a condition similar to that of the intrauterine life. This condition which "automatically" takes place every night indicates, Rank thinks, that even the normal individual never completely overcomes the birth trauma. In dreams we return to and reproduce the intrauterine situation or relive the birth trauma. In fact, dreams represent a more complete return to the original state than the mere act of sleep. The analytical interpretation of dream symbols, Rank believes, gives the strongest support to the theory of the birth trauma.

Every discovery is only a rediscovery of something latent, and the study and understanding of dream symbolism "now enables us to trace back cultural creation to its origin in the depths of the Unconscious." Primitive dwellings, such as caves or hollow trees, for example, "were made or chosen in instinctive remembrances of the warm, protecting womb, analogous to the birds building nests for protective covering." The discovery of implements and weapons, which are a direct imitation of the male sexual organ, represent an attempt to force one's way into substitute material (*materia*), but this enterprise derives its unconscious incentive from "the perpetual insatiable tendency to force one's way completely into the mother." Symbol formation serves as a substitute for the "lost primal reality," while it also "must remind us as little as possible of the primal trauma connected with it." In general, cultural development has involved, in the course of continuous repression, a gradual "withdrawal" from the primal trauma into sublimated forms as a substitution for the primal state.

Rank does not hesitate to follow Freud to the limit of the latter's speculations concerning the "primal horde," the killing of the father, and its consequences. For the former, the "original biological function" of the father was to thwart the sons' desires to return to the mother. For this the sons killed him. The subsequent renunciation of the coveted mother occurred because "although all take possession of the mother sexually (promiscuity), not all can return into her."[4] In fact, only one, the youngest son, can "return into her." But what does this mean? We conjecture its meaning from what Rank has to say about the hero: "His attachment to the mother does not merely rest on the psychical motives of tenderness and pampering (mother's little son), for this has a biological foundation. Physically he remains as it were permanently attached to her, because no one after him has occupied the place, in the mother (motive of virginity). Thus he is really the only one for whom return to the womb and remaining there would be possible, for whom it is, so to say, a reward. The elder brothers, indeed, seek vainly to dispute his place, which in spite of his characteristic 'stupidity' he struggles for and maintains. His superiority really consists in the fact that he comes last, and, so to say, drives the others away. In this he is like the father, with whom he alone, and from the same motives, is able to identify himself."[5]

It appears that, as Freud conjectures, the death of the father was followed by a period of the dominance of the mother or of the women of the family. When the son gained power he broke this dominance and took over the privileges belonging to her. Being spared the fate of the father because he had taken his mother's place and was partially identified with her, he became the leader.

In this loose and abbreviated fashion, Rank, in terms of the birth trauma, attempts to lay the basis for an explanation of certain traits of matriarchy and patriarchy and the change from one to the other. "In the so-called dominance of the Father Right, right or justice — i. e., the privilege of mutual (conciliatory) protection, social forbearance, and care of others — springs from the natural phase of mother attachment which, on the one hand, rests on the protection given by the mother (womb), on the other hand is due to the fear of her caused ultimately by the birth trauma. The peculiar ambivalence towards the lord, the ruler, is thus explained. He is loved, protected, and spared, that is taboo, insofar as he represents the mother. He is hated, tortured, or slain, as representative of the primitive enemy near the mother . . . . The earlier high valuation of woman (her genital), which is still apparent in the ancient worship of goddesses and which has left its traces in the later 'Mother Right,' had to be replaced by the social father-organization traced by Freud from the primitive horde. The strict, just, but no longer violent father must again be set up as the 'barrier to incest' against the desire to return to the mother, whereby he assumes once more his original biological function, namely: to sever the sons from the mother. Anxiety of the mother is then transferred as respect to the King and to the inhibiting Ego (ideal) motives which he represents (justice, state, etc.). The sons' (burghers and subjects) attitude towards him is that of the well-known two-sided Oedipus libido. The systematic social depreciation of woman from her original heights finally results in a reaction against that infantile dependence on her, which the son, now become father, can no longer bear."[6]

We are further told that the development of paternal domination into an increasingly powerful state system administered by men is a continuance of the primal repression, which on account of the painful unconscious memory of the birth trauma has as its purpose the ever wider exclusion of women. But the wish "to return to the mother" remains powerful too. For every revolution against masculine dominance is said to show the tendency to return to the mother.

Religion now is interpreted in terms somewhat different from the earlier view.

"Every form of religion tends ultimately to the creation of a succouring and protecting primal Being to whose bosom one can flee away from all troubles and dangers and to whom

one finally returns in a future life which is a faithful, although
sublimated, image of the once lost Paradise."[7] And this
tendency is said to be most consistently developed "in the
Christian mythology." The son, the *infans*, becomes God,
while the characteristics of the primal father are awarded to
the lord of Hell and those of the primeval mother to Mary.
The crucifixion of Christ, which is a punishment for rebellion
against the father (God the Father) corresponds to a conversion and assimilation to the intrauterine situation, followed by
resurrection, that is, birth (not rebirth). It is a symbolical
repetition and reproduction of the process of birth. The dogma
of the Immaculate Conception represents a concept of the
birth trauma, for it holds that Christ was not born in the
natural way, did not even enter the mother in the natural
way. Thus Christ the hero, according to this explanation,
succeeds "to a great extent" in the mastery of the birth
trauma.

The process of religious development, in fact, "runs
absolutely parallel" with that of social development. In accordance with this notion, Rank conjectures "that the world-wide
historical importance of Christianity rests on the fact that it
was the first to place the Son-God in the centre without
simultaneously attacking the original rights of the mother and
the secondary rights of the father."[8]

Greek, Jewish, and other religions are discussed from a
similar point of view.

The Genesis of Art

The "real root" of art is perceived in the "autoplastic
imitation of one's own growing and origin from the maternal
vessel." We may have to look for the beginning of every art,
according to Rank, in plastic art. In any case primitive man
"first created a vessel for a receptacle and a protection, in
imitation of the womb." The vessel evolved in the direction of
representing a child or its head. Then it "gets a belly, ears,

a beak, etc. . . . " Later art further evolved into representations of complete human beings. In this we are to recognize the tendency to avoid the birth trauma. The artist, in creating human beings after his own image, brings forth ever new, constantly repeated, acts of birth, "and in it brings forth himself amid the maternal pains of creation." The Greek artist "has raised himself in identification with the mother to creator of men, in that he attempts in his works of art to detach himself gradually and under great resistance from the mother, as all the Sphinx-like fabulous beings so convincingly prove. From this 'moment' of simultaneously longed-for and yet not wished-for freeing from the bestial womb, from this eternal sticking fast in birth, which the neurotic constantly experiences afresh, as anxiety of the primal situation, the Greek artist and with him the entire race found the way to idealization by preserving in solid stone this stormy movement, which the Medusa head has kept in all its terrifying significance."9

The deep cultural and historical importance of the development of Greek art lies in the fact that it repeats the biological and prehistorical act of becoming human, the severance from the mother, and the standing upright from the earth via its ideal aesthetic representations of the human body. The original source of the development is anxiety — ultimately primal anxiety and the efforts to overcome it.

The figure of the Sphinx, whose human upper part grows out of the animal-like (maternal) lower body without finally being able to free itself from it, is a mother symbol, and her character as "strangler" is said to make the reference to the birth anxiety unambiguous. "In this meaning the role of the Sphinx in the Oedipus saga shows quite clearly that the hero, on the way back to the mother, has to overcome the birth anxiety, representing the barrier which the neurotic also comes up against again and again in all his attempts to regress." In psychological terms, the Oedipus saga represents a repetition of the primal anxiety at the sexual level, that of the Oedipus complex, while the Sphinx represents the primal trauma. "The hero, who is not swallowed by the Sphinx, is enabled, just through the overcoming of anxiety, to repeat the unconscious wish in the pleasurable form of sexual intercourse with the mother."[10] The riddle of the Sphinx lies in the fact that it represents not only, in its latent content, the wish to return into the mother as the danger of being swallowed, but, in its manifest content, parturition itself and the struggle against it.

The Greeks consistently carried out the tendency to "free themselves from the womb," which means that they were, like Oedipus, able to solve the riddle of the Sphinx.

Tragedy is said to have grown up from the mimic representations of the mythical rites, and symbolized the sufferings and punishments of the mythical hero on account of his tragic guilt, a milder form of the repressed primal wish. "This has become known to us in its unconscious significance from the analysis of mythical tradition, and the origin of tragedy from the dances and songs of the participators in the sacrifice shows clearly what was involved. The skin in which the participators envelop themselves after the sacrifice and disembowelment of the animal is again nothing but a substitute for the protecting womb. This partial realization of the return to the mother has likewise found a lasting pictorial expression in the numerous goat-legged and goat-headed fauns and satyrs of Greek mythology and sculpture. In the art of tragedy which, like the dance, takes the living human being itself as its object, the frightful and primitive character of the repressed primal wish lives on in a milder form as tragic guilt, which every individual mortal spectator can re-enact by continuously re-experiencing it; whereas in epic poetry we see the attempts to overcome the primal wish by fictitious transformations [such as the story of the wooden horse in whose belly the Greek heroes reach the "innermost fortress" of Troy?]. The highest idealization of the birth trauma attained in plastic art is, in compassion-arousing tragedy, resolved once again into the malleable primal element of the anxiety affect, capable of outlet, whereas in epic and satiric poetry the too highly strung idealization breaks out as boastful untruthfulness."

Further examples of the artistic idealization and representation of the primal situation, etc. are given from other cultures, but we shall not reproduce them owing to considerations of space.

The "very root" of the problem of art is a problem of form. And it seems to Rank that all form goes back to the primal form of the maternal vessel, "which has become to a large extent the problem of art."[11] In an idealized and sublimated way artistic form makes the repressed primal form acceptable in that it can be represented and felt as beautiful.[12]

There is a final point we want to bring up before leaving the theme of the birth trauma. Rank has some suggestive things to say about the transition from "mother-culture" to "father-culture":

"Egyptian culture is produced by three factors, which can all be traced back in the same way to the first effort to repress the positive attitude to the mother, which in the Asiatic world view seems to work itself out in a high sexual esteem of the primal mother, and reappears in sublimated form in the Christian mother of God. First, the *religious* factor, appearing in a peculiar cult of the dead, which in every particular detail, especially the preservation of the body, is equivalent to a further life in the womb. Second, the *artistic* factor, appearing in an exaggerated esteem of the animal body (animal cult); third, the *social* factor, appearing in a high valuation of woman ('right of the mother'). These originally purely 'maternal' *motifs*, in the course of a process of development lasting thousands of years and making its contributions to the overcoming of the birth trauma, became masculinized, that is, remodelled in the sense of adjustment to the father libido. Typical of all three manifestations of this mother principle, as of the initial tendency to

overcome it, is the veneration of the moon goddess Isis, along-
side the gradual gain in importance of her brother, son, and
husband Osiris. The same is reflected in the gradual development of the *Cult of the Sun,* which not only allows assimilation with the rebirth phantasy in Jung's sense, but in the
meaning of the more original moon veneration also gives expression to the mother libido. Not only because the sun rises
does the hero identify himself with it, but because it disappears every day afresh into the underworld, and so corresponds to the primal wish for union with the mother-night.
This is proved beyond doubt precisely by the Egyptian sun
worship, with its numerous pictures that represent by preference the sun-ship on its night journey into the underworld,
as also in the texts of the *Book of the Dead . . .*

"But the development of sun worship always goes hand
in hand with a decisive turning from mother-culture to father-
culture, as is shown in the final identification of the new-born
king (*infans*) with the sun. This opposition to the dominance
of the woman both in the social sphere (right of the father)
and in the religious, continues as the transitional process
from Egypt [via Crete] to Greece, where it leads, by means
of the entire repression of woman even from the erotic life,
to the richest blossoming of the masculine civilization and to
the artistic idealization corresponding to it."[13]

The rationale of this is given by Rank in his theory that
the woman through pregnancy and parturition can procure
"the most far-reaching" approach to the primal gratification,
while man, depending on unconscious identification with the
mother and the creation resulting from it of cultural and
artistic productions, has to create a substitute for the production of the primal situation.

The Creation of Individuality

The ensuing fifteen years of Rank's life saw a still
further and more radical deviation from Freudian orthodoxy,

including a criticism of Freudian theory and therapy. To be sure, Rank, like many others, remains tremendously indebted to Freud, and unavoidably, for the latter will always remain a trail-blazer in the wilderness of human problems. But since we are not concerned with an appraisal of the differences between the two men, we shall let Rank speak for himself:

"While at first I was completely under the influence of Freudian realism and tried to express my conception of the creative man, the artist, in the biological-mechanistic terms of Freud's natural science ideology, on the basis of my own experience, I have since been enabled to formulate these common human problems in a common human language as well. 'The Trauma of Birth,' a book written in 1923, marks the decisive turning point in this development. There I compared to the creative drive of the individual as treated in 'Der Kunstler'[14] the creation of the individual himself, not merely physically, but also psychically in the sense of the 'rebirth experience,' which I understood psychologically as the actual creative act of the human being. For in this act the psychic ego is born out of the biological corporeal ego and the human being becomes at once creator and creature or actually moves from creature to creator, in the ideal case, creator of himself, his own personality."[15]

The conception of the trauma of birth has led to a conception of the birth of individuality and autonomous will. In other words, a basic spiritual principle, the gradual freeing of the individual from dependence by a self-creative development of personality replaces the one-sided emphasis of the biological dependence on the mother. Or, as Rank has excellently stated it, the "whole consequence of evolution from blind impulse through conscious will to self-conscious knowledge, seems still somehow to correspond to a continued result of births, rebirths and new birth, which reach from the birth of the child from the mother, beyond the birth of the individual from the mass, to the birth of the creative work from the individual and finally to the birth of knowledge from the work . . . At all events we find in all these phenomena, even at the highest spiritual peak, the struggle and pain of birth, the separation out of the universal, with the pleasure and bliss of procreation, the creation of an individual cosmos, whether it be now physically our own child, creatively our own work or spiritually our own self."[16]

The Concept of Will

The concept of will and will conflict plays an important role in Rank's newer theories.[17] By "will" he does not have in mind any kind of mysterious, metaphysical entity which people are often encouraged to exhibit in using their "will power" in order to overcome difficulties. Negatively, it means that the organism is not a passive, helpless tool of outside influences or of inner drives. Positively, it implies that the individual is, or becomes, an initiating power, which selects, organizes, modifies, and recreates what he assimilates in order to live and flourish. This conception of will implies that "the inner world, taken in from the outside by means of identification, has become in the course of time an independent power, which in its turn by way of projection so influences and seeks to alter the external, that its correspondence to the inner is even more close." Will is "a positive guiding organization and integration of self which utilizes creatively, as well as inhibits and controls the instinctual drives."[18] The relation to the outside world of an active subject, which can give as well as receive, change as well as be changed by, transform while being transformed, is designated as creative. The experience of such a being, acting, suffering, struggling against opposing forces, creating, is signified as will phenomena.

The whole development of man and the process of becoming conscious are said to be marked by a conflict between the will of the individual and supra-individual force, whether the latter be the coercive force of society or the "racial" compulsion of sexuality. In the creative individual a "conflictual separation" from the mass occurs and continues at every step he takes into the new, and this process signifies the never completed birth of individuality. In man nature becomes conscious of herself, but she "becomes even more conscious of herself in a man who at the same time with the increasing knowledge of himself which we designate as individualization, tries always to free himself further from the primitive."

Separation and Individuality

Separation is intrinsic to the developmental process of the individual. At first it is physical separation from the mother but ultimately, from various forms of psychological dependence. "If there is a symbol for the condition of wholeness, of totality, it is doubtless the embryonic state, in which the individual feels himself an indivisible whole and yet is bound inseparably with a greater whole."[19] Birth brings not only the feeling of the loss of connection with the mother but also the feeling of loss of wholeness in himself. Until he can regain a sense of totality in his "ego feeling," his relation to the world remains partial. And furthermore, as a child he depends on the parents, especially the mother, for the satisfaction of all his vital needs. The development of self-dependence is a gradual and conflict-laden process because he leans on the past, which is familiar, which gave him some security, and in which he sees himself "personified." All further steps toward independence from birth to death, weaning, walking, especially the development of the will, are conceived as continuous separations from previous developmental phases of his own ego. Only by the conscious knowledge of this life principle by one who can preserve or call back the past, or in phantasy imagine the future, can the fundamental psychological significance of the concept and the feeling of separation be understood. But the conscious awareness of separation brings guilt consciousness too, and this is where people get into trouble, especially the "neurotics." The latter become conscious that they dare not, cannot, loose themselves because they are bound by guilt.

There is, however, a difference between separating and being separated. Separating is a parting which the individual "works at" himself, which he deliberately initiates, such as in giving up emotional or other ties to parents or others in authority and "love-objects." Being separated implies a forced separation which came upon the individual traumatically, as an abandonment.

Under certain conditions weaning, for example, may be felt as abandonment. In each case the attitude of will is different. Separating oneself, which is an expression of will, is a freeing of oneself, a getting away from dependence. But being separated is felt as compulsory and is resisted. Finally, while in each case there is a feeling of guilt, the quality of the feeling is different. Only in the first instance, where one initiates the separation, does one's ego become "real," that is, does the individual recognize and accept himself as independent of the other (on whom he was previously dependent). In the case where one feels he is being separated from the other, against his will, so to speak, his ego remains "unreal," that is, he cannot accept himself as an independent, self-governing being.

The separating of oneself, the "making real" of one's ego is no child's play, as Rank makes clear:

"To this making real of his own ego, the individual reacts in the actual separation experience with fear which is not an original biological reaction in the sense of the death fear, but on the contrary, is life fear, that is, fear of realizing the own ego [that is, one's own ego] as an independent individuality. Accordingly fear as experienced in birth, is and remains the only fear, that is, fear of one's own living and experiencing. All other fear, whether it concerns death or castration anxiety, represents no biological problem in the narrower sense of the word, but a problem of human consciousness underlying all possibilities of interpretation and explanation. The consciousness problem lying at the root of separation, and the fear reaction following it, is again a problem of human individualization. In the psychic separation experience as it is represented in the development of individuality through the giving up of outlived parts of one's own past, we have to recognize an individualistic expression of the biological principle of growth. With human beings this whole biological problem of individuation depends psychically on another person, whom we then value and perceive psychologically as parents, child, beloved friend. These several persons represent then for the individual the great biological forces of nature, to which the ego binds itself emotionally and which then form the essence of the human and his fate. The psychic meaning of these individuals bound to us in feeling, comprehend in themselves, so to say, all biological, social and moral ties and this so much the more, the more individualistically, that is, however, the more independently, the development of the own ego takes place."[20]

The separation experience has two opposing dynamic characteristics: on the one hand a strengthening of the emotional binding to the other (person), who represents all other ties, because of fear of individuality and the guilt ensuing therefrom; and on the other a striving (will) in the direction of freedom and independence from any one person. The fear of individualization is the fear of being alone, of loneliness, of the loss of kinship with others, and with "the ALL." In the "neurotic," fear of life, of the new, of being alone, is opposed to fear of destruction, of death.[21] In other words, the propulsive creative life impulse terrifies him with its threat of making him different and of apparent loss of kinship with others and with the "all," the totality of things, to the point where it seems a menace to his very existence. These opposing tendencies, the striving for independence and the fear of it, are often so nicely balanced that they paralyze him.

But these two forms of fear, fear of life and fear of death, reduce themselves to a primal fear of loss of connection with a totality, of being an indissoluble part of the whole, of which the embryonic state is a symbol. "This ambivalent primal fear which expresses itself in the conflict between individuation and generation, is derived on the one side from the experience of the individual as a part of the whole, which is then separated from it and obliged to live alone (birth), on the other side, from the final necessity of giving up the hard won wholeness of individuality through total loss in death."22

Three Stages of the Development of Individuality

In freeing himself the individual is said to go through three stages of development. The first step occurs when the individual now wills what he was earlier compelled to, whether the compelling forces come from without, such as the parents and society and their moral code, or from within, such as from urgent sexuality. The "normal, average" man perhaps never gets beyond this stage. Rank thinks it guarantees a relatively harmonious working of the personality. There are fewer possibilities of conflict but also fewer possibilities of creativeness of any kind. Such a man is thought to be largely one with himself and the surrounding world while he feels himself to be part of it.

The next stage is characterized by a feeling of division of the personality, through a disunity of "will and counter will," that is, an inner conflict arises. At this level the person is beginning to strike out on his own, to form ideals, goals, moral and ethical standards which may be other than the socially sanctioned ones. He takes new attitudes toward himself and the world. Here there are possibilities of development not achieved at the first level. This second stage may even-tuate either in creativeness and productiveness or in self-criticism, guilt and inferiority feeling leading to neurosis.

At the third and highest level of development a unified and harmonious working of the personality is achieved once more. While the individual at the second stage is "conflicted," at the final stage, he is fully and completely in harmony with all his powers and his ideals. Here the individual is a man "of will and deed." The creative side of his being is uppermost. (This level is especially characteristic of genius.) "This type in its ideal formation,[23] in its continuous rebuilding or building anew, has created an autonomous inner world, so different and so much its own, that it no longer represents merely a substitute for external reality (original morality) but is something for which reality can offer in every case only a feeble substitute so that the individual must seek satisfaction and release in the creation and projection of a world of his own. In a word, with this type, from all the accepted, the obligatory, from all the wished for, and the willed, from all the aspirations and the commandments is formed neither a compromise, nor merely a summation but a newly created whole, the strong personality with its autonomous will, which represents the highest creation of the integration of will and spirit."[24]

The first type, that is, the person who remains at the first level of development, removes the painful feeling of difference by taking over the social and sexual ideals of the majority for his own. This he does not only by a passive identification of himself with the majority of people in his world but by "an effort of will" which ends in submissiveness of the will toward the compelling power of the culture. He becomes entirely dependent on it. The average man finds the justification of his will in the similarly adjusted wills of the majority.

The person in the third and highest level of development, the creative type, such as the artist or the philosopher, creates a world for himself which he can accept without wanting to force it on others; and he accepts himself. Such a person creates his own inner ideals, which he affirms as his own commandments. At the same time he can live in the world without falling into continual conflict with it.[25]

The second type, the "neurotic" individual, feels himself estranged from the majority of others and cannot accept their standards and justifications for living. Yet he cannot accept the ideals and justifications created by his own will for that would imply that he accept and affirm himself and his own will; and he cannot accept himself. While he fights against external pressure, he also resists the strivings and does not accept the ideals of his own individualized will. Therefore, he is continually at war with himself and society.

The ideal of the average is to be as others are; of the "neurotic," to be himself largely in opposition to what others want him to be; of the creative person, to be that which he actually is.

The Origin of Will

Willing itself—not the willing of this or that, but willing in general, the active operation of will—is said to arise as "an inner primarily negative opposing force against a compulsion." A compulsion may arise from external factors, such as the commands of parents or others, and internally from the urgent, insistent, demanding force of sexuality. The latter is felt to be so strong, so overpowering, especially at puberty, that the person fights against its domination. He fears it would force him under the rule of a strange will, another person, in order to satisfy it. Hence sexuality is felt to be an inner claim of the species opposed to individuality, and the person resists it.

The existence of will is closely dependent on the fact that one cannot have everything without effort and without obstacles and restraints to contend with. Will comes into being because man lives in a world where struggle and effort are necessary in order to live, where every move is met with hindrance, either physical or social, where action and reaction are indissolubly bound together. In Paradise, where life is effortless and without obstacles, there need be no will—and likewise no consciousness. The existence of obstacles, restraints, compulsions marks the first phase of willing. These restraints and compulsions are met with a reaction of resistance, a "counter-will." The parents, for example, set up obstacles to certain of the child's movements and efforts. They in effect say "no, you cannot do this" or "you must not do that." The impulsive striving of the child meets such opposition with a counter-opposition, a "counter-will," which in effect says, "I want what [you say] I cannot have," that which is denied.

But man has needs and hence desire. So a second level of willing is reached. This willing is more definite, particular, directed toward the attainment of particular things. But here also the willing is influenced from without. "We want at that level what others have or want, and this manifests itself as envy or competition in terms of the desire for possessions." We measure our own willing by external obstacles and models; we make comparisons. But only by comparison do we become conscious of our individuality.

Finally a "truly positive willing" is achieved when we give up comparisons and cease to "measure" ourselves by others' standards. When also we understand the nature of our will, we are able to feel the responsibility "with which our own ethical consciousness has to say 'Yes' or 'No' to our individual willing."

The child, unfortunately, is not able to make a distinction between willing as such and particular acts of will, that is, the content of willing. He connects the external restrictions and refusals, which pertain to a prohibition against willing some definite thing at a given moment, determined in terms of content and eventually in terms of time, as a universal

prohibition against willing in general. Every restriction, refusal, or prohibition affects the will itself. Thus he tends to
grow up with a sense of the evilness of his will, of his own
badness.

"The morally proscribed contents themselves are associated originally with the bodily functions. The child must
learn to eat and to control the excretory functions, when the
adults wish, not when he wishes. His counter-will [resistance]
in relation to this is commonly designated as 'bad' and 'hateful,' but this means restricted and eventually punished. Very
soon also the physical expressions of sexuality are drawn in
and then become the most important contents of willing,
perhaps just because these expressions are so violently put
under and forbidden. With regard to the overwhelming part
that the psychic plays in our love life . . . the moral prohibition of the physical expression of sex in childhood, has
perhaps the biologically valuable effect of strengthening the
physical side in its later reaction so that it can stand against
the psychic in general. Possibly we have here the ground for
that separation of sensuality and tenderness which Freud
has described as characteristic of the neurotic, but which I
would characterize rather as the attitude of the average, at
all events, as more wholesome than the indissoluble union of
sensuality with the spiritual which seeks in love the individual
justification of sexuality. Again we see here the separation
of will from content lying at the root of these phenomena.
The tender expressions of love toward certain persons are
permitted to the child, are good; the purely physical element
of the will is evil, bad."26

Hence a person grows up with a will whose contents are
in part "good," that is, approved by the parents and society,
and in part "bad," that is, disapproved. The "bad contents"
of the will, in the case of the child, become manifest at times
in his being "bad," "naughty," while in the adult these "bad"
contents are expressed in phantasy and day dream. These

phantasies and day dreams, as Freud pointed out, may form a preliminary step either to neurosis or to creative activity.

The child, especially, needs the approval of his parents and those who take care of him. Hence only the "good" contents, by and large, may be expressed, while the "bad" are hidden and kept secret because the former imply a moral (parental, social) recognition of will, of the self. Should the will itself, for some reason, such as the unremitting disapproval of the parents, become identified with the "bad" contents, then it remains (that is, is felt to be) evil, is condemned, forbidden, which leads to repression, rationalization, and denial of the autonomy of the self. But this outcome does not always occur. If the person has an originally very strong will, expressed as counter-will, as resistance to authority, the "good contents are not sufficient for the justification of the badness of the will and the individual affirms the forbidden contents also, that is, the bad will itself which they represent." Phantasies and day dreams, previously kept hidden and forbidden are then released from the sphere of "mental will expression" into action, "which in this sense is creative." The self has a chance to operate in its totality and integrity.

Will and Phantasy

While the average man keeps his phantasies to himself, and the "neurotic" represses his, the creative type affirms and reveals them to the world, is in fact compelled to reveal them. For the average man, the content of phantasies is an expression of evil will and thus he has guilt feeling toward others, toward society with whom he identifies himself and his will. The person who represses his phantasies, the "neurotic," is at an intermediate stage of development, in which he neither accepts the judgments of society nor accepts his own self. Hence, he feels his will is bad not so much because he has socially-disapproved phantasies but because they are

an expression of his own will, which he feels is evil.[27] He
therefore has guilt feeling toward himself because he fights
against such a limitation or annihilation of his own autonomy,
of the denial of his will. But the creative person, who affirms
his will, has guilt too, both to others and to himself. Yet he
does not allow guilt to cripple him. He transmutes it, as it
were, into a stimulus for further creative effort. It is "creative
guilt."[28]

The Average Man

Rank's picture of the average man is not a pretty one.
The average man's knowledge about his own psychic processes
and motivations "proves to be so false that it works really
only in its complete spuriousness, in an illusion troubled by
no kind of knowing." He "always plays a role, always acts,
but actually plays only himself, that is, must pretend that
he plays in order to justify his being."[29] The "neurotic," on
the other hand, refuses this pretense, but he is unable to be
himself. His problem is to accept himself and be himself. In
this task psychotherapy, assuming a philosophic character,
must come to his aid. It can give him, that is, enable him
to attain, a world view, a philosophy, a faith in himself.

The Creative Man

The creative type, according to Rank, cannot be understood from Freudian theory. For Freud all "individual expressions," that is, all expressions of individuality, are explained as reactions to social influences, the parents and the
society they represent, or as expressions of biological instincts,
both of which deprive the person of any genuine autonomy
or power of initiative toward self-development. He becomes,
by and large, a passive reflex of forces beyond his control.
Or, in other words, he is "a wrestling ground" of the id
(biological instincts) and the superego (the parents and
society). No wonder then, the ego, according to this view

of Freud's, is weak. Such a notion, says Rank, may be a possible description of the great mass of men whom the "average man" represents, but it cannot properly and convincingly explain the creative type. For he is able "to create voluntarily from the impulsive elements and moreover to develop his standards beyond the identifications of the super-ego morality to an ideal formation which consciously guides and rules this creative will in terms of the personality. The essential point in this process is the fact that he evolves his ego ideal from himself, not merely on the ground of given but also of self-chosen factors which he strives after consciously."[30]

Ego and Consciousness

According to Rank, the ego, far from being a helpless tool, driven by the id and restrained by the superego, develops its own autonomy and expresses itself creatively. It is the autonomous representative of the will.

While he does not deny the importance of unconscious processes, Rank gives the conscious ego a central role and importance. Acting, feeling, and thinking, he says, are comprehended in and through consciousness. Freud explained consciousness genetically as a sense organ for the perception of psychic qualities. Earlier, Rank surmises, it was entirely a sense organ for the perception of external qualities. Then the perception of inner qualities was added. A further developmental level supervened when it became an independent and spontaneous entity for partial control of the outer and inner worlds. As a crowning achievement, consciousness became an instrument of observation and knowledge of itself; self-consciousness arose. Thus the power of consciousness has grown as an instrument of understanding, controlling and re-creating the external and internal world.

Thus consciousness is more than an expression and tool of the will. It has become a "self-dependent power," which

can either support and strengthen the will by rationalization
or repress it by denial of its strivings. The next step occurs
when the ego not only represses certain will strivings but
determines what should be, how the person should act, in
terms of its own ideal formation. But with the growth of
self-consciousness, a conflict between knowing and experiencing, between ego and will, arises. Man's knowledge of himself,
of his difference, of his separation from others and from
nature, interferes with naive action, restrains him and torments him. And so he suffers guilt on two counts, from the
side of will and from consciousness. His experiences in childhood convince him that his will is bad; from this he feels
guilt. But his own consciousness, or self-consciousness, also
acts to restrain him, which then he comes to feel is also bad;
hence, he has guilt on this account.

The active hero, who performs prodigious exploits, and
who represents the conscious power of will, can act since he
knows only his will, although he eventually comes to grief
because he cannot foresee the consequences of his act. He
represents unreflective experience. Nor does he want to know,
because it might preclude his acting. The "passive man of
suffering," the "neurotic," cannot act because his self-consciousness restricts him, and for such impotence he suffers
with feelings of guilt. The creative type lives in constant conflict between the two possibilities. He solves this conflict "for
himself and others since he transposes the will affirmation
creatively into knowledge, that is, expresses his will spiritually
and changes the unavoidable guilt feeling into ethical ideal
formation, which spurs him on and qualifies him for ever
higher performance in terms of self-development."[31]

Self-Knowledge and Sin

As everyone knows, the problem of evil, sin, guilt is an
ancient one. Both mythology and religion have attempted to
give a solution to this problem, for, according to Rank, man

longs for naive unconsciousness as the source of happiness and curses the knowledge of good and evil bought so dearly. Mythology and religion say "that the conscious will, human willing in contrast to natural being, is the root of the arch evil which we designate psychologically as guilt feeling . . . This transformation is related to the development of conscious willing just outlined whose first externalization we recognized as a denial, a negation. On account of its negative origin the will is always evil as, for example, with Schopenhauer who harks back to the corresponding oriental teachings. The idea of sin as the biblical presentation teaches, is related to the next developmental level where will, consciously defiant, is affirmed, that is, where knowedge thereof already introduces pride. Finally the Christian idea of guilt under whose domination we still live just as under that of the Jewish idea of sin, is the reaction to the positively creative will tendencies of man, to his presumption in wanting to be not only omniscient like God, but to be God himself, a creator."[32]

Self-knowledge leads finally to a constant awareness of itself, and this self-knowledge present in immediate experience disturbs the latter, if it does not completely block it. If the will is bad and its denial the cause of all suffering, conscious knowledge of ourselves and our problems, insight into the denial process, constitutes evil, sin, guilt. Thus for the "neurotic," consciousness means awareness of difference, of separation, of impotence of his will, thwarted, blocked, denied and denying, resulting in feelings of inferiority and guilt.[33]

On the other hand, the "putting over" of will in living, its fulfillment, added to the consciousness of this potency of will in experience, constitutes pleasure and happiness.

Impulse, Emotion and Will

Rank characterizes the personality in terms of impulse, emotion and will. The child brings into the world a primitive impulse life. By its nature it tends immediately to motor discharge, resulting in a feeling of gratification. An impulse excitation "naturally passes through the two phases of tension and discharge, which the ego on the whole experiences as pain and pleasure." In emotion which gradually develops also there are pain-tension and pleasure-discharge, but the "accentuation" is different. The essence of emotion consists in wanting to preserve tension in order to prolong the pleasure phase until the point is reached when it becomes unbearable and has to be discharged.

The emotional life corresponds to an inhibited or dammed-up impulse-life. The damming up may come from external obstacles or from within because the individual soon learns to make use of impulse-inhibition for the sake of developing emotion.[34] Emotion arises out of a blocked impulse.[35] Its essence "consists of the union of the ego with the Thou, of the individual with his fellow men, in the broadest sense, with the community."

The real emotional life, as an inner experience, can occur only at the stage of the formation of will. The will "is an impulse, *positively and actively* placed in *the service of the ego*, and *not a blocked impulse, as is the emotion*. . . . [Will develops] parallel to the subjection of the impulse life originally dominating the individual, but now under the dominance of the ego." The child, by learning to control its bodily functions, manifests the beginning of the process of will development. "This necessary physical training thus proves to be not only the individual's restriction of the impulse through education, but also the strongest factor of early childhood's formation of will, the result of which represents for the child a pleasurable victory over the racial impulse life, in so far as he is in the position to value it as his own achievement, and not consider it as a compulsion of education." The will may be designated as "individual impulse" because it strives for the control of the whole impulse life by one's own self. But the will, which is formed for the dominance and subjection of one's own impulse life, turns outward also, "and there becomes negative counter-will in the form of stubbornness and resistance, wilfulness and disobedience."

Love and Hate

There are two kinds of "emotional formation," namely, "uniting emotions" such as love, gratitude, longing, tenderness, "submission," repentance (collectively comprehended under the heading of love-emotions); and "separating reactions" like stubbornness, rage, pride, fear, scorn, anger (collectively characterized as hate-affects). Rank thinks that the child inclines toward the latter "because they permit of an outer discharge which is less possible and natural in the uniting feelings of love."[36] Hate-affects are not only negative feelings, but they in general prevent the formation of love-emotion or at least its expression. The unitary-feelings are said to presuppose a higher stage of development of the personality than one generally finds in the child.

The affirmation of love-emotion leads to a "kind of beneficent release of will,"[37] while the hate-affects represent a "hardening" of the will. In the latter case, will, in the negative sense, diverts emotion from its softening influence into a defense of itself. The love-emotions are characterized by a yielding of self-will, although this does not mean a yielding to the will of another, while the hate-affects represent an exaggeratedly defensive, negative expression of will.[38] Where the will denies the emotional "yielding" without increasing this denial into a "hardening" of the will in an affect, the resulting partial denial manifests itself as a transformation of positive emotion (love) into guilt feeling.

The emotional life represents the strongest inner force, a force that is stronger than the sexual instinct; the latter is always capable of being controlled and satisfied somehow, while the former is uncontrollable and insatiable. In fact, the very essence of the emotional life is that it cannot be controlled and satisfied.

Sexuality and Individuality

Sexuality is said to be the only "natural" method of healing or at least for alleviation of the will conflict which arises in regard to the other person and to the world, to the problem of individuality, the "primal ethical conflict."[39] Neurotic sex conflicts are to be understood as manifestations of the primary will conflict.

"The neurotic individual of either sex is incapable of surrender to the other, or to unity with himself, because in him the inner will conflict with its predominantly negative character is so intense that neither outer good fortune nor inner release can protect him from his own destructive reactions. He is incapable of surrender and unity because he cannot get free from the consciousness of himself." In therapy the other person, the therapist, "justifies our will, makes it good." The patient is enabled to accept himself, to regain a unity with himself, to free himself from excessive self-consciousness and, in general, from various destructive reactions toward himself and others. And he can accept his sex role without fear of loss of individuality, partly because in the love relation a far-reaching identification is reached and emotional differences are removed, partly because there is an affirmation and increase of difference which works happily since there is a voluntary submission of will, a lack of defensiveness.

In every kind of emotional relation two great principles, love and force, are opposed. "In love and through love, whether it be divine or human, the individual can accept himself, his own will because the other does, an other does." Force or "will compulsion" is exactly opposed to love and works destructively.

Modern man uses sexuality not simply for pleasure or

for procreation but as an outlet for emotion and an instrument of will. In the ideal love experience, "both sexes enjoy the beneficent feeling of will accomplishment," but also release from individual consciousness in ecstasy and emotional yielding, and finally free themselves from guilt through the creation of a child. While the creation of a child is a generic, biological function, it becomes an individual creation in the training and education of the child. Unfortunately, the clash of wills of the two partners often makes this three-fold experience a brief one.

The creative individual, however, does not satisfy himself with the creation of another individual being. Both sexuality and love are insufficient for the creative man because in them the individual creative urge is limited by alien counter-wills. "Moreover, creativity is not something which happens but once, it is the constant continuing expression of the individual will accomplishment, by means of which the individual seeks to overcome self-creatively the biological compulsion of the sexual instinct and the psychological compulsion to emotional surrender."[40] This is the explanation for the guilt which the creative personality necessarily produces by his development and affirmation. In his will accomplishment he goes "beyond the limits set by nature" in overcoming the biological sexual instinct to which the ego reacts with guilt. In the "spiritual psychic creation" the ego is opposed to the world and rules it in terms of its will. The creative person commits the sin of Adam, namely, he forces the sex instinct into the service of his individual will.[41]

The Oedipus Complex

In interpreting the Oedipus complex Rank urges the importance of the given family situation. In fact, the entire relation of the child to the parents, he says, had better be called the Oedipus situation. Thus, while according to Freud, the boy wants to separate the parents, to get rid of the father, according to Rank, he may, in some circumstances, want to bring the parents together. If, for instance, the child feels that the conflicts of his parents are a threat to his own welfare, he will try to bring them together or to keep them together.

There is another side to the problem: the problem as to what the child signifies for the parents ideologically, in what light they see him, and for what they want to use him. Rank states explicitly that the child has always been used for something, at times by the community (as its "collective soul-bearer"), at times by the parents or one of them. He is often psychically misused and exploited, for many marital conflicts are "projected" on to him. But he also takes advantage of the parents' guilty feeling about exploiting him. Thus he "recreates" a given situation in terms of his needs and wishes.

The Oedipus complex will have a different significance for the individual at various times in his life, such as childhood, puberty, maturity. And it will have a different significance for different people, such as for the artist and the "neurotic." Furthermore, the incest wish is to be distinguished from "the father ideology." The former is a symbol of individual immortality to which one clings in order to escape "the compulsion of the racial immortality in sex." Simultaneously one defends oneself against the acceptance of the new father role.

But the Oedipus complex also has a different meaning when considered from different angles, that is, from the point of view of the individual, or from that of the father, or from that of the son. "As an individual one does not want to put oneself in the father's place and to become father, that is the husband of the mother. As son, one may desire it but only to deny with it the role of the son; that is to say, if one must have a racial function then at least to have that of the father. Finally with the complete acceptance of the father role, the man will naturally love the son more (and not according to the Oedipus scheme, the daughter) because he sees in him his direct successor and heir."[42]

Preference for the daughter by the father is said to show less willingness to accept the role of father, for it represents a desire of the father to be reborn in the daughter instead of the mother.

Hence the "biological Edipus tendency" is "complemented" by a psychical one which is directed toward the child of the same sex.

The child is said to react to this state of affairs in an ambivalent fashion. The son takes refuge in the mother not only from fear of the father but also from a too great love for the father, which he fears. Thus he develops a "mother fixation" in order to protect his individuality from being engulfed completely in the role of son to the father, a continuation of the father's ego. In other words, the father attempts to force the son to become his identical successor. The child rebels at this role of being only a son and not an individual in his own right. Hence, there is a duel between father and son. For similar reasons, the daughter often leans toward the father. So the child uses such stratagems in order to protect his integrity, but in the process he also is pushed in the direction of biological dependency, that is, on the parent of the opposite sex. "The parents fight openly or tacitly for the child's soul, whether in the biological (opposite sex) or in the egoistic sense (the same sex), and the child uses the parents correspondingly, and plays them one against the other, in order to save his individuality."[43]

Therefore the child needs both parents in order to save himself from being "devoured" by either one.

The Psychology of Women and Men

We conclude this part of the discussion with Rank's differentiation between men and women, their basic psychology,

he says, being different. Man's strength lies in his creative
power, woman's in her sex. Since sex signifies for the man
mortality, he fears it, both in her and in himself. She, on
the contrary, accepts sex and finds her immortality in sexual
procreation, a continuation of her biological self, while she
fears the will of the man. In order to pursue his supernatural
aims, man has masculinized the world, including woman, and
has forced a masculine ideology on her, who still preserves
the "irrational" elements in human nature. Man has never
accepted the fact of being mortal, that is, "never accepted
himself." Hence, his basic psychology is "denial of his mortal
origin and a subsequent need to change himself in order to
find his real self, which he rationalizes as independent of
woman."[44] Woman, however, has accepted her basic self, that
is, motherhood, while, having accepted a masculine ideology,
she needs constant assurance that she is acceptable to him,
which she can only get by living up to his ideals and
standards. At the same time she conceals her own psychology
partly as a weapon against the man, which she needs as a
refuge of her crushed self, partly because her own psychology
is a secret to her too.

Woman, because of her biological make-up, is fundamentally conservative. Man, on the other hand, dictated by his
more selfish need for the preservation of his own ego, strives
to control and create.

Hence, the question of the equality of men and women
is wrongly conceived, for the only equality is the equal right
"of every individual to become and to be himself, which
actually means to accept his own difference and have it
accepted by others."[45]

The Struggle For Self-Perpetuation

Rank sees a struggle for self-perpetuation, some kind of
spiritual perpetuation, as elemental and fundamental to mankind. Man fears final destruction, not so much natural death,

for in the belief of many peoples the soul lives on after death. What he fears is destruction of his spiritual self. Racial survival in one's children and their descendants is not sufficient; it is non-personal and limited by death. Mankind yearns for some kind of eternal spiritual survival.

The belief in immortality has expressed itself in various forms. Thus totemism, says Rank, the first form of religion, established a kind of "collective immortality" in the rebirth of the souls of the dead through the totem of the clan. Through religion they became alike thus gaining a "new kind of collective immortality" in the clan-totem. For Rank incest is a symbol of man's self creative urge, drawing its strength from the belief in immortality.

Before we outline his views on incest and the Oedipus myth, we must first introduce some other ideas of his adopted from the researches of a Swiss scholar, Bachofen, the American anthropologist, Morgan, and others. Rank very briefly attempts to trace the fate of the child from its status in the "primal family" (not to be confused with Freud's "primal horde") which he reconstructs "according to the newer views of sociology," to our modern small family unit.

In this primitive community neither monogamy nor promiscuity in the usual sense existed but a kind of group marriage, in which the regulation of the sexual life was "closely connected" with the religious ideas of the group. And these religious ideas also determined the prevailing attitude toward the child. In this group-family the children belonged in common to all the mothers. Sometimes when they were bigger the children were assigned to a "father of choice" who apparently acted as tutor for further training. The "father-ideology" hardly existed.[46]

Then a transitional phase developed, the matriarchy, during which the mother's brother was the male head of the family instead of the father.

This transitional phase was succeeded by our present-day small family unit characterized by the acceptance of the father's role as begetter of his children. This role "was formerly denied from religious reasons of the belief in immortality. . . . Today with the enfeeblement of the patrias potestas and the strengthening of the individualistic tendency, the child is an individual for himself although he is lawfully the father's successor and is claimed as a collective being by the State."[47] Nowadays the mother trains the child in the early period, while the father "claims" him later, but he has to share the upbringing of the child with the school, that is, the community.

So we see the child developing in different situations. Today he is made "an individual vindication" of marriage, while formerly as a "collective being" he made marriage unnecessary.

Rank suggests that for a long time preceding the "patriarchal ideology," personal fatherhood was not only unknown but denied in order to maintain the individual ideology of immortality. In very early times a second self was ascribed to one's shadow. The individual's shadow was protected from injury like the real self, but the death of the latter (physical death) did not affect the shadow, which survived it. The shadow not only had an independent life but was considered the most vital part of the human being, namely, his soul. The notion of the soul's surviving after death took two forms. In one form life after death continued much as it was on earth; the Indians, for example, at death went to heavenly hunting grounds. In the other, there was a return to earth. The latter notion triumphed when the belief in an immortal soul in its naivest form of the shadow was shattered in totemism, according to which the soul of the father or grandfather lived again in the newborn child. However, both notions may exist side by side. In totemism, sexual procreation is denied; the woman is impregnated by the spirit of the dead surviving in animals or plants which enter the mother's womb. Thus, the ego continues to exist, perhaps in a somewhat different form, in an animal or plant, or in a newborn child. The function of primitive systems of religion and social organization, then, according to Rank, seems to have been to deny personal fatherhood. As the patriarchal society developed with its recognition of the real father, strife arose, a struggle of man against the role of father thrust upon him, which reaches its highest in Greek mythology.

Rank has thrown these ideas together in a rather loose, abbreviated fashion. Perhaps we can make them a little clearer from the following. The "institution of group marriage fortified the position of women. The gradual dominance of the mothers, not only over the children of the clan but ultimately over the men, as borne out by the 'matriarchal organization,' was seemingly a slow process resisted by man who still defended his supernatural origin and survival. As he was conceived from the spirit of the dead and lived on in his double [the shadow] he had to keep free from the mortal origin of woman, the mother. Thus motherhood . . . was not accepted from the beginning as a matter of course; the conception of the mother as the bearer of life appears comparatively late, although at an earlier stage than the conception of fatherhood . . . Originally, 'the mother herself is no more than the host, as it were, of the child who decided to be born of her body; she is in no sense its shaper or genetrice. Motherhood and fatherhood both, in Australia, are essentially social; they are based upon and fulfil certain fundamental social needs . . . there is nothing of any biological or physiological nature nor any concepts of consanguinity associated with these relationships.' From this denial of motherhood on the part of the man leads a long uneven way to the modern individual's famous 'mother-complex.' This emotional tie— far from being natural—is the ultimate result of a development which started when man first accepted biological fatherhood in place of his own self-perpetuation . . ."[48]

The Oedipus Saga

Hence, the Oedipus saga from a sociological point of
view is a "heroic defense" of the man against the role of
father. "The father of Edipus, Laios, represents the type of
man rejecting the sexual ideology . . . On account of the
prophecy that the son would be his successor, he abstains for
years from sexual intercourse with his wife, with whom he
cohabited only once in drunkenness or when seduced by her
so accidentally begot Edipus. The boy was immediately exposed after birth, because the father wanted no successor,
but wanted to be his own immortal successor, a desire which
the myth presents in the incest of Edipus with his mother.
This concept makes Edipus himself a representative of the
father who wants to have no children, yet tries to preserve
himself indefinitely. The incest with the mother from which
also children sprang up, proves to be . . . a compromise
between the wish to have no children at all (Laios) and the
necessity to renounce one's own immortality in favour of the
children. This compromise to beget oneself as the mother's
son and to be reborn from her, must naturally fail tragically.
This is the veritable guilt of Edipus, not that he slew the
father and took his place with the mother. For as little as the
father wants to continue to exist only in his sons, just as
little has the son an inclination to play only the part of a
successor to the father. In this sense Edipus rebels likewise
against the role of son as against that of father and not as
son against his father. This double conflict in the individual
himself who wants to be neither father nor son, but simply
Self, is portrayed in the myth in all its features which one
cannot understand from the individual psychological viewpoint but only when one regards it as a sediment of sociological development. In this sense the resistance against the
begetting of a son signifies also one's own resistance to come
into the world as son; the exposure signifies the son's wish
not to be brought up in the parental home as son but to

THE THEORIES OF OTTO RANK

grow up a free man in the wilderness. In this sense finally
the fate or destiny that compels him to slay the father and
to marry the mother signifies not only the son's individual
wish as Freud has it, but also the coercion of the species that
prescribes marriage and fatherhood against the individual's
will."[49]

Rank believes that the myth portrays a struggle between
the "individual ego" believing itself immortal and the "racial
ego" embodied in the "sexual ideology," which renounces individual immortality in favor of marriage and children. This
inner struggle is presented symbolically in the Oedipus saga
as an external strife between father and son. Such a struggle
could arise only with the full development of individuality
as represented in Hellenism. The Oedipus saga embodies a
long tradition, and Sophocles' version is an end-product of
that tradition. The Greek Oedipus tradition simply represents
a re-interpretation of an ancient creation-rite. "The Oedipus
of the primitive seasonal myth was originally a phallic vegetation spirit, an offspring of the earth-mother whose son
was also her husband."[50] In his presentation of the Oedipus
material Sophocles, who also may have had an Oedipus complex, was as much influenced by the old traditions as by the
contemporary attitude toward it.

The Oedipus of the tragic poets portrays a further
development of the saga. Here Oedipus represents the man
already forced into the part of father and into matrimonial
laws. Sophocles' "Oedipus at Colonus," for example, suggests
this. "Deprived of his individual immortality and with the
approach of age and of death he tries to abandon his
fatherhood in order to regain his individual immortality."
In the play, the hero not only recalls his own childhood but
also the "mythical hero Oedipus," whose incest with the
mother he wants to imitate.[51] (Incestuous origin was considered an earmark of supernatural origin, according to Rank.
Furthermore, through incest "the individual once more tries

to recapture heroic stature, thus overcoming the fear of death by being reborn through his own mother.") The poet Sophocles, who is supposed to have been accused by his own sons of senile incompetence, has, furthermore, expressed his own psychology in the play. Nevertheless, he has described only a general motive, that of the father who will not be replaced by his son and of the son who will not be the father's successor.

The ancient myth of Oedipus may be said in summary to have gone through three stages: the heroic, the poetic, and the psychological. In the heroic stage, certain exceptional individuals, who had made themselves immortal in their work (heroes) were granted the privilege of incest, which originally and during the transitional period served as an attempt to achieve one's own immortality. "The father principle was not yet fully accepted by the man, he was only father of the son begotten of the mother, thus he was father of himself, who wanted to continue to exist in the son."[52] In the next stage, the collective ideology gives way to the patriarchal family organization, in which personal immortality is renounced for immortality in the children. This in turn implies a "racial fetter" because only through "racial sexuality" and hence marriage and family can one achieve this kind of immortality. But at this stage of development the man still yearned for "the good old times," to be like Oedipus of the ancient myth. "Finally, in the present-day individual who with his victorious individualism has precipitated the downfall of the father's rule and of the famly organization, we find the same motive interpreted [by Freud] as a wish for the father role, a motive which originally gave expression to the horror of it."

These three stages of development are said to correspond to the development of the individual. "Thus a young poet is likely to be heroic, the ageing writer more psychological, the one represents the attitude of the independent ego, the other acknowledges the necessary adjustment and submission to law."[53]

Oedipus, unlike his father, accepted his sons and wanted to be father of his family, but in his old age "the old Adam" got the better of him. He (the creation of the poet) then wanted immortality like the mythical hero Oedipus. Having been sacrificed to the "family ideology," in old age he rebelled; after he had cast out the wife and cursed the sons, he found consolation in his daughters. In other words, the Oedipus of the historical saga reflects a different and earlier stage of development of society than that of the Oedipus of Sophocles, who created him, at least in part, according to the state of society and family development of his own time. And, we may add, as Rank noted, the Oedipus of Freud's interpretation likewise reflects the conditions of his culture in his time.

The Role of Illusion and Truth

Rank professes a "relativity" theory of knowledge. He holds to the view that the nature of will determines truth and falsity, not the nature of the world. Truth is subjective— what I will to be true is true. "Truth is what I believe or affirm, doubt is denial or rejection. But the reality which penetrates consciousness through our sense organs can influence us only by way of the emotional life and becomes either truth or falsehood accordingly; that is, is stamped as psychic reality or unreality. In the interaction of will and consciousness as it manifests itself in the emotional life we find a continuous influencing of one sphere by the other. Even the purely sensory consciousness is not merely receptive, but is guided and restricted by will. I see or hear what I want to, not what is. What is can only be learned by overcoming the tendency to deny all that I do not want to see or hear or perceive. Still more clearly is intellect influenced by will, for logical, causally directed thinking, going beyond the effort to shut out the painful is the positive, active expression of the will to control reality. The third level of creative consciousness or phantasy is the most positive expression of the counter-will, which not only says 'I will *not* perceive what is,' but 'I will that it is otherwise, i.e. just as I want it. And this, only this is truth."[54]

Rank mixes up terms badly in this connection. Truth is used in several senses: in "its practical meaning," that is in terms of "psychic reality" (what I will to be true is true), in an epistemological sense (how I know), and finally in a logical or perhaps ontological sense (that which is or exists, not what I want to believe). Often he confuses these meanings, so that one cannot be sure in which sense he is using truth. The height of confusion is reached when he speaks of not only art, religion, and love as "illusions" but philosophy and science too. Furthermore, there are inner illusions (unspecified) which "condition" the outer.

Deeply pessimistic, he says that with the truth (apparently here he means truth as what is really so, not what we should like to believe is so) we cannot live. In order to live, one needs illusions. Seeking the truth in human motives for acting and thinking is destructive. "The more a man can take [seeming] reality as truth, appearance as essence, the sounder, the better adjusted, the happier will he be." Failure to do so results in suffering and disaster. The constantly effective process of self-deceiving, pretending and blundering is the essence of "reality," which is, so to speak, a continuous blunder.[55]

This is in essence what the Greek myth says. Oedipus would have lived happily in his world of appearance had he not been driven by intellectual pride, the will to truth, "to expose his reality as lies, as appearance, as falsehood."[56]

The trouble with the "neurotic" is not that he suffers from pathological mechanisms—these are necessary and wholesome for living—but in the failure of these mechanisms to maintain illusions important for living. The average well-adjusted person can make the culturally accepted reality into his own; it becomes his "truth." Finally, the creative man seeks and finds "his own truth," which he then proposes to make general, real.

In this way Rank, if we accept his ideas on the subject, completely destroys any objective criterion for determining truth—including the truth of Rank's ideas.

8. THE THEORIES OF KAREN HORNEY

Karen Horney for over fifteen years was an orthodox Freudian practicing psychoanalyst. But eventually, as in so many other cases, doubts arose as to the adequacy and usefulness of many of Freud's theoretical formulations and ideas. Her coming to America seems to have been one of the decisive factors in her final revolt. "The greater freedom from dogmatic beliefs which I found in this country alleviated the obligation of taking psychoanalytical theories for granted, and gave me the courage to proceed along the lines which I considered right. Furthermore, acquaintance with a culture which in many ways is different from the European taught me to realize that many neurotic conflicts are ultimately determined by cultural conditions."[1] The early work of Erich Fromm, among others, seems to have been another influence to strengthen her misgivings concerning Freud, and to develop her own ideas.

In any case her first book, *The Neurotic Personality of Our Time*, attempted to explain "neurotic" phenomena not primarily in terms of the Oedipus complex (which, according to Freud, is the kernel of every neurosis) but in terms of a "basic anxiety." We shall discuss this below.

THE CONCEPT OF NEUROSIS

The term "neurotic" has become almost a catchword. Among laymen it is often used to "explain" nearly every unusual or unconventional act, feeling, or thought. Worse still, it has become a term of abuse. If you want to disparage a person, you call him a neurotic—and that puts him in his place. This points to the fact that many people have a contemptuous attitude toward one who has certain kinds of problems in living, the "neurotic" personality.

The concept of neurotic (abnormal) implies there is such a thing as a normal person. Horney proceeds to show that the notion of what is normal is rather elusive. For example, behavior considered neurotic in one culture may be considered normal elsewhere and conversely. "With us a person would be neurotic or psychotic who talked by the hour with his deceased grandfather, whereas such communication with ancestors is a recognized pattern in some Indian tribes."[2] Furthermore, what is considered normal in a given culture varies in the course of time. And at a given time it varies in different classes within the culture.

The concept of normality, therefore, poses serious problems. To mistake what is considered normal in one's own culture as the universal standard of normality can lead to serious theoretical and therapeutic consequences. Unfortunately, Freud did assume that certain traits he found in people, like the greater jealousy of women, are to be explained on a biological basis and hence are universal.

Horney, however, categorically asserts that there is no such thing as a universal normal psychology. The normal human being does not exist, she says. In this case, then, how can one say that any person is neurotic? Does it not appear that at most all one can say in regard to alleged neurotics is that they are unconventional? Without attempting to meet this problem directly, Horney mentions two characteristics which she says one can discern in all neuroses: "a certain rigidity in reaction and a discrepancy between potentialities and accomplishments."[3]

While a "normal" person reacts according to the requirements of the objective situation, a neurotic brings to all situations involving people a predetermined attitude by which, or according to which, he tends to react. Thus a "normal" person will be suspicious only when the situation calls for it, when, say, the other person manifests signs of insincerity, evasiveness, or falsehood. When no such signs exist, a "normal" person is not very likely, if at all, to suspect the good faith of another. But a neurotic may bring to any situation an attitude of suspiciousness (or apprehensiveness or hostility, depending on circumstances). He will be consciously or unconsciously on the watch for signs of insincerity or bad faith, and even if he finds no evidence, he will still tend to assume, perhaps unconsciously, that the other person cannot be trusted. The "normal" person is flexible in his attitudes and behavior concerning the situations in which he finds himself; the neurotic is rigid, inflexible.

But Horney goes on to say that rigidity is indicative of a neurosis only when it differs in degree from prevailing patterns of rigidity, or as she puts it, deviates from the cultural patterns. A large proportion of peasants in Western civilization are said to have a rigid (inflexible) suspicion of the new and strange. Hence, in such a community of peasants, Horney implies, rigidity would tend to be "normal."

"In the same way, a discrepancy between the potentialities of a person and his actual achievements in life may be due only to external factors. But it is indicative of a neurosis if in spite of gifts and favorable external possibilities for their development the person remains unproductive; or if in spite of having all the possibilities for feeling happy he cannot enjoy what he has; or in spite of being beautiful a woman feels that she cannot attract men. In other words, the neurotic has the impression that he stands in his own way."[4]

Unfortunately, Horney does not explain what she means by "productive" here, taking it for granted that the reader will understand, but the meaning is not clear. There is said to be one essential factor common to all neuroses: anxieties and the defenses built up against them. Anxiety is character- ized as being the efficient cause or "motor" to set the neurotic process going and to keep it going. However, Horney later adds another essential characteristic of neurosis: the presence of conflicting tendencies. The person who has these conflicting tendencies is unaware of them, or at least of the precise conditions necessary for their occurrence. For such tendencies he "automatically" tries to achieve compromise solutions. While everyone may have some conflicts which are generated by the culture, in the neurotic they are sharper and more accentuated. So Horney reaches a tentative "description" of a neurosis: it is "a psychic disturbance brought about by fears and defenses against these fears, and by attempts to find compromise solutions for conflicting tendencies."[5]

CHARACTER AND SITUATION NEUROSES

In speaking of neuroses, she refers to "character neur- oses" rather than "situation neuroses." A situation neurosis is said to be primarily the reaction of a person whose person- ality is otherwise intact and undisturbed to an external situation filled with conflicts. No example is given so we shall invent a simplified one for the sake of illustration. In a period of great unemployment a person out of work may be offered a good job in a foreign country which involves his leaving some loved one behind for a long time. The desire to remain with the loved one may be as great as, or greater than, the need to take the position, thus arousing an intense conflict.[6] In a character neurosis, the chief trouble lies in deformations of character, not primarily in the external life situation of the person, though the latter, when difficult, may reveal hitherto hidden problems and disturbances or accen- tuate them. Character deformations are the result of a long history, beginning usually in childhood and involving "greater or lesser parts of the personality in a greater or lesser intensity." Superficially, the character neurosis may look like a situation neurosis. In other words, at first view a difficult external situation may seem sufficient to cause the neurosis in an otherwise "normal" person. But "a carefully collected history of the person may show that difficult character traits were present long before any confusing situation arose, that the momentary predicament is itself to a large extent due to previously existing personal difficulties, and furthermore that the person reacts neurotically to a life situation which for the average healthy individual does not imply any conflict at all."[7]

It is the character disturbances and deformations with which Horney (like Freud in part as his discoveries increased) concerns herself, not symptoms, for one may "cure" symptoms without curing a disease. In other words, one may be able to remove symptoms without removing their underlying causes. In fact, there may be no clinical symptoms, or they may vary, while a serious character disturbance exists. Furthermore, it is character, she says, not symptoms, which influences human behavior.

Horney, like Jung and others, in contrast to Freud, puts the emphasis on a functional understanding of neurosis. A genetic understanding is necessary—a knowledge of how people, so to speak, "got that way"—but it is not sufficient. One must know the "actually existing unconscious tendencies and their functions and interactions with other tendencies that are present, such as impulses, fears, and protective measures." Freud, she says, put the emphasis on an analysis of the sexual roots of an impulse or the infantile pattern of which the impulse is supposed to be a repetition.

But these unconscious tendencies are said to have a common basis; the contents of the "dynamically central conflicts" and their interrelations are essentially similar in all neuroses. These conflicts refer to specific life conditions in a given culture, not to problems common to human nature, since, as she puts it, the motivating forces and conflicts in other cultures are different. Horney implies she does not believe in a human nature common to all men, or at least suggests that neuroses do not represent problems common to all men. The concept of neurotic personality, then, only means "that there are neurotic persons having essential peculiarities in common, but also that these basic similarities are essentially produced by the difficulties existing in our time and culture."[8]

CONCEPT OF ANXIETY

If anxiety and the defenses set up against it are essential to neurosis, the problem of anxiety needs clarification. Freud at one time believed that the frustration of libidinal drives caused anxiety. In other words, he believed that repressed libidinal energy became converted into anxiety or discharged in the form of anxiety. Later he came to the conclusion that anxiety is not the result of repression but the cause of repression. However, his account of the anxiety process is complicated and rather vague.[9]

Horney distinguishes between fear and anxiety. Fear is a "proportionate" reaction to a dangerous situation, the danger being transparent and objective. But anxiety too is said to be a "proportionate" reaction to a situation of danger, but in this case the danger "is hidden and subjective." The intensity of the anxiety "is proportionate to the meaning the situation has for the person concerned, and the reasons why he is thus anxious are essentially unknown to him."[10]

Some people are well aware of feelings of anxiety; others are quite unaware of them, though they may recognize feelings of depression or disturbances in the sexual life. Anxiety may be concealed by various experiences, such as anger or suspicion or feelings of inadequacy. Many people spend a great deal of time and energy trying to escape anxiety.

"In fact, we seem to go to any length to escape anxiety or to avoid feeling it. There are many reasons for this, the most general reason being that intense anxiety is one of the most tormenting affects we can have. Patients who have gone through an intense fit of anxiety will tell you that they would rather die than have a recurrence of that experience. Besides, certain elements contained in the affect of anxiety may be particularly unbearable for the individual. One of them is helplessness. One can be active and courageous in the face of a great danger. But in a state of anxiety one feels—in fact, is—helpless. To be rendered helpless is particularly unbearable for those persons for whom power, ascendancy, the idea of being master of any situation, is a prevailing ideal. Impressed by the apparent disproportion of their reaction they resent it, as if it demonstrated a weakness."[11]

The apparent irrationality of anxiety is also intolerable to some people, who find it hard to endure the existence of irrational forces within them, and who may have automatically trained themselves to exercise strict intellectual control over their conscious thoughts and feelings. Since our culture stresses rational thinking and behavior and regards irrationality whether real or apparent as inferior, the neurotic has an added incentive for intellectual control of himself and is further bedeviled by the contrasting, conflicting drives within him which render him helpless.

Finally, the very existence of irrational anxiety is an implicit warning that there is something "out of gear" within the person. Yet the neurotic will strenuously reject any insinuation that all is not right with him. Because of his feeling of being trapped and helpless, he will especially resist any suggestion of change. To change a fundamental attitude is for anyone usually, if not always, a difficult prospect, and this becomes doubly difficult for one who is already burdened with problems.

Ways of Escaping Anxiety

There are said to be four main ways in our culture for escaping anxiety: to rationalize it, to deny it, to narcotize it, and to avoid thoughts, feelings, impulses and situations which might arouse it. Rationalization is said to consist in turning anxiety into a rational fear. An over-solicitous mother, one who lavishes attention on and has excessive "concern" for her children on any and all occasions, turns her own anxieties into a fear that the children are in constant danger of something or other.

People deny anxiety, sometimes consciously, sometimes unconsciously. In the latter case, it is "denied" by keeping it out of consciousness. Only the "concomitants" of anxiety are present, such as shivering, sweating, accelerated heartbeat, choking sensations, a frequent urge to urinate, diarrhea, vomiting, a feeling of restlessness, of being rushed or paralyzed. When one consciously denies anxiety, one may make a conscious decision to overcome it. Thus a girl who was tormented by anxiety until close to puberty, especially concerning burglars, decided to sleep alone in the attic, to walk alone in the empty house. Of course she only lost her fear of burglars.

In narcotizing anxiety one may do so literally by taking to alcohol or drugs. But there are various other ways, such as indulging in a ceaseless round of social activities, burying oneself in work, sexual promiscuity.

An example of the fourth way of escaping anxiety is that of a girl who fears that if she goes to parties she will be neglected. So she makes herself believe she dislikes social gatherings and may avoid going to them. Avoidance of anxiety-provoking situations may automatically occur, and this is called inhibition. "An inhibition consists in an inability to do, feel or think certain things, and its function is to avoid the anxiety which would arise if the person attempted to do feel or think those things."[12] There are various kinds of inhibition, but we shall give only one example. One who has strong inhibitions about approaching women or being sexually intimate with them may automatically assume that he is deferring to the cultural dogma of the sacredness of women.

Certain effects of anxiety are worth mentioning at this point. An anxiety-provoking activity produces a feeling of strain, fatigue or exhaustion. Anxiety impairs the effectiveness with which one perfoms such an activity. And it will spoil most of the pleasure the activity might have.

The Role of Hostility

Since anxiety is said to be a fear which involves a subjective factor, the problem arises as to what that factor is. It is hostility. According to Horney, "*hostile impulses of various kinds form the main source from which neurotic anxiety springs.*"[13] These hostile impulses are usually repressed. When one thus pretends, so to speak, that everything is all right and refrains from fighting when he should or wishes to, it reenforces a preexisting sense of defenselessness. If a neurotic's interests are attacked, he may feel powerless to defend himself because awareness of hostility may be unbearable to him. The hostile impulses are expressed, perhaps afterwards, in fantasy or dream.

Repressed hostility, however, usually becomes intensified. If one represses his hostility against, say, an aggressive, domineering person (and the number of aggressive, domineering people in this culture is not small), that person may go right on taking advantage of him in one way or another whenever an opportunity occurs, thus increasing the repressed hostility. For one cannot fail to "register" (experience unconsciously) hostility or rage when one's interests or one's integrity is violated, if it is not possible to feel hostility directly and consciously. Repressed hostility may itself arouse anxiety, if there is a possibility that the hostility would endanger other interests by its expression, such as a job or the love of a spouse. More often it is "projected," sometimes on those against whom one feels hostile, frequently on other objects. When the projection has occurred, various other complications may arise.[14]

By this time the reader probably will wonder where the original anxiety and hostility came from. The answer to this requires discussion of Horney's concept of the basic structure of neurosis.

BASIC STRUCTURE OF NEUROSIS

While some forms of anxiety may be fully accounted for by conflict-laden objective situations, these are not or at least in the past were not the primary problem in psychiatry. Unless prolonged, they may provoke only a situation neurosis. The anxiety experienced in a character neurosis has to be understood with reference to the past history of the person.

The childhood experiences of a great number of persons with a character neurosis show that their environment has certain typical characteristics.

"The basic evil is invariably a lack of genuine warmth and affection . . . The main reason why a child does not receive enough warmth and affection lies in the parents' incapacity to give it on account of their own neuroses. More frequently than not, in my experience, the essential lack of warmth is camouflaged, and the parents claim to have in mind the child's best interest. Educational theories, oversolicitude or the self-sacrificing attitude of an 'ideal' mother are the basic factors contributing to an atmosphere that more than anything else lays the corner-stone for future feelings of immense insecurity.

"Furthermore, we find various actions or attitudes on the part of the parents which cannot but arouse hostility, such as preference for other children, unjust reproaches, unpredictable changes between overindulgence and scornful rejection, unfulfilled promises, and not least important, an attitude toward the child's needs which goes through all gradations from temporary inconsideration to a consistent interfering with the most legitimate wishes of the child, such as disturbing friendships, ridiculing independent thinking, spoiling its interest in its own pursuits, whether artistic, athletic or mechanical—altogether an attitude of the parents which if not in intention nevertheless in effect means breaking the child's will."[15]

A child who experiences no love and no respect in his early years will tend to develop a "reaction of hatred" toward his parents and other children and a distrustful or spiteful attitude toward everyone. And he will grow up with expectations of evil from everyone, unless some mitigating circumstances occur such as contact with an understanding teacher. Because the child is helpless and depends on the parents in all vital matters, including love, he may have to disguise his hatred or repress it, depending on parental vicissitudes, their "tolerance" of hostile expressions, and so on. In other words he fears they may desert him or turn against him if he expresses hostility. If he is "bad," the parents, at least in our culture, will usually make him feel guilty, unworthy and contemptible. When the child manifests sexual curiosity or indulges in other sexual activity, such as masturbation, he is informed, directly or indirectly, that it is forbidden, and that he is dirty and despicable if he engages in such sexual activities.

For such reasons a child may be compelled to repress his hostility, and eventually, because of his precarious situation, he develops anxiety. His helplessness, his fear, his need of love, his feelings of guilt all combine to bring about a repression of hostility. And the danger for the child's character is said to lie in the repression of any protest against the actions of parents.

While infantile anxiety is a necessary condition for

the development of a neurosis, Horney believes it is not in itself sufficient. An early change in surroundings, counteracting influences like the affection of a loving grandmother may forestall a definite neurotic development.

The child who, without the intervention of more favorable influences, grows up in the kind of destructive environment described above, not only develops anxiety but he projects it on to the outside world. He becomes convinced that the world in general is dangerous and frightening. In general also, he will be less enterprising and self-assertive.[16] "He will have lost the blissful certainty of being wanted and will take even a harmless teasing as a cruel rejection. He will be wounded and hurt more easily than others and will be less capable of defending himself." Such a child acquires "an insidiously increasing, all-pervading feeling of being lonely and helpless in a hostile world. The acute individual reactions to individual provocations crystallize into a character attitude. This attitude as such does not constitute a neurosis but it is the nutritive soil out of which a definite neurosis may develop at any time. Because of the fundamental role this attitude plays in neuroses I have given it a special designation: the basic anxiety; it is inseparably interwoven with a basic hostility."

In character neuroses this basic anxiety is said to underlie all relationships to people, while in "simple" situation neuroses it is lacking. Basic anxiety is characterized roughly as "a feeling of being small, insignificant, helpless, endangered, in a world that is out to abuse, cheat, attack, humiliate, betray, envy."[17]

There is said rarely to be an awareness of basic anxiety and of basic hostility in the person who has them, or at least of their significance. The basic anxiety and hostility may be concealed by a superficial conviction that in general people are quite likable, or by a readiness to admire. This basic anxiety may also be transferred to things other than people such as thunderstorms, political events, germs, canned food, or manifested in a feeling of being doomed by fate, the anxiety being at the same time "divested of its personal character."

Generally speaking, basic anxiety has the following consequences: "It means emotional isolation, all the harder to bear as it concurs with a feeling of intrinsic weakness of the self. It means a weakening of the very foundation of self-confidence. It carries the germ for a potential conflict between the desire to rely on others, and the impossibility to do so because of deep distrust of and hostility toward them. It means that because of intrinsic weakness the person feels a desire to put all responsibility upon others, to be protected and taken care of, whereas because of the basic hostility there is much too much distrust to carry out this desire. And invariably the consequence is that he has to put the greatest part of his energies into securing reassurance."[18]

NEUROTIC TRENDS

Since anxiety tends to be unbearable there are various ways of escaping, or trying to escape, from it. According to Horney there are in our culture four principal modes of protection or "trends" against it: affection, submissiveness, power, withdrawal. These trends themselves are interrelated, reenforce one another and create conflicts. In neuroses, the craving for affection and the craving for power and control are said to play the greatest roles.[19]

The Neurotic Striving for Affection

While Horney discusses these four main ways of escaping anxiety and their various ramifications in considerable detail, we can only indicate in a brief fashion how they operate. For the neurotic as a defense against anxiety affection implies: "If you love me, you will not hurt me." For this reason, among others, he has an inordinate need of affection, and he never can get enough of it.[20] He fears dislike or disapproval and he will go to great lengths to avoid them, even though his basic hostility will manifest itself again and again to thwart him. As a rule he cannot bear to be alone, he needs continual contact with others and their friendly reassurance. Hence, he will tend to have little discrimination in his choice of friends. He will be eternally dependent emotionally on some one. Perhaps he will "slide from one sexual relation into another," or be inhibited sexually, or remain within the range of "normal" sexual behavior. But in any case his sexual activity, like all of his human relationships, will be indiscriminate and compulsive and will often serve as a substitute for emotional intimacy. Yet in spite of his overwhelming craving for affection, when affection is offered he very often cannot accept it, if ever, because he has a deep conviction of his own unlovability, and because he fears emotional dependency, which, to him, an intimate relationship implies. Eventually he may withdraw from close human contact.

The neurotic demands unconditional love. In other words, he wishes to be loved regardless of any provocative behavior on his part, to be loved without any return of love, and to be loved without any advantage for the other person. The demand of unconditional love ultimately springs from his need of reassurance because he has a deep conviction of his own inability to love.

The Neurotic Striving for Power

The quest for power, prestige, and possession, in the neurotic sense, is so common that not a great deal needs to be said by way of illustration, and in any case we have discussed it elsewhere in this book. According to Horney, the wish to dominate, to win prestige, and to acquire wealth—all three of course go together in our culture—is not necessarily neurotic. The feeling of power in a normal person may be based on superior physical strength, ability, mental capacity, and so on. The striving for power may also be connected with a cause: family, native land, a religious or scientific idea. But the neurotic striving for power springs from anxiety, hatred, and feelings of inferiority. He feels that by having power no one can hurt him.

A cultural factor also enters into the picture. In our culture the striving for power and possessions is applauded, highly prized, and in various ways carefully nurtured—at least among certain groups. But among the Pueblo Indians there is little difference in individual possessions, and the striving for prestige is actively discouraged. Hence, in such a culture power and possessions would be of little use to the neurotic in his struggle to allay anxiety.

The power-driven neurotic is constantly preoccupied with inflating his ego—everything else is secondary—in order to protect himself from unbearable feelings of insignificance and helplessness. The striving for power manifests itself in numerous ways. A power-driven person wants to be right all the time, to have his own way in almost any situation, to control people and things, never to give in even when he is wrong; hence, he is incapable of "fifty-fifty" relationships. Since, according to Horney, love implies surrender, a power-driven neurotic will tend to have difficulties in love relationships. In fact, he will want to manipulate love relationships to serve his drive for power.

The neurotic striving for prestige takes many forms, such as lavish display of wealth, of knowledge, or of anything else. A person who craves prestige will want to know prominent people. Generally, the need to be admired will be great. In short, one who craves prestige wants to be "just wonderful."

Wherever possible the neurotic's hostility is pressed into "civilized" forms. Hostility takes the form of a tendency to domineer, to humiliate, or to deprive others. Hostility is expressed in the neurotic striving for possessions, usually as a tendency to deprive others, along with a begrudging envy of them, and a person may spend much time and energy for the sake of gaining a trivial advantage over someone. While cheating, stealing, exploiting or frustrating others, according to Horney, are not necessarily, for example, neurotic since they may be culturally patterned, for the neurotic person they are highly charged with emotion.[21] However, such a person may be consciously unaware that he deprives others. It is not surprising that frequently he will develop anxiety lest he be cheated or exploited by others.

As everyone knows, competition is an outstanding characteristic of our culture. Indeed competition is or is at least alleged to be the mainspring of our economic system. "From its economic center competition radiates into all other activities and permeates love, social relations and play." Likewise competition is said to be "an unfailing center" of neurotic conflicts.

Neurotic competitiveness in our culture differs from the "normal" in three ways. The neurotic competes even against people who are not even potential competitors, persons who do not strive for the same goal as he. The neurotic's "feeling toward life can be compared to that of a jockey in a race, for whom only one thing matters—whether he is ahead of the others."[22] But the neurotic's ambition exceeds all bounds. He is not content to outdo others; he wants to be unique and exceptional. Finally, hostility is inherent in his competitiveness. He has a blind, indiscriminate and compulsive drive to disparage others, to frustrate them, to defeat them. Such a person will even go to any length to defeat an analyst who tries to help him.

He will also fear retaliation from others. Since he has a craving to be loved as well, he finds himself in a dilemma. The dilemma cannot be escaped, however, without renouncing one aspect of it. Yet he clings, as well as he can, to both factors causing the dilemma, inordinate ambition and an inordinate need for affection. He attempts to escape in two ways, by trying to justify his drive for dominance and the grievances resulting from his failure to achieve dominance, or by checking his ambition for fear of envy of others. His efforts have many further ramifications which we cannot go into; but the net result is inevitable disappointment and frustration. He is a prey to tormenting inner conflict.

"Thus the conflict situation of the neurotic person derives from a frantic and compulsive wish to be the first in the race, and at the same time an equally great compulsion to check himself as soon as he gets well started or makes any progress. If he has done something successfully he is bound to do it poorly the next time. A good lesson is followed by a bad lesson, an improvement during treatment by a relapse, a good impression on people by a bad one. This sequence keeps recurring and gives him the feeling that he is waging a hopeless fight against overwhelming odds. He is like Penelope, who unravelled every night what she had woven during the day."[23]

Neurotic Submissiveness

Submissiveness can be manifested toward a particular institution or person or in a general compliance with the "potential wishes" of everyone and an avoidance of anything that might arouse resentment. In the former case people accept the authority of standardized traditional views or that of a powerful person. In the latter case, "the individual represses all demands of his own, represses criticism of others, is willing to let himself be abused without defending himself and is ready to be indiscriminately helpful to others."[24] In both cases people believe that by submitting they will not be hurt or sometimes that they will get affection from people to whom they submit.

Neurotic Withdrawal

Finally, one may seek protection and relief from anxiety by achieving independence of others in regard to external and internal needs. One may amass wordly goods and become emotionally detached from people for this purpose. He feels that if he withdraws nothing can hurt him.

Secondary Satisfaction

According to Horney, any one of the four ways discussed can be effective in bringing reassurance if circumstances are favorable and if conflicts do not arise. They furnish a "secondary satisfaction." Thus a submissive woman may find a great deal of secondary satisfaction in obedience to her husband, when her culture favors such obedience. As a rule people will seek reassurance in several ways. But any and all of the four devices entail an impoverishment of the entire personality.

Culture and Neurosis

In her second book, *New Ways in Psychoanalysis*, Horney undertakes an important critical re-evaluation of Freudian theory. But except for special points, this aspect of her work exceeds our purposes here. Summarily, she agrees with Fromm that "particular needs which are relevant to understanding the personality and its difficulties are not instinctual in character but are created by the entirety of conditions under which we live."[25] It is the conflicting trends in the personality, developed for reasons which we discussed above, that constitute or determine neuroses.

The Oedipus Complex

Fixations on the parents, she believes, do not arise for biological reasons. The fixations, the attachment of the boy to the mother, of the girl to the father, arise from describable conditions in the family relationships. There are said to be two main series of conditions. The first is sexual stimulation by the parents. The sexual stimulation may consist of a "gross sexual approach," sexually-tinged caresses, or "an emotional hothouse atmosphere" surrounding all or only some of the members of the family; certain children may be singled out, while the others may be regarded with animosity by the parents.

The second series of conditions springs from anxiety. For reasons we discussed above, some children grow in a highly unfavorable psychological family set-up, resulting in a conflict between dependency on the parents and hostile impulses against them. This arouses anxiety, often compelling the child to cling to one of the parents if there is thus a possibility of receiving reassurance. This clinging to the parent is not love. It may or may not have a "sexual coloring," but the sexual element is not essential to it.

In the case of sexual stimulation the attachment of the child goes to the parent who elicits love or sexual desires. In the second case, the attachment usually goes to the more powerful or more awesome parent, since the winning of his affection promises more protection. The goal of the child in the former instance is love; in the latter, mainly security. In her experience, Horney says, the vast majority of the attachments of neurotics in childhood were of the second kind. A girl who in childhood was attached to a domineering mother manifests a similar attitude toward her husband.

The attachment to the parents in both cases is not a biologically given phenomenon "but a response to provocations from the outside." Although Horney is inclined to think there is no good reason why a child should not have sexual leanings toward the parents and siblings, she doubts that they reach an intensity sufficient to meet Freud's description of the Oedipus complex. The important point is that early relationships in their totality mold the character. The classic formulation of Freud can have dangerous consequences. While it has helped to make parents conscious of the lasting harm to children by exciting them sexually, by being over-indulgent or too prohibitive in sexual matters, it has fostered the illusion that it is enough to enlighten their children about sex, for example, or to refrain from whipping them, from forbidding masturbation, or from attaching them too strongly to the parents. The danger is that the most important things will be overlooked: a real interest and respect for the child, the necessity for real warmth, reliability and sincerity by the parents.

FEMININE PSYCHOLOGY

Unless one is bemused by theoretical preconceptions, a reading of Freud's comments and theories concerning women will raise doubts as to his understanding of feminine psychology.[26] Horney discusses the views of one psychoanalyst, Helene Deutsch, who seems to have outdone Freud. Deutsch believes "that what woman ultimately wants in intercourse is to be raped and violated; what she wants in mental life is to be humiliated; menstruation is significant to the woman because it feeds masochistic fantasies; childbirth represents the climax of masochistic satisfaction." Motherhood is a long-drawn-out masochistic gratification. Unless, Deutsch believes, women are or feel that they are being raped, injured or humiliated in intercourse, they are likely to be frigid.[27]

The work of recent women psychoanalysts, including Horney and Clara Thompson, nevertheless is likely to increase one's skepticism as to such views. Furthermore, theoretical preconceptions have, of course, important consequences for therapy. The theory of penis-envy in women offers a good example of this. Patients quite naturally seize upon comparatively harmless and simple solutions of their problems in order to avoid the pain of facing their inadequacies and the need to change. "It is so much easier for a woman to think that she is nasty to her husband because, unfortunately, she was born without a penis and envies him for having one than to think, for instance, that she has developed an attitude of righteousness and infallibility which makes it impossible to tolerate any questioning or disagreement. It is so much easier for a patient to think that nature has given her an unfair deal than to realize that she actually makes excessive demands on the environment and is furious whenever they are not complied with."[28]

Acording to Horney, specific cultural conditions engender specific qualities and faculties in both men and women. The wish to have a penis, that is, to be a man, may express a desire (often a yearning desire) to have those qualities which we in our culture regard as masculine: strength, courage, independence, success, sexual freedom, the right to choose a partner. Neurotic women also tend to base their inferiority feelings on the fact that they are women, a less-privileged group, than on the more direct and specific interpersonal relations which engender feelings of inferiority. Again, the wish to be a man may be a disguise for repressed ambition— in neurotics of both sexes an ambition perhaps so destructive that it provokes anxiety and has to be repressed. Then the repressed ambition will often take culturally permissible forms of expression. Masochistic trends in men and women primarily signify an emotional dependence on others.

However, women in our culture for centuries have been deprived of great economic and political responsibilities and kept to a private emotional sphere, the family and home. Hence, they have had to rely on love, for example, as the only value that counts in life, a situation which makes them especially vulnerable to the vicissitudes of life in our culture.

Nevertheless, the obsession with love and love relationships, Horney claims, has nothing to do with femininity or masculinity. It is a neurotic phenomenon.

NARCISSISM

For Horney, narcissism primarily means not self-love nor self-admiration, as the Freudians believe, but self-inflation.

"It means that the person loves and admires himself for values for which there is no adequate foundation." Such a person expects love and admiration from others, in Horney's meaning of the term, for spurious reasons, for qualities he does not have, or not to the degree he believes he has. To value a quality in oneself which one has, or to want to be valued by others for such a quality, she says, is not narcissistic. She does not think, with Freud, that narcissism is an instinctive development; she thinks it is a neurotic trend.

An unfavorable environment such as we discussed above produces a narcissistic trend. A derogatory attitude, preference for other siblings, and so on combine to render the child weak and dependent. Being exploited as a child by the parents to serve their own neurotic needs, he becomes alienated from others. His emotional relationships become thin and he loses the capacity to love. If a child does not experience love and respect, he cannot develop those qualities in himself. He loves neither himself nor others. Parents make the child feel that to be accepted or liked he must be as others expect him to be. Consequently, he cannot develop his own will, his own likes and dislikes, his own self.

Such a person has to "aggrandize" himself, fancy he is something outstanding, in order to escape an unbearable feeling of nothingness. He may in phantasy think of himself as a genius or a prince, or quite inarticulately feel that he is significant beyond compare. These false notions serve as a substitute for the genuine sense of self of which he was deprived. The more alienated from others he becomes, the more of "psychic reality" his phantasies acquire. In this way he consoles himself for not being loved and appreciated. He is too superior to others for them to love and appreciate him.

Perhaps, Horney suggests, these secret substitute satisfactions save him from being entirely overwhelmed by his fundamental feeling of isolation and littleness. But, as in all other neurotic trends, he develops neurotic needs which cause

him no end of difficulties, such as the need for unlimited
admiration as a substitute for love.[29]

CONCEPT OF A BASIC CONFLICT

It is not possible, short of an entire book, to discuss all
of the neurotic trends described by Horney and their ramifications and consequences. So we shall restrict ourselves to an
exposition of the main points in her more recent theories. The
newer theories, except for a few points, seem to be in the main
a reworking and refinement of ideas put forth in *The Neurotic
Personality of Our Time* and *New Ways in Psychoanalysis*.

Certain neurotic trends combine to reenforce one another
and to determine a basic attitude towards the self, toward
others and a philosophy of life. One grouping of trends is
said to combine to form an attitude of "moving toward
people." Another results in an attitude of "moving away from
people," and a third, in an attitude of "moving against
people." But these three incompatible attitudes will be found
in the same person although one will usually predominate.
The existence of three incompatible attitudes sets up what
Horney calls a "basic conflict" in the personality. This makes
for ever-increasing difficulty in living. "Because of his fear of
being split apart on the one hand and the necessity to function
as a unity on the other, the neurotic makes desperate attempts
at solution. While he can succeed in this way in creating a
kind of artificial equilibrium, new conflicts are constantly
generated and further remedies are continually required to
blot them out. Every step in this struggle for unity makes the
neurotic more hostile, more helpless, more fearful, more alienated from himself and others, with the result that the difficulties responsible for the conflicts become more acute and their
real resolution less and less attainable. He finally becomes
hopeless and may try to find a kind of restitution in sadistic
pursuits, which in turn have the effect of increasing his hope-
lessness and creating new conflicts."[30]

While Freud believed there is a "basic conflict" between life and death instincts, which is universal and ultimately insoluble, Horney's theory differs. She does not believe that a basic neurotic conflict need arise when proper environmental conditions exist, and that when it does occur, it is, in principle, capable of resolution.

The basic conflict, in Horney's sense, stems from the basic anxiety. In attempting to cope with the pathogenic factors in his world, the child develops permanent character trends which, for reasons we have indicated, Horney calls neurotic trends. In trying to "move" in his environment, the child can move toward people, against them, or away from them. If, despite fears and estrangements, he moves toward people, he accepts his own helplessness and develops an attitude of dependency, perhaps upon one or more of the more powerful members of the family. He becomes compliant; but in this way he attains a feeling of psychological support and belonging. The child may also accept and take for granted the hostility around him, and, whether consciously or not, determine to fight. Partly for his own protection, partly for revenge, he wants to defeat those around him. Hence, he becomes rebellious and moves against people. The third possibility is to keep apart, to move away from people. Such behavior is based on the fact that the child feels he does not have much in common with others, and that they do not understand him. And so, in a manner of speaking, he creates and lives in a world of his own: nature, books, day-dreams, music.

But, psychologically speaking, these three modes of coping with the environment are not mutually exclusive. The child cannot wholeheartedly accept any one of them—he is much too helpless in a realistic sense to take such a stand. Elements of all three will be found: exaggerated helplessness, hostility, and isolation. He will oscillate between them. As he develops, however, one of them usually becomes manifestly predominant.

Barring the intervention of mitigating circumstances, such as the devotion of a relative, these trends develop into an inflexible pattern.

In the adult neurotic, these three incompatible modes of behavior and experience generate conflict. He has to maintain some kind of "equilibrium," and the various trends clash and make for tormenting conflicts. The conflicts springing from these incompatible attitudes and modes of behavior are said to constitute the core of neurosis and are therefore called basic.

THE COMPLIANT TYPE OF PERSONALITY

In order to avoid repetition, we shall not discuss the three basic life-attitudes in any detail. Since the various trends are found in the same person and interrelated, a discussion of any one trend necessarily involves some—if the analysis is pushed far enough, all—of the other trends. When an attitude of moving toward people is manifest, such a person may be called the compliant type. He shows a marked need for affection and approval and a "partner" on whom he can lean, an inability to stand alone, a tendency to subordinate himself, to feel weak and helpless, to feel that others are stronger, superior, more attractive, to rate himself by others' standards and attitudes. Yet strong aggressive drives exist but are repressed in order to preserve his sense of unity, for example, and to avoid the possibility of hostility from others.[31] Hence, he cannot really love others.

THE AGGRESSIVE TYPE

Those who move against people, the aggressive type, take it for granted that everyone is hostile. Life is a bitter struggle against others. Therefore, the primary need of the aggressive person is to control others. While the particular kind of control he will try to exercise depends in part on native gifts, in part on his conflicting trends, control people he will by hook or crook if he possibly can manage it. He will endeavor to excel others in any way, to outsmart them, and to belittle them. Everything is viewed in the light of what he can get out of it. He tries to be a good fighter; he is "realistic" within certain limits, often efficient and capable. Since he regards affection, sympathy, all the "softer" feelings as weak or ridiculous, he will fight them in himself or repress them.[32]

THE DETACHED TYPE

People who manifest the need to move away from others are called detached. They have a compelling inner need to put "emotional distance" between themselves and other people. They do not want to get involved in any way with others. Closeness arouses unbearable anxiety. Consequently, they tend to have a compelling need to be self-sufficient. In order to accomplish this, such a type will struggle to be resourceful or, if necessary, to restrict his needs. Quite in contrast to the compliant type, he has a considerable need for privacy. He dislikes sharing experiences, and he is very sensitive to anything that may resemble coercion, influence, obligation. Although all neurotics have a need to feel superior, his is intense. He must at least feel very strong or uniquely significant in order to bear isolation. If his feeling of superiority is temporarily shattered, he may be unable to bear isolation and become compliant.

The detached person tends to suppress all feeling for people but not necessarily for other things, although if he is capable of deep and passionate emotion he may have to suppress it in all areas of life in order to keep it out of his relationships with people. Sexual relationships can sometimes be enjoyable if they are transitory. In other cases they may not be possible. Any desire or interest may constitute a threat of dependency.

The detached person is no automaton. He refuses to concur blindly with the majority, and in this way he preserves some integrity—even against the corrosive force of a neurosis. His detachment may allow him, if he is talented, to achieve some degree of original thinking and feeling. Such factors, combined with a contemplative attitude, may, in some circumstances, contribute toward the development and expression of creative abilities.

However, the detached person's condition is not enviable. In a difficult situation he "can neither appease nor fight, neither cooperate nor dictate terms, neither love nor be ruthless. He is as defenseless as an animal that has only one means of coping with danger—that is, to escape and hide."[33]

All other neurotic trends are said to constitute attempts to deal with life "in a positive way." But detachment renders one so helpless that eventually defensive measures become uppermost. A threat to detachment may in certain circumstances result in a disintegration of personality in psychotic episodes.

In the life history of the detached type contradictory strivings occur. Periods of compliance will alternate with periods of aggressiveness. Detachment is a defense which people develop against the two more active partners in the basic conflict. Detachment has the all-important function of keeping major conflicts out of operation. But the compulsive cravings for affection and for aggressive domination remain, though repressed, to harass one. Hence, as long as these two contradictory trends exist, no real peace or freedom is possible.

Four Attempts at Solution

In Horney's latest formulation, there are said to be four major attempts at solution of conflict. They are: 1) to "eclipse" part of the conflict and give its opposite predominance; 2) to "move away from" people; 3) to move away from oneself (idealized image); 4) to effect a still more radical divorce (externalization). There are others which are said to be of less significance, some of which we have discussed.

It appears that in regard to (1) the conflict is between the three attitudes which we have discussed. Yet Horney lists "moving away from" people as the second attempt at solution, apparently implying that there is a difference between this and the basic neurotic trends to withdraw. While there is a similarity, the second major attempt at solution is practiced in order to avoid the danger of becoming aware of inner feelings.[34]

We shall go on to discuss the other two major attempts at solution of conflict.

THE IDEALIZED IMAGE

Another attempt to solve or rather deny the existence of conflicts is represented by the idealized image. In order to preserve a feeling of unity in himself by which he can function, regardless of the cost, a person creates an "image" which, though deceptive, he believes is really he or which he feels he can or ought to be. This image is largely, though not entirely, unreal. An example of this which Horney offers is that of the large middle aged woman who, peering into the mirror, sees herself as a slender young girl. The kind of image a person has will depend on the structure of his personality. One will have an image of himself as a master mind, a genius; another as a saint; and still another as a Casanova. To the degree to which the image is unrealistic it makes one arrogant; one arrogates to oneself qualities that one does not have or has only potentially. The more unrealistic the image is, the more vulnerable a person is and in need of affirmation and recognition. Essentially the neurotic is unaware that he is idealizing himself. For him the image has the "value of reality."

It serves as a substitute for the genuine self-confidence
and pride which he lacks, as an illusory kind of fulfillment of
the need to feel superior, and as an obligating power or ideal
which saves him from feeling lost in the world, as a guide or
purpose in life, and as a facade to hide his inner conflicts. In
the latter case, a compliant person, for example, has an image
of himself as a loving and generous person. He can thus hide
his aggressiveness from himself. Finally it reconciles opposing
trends. The detached person, for example, becomes in his own
eyes a wise leader who meets out a stern but just discipline,
while he himself remains aloof.

Like all neurotic trends, the idealized image has serious
drawbacks. The worst drawback probably is that it alienates
him from his real self. Furthermore, it makes it all the more
difficult for him to accept himself as he factually is. Since he
has put himself on a pedestal, the contrast becomes all the
greater. The idealized image comes into being because he cannot tolerate himself as he really is. Now the image makes
the actuality all the more unbearable. And so he rages against
himself and despises himself. A new conflict is thus created. As
a result of the intensified conflict, he may become narcissistic,
or perfectionistic, or erratic, irresponsible and negativistic.

EXTERNALIZATION

When the idealized image technique fails, resort may be
had to what Horney calls externalization. Internal psychological processes may be experienced "as if they occurred outside oneself." As a rule also external factors are presumed to
cause one's difficulties. In this way one runs away, so to speak,
from oneself. Externalization is in part projection, but it is
more. Not only are one's faults but also to some degree all
one's feelings experienced "in others." Such a person is said
to be unaware of his own attitudes toward himself. For
example, he will "feel that some one else is angry with him

when actually he is angry with himself." Or he may be aware of anger at others when actually he directs it at himself.[35] Such a person may be profoundly disturbed at the oppression of small countries and unaware of his own sense of oppression. He pays for this process of externalization by a sense of shallowness and emptiness and by overdependence on external circumstances. While inner conflicts are removed from awareness, external ones take their place, since the outside world is held responsible for one's troubles, and he becomes more reproachful, vindictive and fearful in respect to others. His original conflict between himself and the world becomes exaggerated.

CONCLUDING REMARKS

There is a final point to be mentioned. Horney, like Fromm, claims that moral problems play an important role in neurosis.[36] This is a very significant advance over older ideas.

Horney, like some other recent writers on psychoanalysis, is more optimistic than Freud in regard to man's nature and destiny. "Freud's pessimism as regards neuroses and their treatment arose from the depths of his disbelief in human goodness and human growth. Man, he postulated, is doomed to suffer or to destroy. The instincts which drive him can only be controlled, or at best 'sublimated.' My own belief is that man has the capacity as well as the desire to develop his potentialities and become a decent human being, and that these deteriorate if his relationship to others and hence to himself is, and continues to be, disturbed. I believe that man can change and go on changing as long as he lives. And this belief has grown with deeper understanding."[37]

9. THE THEORIES OF ERICH FROMM

In the last fifty years there has been a tremendous growth in our knowledge of anthropology and sociology. One of the handicaps under which Freud labored in his earlier years was a lack of this knowledge. Since the 1880's and 1890's when Freud began to make his great discoveries and observations concerning the psychology of man, students of the social sciences at home and abroad have amassed a vast amount of material from every part of the world concerning man's nature and behavior. To be sure, Freud, Jung and Rank made use of a good deal of anthropological data acquired earlier but not a little of their work is marred by hasty interpretations based on inadequate or insufficient material. But the years have brought more cautiousness to psychoanalysis. The earlier exuberance has been replaced by a more careful, more precise formulation of theory based on much more empirical knowledge. Among those who apply contemporary knowledge of sociology and anthropology to psychoanalysis are Fromm, Kardiner,[1] Horney and H. S. Sullivan.

With the publication of *Escape from Freedom* Erich Fromm immediately became, in the judgment of many people, one of the foremost thinkers in psychoanalysis. In this work he asserts that Freud and most of his disciples had only a very naive notion of what goes on in society and that most of his applications of psychology to social problems were misleading constructions.

"Freud went further," he says, "than anybody before him in directing attention to the observation and analysis of the irrational and unconscious forces which determine parts of human behavior. He and his followers in modern psychology not only uncovered the irrational and unconscious sector of man's nature, the existence of which had been neglected by modern rationalism; he also showed that these irrational phenomena followed certain laws and therefore could be understood rationally. He taught us to understand the language of dreams and somatic symptoms as well as the irrationalities in human behavior. He discovered that these irrationalities as well as the whole character structure of an individual were reactions to the influences exercised by the outside world and particularly by those occurring in early childhood."[2]

Yet Freud, like every one else, even a genius, was so imbued with the spirit of his culture that he could not transcend certain limits set by that culture. As the earth carries the atmosphere around with it, all of us carry within us the virtues and limitations of our culture, by means of which, as it were, we live and breathe. Hence, the limitations of Freud's culture circumscribed his understanding of the sick individual as well as the "normal" one; they also handicapped his understanding of the irrational phenomena which operate in society.

Fromm goes on to press his analysis of Freud into the details of the latter's theories:

"Freud accepted the traditional belief in a basic dichotomy between man and society, as well as the traditional doctrine of the evilness of human nature. Man, to him, is fundamentally antisocial. Society must domesticate him, must allow some direct satisfaction of biological—and hence, ineradicable—drives; but for the most part society must refine

and adroitly check man's basic impulses. In consequence of
this suppression of natural impulses by society something
miraculous happens: the suppressed drives turn into strivings
that are culturally valuable and thus become the basis for
culture. Freud chose the word sublimation for this strange
transformation from suppression into civilized behavior. If
the amount of suppression is greater than the capacity for
sublimation, individuals become neurotic and it is necessary
to allow the lessening of suppression. Generally, however,
there is a reverse relation between satisfaction of man's drives
and culture: the more suppression the more culture (and the
more danger of neurotic disturbances). The relation of the
individual to society in Freud's theory is essentially a static
one: the individual remains virtually the same and becomes
changed only in so far as society exercises greater pressure
on his natural drives (and thus enforces more sublimation)
or allows more satisfaction (and thus sacrifices culture)."[3]

The founder of psychoanalysis erected a conception of
human nature on the basis of the most important drives he
discovered operating in modern Western man. For him the
individual of his culture represented "man," that is, mankind,
and he thought that the passions and anxieties of people in
his culture were eternal forces rooted in the biological constitution of man.

THE CONCEPT OF INSTINCT

Fromm proceeds to lay the basis for his own theories by
a clarification of the concept of instinct. If by instinct one
means a physiologically determined need or urge like hunger,
thirst, sex, then there can be no quarrel with such a notion,
for, of course, man has such biological needs. However, the
form of expression and satisfaction of these needs is culturally
determined. And this form of expression and satisfaction varies
enormously throughout the world. But when people talk about

instincts, they often confuse a specific action pattern determined by inherited neurological structures, such as is found
in the animal kingdom, with biological needs; the latter in
the human being do *not* have specific, fixed, inherited action
patterns by which they are satisfied. Such a confusion has
enormous theoretical and practical consequences which we
cannot enter into here. Fromm is careful to point out that
the higher we go in the scale of animal development, the less
completeness of structural development do we find at birth.
With human beings the lack of structural adjustment at birth
is at a maximum. And he quotes another writer (L. Bernard)
to the effect that instinct is a diminishing if not a disappear-
ing category in higher animals—especially in human beings.
This means that man's adaptation to nature is based essentially on the process of learning, on culture, not on instinct.

THE KEY PROBLEM OF PSYCHOLOGY, RELATEDNESS

Hence the key problem of psychology for Fromm is *the
specific kind of relatedness of the individual towards the world
and to himself.* This relatedness is acquired in the process
of human learning, human acculturation. To be sure, he says,
man has certain fundamental needs, which have to be satisfied, but the significant problems of psychology are located
elsewhere: in the relationship of man to his world. And this
relationship is not fixed. To say or imply that the fundamental problem of human psychology lies in the problem of
the satisfaction or frustration of instinctual needs and drives
is to oversimplify matters enormously. For the very fact of
human learning generates new needs and problems as imperative—or even more so—than the needs of hunger and thirst.
In a world that is not fixed, static but ever changing and
dynamic, new problems and possibilities arise.

Fromm has put this so well that we quote his own words.
"It is not as if we had on the one hand an individual equipped

by nature with certain drives and on the other, society as something apart from him, either satisfying or frustrating these innate propensities. Although there are certain needs, such as hunger, thirst, sex, which are common to man, those drives which make for the *differences* in men's characters, like love and hatred, the lust for power and the yearning for submission, the enjoyment of sensuous pleasure and the fear of it, are all products of the social process. The most beautiful as well as the most ugly inclinations of man are not a part of a fixed and biologically given human nature, but result from the social process which creates man. In other words, society has not only a suppressing function—although it has that too—but it has also a creative function. Man's nature, his passions, and anxieties are a cultural product; as a matter of fact, man himself is the most important creation and achievement of the continuous human effort, the record of which we call history."[4]

The animal lives in an harmonious relation with its world, not in the sense that it does not have to make any effort in order to survive, but in the sense that its inherited instinctual equipment makes it a fixed and unchanging part of its world. The emergence of man from the purely animal state has brought with it new qualities which distinguish him from the animal. These qualities include "his awareness of himself as a separate entity [from the rest of nature], his ability to remember the past, to visualize the future, and to denote objects and acts by symbols; his reason to conceive and understand the world; and his imagination through which he reaches far beyond the range of his senses." Although he is the most helpless of all beings at birth, his biological weakness thus becomes the prime cause for the development of his specifically human qualities.

Since man is not a fixed, unchanging part of his world like an animal, reason, imagination and self-awareness, which he has developed in the place of relatively unchanging action patterns by which the animal is adjusted to its world, have concomitantly and further disrupted man's harmonious adjustment with the rest of nature. He has become an anomaly, "a freak of the universe." "He is part of nature, subject to her physical laws and unable to change them, yet he transcends the rest of nature. He is set apart while being a part; he is homeless, yet chained to the home he shares with all creatures. Cast into this world at an accidental place and time, he is forced out of it, again accidentally. Being aware of himself, he realizes his powerlessness and the limitations of his existence. He visualizes his own end: death. Never is he free from the dichotomy of his existence: he cannot rid himself of his mind, even if he should want to; he cannot rid himself of his body as long as he is alive—and his body makes him want to be alive."[5]

Thus the conditions of human life—being a part of nature, yet transcending the rest of it, "homeless," yet chained to this natural world, longing for immortality, yet condemned to death, possessing a rational mind which tells him of his brief hour and a body that makes him want to be alive, a craving for oneness with the world and a self-awareness which sets him apart—such conditions constitute incompatibilities which Fromm calls existential dichotomies because they spring from the nature of human existence. These conditions cannot be eradicated but man must face them. He cannot return to the prehuman state of animal existence in which reason, self-awareness, and imagination do not exist to remind him of his powerlessness, aloneness, and mortality. Thus the human situation impels man everlastingly to strive for a solution to these incompatible conditions of life. Reason, which is his blessing, is also his curse. Human history is a record of the struggle to overcome, or at least to come to satisfying terms with, the incompatible conditions of human existence. This is in part also what Fromm means by saying that the relationship of man to his world is not static but dynamic. As humanity strives to solve some of the basic "contradictions" or incompatibilities of human existence, new problems are generated. No final solutions are reached. Reason is constantly reminding man of his failures, of his powerlessness, of his aloneness in a world indifferent to his fate. And this is intolerable. Hence, man cannot rest; he must struggle to overcome or somehow find a way to make these tormenting conditions bearable. "The dynamism of his history is intrinsic to the existence of reason which causes him to develop and, through it, to create a world of his own in which he can feel at home with himself and his fellow men. Every stage he reaches leaves him discontented and perplexed, and this very perplexity urges him to move toward new solutions."[6]

Although there is no innate drive for progress, man must proceed on the way he set out—a road that leads farther away from animal existence—toward another kind of harmony with nature, his fellows and himself. One way by which he has attempted to negate or deny his fate is by creating religions which promise an eternal life in the hereafter. Another is by attaining ever increasing knowledge and understanding, by which he can control or at least modify some of the conditions of his life and make it more bearable and satisfying, and by which, comprehending the conditions of human life, he attains a sense of community and relatedness with all men who share the same fate.

EXISTENTIAL AND HISTORICAL DICHOTOMIES

Fromm makes a distinction between existential and historical dichotomies. Life versus death is the most fundamental existential dichotomy. Another existential dichotomy results from the fact that man lives for only a brief period in the historical process. The limitations of any historical period become his limitations. By and large, the realization of human potentialities cannot exceed the limits of the culture which is reached at any given time. Only if the life span were identical with the entire historical process could one realize his potentialities to the fullest. And of this fact man has at least a dim perception.

The conditions which generate existential dichotomies cannot be changed. Death is unalterable, and all life is limited to a small sector of space and time. No power of reason, no magic of rite and ceremony can alter these facts. But there are other incompatibilities in human life which are not eternal and unchangeable. These are "historical dichotomies" which can be overcome, given intelligence and courage, either at the time they occur or at a later historical period. The contemporary abundance in our world of material and technological resources and our inability to use it for peace and general welfare are incongruous facts. Fromm adds that those who benefit from historical dichotomies strive to convince mankind that they are an unavoidable and ineradicable part of human existence, that they are existential dichotomies.

Now, according to Fromm, one of the peculiar qualities of the human mind is that when confronted with incongruities, incompatibilities and contradictions, it cannot remain passive. It must try to resolve them. All human progress, he says, is due to this. If man is to be prevented from reacting to the awareness of contradictions by action, they must be denied. In individual life rationalization (more or less plausible but spurious reasoning and explaining) serves this function. In society, "ideologies"(socially patterned rationalizations) have the same function. A widespread acceptance of ideologies or the say-so of authority will persuade people to accept them; their minds become appeased, though not entirely set at rest.

Historical dichotomies can be eradicated given courage and wisdom, but existential dichotomies cannot. People may deaden and appease their minds with soothing ideologies which, for example, may stifle their fear of death, but unconsciously (and often consciously) they remain restless, dissatisfied and anxious. It is pretty difficult to explain death away—or starvation in a land of plenty. Eventually man must face the truth about himself; it is the only genuine solution. He must recognize his aloneness in a universe indifferent to his fate.

THE HUMAN SITUATION

Fromm's attitude and outlook in this problem of the human situation is uncompromising. The only meaning life has is what the individual gives it by the unfolding and realizing of his powers of reason, love, and productive work. This unfolding and realizing of man's powers constitutes the basis of man's happiness and salvation.

In contrast to Freud, Fromm believes, in accordance with the ideas we have discussed, that a large part of man's strivings cannot be explained by the force of his instincts. When man's needs for food and drink and sex are satisfied, then, says Fromm, his most compelling problems *begin.* "He strives for power, or for love, or for destruction, he risks his life for religious, for political, for humanistic ideals, and these strivings are what constitutes and characterizes the peculiarity of human life."[7]

Since the disharmony of man's existence with the rest of nature generates needs which far transcend those of his animal origin, such as an imperative drive to restore a unity and equilibrium between himself and the rest of nature, he has to erect a mental reference-frame, an orientation, from which he can derive an answer to the question of where he stands and what he ought to do. Having a body as well as a mind, he must also create this reference-frame to contain answers and solutions to every aspect of his existence, not only in thinking, but in his feelings and actions. Such a system attempts to give an answer to the human quest for meaning. And Fromm calls such a system a frame of orientation and devotion. The need for such a system is common to all men. Some find it in organized religion, others in systems whose contents are secular although they fulfill the same fundamental need: to be significantly related to the world, to oneself and one's fellow men.

While Freud explained religion as a form of neurosis, Fromm maintains that neurosis is a form of religion (a frame of orientation and devotion) which differs mainly from organized religion by its individual, non-socially-patterned characteristics. For Fromm this need for a frame of orientation and devotion is the most fundamental and all-inclusive need of mankind. And this concept is the key to understand Fromm's thought.

Since frames of orientation and devotion differ in content, by what criterion can we judge them? By their truth, by the extent to which they further the development of man's powers of reason, love, productive work, etc., and by the degree to which they offer a genuine solution to man's need for equilibrium and harmony in his world.

THE GROWTH OF INDIVIDUALITY

We now can go on to discuss in more detail the problems and possibilities of mankind which have arisen from its emergence from a pre-human existence. We have pointed out that the history of man began with his emerging from a state of oneness with the rest of nature to an awareness of himself as a separate entity. But this awareness came about very gradually. It remained dim over long periods of history. Man remained closely tied to the natural and social world in which he lived. For a long period of history he was only partly aware of himself as a separate being; therefore, he still felt himself to be an indissoluble part of the rest of nature. But the time came when man became sharply aware of his separateness and uniqueness. This process of the emergence of mankind from its original ties with nature is called by Fromm the process of individuation, which he thinks reached its peak between the Reformation and the present. The process has been described as follows:

"From the beginning of his existence man is confronted with the choice between different courses of action. In the animal there is an uninterrupted chain of reactions starting with a stimulus, like hunger, and ending with a more or less strictly determined course of action, which does away with the tension created by the stimulus. In man that chain is interrupted. The stimulus is there but the kind of satisfaction is 'open,' that is, he must choose between different courses of action. Instead of a predetermined instinctive action, man has to weigh possible courses of action in his mind; he starts to think. He changes his role toward nature from that of a purely passive adaptation to an active one: he produces. He invents tools and, while thus mastering nature, he separates himself from it more and more. He becomes dimly aware of himself—or rather of his group—as not being identical with nature. It dawns upon him that his is a tragic fate: to be part of nature, and yet to transcend it. He becomes aware of death as his ultimate fate even if he tries to deny it in manifold phantasies."[8]

Primitive religions and myths bear testimony to man's original ties to nature, what Fromm calls "primary ties," to the soil he lives on, the sun and moon and stars, the trees and flowers, animals, and the people with whom he is related by ties of blood. This feeling of identity with nature, clan, religion gives him security and a sense of belonging. He is rooted in an organized, structuralized totality, in which he has an unquestionable place. Thus, he is protected from the most awful human predicament: complete aloneness, complete isolation, and tormenting uncertainty and doubt.

But there is another side to the picture. These primary ties stand in the way of the development of his reason and his critical capacities, for he has no impelling reason to use them. The primary ties "let him recognize himself and others only through the medium of his, or their, participation in a clan, a social or religious community, and not as [self-governing] human beings; in other words, they block his development as a free, self-determining, productive individual."[9]

According to Fromm, European and American history since the end of the Middle Ages marks the full emergence of the individual. And he devotes considerable space to an analysis of this process of growing freedom—and growing isolation. Unfortunately we cannot discuss it here.

Let us sum up the process which we shall see again, or at least its analogue, in the individual. The emergence of man resulted in a process of growing strength and integration, mastery of nature, a growing power of reason, and growing solidarity with others. But the process of increasing individuation also meant growing isolation, insecurity, and doubt concerning one's role in the world. Doubt arose as to the meaning of one's life, and an increasing sense of one's own powerlessness and insignificance. In other words, Fromm, borrowing from Hegelian philosophy, says that the process of individuation has a "dialectical" or dichotomous character.

In the history of the individual, a similar or at least analogous process is to be found. The beginning of individual human existence occurs with physical separation from the mother, a condition analogous to that of the emergence of man from the animal state of instinctual adaptation. Yet the child remains functionally one with the mother or her surrogate for some time, for he is fed and cared for in every vital respect by her. Gradually the child becomes aware of himself as an entity separate from the mother and other objects. By means of his own developing equipment, activity, and education, the child begins to experience a world outside himself and to make distinctions. The process of education, involving frustration and prohibition, especially sharpens the child's awareness of the difference between the "I" and the "Thou," between the developing self and others. The growing self-awareness of the child is analogous to the growing self-awareness of mankind.

A very important point needs to be noted here. Education necessarily involves some frustration and prohibition. It is the kind of frustration and prohibition and especially the attitude of the mother or nurse which are all-important. If the mother is a loving person, no real damage to the child's developing personality will occur. Short of being an imbecile, a loving mother will "instinctively" do the right thing, at least within certain limits ordained by the culture. Growing up in an atmosphere of self-respect and love, the child will "naturally" develop into a self-respecting, healthy human being with respect and regard for others.

The hateful, destructive, or "overprotective" mothers and fathers are the ones who do the damage. "It is the thwarting of expansiveness, the breaking of the child's attempt to assert himself, the hostility radiating from parents—in short, the atmosphere of suppression which create in the child the feeling of powerlessness and the hostility springing from it."[10]

And so the child gradually develops his capacities within the limits ordained by the culture, family, and native constitution. More and more he becomes aware of himself as a separate being, different from others. From growing experience he learns something of his powers and how to use them. New possibilities of experience continually occur. For the healthy child, at any rate, the world is a strange and fascinating place in which to exercise his powers. The various spheres of his being, physical, mental, emotional become more and more integrated. An organized and integrated structure, the self, develops. Given fortunate circumstances, he becomes an individualized person, his personality guided by reason and will. The dependency on the parents is shed, as it were, layer by layer, until as an adult the person becomes a free, self-governing being.

But here, too, alas! there is another side to the picture. The primary ties, the feelings of oneness and dependency on the parents and others, give the child a sense of security and belonging. The process of growth and individualization destroy this kind of security and sense of belonging. As the child emerges from a state of un-self-conscious unity with his milieu, he becomes aware of being alone, of being an entity separate from all others. "This separation from a world, which in comparison with one's own individual existence is overwhelmingly strong and powerful, and often threatening and dangerous, creates a feeling of powerlessness and anxiety. As long as one was an integral part of that world, unaware of the possibilities and responsibilities of individual action, one did not need to be afraid of it. When one has become an individual, one stands alone and faces the world in all its perilous and overpowering aspects."[11] The more the child has experienced hostility, the more his developing capacities have been blocked, the more he has been deprived of self-confidence and self-respect, the more difficult will this problem of a threatened isolation be. For many it will be a tormenting, agonizing prospect and a problem they will never solve. On the other hand, those children who are reared in healthy surroundings will have far less of a problem and, having greater inner strength, they will tend toward a more genuine solution.

As a result of this threat of unbearable isolation and powerlessness, impulses to abandon one's individuality, one's state of being a self-governing entity, by completely submerging oneself in the world outside arise. We shall study some of these forms of escape, but we can now say that the submersion of oneself in something or someone else can never be identical with one's primary ties. The process of individuation cannot be reversed. The only adequate solution, according to Fromm, is a relationship with man and nature, chiefly by love and productive work, which strengthens the total personality, sustains the person in his sense of uniqueness, and at the same time gives him a feeling of belonging, a sense of unity and common destiny with mankind.

Were every degree of progress of the child toward separation and individuation marked by a corresponding growth of self, his development would be harmonious, without anxiety and fear of aloneness and powerlessness. But this does not happen for various reasons, such as an unhealthy, that is, a hostile and anxiety-laden family situation, or because of irrational, pathogenic factors in society, which are communicated to the child by the family, school or church. There is, therefore, a lag between increasing individuation and the progress of self security. This, in turn, leads to the development of various mechanisms of escape, some but not all of which are often labeled as "neurotic."

An analogous problem arose in connection with the development of mankind or at least a large section of it. Due to certain economic, social, and political conditions, which Fromm discusses, there has also been a lag in phylogenetic development. Here, too, there has been an imbalance in man's growth toward self-strength and security. And since the family is the "psychic agency" of society, this lag is, as we indicated above, conveyed to the child.

MECHANISMS OF ESCAPE

We shall now indicate the various "psychic mechanisms" by which the person attempts to escape unbearable feelings of aloneness and powerlessness due to pathogenic conditions in his familial and social worlds. These mechanisms are (moral) masochism, sadism, destructiveness and automaton conformity. Since masochism and sadism are regularly to be found in the same person, such a one is labeled sado-masochistic, or, for reasons we discuss below, authoritarian. Masochistic strivings usually appear in the form of feelings of inferiority, powerlessness and individual insignificance. This is analogous to the feelings of the helpless child, but there is a difference. The feeling of helplessness, or relative helplessness, of a young child is factual, that is to say, because of his limited equipment and experience there is nothing he can do except to depend on the parents, the authorities on whom he leans for the necessities of life. Furthermore, he is yet only dimly aware of himself as a separate being. The parents still appear to be an integral part of the child's universe. Submission to them, therefore, has a different quality from that of the submissiveness of a grownup who leans on an authority. While the moral helplessness of the adult is also causally determined, it is now his orientation to the world—his unconscious longing to return to or to remain in a state of dependency and helplessness—which causes him to feel and act as he does. And there is another difference. He can no longer accept the closed world of the child. Awareness of himself as a separate, isolated being has entered the picture.

Masochism

People with strong masochistic strivings may complain about their feelings of inadequacy and consciously want to get rid of them, but unconsciously they are impelled to feel inferior or insignificant. They have never really *experienced* to the depths of their being the happiness and fulfillment of being independent and free. Their minds tell them that the way they feel and act is foolish and thwarts their chances of happiness. They suffer intensely. But man has a great fear of the unknown, and they unconsciously fear that which they have never known, independence. In other words, they have no real insight or at least not enough into the nature of their problems and the genuine possibilities for their solution. However inadequate, thwarting, and tormenting their state may be, it gives them some feeling of being related to others, of not being completely isolated and alone in the cosmic setting. Never having experienced independence, they cannot believe it promises a far more satisfactory and fulfilling kind of relatedness. And so they tend to remain weak, helpless and to depend on powers outside themselves, on other people, or institutions, or nature.

In order to avoid confusion, it must be pointed out that everyone is in a sense dependent, but it is a different kind of dependency, and to this matter we shall return later.

There are all sorts of disguises for masochistic feelings —"love," "loyalty," "devotion," etc. There are also extreme forms of masochism which we need not go into here.

Sadism

Sadism is, so to speak, the other side of the penny. People who have masochistic strivings will also be found to have sadistic strivings, varying in strength. Fromm distinguishes three kinds of sadistic strivings. "One is to make others dependent on oneself and to have absolute and unrestricted power over them, so as to make of them nothing but instruments, 'clay in the potter's hands.' Another consists of the impulse not only to rule over others in this absolute fashion, but to exploit them, to use them, to steal from them, to disembowel them, and, so to speak, to incorporate anything eatable in them. This desire can refer to material things as well as to immaterial ones, such as the emotional or intellectual qualities a person has to offer. A third kind of sadistic tendency is the wish to make others suffer or to see them suffer. This suffering can be physical, but more often it is mental suffering. Its aim is to hurt actively, to humiliate, embarrass others, or to see them in embarrassing and humiliating situations."[12]

One might think that the sadistic person is strong and independent in contrast to the masochist, who seems weak and helpless. But the sadist is weak and helpless too. He needs some one to dominate, hurt and humiliate. Without such a relationship, he feels lost and alone.

As we have already mentioned, the two kinds of tendencies will be found in the same person, though usually one will predominate. Hence, in a sado-masochistic relationship between people, the roles will not infrequently be reversed. In either case, the person cannot bear the isolation and weakness of his own self. He has to "submerge" his real self, as Fromm puts it, thus losing his integrity. When the person is neither submitting to nor dominating another, he becomes anxious and afraid. He has no peace, no rest, and his life is taken up with either one or the other.

Although probably some masochistic and sadistic traits are found in everyone, only the person in whom they predominate can be called sado-masochistic.

Destructiveness

Since sado-masochistic strivings are often found along with the phenomenon which Fromm calls destructiveness, it is not easy to elucidate its special characteristics. In fact, in one sense all the "mechanisms of escape" we discuss are destructive since they thwart and block the development of man's powers and deprive him of any genuine and unalloyed happiness. But destructiveness in the sense in which Fromm uses it has some special characteristics. The destructive person tries to eliminate or destroy the other person or object, not to dominate, nor to submit, nor to conform like a robot. Since destructiveness too is based on unbearable feelings of powerlessness and isolation, the destructive person aims to remove any basis of comparison or any possible threat. "I can escape the feeling of my own powerlessness in comparison with the world outside of myself by destroying it. To be sure, if I succeed in removing it, I remain alone and isolated, but mine is a splendid isolation, in which I cannot be crushed by the overwhelming power of the objects outside of myself. The

destruction of the world is the last, almost desperate attempt
to save myself from being crushed by it."[13]

Here too we find destructiveness masquerading under
various disguises: "love," "duty," "conscience," "patriotism."

It is necessary to distinguish between two forms of destructiveness: what Fromm calls irrational and rational destructive tendencies. The former we have discussed above.
"There are destructive tendencies which result from a specific
situation; as reaction to attacks on one's own or others' life
and integrity, or on ideas which one is identified with. This
kind of destructiveness is the natural and necessary concomitant of one's affirmation of life."[14] This is rational.

According to Fromm, when man's sensuous, emotional and
intellectual capacities are stunted, when the drive to live
productively, lovingly, happily, which depends on the development of man's powers, is thwarted, the energy directed toward
life-furthering activities undergoes a process of reorganiza-
tion and becomes directed toward irrational destructiveness.

Automaton Conformity

Automaton conformity is difficult to elucidate, partly
because it is so widespread that it seems the "natural" way
of life, partly because some conformity is necessary in any
culture, partly because one must have some patterns of
thought, feeling, and action as materials to go on in order to
become a human being. But more of this below.

The mechanism of automaton conformity is characterized
by the fact that one adopts entirely the kind of personality
offered him by cultural patterns; "and he therefore becomes
exactly as all others are and as they expect him to be."[15]

The automaton conformist wipes out or attempts to wipe
out the difference between himself and others, thus overcoming the conscious—but not unconscious—fear of aloneness
and powerlessness. Such a person aims to think, feel, imagine,
and act exactly like all others of his culture or class. To be

sure, in American society, where there is a variety of clashing
culture patterns, such a person may have to exercise some
ingenuity. But here the schools, the radio, the newspapers, the
movies come in handy. They can teach him. It is true, also,
that some people have local or other loyalties because of such
things as religion or foreign origin. But by and large they
will strive to become exactly as all others are. In other words,
they substitute a pseudo-self for their own real self.[16]

ASSIMILATION AND SOCIALIZATION

Before discussing Fromm's theory of temperament and
character we need to introduce some other ideas. In the
process of living, he says, man relates himself to the world by
(1) acquiring and assimilating things, and (2) relating himself
to people and himself. The former is called the process of
assimilation, the latter, socialization. The two processes are
conjunctive. "Man can acquire things," he observes, "by
receiving or taking them from an outside source or by producing them through his own effort. But he must acquire and
assimilate them in some fashion in order to satisfy his needs.
Also, man cannot live alone and unrelated to others. He has
to associate with others for defense, for work, for sexual satisfaction, for play, for the upbringing of the young, for
the transmission of knowledge and material possessions. But
beyond that, it is necessary for him to be related to others, one
with them, part of a group. Complete isolation is unbearable
and incompatible with sanity. Again man can relate himself to
others in various ways: he can love or hate, he can compete or
cooperate; he can build a social system based on equality or
authority, liberty or oppression; but he must be related
in some fashion and the particular form of relatedness is
expressive of his character."[17]

Except for the kind of relatedness referred to under the
heading of spontaneous love and productiveness, which we
discuss below, the various forms of socialization have been

outlined. But for the sake of clarity we mention the various kinds of socialization and assimilation at this point. In the process of socialization there are five orientations, two of which, masochism and sadism, are interrelated: masochism, sadism, destructiveness, automaton conformity, and love. There are also five kinds of orientation in the process of assimilation: the receptive, the exploitative, the hoarding, the marketing, and the productive. The orientations in both the process of assimilation and socialization are respectively related. Thus, the receptive character is masochistic, the productive character is a loving person.

CHARACTER AND TEMPERAMENT

The various character types are "ideal constructions," that is, they are never found in a pure state. Everyone is a mixture of more than one type, although one usually, if not always, predominates.

For Fromm, personality designates the totality of inherited and acquired psychic qualities of the person which make him unique. The difference between inherited and acquired psychic qualities is in the main equivalent to the difference between temperament, endowment and all constitutionally given psychic qualities, and character. Temperament as a concept refers to the mode of reaction to experience. Following Hippocrates, Fromm classifies temperaments as choleric, sanguine, phlegmatic, and melancholic. Thus a choleric person's reaction will be "quick and strong," with rapidity and intensity of feeling, and resulting generally in quick vigorous action. But this does not tell us what the reaction refers to. Here one has to know something of the person's character as well as the situation. The loving person, the productive character, with a choleric temperament, will react quickly and strongly to love; the sadistic person who has a choleric temperament will react perhaps just as vigorously to submissiveness.

The fundamental basis of character lies in the specific kind of relatedness of a person to the world. Character is defined "as the (relatively permanent) form in which human energy is canalized in the process of assimilation and socialization."[18] The character system is the human substitute for the instinctive apparatus of the animal. Once energy is organized into a character system, the person's orientation toward life, which constitutes his character, is extraordinarily difficult to change. The quality of his experience and behavior will be determined by his character.

The character of the child is moulded by the family, but the latter, according to Fromm, is the "psychic agency" of society. By adjusting himself to the family situation, the child acquires the kind of character which makes him want to do what he has to do in order to function with some social effectiveness. In thus adjusting himself, he acquires a character whose core is common to most members of his social class and culture. This common core is by Fromm called the "social character." It is constituted by or derived from the dominant social and cultural patterns of his world.

On this common core are "superimposed" all the variations of the individualized character. Since the personalities of the parents differ, perhaps only to a trivial degree, perhaps considerably in some cases, and since there are psychic and material differences of the specific, local social environment, and finally, since each person will have constitutional differences, there will be various degrees of individuation and differentiation constituting the individual character. One may think of the difference between the social and individual character as a continuum. Near one end of this continuum are people whose personalities are constituted mainly, almost exclusively, by conventional social patterns, and near the other end those who depart widely from some of them, for example, geniuses. However, difference of itself tells nothing—it is the

kind of difference that matters. A "deviant" may be a creative
artist or an idiosyncratic and ineffectual nonentity.

We can put this another way by saying that every
person, by reason of his acculturation, which means by reason
of his being human, must acquire the various materials of his
culture. If he grows up in fortunate circumstances where he
is given a fair chance to develop his capacities (which in turn
depend on native endowment), he will be able to reorganize
and work over and recreate these materials to such a degree
that he will become what Fromm calls a productive human
being. Otherwise he will develop one of what Fromm calls the
non-productive orientations, although even here there will be
differences. But as we said above, whether the difference be
great or small, it is the kind of difference that matters. Just
which type of non-productive orientation a person develops
will depend on his particular family situation, but ultimately,
by and large, on the dominant social and cultural patterns.

As to why certain social and cultural patterns do predominate is a problem for sociology. Fromm has discussed
these matters to some extent, but they are beyond the scope
of this book.

The Receptive Character

We now take up the various orientations from the point
of view of assimilation. In the receptive orientation, the person
believes that everything he needs or wants, material goods,
love, knowledge, or pleasure, must come from an outside
source which he passively accepts, not from his own efforts.
He believes that the only way he can get anything is by someone's giving it to him. Such a person leans on authority for
knowledge and help and on people in general for any kind of
support. Love for him means being loved, not the active
process of loving. Since the receptive person feels so inadequate, he will easily "fall for" anyone who gives him anything
that looks like affection or love. In general, such a person is

passive, and feels paralyzed when left alone. He is always in search of a "magic helper," someone to "take care of" him. Needing many people for help, he will be loyal to many people, and he cannot say "no" to requests and demands. The receptive person has great fondness for food and drink, as if to overcome anxiety by eating and drinking. In the dreams of such a receptive person, being fed is a frequent symbol of being loved.

Receptive characters are friendly and optimistic, but they become anxious when their source of supply is threatened.

The Exploitative Character

The exploitative person, on the other hand, tries to take everything from people by force or cunning. Whatever sphere of life he is concerned with, he will want to grab or steal: another's spouse or friend, another's ideas, another's material goods. Everyone is an object of exploitation. Anything the exploitative person can take or steal is more attractive than what he can produce by his own efforts. His attitude is one of hostility and manipulation. While the receptive person is confident, the exploiter is suspicious, envious, jealous, and cynical.

The Hoarding Character

In the hoarding orientation, people have little faith in anything new they can get from outside. Security is based on hoarding and saving, keeping what they have, while spending is felt as a threat and arouses anxiety. They are misers with money, thoughts and feelings. Love means possessiveness. They are said to know everything but are incapable of creative thinking. They can show a kind of faithfulness toward people, but they are suspicious. Although they have no faith in the future, they are sentimental about the past.

The hoarder is orderly, pedantic, punctual, and he cannot endure having things out of place. He may indulge in compulsive washing, another way to undo contact with the outside world. In general, the outside world is experienced as a threat to his orderly, fortified, insulated self. The hoarder tends to believe he possesses only a fixed quantity of strength or mental capacity, which is diminished by use and which cannot be replenished. Hence, he has no faith in the self-replenishing power of living things. He does not realize that activity and the exercise of one's powers are strengthening, and that they deteriorate with inactivity. Creation is unreal. With people, intimacy is conceived of as threatening; remoteness or possession, to the hoarder, implies security.

The Marketing Character

The marketing orientation is the counterpart in the process of assimilation to that of automaton conformity in the process of socialization. People of this kind feel that their personalities are commodities to be bought and sold like a bale of hay. Our education fosters this orientation. We are taught to be "adaptable" and sensitive to the changing expectations of other people. To be "successful" is to be valuable; to be unsuccessful is to be worthless. Such people try to be experts at "selling" their personality, and so their personality is constituted by whatever qualities are in demand. But this means one has no stable and genuine personality. Hence, one has no real experience of self as an autonomous being capable of guiding one's own destiny. Such a person is bound to feel empty and anxious.

The Productive Character

Thus far we have discussed what Fromm calls the non-productive orientations in the conjunctive processes of assimilation and socialization. Before discussing the last orientation in both spheres, the productive, we wish to outline his views on selfishness and self-love.

Fromm aptly points out that modern culture is pervaded by a taboo on selfishness. While we are taught that it is virtuous to love others, we are also taught that to love ourselves and to be selfish is sinful. Yet this is in flagrant contradiction to another doctrine which we imbibe, namely, that the most powerful and legitimate drive in man is selfishness and that by following this imperative drive we make the best possible contribution to society. Again, it is usually implied that loving oneself is incompatible with love for others.

First of all, Fromm asserts, it is fallacious to claim that self-love and love for others are incompatible. If it is a virtue to love another as a human being why should not one love oneself as a human being also? Furthermore, "not only others, but we ourselves are the 'object' of our feelings and attitudes; the attitudes toward others and toward ourselves, far from being contradictory, are basically *conjunctive* . . . Love of others and love of ourselves are not alternatives. On the contrary, an attitude of love toward themselves will be found in all those who are capable of loving others. *Love*, in principle, *is indivisible as far as the connection between 'objects' and one's own self is concerned.* Genuine love is an expression of productiveness and implies care, respect, responsibility, and knowledge. It is not an 'affect' in the sense of being affected by somebody, but an active striving for the growth and happiness of the loved person, rooted in one's own capacity to love."[19]

Nor is it true, as the notion of romantic love has it, that there is only one person in the world whom one can love, and, if that person be discovered, that love for him entails a withdrawal of love from all others. Love of one person implies love of mankind, since he embodies all the essential attributes of man, and since love of mankind is the basis of individual love and not conversely. Genetically, the ability to love is acquired in loving specific individuals, members of one's own family, for example, but one loves them primarily for their qualities as human beings. In other words, love of man is, logically speaking, the premise of individual love.

From all this it follows that if a person can love others, he necessarily loves himself too. If he can "love" others, but not himself, and conversely, if he "loves" himself but not others—then in either case he cannot love at all.

As for selfishness in the usual sense, it does not imply self-love but self-hatred. Psychoanalysis reveals that selfish people in the usual sense are profoundly anxious, self-contemptuous, empty and frustrated. Hence, they are eager to snatch from life whatever they can get to compensate for their feelings of powerlessness and incapacity to love. Since they lack self-respect and self-love, they necessarily have no respect for the dignity, integrity and rights of others.

In general, says Fromm, the trouble with modern culture "lies not in its principle of individualism, not in the idea that moral virtue is the same as the pursuit of self-interest . . . *not in the fact that people are too much concerned with their self-interest, but that they are not concerned enough with the interest of their real self; not in the fact that they are too selfish, but that they do not love themselves.*"[20]

We return now to the concept of productiveness and love in the process of assimilation and socialization. Man is not only a rational and social being, he is also a producing being. He must produce in order to live. Using his imagination and reason, he transforms the material he finds. Material production, however, is only one aspect of man's productiveness. In a wide sense, productiveness "is man's ability to use his powers and to realize the potentialities inherent in him."[21] These powers are mental, emotional, and sensory, involving responses to other people, to oneself, and to things. Hence, the productive orientation refers to one's mode of relatedness in all realms of experience. We can put this another way by saying a person is born with certain inherent capacities.

Depending on circumstances, mainly those of family and culture, he may develop these capacities to the maximum, within the scope of development of the culture. Certain it is that if a person in childhood is mistreated and uncared for, he will tend to grow into a warped human being, his innate capacity for love stunted, and his capacity to think independently limited or destroyed. But to be able to develop one's powers, such as reason and love, and to use them, is to be productive. This does not mean one has to become a great scientist or artist. It simply means that one is able to think independently and critically, to feel intensely without serious emotional warp, to respect oneself and one's fellow men, to enjoy sensuous pleasures without anxiety and repression, to delight in the works of nature and art—in a word to affirm oneself and life and to find life good. Of course many of us, for a variety of reasons, chiefly cultural, never develop any of our powers to a significant degree, to a point where we can think critically and independently, or to experience the full ecstasies of imagination and feeling.

On the subject of love it is easy to get confused or sentimental. Fromm quickly disposes of the usual drivel about love. "There is hardly any word which is more ambiguous and confusing than the word 'love.' It is used to denote almost every feeling short of hate and disgust. It comprises everything from the love for ice cream to the love for a symphony, from mild sympathy to the most intense feeling of closeness. People feel they love if they have 'fallen for' somebody. They call their dependence love, and their possessiveness too. They believe, in fact, that nothing is easier than to love, that the difficulty lies only in finding the right object, and that their failure to find happiness in love is due to their bad luck in not finding the right partner. But contrary to all this confused and wishful thinking, love is a very specific feeling; and while every human being has a capacity for love, its realization is one of the most difficult achievements.

Genuine love is rooted in productiveness and may properly be called, therefore, 'productive love.' Its essence is the same whether it is the mother's love for the child, our love for man, or the erotic love between two individuals . . . Although the objects of love differ and consequently the intensity and quality of love itself differ, certain basic elements may be said to be characteristic of all forms of productive love."[22]

Love is an activity in which one respects and cares for another. To care for someone implies that one will foster his growth and development and not hinder or destroy it, as in other kinds of relationships, such as the sado-masochistic. A good example of caring is that of the mother for her child, who labors for the child's growth. While an adult is not as helpless as a child, the difference is relative. All men depend on one another. The caring is mutual, and this is one way in which such relationships differ from neurotic dependency, where one wants everything from a "magic helper," who, if he accepts the role, dominates and exploits the former instead of fostering his growth and independence. In a loving relationship both labor for the further development of the other's capacities. In this sense they genuinely "care for" each other.

Love is also characterized by responsibility and knowledge. To be responsible means one is willing to answer to oneself for the welfare of the other, to exact of oneself the duty of helping him to flourish mentally and emotionally. Finally, in order to help another person one must understand him, know him. Efforts at assistance made in ignorance can be hurtful or at best merely sentimental busyness.

We conclude our discussion of the various orientations or character types by observing that when the productive orientation in a person is dominant, any elements of the four non-productive orientations also existing in the person become transformed and take on positive, life-furthering qualities. For example, a minor tendency toward submissiveness becomes devotion, stubbornness becomes steadfastness, opportunism becomes purposefulness. There are further possible combinations and permutations which we omit here.[23]

AUTHORITARIANISM

Any account of Fromm's theories which omits a discussion of authoritarianism would be seriously defective. There is a very important difference between rational and irrational authority. Rational authority is based on competence. The person who has such authority functions adequately in the task with which he is entrusted. Rational authority requires constant scrutiny and criticism of its role. Being temporary, when the tasks and functions assigned to it have been carried out, it ends. It is based on equality, except for some difference of knowledge or skill between the person entrusted with authority and those subject to him. An example of rational authority is that of a competent teacher who imparts his knowledge without dominating or overawing his pupils, who in principle can become as expert as he.

Irrational authority is based, not on competence to fulfill specific tasks and functions, but on power over people. The power may be physical, mental or "moral," actually employed by a person to manipulate people, or irrational attributions of power to another, springing from the anxiety and helplessness of the submissive person. Irrational authority claims eternal sway. It intimidates its subjects and at the same time arouses their admiration by seemingly magic qualities. Criticism by its subjects is forbidden. Hence irrational authority is based on inequality. "The Church," "The Party," "The Family," among others, are examples of irrational authority. Sometimes an institution combines elements of both, as is often the case in the family situation. But irrational authority does not have to be a person or institution which tells one what to do and what not to do. It can be an attitude, a "philosophy" of life which one adopts, not from critical thinking and reflective experience, but from anxiety. Thus certain elements of Kantian ethics, which we cannot discuss here, can be adopted uncritically and be as impelling as the dictates of a church or Party.

The person submitting to irrational authority internalizes the commands and taboos of the authority. "The laws and sanctions of external authority become part of oneself, as it were, and instead of feeling responsible to something outside, one feels responsible to something inside, to one's conscience."[24] Furthermore, because man has a need to admire and have an ideal, and to strive for some kind of perfection, the image of such perfection becomes projected onto the authority, resulting in an unshakable conviction as to its ideal character.

The person who submits to irrational authority has a sado-masochistic ("symbiotic") or "authoritarian" character structure.[25] The authoritarian character finds "inner security by becoming, symbiotically, part of an authority felt to be greater and more powerful than himself. As long as he is part of that authority—at the expense of his own integrity— he feels that he is participating in the authority's strength. His feeling of certainty and identity depends on this symbiosis, to be rejected by the authority means to be thrown into a void, to face the horror of nothingness. Anything, to the authoritarian character, is better than this. To be sure, the love and approval of the authority give him the greatest satisfaction; but even punishment is better than rejection. The punishing authority is still with him, and if he has 'sinned,' the punishment is at least proof that the authority still cares. By his acceptance of the punishment his sin is wiped out and the security of belonging is restored."[26]

Authoritarianism is usually pyramidal, especially in certain societies like Nazi Germany. But there is such a thing as "anonymous authority" such as "the market" but we cannot discuss it here.[27] Our own society is said to be dominated by the authority of the market—and hence the marketing orientation predominates.

Freud's super-ego, according to Fromm, represents the authoritarian conscience.[28] As we shall see below, the essence of the Oedipus complex represents the struggle of the son against the father in the former's efforts to escape the latter's domination and exploitation.

SEX AND HAPPINESS

We have had little to say about sex in our discussion of Fromm's views. This does not mean that he slights the role of sexual needs. For Fromm, however, sex is only one of man's imperative needs, and, as we have seen, is not the nuclear explanatory concept in understanding human behavior that it was for Freud (along with the "death instinct").

Furthermore, for Freud the essence of pleasure, including sexual pleasure, is relief from painful tension. But for Fromm pleasure, including sexual pleasure, is based on the use of surplus energy along with, or after, the satisfaction of bodily needs. Happiness is an expression of freedom and productiveness.[29]

ETHICS AND HUMAN NATURE

Before we come to the last theme to be discussed, Fromm's interpretation of the Oedipus myth and complex, we wish to discuss his views on the relation of ethics to psychoanalysis. He maintains that ethical norms and values have a vital relationship to man's self-realization and the fulfillment of his potentialities. He also believes that problems of ethics and ethical validity cannot be divorced from the study of personality. "The value judgments we make," he says, "determine our actions and upon their validity rests our mental health and happiness. To consider evaluations only as so many rationalizations of unconscious, irrational desires [as do certain psychoanalysts[30]]—although they can be that too—narrows down and distorts our picture of the total personality. Neurosis itself is, in the last analysis, a symptom of moral failure (though 'adjustment' is by no means a symptom of moral achievement). In many instances a neurotic symptom is the specific expression of moral conflict, and the success of the therapeutic effort depends on the understanding and solution of the person's moral problem."[31]

These neurotic symptoms are often typical expressions of some of the problems of modern man. Modern man is uneasy and more and more bewildered; and he is dimly aware of a sense of futility about the way he lives and the goals he strives for. "While his power over matter grows, he feels powerless in his individual life and in society. While creating new and better means for mastering nature, he has become enmeshed in a network of those means and has lost the vision of the end which alone gives them significance—*man himself.* While becoming the master of nature, he has become the slave of the machine which his own hands built. With all his knowledge about matter, he is ignorant with regard to the most important and fundamental questions of human existence: what man is, how he ought to live, and how the tremendous energies *within* man can be released and used productively."[32]

For Fromm the character structure of the mature and integrated personality, the productive character, constitutes the source and basis of virtue. In other words, to live productively, in the sense we elaborated above, is to live virtuously. Vice, on the other hand, springs from indifference or contempt for oneself and from self-mutilation.

THE OEDIPUS MYTH[33]

Fromm claims *"that the [Oedipus] myth has to be understood not as a symbol of the incestuous tie between mother and son, but as the rebellion of the son against the authority of the father in the patriarchal family; and that the marriage of Oedipus and Jocasta is only a secondary element, only one of the symbols of the son's victory, who takes over his father's place and with it all his privileges."*[34]

He begins by pointing to certain difficulties in Freud's interpretation. If the myth is a symbolic expression of the incestuous tie of the boy to the mother with rivalry toward the father, why is there no indication in the myth that Oedipus is attracted by or falls in love with Jocasta? While he marries her, according to Sophocles' version, actually it seems that she merely, so to speak, "goes with the throne." In all except one of the older versions of the myth, he does not marry his mother at all. Another question: since Oedipus is the courageous and wise hero who defeats the Sphinx and is therefore the benefactor of Thebes, why is he the man who commits the crime which is considered to be the most horrible by his contemporaries? The fact that in Greek tragedy the powerful and strong are suddenly struck by disaster does not seem to Fromm to provide the most satisfactory answer.

If we consider the trilogy, not merely "King Oedipus" as Freud did, we find that the theme which runs through the three works is the conflict between father and son. In "King Oedipus" the conflict is expressed by the killing of Laios. In "Oedipus at Colonus," the conflict is between Oedipus and his two sons. In "Antigone" it is the conflict between Creon and Haemon. There is no incest problem between Oedipus' sons and their mother or between Haemon and his mother. It is plausible to assume, then, that in "King Oedipus," the conflict between father and son, not the problem of incest, is the real issue. "An analysis of the whole Oedipus trilogy will show," Fromm says, "that the struggle against paternal authority is its main theme and that the roots of this struggle extend far back into the ancient struggle between the patri-archal and matriarchal systems of society, family and reli-gion." Furthermore, Oedipus, Haemon and Antigone represent

the matriarchal world. These representatives of the matriarchal world "attack a social and religious order based on
the powers and privileges of the father, represented by Laios
and Creon."[35]

Fromm here, of course, is drawing upon Bachofen's theory
of "Mother-right" as a basis for his own interpretation of
the Oedipus myth. Since we have discussed "Mother-right"
in connection with other writers, especially Rank, we need
not repeat what was said then in regard to the social organization of matriarchy.[36] Eventually men defeated, subdued and succeeded women, themselves becoming rulers in a
social hierarchy. "The patriarchal system which was thus
established," Fromm relates, "is characterized by monogamy
(at least as far as women were concerned), by the authority
of the father in the family and the central role of men in a
hierarchically organized society." Religion corresponded to
the social organization in the patriarchal culture. Male gods
are the supreme rulers of men (instead of goddesses as during
the matriarchy), like the father in the family.

The difference between the matriarchal and patriarchal
order extends to social and moral principles. "Matriarchal
culture is characterized by the emphasis on ties of blood,
ties to the soil and the passive acceptance of all natural
phenomena. Patriarchal society in contrast is characterized
by respect for man-made law, by the predominance of rational
thought and by the effort to change natural phenomena by
man." While these principles of patriarchy represent an advance over matriarchy, in other respects the latter was
superior. "In the matriarchal concept all men are equal since
they are all the children of mothers and each one a child of
Mother Earth. A mother loves her children all alike and
without [limiting] conditions, since her love is based on the
fact that they are all her children and not on any particular
merit or achievement; the aim of life is the happiness of
men and there is nothing more important or dignified than

human existence and life. The patriarchal system, on the other hand, recognizes obedience to authority as its main virtue. The principle of equality is replaced by a hierarchical order in society and state, ruled by an authority just as the family is dominated by the father."[37]

In the various versions of the myth, upon which Sophocles built his work, the figure of Oedipus was always connected with the cult of the Earth Goddess, who, according to Bachofen, represents matriarchal religion. Fromm offers two examples which we need not give here.

The Sphinx episode also, according to Fromm, points to a connection between the matriarchal principle and Oedipus. When he arrives in Thebes, the Sphinx is devouring the young men and women of the city. She will cease only when someone can give a correct answer to the riddle she is asking: "What is it that first goes on four, then on two and eventually on three?" Anyone who can solve the riddle and free the city is to be made king and to have the king's widow as a wife. Oedipus discovers the answer to the riddle. The answer is man, who first as a child walks on all fours, then as an adult on two legs, and in old age on three legs (that is, with a cane). When Oedipus solves the riddle, the Sphinx throws herself into the sea, and Thebes is saved.

However, not the riddle itself, but the answer to the riddle is important, Fromm believes, basing his interpretation on psychoanalytic principles of symbolic interpretation of dreams and myths. There is, he says, a displacement of accent from the important element in the latent content of the riddle, to a minor element in the manifest content. The translation of the Sphinx' words is: "He who knows that the most important answer man can give to the most difficult question he is confronted with is man himself can save mankind." The answer stresses the importance of man, which reflects an attitude and a principle characteristic of matriarchy, and which shows that Oedipus belongs to the matriarchal order.

The principle of man's importance is likewise expressed in "Antigone" by Sophocles; Oedipus' daughter, Antigone, cares only for man himself, the natural law and love. She holds to these principles in contrast to the position of Creon, who represents the authoritarian principle in the family and state, against which Haemon likewise rebels.

The question arises as to why Jocasta is destroyed instead of being victorious, assuming she symbolizes the motherly principle. She is destroyed because she failed to fulfill her duty as a mother, being ready to kill her child in order to save her husband, which from the patriarchal point of view is legitimate, but which from the matriarchal standpoint is the unforgivable crime. "It is she who by committing this crime starts the chain of events which eventually lead to her own end and to her husband's and son's destruction."[38]

In other words, Fromm seems to imply, Sophocles who represents or favors the matriarchal principle in the play has Jocasta destroyed because in a matriarchal society the fate of a mother who would kill her child is death. Furthermore, this being the greatest crime in a matriarchal society, disaster to those close to her, which psychologically speaking, means a further disaster to her, would naturally follow.

Stated from another point of view, we must not lose sight of the fact, Fromm says, that the myth "as it was known to and formulated by Sophocles had already been changed according to the patriarchal pattern, that the manifest and conscious frame of reference is that of a patriarchy and that the latent and older meaning appears only in a veiled and often distorted form. The patriarchal system had been victorious and the myth explains the reasons for the downfall of matriarchy. It proposes that the mother by violating her paramount duty brought about her own destruction."[39] It is not clear to us whether Fromm wants to imply also that the latent content has a still deeper meaning, namely, that the matriarchy was defeated by the patriarchal

form of society when the former began to betray its own
principles. If the mother symbolizes the motherly principle,
this latter interpretation seems plausible.

In "Oedipus at Colonus," Oedipus arrives at, dies in a
mysterious way and is buried in the grove of the goddesses
of the earth. These "awful" goddesses "of dread aspect" are
representatives of the old mother-goddesses and the matriarchal principle. If an element appears in a myth belonging
to an earlier phase of development and which is no longer
part of people's conscious frame of reference at the time of
final formulation, it may often have the quality of dread
and awfulness (analogous to what happens in dreams).
"Touching upon something hidden and tabu," as Fromm puts
it, "the conscious mind is affected by a fear of a particular
kind—the fear of the unknown and the mystifying."[40]

The scene at the grave makes a plain allusion to matriarchy. Oedipus praises his daughters as true images of the
ways of Egypt, where men weave in the house and the wives
go forth to win the daily bread—a reference to Egyptian
matriarchy. Further, he alludes to his daughters who preserve
him as men, not women.

As Oedipus dies the emphasis again is upon something
awful and mystifying. The messenger who reports how Oedipus
dies sees Theseus, King of Athens, who accompanied Oedipus
to the holy place of the goddesses, holding his hand before
his face to screen his eyes as if he had seen something dreadful and not to be beheld.

Theseus, the messenger reports, prayerfully salutes the
earth and the heavens above, both at once. The passing of
Oedipus is wonderful and mystifying. The messenger cannot
tell whether he was removed from the earth by the gods above
or below, by the world of the fathers or that of the mothers.
But in a formulation written centuries after the mother-goddesses had been conquered by the Olympian gods, the uncertainty of the messenger, Fromm says, can only be a (dis-

guised) expression of a secret conviction that Oedipus was brought back to where he belongs, to the mothers.

In "Antigone," the two principles for which Creon and Antigone stand are clearly those which Bachofen character-ized as patriarchal and matriarchal. Creon represents the patriarchal principle of the supremacy of the law of the state, of obedience to authority, over the allegiance to the natural law of humanity, of the precedence of the tie between man and wife, between ruler and ruled, over ties of blood. The patriarchal principle "is the principle of order and authority, of obedience and hierarchy."[41] Antigone stands for the matriarchal principle of blood relationship as the most fundamental and indestructible tie, of the equality of all men, of the respect for human life, and of love. Hence, she is Creon's uncompromising antagonist. Her laws are of all time, and as the play puts it, no man knows when they were first put forth; they are not those of an authoritarian state. The law of burial, which she passionately affirms, of returning the body to the earth, likewise originates in the religious principles of matriarchy. It is her nature to love, as she says, not to hate. "She stands for the solidarity of man and the principle of the all-embracing mother love."[42]

Creon's values are the two interrelated values of authority in the family and in the state. Sons are regarded as the property of their fathers and their function is to be "service-able" to their fathers. Likewise citizens are the property of the state and its ruler. Their disobedience is regarded as the worst of evils. From these principles and from his father's authority, Haemon eventually rebels. He relies on reason, which he says is the highest of all things we possess, and on the will of the people.

As the tragedy nears its end, Creon has Antigone buried alive, another symbolic expression of her connection with the earth and the goddesses of the earth. Again Tiresias appears, this time to make Creon aware of his crime. With the death of Antigone, Haemon, and Creon's wife, Eurydice, Creon recognizes the "complete collapse of his world and the defeat of his principles."

THE OEDIPUS COMPLEX

Freud made three factually correct observations concerning what he called the Oedipus complex, according to Fromm, but the theory by which he explained them was fallacious. He observed, first, the presence of sexual strivings in children. Second, he observed that the ties by which a child is bound to his parents often are not severed when as a result of his development they normally should be, with the growth of independence. Freud saw that this irrational fixation of children to their parents is found in all neuroses, and that it is one of the causes of neurotic symptoms and neurotic character traits. As Freud put it, the Oedipus complex is the kernel of every neurosis. Third, he recognized that the father-son conflict is characteristic of patriarchal societies, and he also observed how the son's unsuccessful rebellion against his father's authority and the son's fears following defeat established the basis for a neurotic development.

Freud explained all three on the assumption that the attachment to the mother is based on the sexual strivings of the child, and that the conflict between father and son is a result of sexual rivalry. However, data since gathered by certain psychoanalysts and child psychologists, for example, as well as by anthropologists, have thrown grave doubt on the correctness of the explanation.

Fromm points out that the recent data show that the Freudian Oedipus complex is not universal, that the rivalry between father and son does not occur in societies where strong patriarchal authority does not exist, and that the tie to the mother is not essentially sexual. When not suppressed, infantile sexuality, instead of being directed primarily toward the mother, is normally satisfied auto-erotically and by contact with other children. Furthermore, it seems that the fixation or pathological dependence on the mother is caused particularly by a dominating attitude of the mother, making the child helpless and in greater need of her protection and love.

The conflict between father and son is a product of authoritarian patriarchal society, where especially the son is regarded as his father's property, whose interest he should serve "like a thing," like a chattel or a beast of burden. The conflict has little to do with sexual rivalry. Such an attitude and the treatment by the father of the son which springs from it are opposed to man's wish to be free and independent. Hence, a conflict whether open or unconscious necessarily occurs. The greater the pressure by the father to make his son a means to his (the father's) own ends, the greater will be the conflict.

Freud interpreted neurosis and the Oedipus complex as a result of the conflict between the irrational passions of the child and "reality" as represented by parents and society. Fromm regards both the Oedipus complex and neurosis as expressions of a conflict between man's legitimate striving for freedom and independence and those social arrangements which frustrate man's striving for self-fulfillment, happiness, and independence.[43] When the social arrangements which thwart self-fulfillment and independence are successful, they create in man a destructive passion, which, in turn, must be suppressed by external or internal force.

To conclude, when we have a society in which the respect for the integrity of every individual, including every child, is realized, then, says Fromm, the Oedipus complex, like the myth, will belong to the past.

10. THE THEORIES OF
HARRY STACK SULLIVAN

The writer in some ways most difficult to understand of the several psychiatrists and psychoanalysts we discuss is Harry Stack Sullivan. There are many reasons for this. Sullivan is not, as a reviewer put it, one of the writing psychoanalysts who can write a book "between patients." He has written little; his language is highly technical, and his thought, as a rule, very complicated, subtle and highly compressed.[1] But there is another and still greater difficulty, which we can only gradually indicate, and with which we shall be concerned throughout the chapter. This relates to his theory of interpersonal relations. At first blush it appears that the statement that psychiatry is the study of processes that involve or go on between people, interpersonal relations, is simple and obvious. Yet it is the most complicated psychiatric theory known to us. We shall approach this theory deviously, and from various angles.

Unless we have devoted a good deal of study and thought to the matter, we tend to think of ourselves as self-contained, physically and mentally isolated beings, looking out upon the world, as it were, from a tower in our own private castle, save perhaps for periodic excursions outside to satisfy physical, emotional and mental needs and desires. And then, further, we tend to assume that these contacts with the outside world are superficial, that our contacts with the world for food and drink, for sex, for conversation, for friendly intercourse, when we are at work or at play, whenever we are actively engaged with people and things, leave us relatively untouched, the same person as before, our personalities essentially unchanged. Usually it takes a crucial occurrence—the loss of a loved one, removal to a foreign country, a severe illness, intense and prolonged loneliness—to give us a hint that we are more intimately related to the world in which we live than everyday, routine living might lead us to assume. (There are good historical reasons for this which we cannot go into.)

However, Sullivan holds that the opposite is the case. As long as life lasts, we are, as the psychological jargon has it, "interacting" with our physical and social worlds in such intimate fashion, that if, *per impossibile*, we could be absolutely isolated from the physical and mental world in which we have our being, our very life on this earth would be a matter of minutes. Complete isolation is synonymous with death.

We are always interacting with and in the world; we are always undergoing experience. In fact, we are our experience.

THE GOALS OF HUMAN BEHAVIOR

We begin our exposition of Sullivan with some preliminary distinctions and assumptions. He differentiates "human performances," which include revery processes, such as day dreaming, and thought, into a two-part classification. In more popular language, the purposes, the goals or end states of human behavior are divided into two actually interrelated classes. These two classes refer to the pursuit of satisfactions and the pursuit of security. Satisfactions include sleep and rest, food and drink, sexual fulfillment (the satisfaction of lust). Loneliness is also listed as a "middling example." These satisfactions are closely connected with the bodily organization of man. Hence, loneliness is included by Sullivan because, among other things, we have a desire to touch one another and to be physically close.

The class of pursuits pertaining to security refer more directly to man's cultural equipment than to bodily organization. The concept of security, in Sullivan's sense, is not easy to explain. Roughly, it refers to the state of well-being, of "good feeling," of euphoria. All "those movements, actions, speech, thoughts, reveries and so on which pertain more to the culture which has been imbedded in a particular individual than to the organization of his tissues and glands, is apt to belong in this classification of the pursuit of security."[2]

The process of becoming a human being, for Sullivan, is synonymous with the process of acculturation or socialization. The need for security arises from the fact that every person undergoes this process of acculturation which begins at birth. From the very beginning of life in this world, everyone, at first through "empathy," which we discuss below, is made to feel some of the effects of the culture by the attitudes of the significant person or persons who take care of him: mother, nurse, or their surrogates. The attitudes of those who take care of the child are themselves socially conditioned. Because of empathy, long before the infant can understand what is happening, he experiences something of the attitudes of the significant people around him. Later he is deliberately taught what is right and wrong, "good" and "bad." In this way, the impulses, the biological strivings of the infant are socially "conditioned," that is, moulded, both as to form of expression and fulfillment, according to the culturally approved patterns. As we shall see, because of the experiences of approval and disapproval from the parents or their surrogates, the achievement of satisfactions according to the culturally "correct" or approved patterns causes a profound feeling of well-being, of good feeling, of security.

When, for certain reasons, the felt needs of a person, the biological strivings, cannot be fulfilled according to culturally approved patterns, which he learned in early life, he feels intense and painful uneasiness and discomfort, insecurity, or *anxiety*.

It is not very difficult to see that the distinction between the pursuit of satisfactions and the pursuit of security and their attainment is logical or conceptual. The two are inextricably bound up together. But these two broad classifications are helpful for preliminary discussion. In general terms they explain what one is after in any situation with other persons, whether real or "fantastic" or a blend of both ("eidetic"). Hence, they represent "integrating tendencies." They explain why a situation in which two or more people— "all but one of which may be illusory" (or eidetic)—are involved or "integrated" becomes an interpersonal situation. It is because of these needs that one cannot live and be human except in communal existence with others.

THE CONCEPT OF TENSION

Because of the great role which anxiety and tension play in Sullivan's theories, we need first to mention some of his ideas about the latter. The achievement of satisfactions causes a decrease of tonus, tension, of the unstriped, involuntary muscles. But the effort at warding off anxiety (insecurity) is accompanied by heightened tonus, often of the striped, skeletal muscles, often of the unstriped, visceral muscles.

"The facts seem to indicate that tonic changes in the unstriped, involuntary muscles of the viscera—the internal organs of the body—are, from birth onward, intimately related to the experiencing of desires, needs for satisfaction. Heightened tone of the stomach wall is called out by depletion of our chemical supplies and the occurrence of vigorous contractions in these tense muscles gives rise to the 'pangs of hunger.' The taking of food—the ingestion of which probably leads to a release of nutritive substance stored in the liver—promptly relieves the excess tone and the contractions quiet down to the churning of the stomach contents. Hunger, in a way of speaking, is from the first influx of food, more a matter of the oral dynamism than of the stomach. In infants, at least, once this dynamism has discharged itself, alertness disappears, vigilance is withdrawn from circumambient reality, and sleep supervenes. Throughout life the pursuit of satisfactions is physiologically provoked by increased tone in some unstriped muscles; and the securing of the satisfactions is a relaxation of this tone, with a tendency towards the diminution of attention, alertness, and vigilance, and an approach to sleep."[3]

In the securing of satisfaction, the striped, skeletal muscles are "of relatively instrumental value" in very early infancy. They are said to do what is necessary—we are not told what that is—and then relax. But as soon as the mother begins to include prohibitions and disapprovals in educating the youngster, things get complicated. He develops a need for security against primarily "noxious emotional states empathized from the personal environment." Here the skeletal muscles take on a new function.

This function is to get rid of empathized discomfort and painful tension of various origins. "The oral dynamism [the respiratory apparatus, the food-taking apparatus, from which the speaking apparatus is evolved] has been the channel for performances needed to appease hunger—and pain and other discomforts. It may be presumed that its function in emitting the cry has been quite automatic. This may not have worked too well, and delayed response to the cry may be one of the first experiences that tend to focus alertness. But in any case, the oral dynamism is not now effective in securing relief from the discomfort set up by empathy; on some occasions, it is simply ineffectual, and on other occasions, its activity is accompanied by increase of the empathized discomfort. This leads gradually to a differentiation of empathized from other discomforts, and to the *inhibition* of the cry as a universal tool. The inhibiting of a complex pattern of behavior is not as simple as was its automatic initiation. Some of the movements are cut off, but the increase of tone in the appropriate muscles may not be inhibited. The experience of empathized hostility or unfriendly prohibition or, as it later comes to be observed, a forbidding gesture becomes colored by and associated with heightened tone in some striped muscles—at first those concerned with the cry.

"The course of acculturation, in so far as it pertains to toilet habits, is also a learning to suffer increasing tension in the bladder and rectum, and to resist the automatic relaxation of the sphincter muscles concerned in retaining the urine and feces. Failures in this are often accompanied by empathized discomfort [due to parental disapproval], and success is often the occasion of empathized comfort which is added to the satisfaction from relief of the tension."[4]

Action which avoids or relieves any of these tensions is experienced as continued or enhanced *self-respect* or self-esteem. Thus a person who has become tense at an expression of hostility from someone he is talking to may subsequently, let us say, be made to laugh heartily at some remark or occurrence. When this happens, he suddenly feels a relief from tension; he "feels better" about himself and others. While the effort to ward off anxiety involves an increase of tension, the relief from anxiety is associated with actions which, among other things, decrease muscle tension.

Anxiety is not synonymous with muscle tension, but the latter is a necessary condition for its experience. As we shall see, *anxiety is always related to interpersonal relations.*

THE POWER MOTIVE

Even more important and logically more fundamental than the impulses resulting from a feeling of hunger or thirst is the "power motive," the impulse to obtain and maintain a feeling of ability. To be able to obtain satisfactions and security is to have power in interpersonal relations; not to be able to do so is to be powerless, helpless. According to Sullivan, the development of actions, thoughts, foresights, etc., which are "calculated" to protect one from insecurity, is based on and springs from the disappointments and frustrations of early infancy. When one achieves power or ability in interpersonal relations, one respects oneself and therefore others. While the attitude toward the self is first determined by the attitude of those who take care of the child, his subsequent attitude toward others is determined by the attitude he has toward himself. "If there is a valid and real attitude toward the self, that attitude will manifest as valid and real toward others."[5]

EMPATHY

There is said to be "a peculiar emotional relationship" between the infant and those who take care of him. Long before he can understand what is happening to him, this "emotional contagion or communion" between him and the significant adult, the mother or nurse, exists. Sullivan surmises its greatest importance is between the ages of six and twenty-seven months. For example if a mother looks with disfavor on her offspring or she suffers a fright around feeding time, there may be great feeding difficulties. This unclear mode of emotional communication is thought to be biological, for certain animals are said to exhibit a similar phenomenon. Since the attitudes of the mother or nurse are socially conditioned, this mode of emotional communication, which does not seem to occur, in Sullivan's view, through

ordinary sensory channels, is very important for understanding acculturation. In later years, however, empathy is not
much in evidence.

THREE MODES OF EXPERIENCE

All experience occurs in one or more of three "modes"—
the prototaxic, parataxic, and syntaxic. As the Greek roots
of this horrendous term indicate, the prototaxic mode refers
to the first kind of experience the infant has and the order
or arrangement in which it occurs. As grown-ups, we experience things in terms of time and space, of here and "out
there," of before and after. We break up our experience, so
to speak, into constituent elements for the purposes of getting
along in the world. Furthermore, our experience, or at least
much of it, is referable to a self who does the experiencing,
the self being a center of reference. "I went for a walk in
the park at four o'clock." These are examples of every day
distinctions we make. Others, of course, are much more subtle
and refined.

Now in the beginning, the infant, Sullivan hypothecates,
makes no such distinctions for a variety of reasons. Aside
from structural and functional limitations, the organism at
birth has had, of course, no direct experience with the cultural heritage. We shall avoid saying he has no mind as
yet—for we shall not deal here with the problem of the
nature of mind nor with the problem of what he inherits
from his life in the womb, concerning which apparently not
a great deal is known, at least regarding mind.

According to Sullivan's hypothesis all that the infant
"knows" are momentary states, the distinction of before and
after being a later acquirement. The infant vaguely feels or
"prehends" earlier and later states without realizing any
serial connection between them. He has no ego in any dis-
tinctive sense because the self has not yet developed. For such

reasons, he has no awareness of himself as an entity separate from the rest of the world. In other words, his felt experience is all of a piece, undifferentiated, without definite limits. It is as if his experiences were "cosmic." This mode of experience is often marked in certain schizophrenic states.

The terms "parataxic" and "syntaxic"[6] also are etymologically related to the order and arrangement of experience. At the risk of confusion, we shall remind the reader that parataxic (like syntaxic) is a grammatical term as well, which refers to the ranging of clauses or propositions one after another without connectives such as "and," "or," "since," etc. to show the relations between them.

Gradually the infant learns to make some discrimination between himself and the rest of the world. As Sullivan puts it, he no longer reaches out to touch the moon. In other words he gradually learns to make elementary differentiations in his experience.

"We learn in infancy that objects which our distance receptors, our eyes and ears, for example, encounter, are of a quite different order of relationship from things which our tactile or our gustatory receptors encounter. That which one has in one's mouth so that one can taste it, while it may be regurgitated to the distress of everyone is still in a very different relationship than is the full moon which one encounters through one's eye but can in no sense manage."[7]

As the infant develops and maturation proceeds, the original undifferentiated wholeness of experience is broken. However, the "parts," the diverse aspects, the various kinds of experience are not related or connected in a logical fashion. They "just happen" together, or they do not, depending on circumstances. In other words, various experiences are felt as concomitant, not recognized as connected in an orderly way. The child cannot yet relate them to one another or make logical distinctions among them. What is experienced is assumed to be the "natural" way of such occurrences, without reflection and comparison. Since no connections or relations are established, there is no logical movement of "thought" from one idea to the next. The parataxic mode is not a step by step process. Experience is undergone as momentary, unconnected states of being.

The parataxic mode of organizing experience occurs mainly through visual and auditory channels. Dreams are often examples of this mode of experiencing. But it occurs a good deal of the time in waking life. In other words, we do not—and cannot—always organize our experience into a logically connected, related totality, in which the various elements are compared, contrasted, and ordered in a precise fashion. Ordinarily we do not indulge in careful ratiocination as we dress in the morning, proceed to work, and so on. It is not necessary, and in any case there is not enough time.

As the infant learns the rudiments of language, he is said to pass into the "epoch" of childhood. And here we introduce another term, the "autistic." The autistic is a verbal manifestation of the parataxic. But the capacity for verbal communication is just beginning to be manifested, and the tools, vocabulary, grammar, etc. are scarcely formed and learned. Because of the child's limited equipment and experience with the symbol activity and experience of others, his own symbol activity is arbitrary, highly personal, unchecked and untested. Hence his imagination is not curbed to conform to everyday "reality." Autistic symbols, however, are useful in recall and foresight.

Let us take an example of a child who has been given a picture book also containing words, say, to name or describe the pictures. It will have a picture of a cat, and below or above or somewhere on the page there is written what the child eventually learns is c-a-t. Then, too, to complete the example, the animal who runs around the house also is referred to by the same name as that of the colored or black and white pattern in the book. Sullivan comments on the significance of such a frequent phenomenon in our culture as follows:

"I am sure no child who can learn has not noticed an enormous discrepancy between this immobile representation in the book which, perhaps, resembles one of the momentary states that kitty has been in on some occasion. I am certain that every child knows that there is something very strange in this printed representation being so closely connected with the same word that seems to cover adequately the troublesome, amusing, and very active pet. Yet, because of unnumbered, sometimes subtle, sometimes crude experiences with the carrier of culture, the parent, the child finally comes to accept as valid and useful a reference to the picture as 'kitty' and to the creature as 'kitty.'

"The child thus learns some of the more complicated implications of a symbol in contradistinction to the actuality to which the symbol refers, which is its referent; in other words, the distinction between the symbol and that which is symbolized. This occurs, however, before verbal formulation is possible.

"From the picture book and the spoken word in this culture one progresses to the printed word and finally discovers that the combination of signs, c-a-t, includes 'kitty' in some miraculous fashion, and that it always works. There is nothing like consistent experience to impress one with the validity of an idea. So one comes to a point where printed words, with or without consensually valid meaning, come to be very important in one's growth of acquaintance with the world.

"There was first the visually and otherwise impressive pet, which was called 'kitty' (an associated vocalization): then came the picture of the kitten; now comes the generic *c a t* which includes kitty, picture of kitten, a kitten doll, and alley cats seen from the windows. And all this is learnt so easily that—since no one troubles to point it out—there is no lucid understanding of the sundry types of reality and reference that are being experienced. Familiarity breeds indifference in this case. The possibilities for confusion in handling the various kinds of symbols, naturally, remain quite considerable."[8]

The child gradually begins to catch on to patterns of relationships, to the grammatical structure of the language, and to the usual relationships and distinctions obtaining in his society. There is a more discriminating realization of the other fellow, the responder. The child now more clearly realizes that, for example, when he cries "dada," the other person responds in a more or less characteristic fashion. And so the child learns to anticipate the responses of others. These responses become associated with the use of certain words and gestures. In other words, the characteristic reactions of the other people give meaning to the language, a meaning that is thus implicitly agreed upon. Of course, the child does not set out systematically to learn the everyday meaning of the language. He learns by the trial and error method. Hence, he also learns that not only one's own experience is important, but that of others. He also learns to use verbal symbols as an economical way to get a lot to happen in a short time, with little use of energy.

Of course, there is a great deal more than this to be said about the learning process, but this sketch may indicate some of the ways by which, according to Sullivan, a child learns to use language with an interpersonal reference.

In any case, the child gradually learns the "consensually validated" meaning of language—in the widest sense of language. These meanings have been acquired from group activities, interpersonal activities, social experience. Consensually validated symbol activity involves an appeal to principles which are accepted as true by the hearer. And when this happens, the youngster has acquired or learned the syntaxic mode of experience.

But the learning process is not always consistent—because the significant others are not always consistent in their behavior. Furthermore, as we know, people do not always take the trouble to teach the child the distinctions between various symbols and that to which they refer. The trial and error method by which a good deal of learning necessarily occurs is not ideally suited for acquiring precise distinctions. For such reasons, language thus comes to have a double meaning—a personal meaning and a consensually validated meaning or a blend of both. In this way, among others, people come to maintain a wide margin of misinformation and illusion about others, themselves, and the world.

Tension, when it occurs in connection with needs, such as those of food and sex, is experienced in the syntaxic and parataxic modes. The tension of anxiety, however, is experienced by grown-ups mainly in the parataxic mode.[9]

THE MEANING OF DYNAMISM

Before taking up an exposition of the self dynamism (or self system or, simply, self), we must try to indicate what the term "dynamism" means. It has been defined as "a relatively enduring configuration of energy which manifests itself in characterizable processes in interpersonal relations."[10] In other words dynamism refers to the way energy is organized and channeled in the human organism. Dynamism implies only a relatively enduring capacity to bring about change. It is analogous to any structure or organization of processes which always contains numerous sub-structures.

For Sullivan energy always means physical energy. He rejects the notion of "psychic energy."

THE EVOLUTION OF THE SELF

As everyone knows, certain restraints are put on the young offspring's freedom which are or are considered to be necessary for his socialization, for training him and making him the sort of person considered right and desirable in the society in which he will live and have his being. These restraints, above everything else, bring about the evolution of the self dynamism. In this evolution, other aspects of the personality, such as *the selectively inattended* and *disassociated* processes, those which occur outside of self-awareness, are also developed.

We shall begin our exposition of Sullivan's theories concerning the evolution of personality with the "epoch" of infancy. Infancy refers to the period from birth to the maturation of the capacity for language behavior. During this period certain of the attitudes of the parent or nurse are said to be conveyed empathically. Suppose the mother is tired or upset or angry when she is in close contact with the infant, let us say, when she nurses or bathes him. Something of her attitude is then conveyed to him. His sense of well-being, his euphoria, is markedly decreased. The mother who observes or at least senses this gets anxious, which state is then communicated to the infant, further lowering his feeling of well-being, further increasing his insecurity. And so the process goes on. It is "dynamic."

Euphoria and anxiety are, conceptually, direct opposites, "polar constructs." In actuality there is no such thing as "pure" euphoria, in which there is no tension and therefore no action, something like an empty state of bliss. Perhaps the nearest approximation to euphoria in the "ideal" sense is deepest sleep. Nor is there any actual state of absolute anxiety. In the state of terror—in which there is a complete but temporary disorganization of personality—the most extreme degree of tension ordinarily observable occurs. Euphoria and anxiety are inversely related.

It is not difficult to see that a chronically hostile mother will induce an intense and more or less chronic anxiety in the offspring. Furthermore, such a mother will deprive him of the experience of tenderness—a deprivation which will have fateful consequences for his future well-being and happiness.

One of the characteristics of anxiety is that it interferes with observation and analysis, with the acquisition of information and understanding and with recall and foresight. It interferes with alertness to the factors in a situation that are relevant to its occurrence. Therefore it interferes with effective action.

Sooner or later the infant is recognized as educable. And when this happens, there is said to be a restriction of tender cooperation. The exhibition of tenderness by the parents tends to be modified so that it will be used more on "suitable" occasions. The mother, for example, begins to train the child in the "proper" toilet habits, those considered proper in the society in which she lives. She will express or withhold tenderness and approval as the child learns to conform or not to her desires and methods in this matter. Thus, training involves the expression of tenderness and approval for some acts and disapproval and the withholding of tenderness for others. In other words, some performances bring tenderness and approval with the consequent increase of euphoria, while others bring disapproval and hence anxiety. These experiences of rewards and punishments come to be regarded as something special. Gradually the child catches on to the fact that they are related to his feelings of euphoria and anxiety. The more or less abrupt supervention of anxiety gradually teaches or forces him to focus awareness on the performances which bring approval and disapproval. He learns, for example, to recall incidents occurring before anxiety. After a while a forbidding gesture will be sufficient to change his behavior.

In other words, as his observation improves, his grasp on the patterns of approval and disapproval becomes more refined. He learns that when anxiety is present and something is done which brings tenderness and approval, the painful discomfort is assuaged or banished.

Hence, the child gradually learns to focus attention on behavior which brings approval and disapproval in order to win rewards, tenderness and approval, and escape punishment, disapproval and disapprobation.

In infancy a vague idea of "my" body arises. From the sentience of the body as a basis, there gradually evolve three "personifications" of "me"—"good me," "bad me," and "not-me." The "good me" is an organization of experiences of approval, tenderness, and general good feeling. The "bad me" is an organization of experiences related to increasing anxiety states. The "rudimentary personification" of "not-me" evolves very gradually. The processes labeled "not-me" belong to the most poorly grasped aspects of living and refer to "uncanny" experiences like horror, dread, loathing, awe. What these uncanny experiences are about is not known, but they seem to originate in the experiences of anxiety in infancy, "primitive anxiety." They occur in the parataxic mode. The personification, "not-me," is not constituted by communicative processes and hence not much can be said about it. Nightmares and certain schizophrenic experiences are examples of uncanny experiences of the "not-me."

The "personifications" of "good me" and "bad me" belong to the self system. In other words, to put this crudely, there are times when "I" am "good me" and times when "I" am "bad me." Whether or not the self is predominantly one or the other depends on the course of experience, especially in early life. But the "good me" is essentially desirable, for it is organized on the basis of experiences of security. Hence "I" shall tend to regard "my" self as essentially the "good me"—at least unless my life experience has been extraordinarily unfortunate.

We can now state in general terms the origin, nature, and function of the self dynamism. It has its basis in the need for alertness to approval, tenderness and disapproval. We should like, too, to call attention to its *restrictive* function. "The self-dynamism is built up out of this experience of approbation and disapproval, of reward and punishment. The peculiarity of the self-dynamism is that as it grows it functions, in accordance with its state of development, right from the start. As it develops, it becomes more and more related to a microscope in its function. Since the approbation of the important person is very valuable, since disapprobation denies satisfaction and gives anxiety, the self becomes extremely important. It permits a minute focus on those performances of the child which are the cause of approbation and disapprobation, but, very much like a microscope, it interferes with noticing the rest of the world. When you are staring through your microscope, you don't see much except what comes through that channel. So with the self-dynamism. It has a tendency to focus attention on performances with the significant other person which get approbation or disfavor. And that peculiarity, closely connected with anxiety, persists thenceforth through life. It comes about that the self, that to which we refer when we say 'I,' is the only thing which has alertness, which notices what goes on, and, needless to say, notices what goes on in its own field. The rest of the personality gets along outside awareness. Its impulses, its performances are not noted."[11]

Among the peculiarities of anxiety is the fact that it is always "at 180° to any other tension with which it coincides."[12] In other words, it directly opposes the tensions of somatic needs and thereby prevents or hinders the satisfaction of somatic needs. An extremely anxious person cannot obtain proper sexual satisfaction or may be prevented from enjoying food by nausea, vomiting, etc. While all other tensions are followed by activities, either overt or covert, which resolve the tensions and satisfy needs, the tension of anxiety, in Sullivan's language, does not result in energy transformations directed to its relief by the removal of the situational factors obviously concerned in its provocation. The tension of fear, on the other hand, is often manifested in activities which remove the situational factors provoking fear, escapes them, neutralizes their importance or defers being afraid until the near future when the real or apparent danger is over.

As one grows, one learns, if only in a dim way, how to avoid most situations which provoke intense anxiety, but the capacity for it remains. And it will manifest itself throughout life. In this respect, the difference between the "normal" person and the "neurotic" is only one of degree.

Because experiences of approbation and disapproval occur long before one can think, long before one can discriminate what occurs, the earliest attitudes, and the most "deep seated" and pervasive, are acquired unthinkingly, with little or no discrimination. Furthermore, the infant, and to a large extent also, the child, is biologically and psychologically helpless. Not only does he depend on the parents for the necessities of life itself, but he has no or only an incipient ability to think and no or insufficient social experience. Hence, in earliest years the attitudes, codes, and behavior of the parents and their surrogates are necessarily accepted without criticism or discrimination. In Sullivan's language he is still pretty much restricted to the parataxic mode of experience. Later, at least to some degree, he will develop the ability to question, compare and relate his experiences.

The "facilitations and deprivations," that which is approved and disapproved by the parents and others close to the child, becomes the source of the material built into the self dynamism. By and large their behavior will be sufficiently consistent to give the self-system a form and direction which it will maintain throughout life. Any experience which promises to threaten the form and direction of the self will provoke anxiety. When this happens, the person will not clearly notice what is happening; its significance will not be realized. And he will usually, without being aware of it, indulge in behavior calculated to nullify the experience or its importance.

Thus, anxiety is the instrumentality by which the self limits and restricts awareness. It functions so as to maintain its own form and direction. "Even when the self is a derogatory and hateful system it will inhibit and misinterpret any disassociated feeling or experience of friendliness towards others; and it will misinterpret any gestures of friendliness from others. The direction and characteristics given to the self in infancy and childhood are maintained year after year, at an extraordinary cost, so that most people in this culture, and presumably in any other, because of inadequate and unfortunate experience in early life, become 'inferior caricatures of what they might have been.' Not only the family, but various other cultural institutions less directly, all combine, more or less unwittingly, to produce this effect."[13]

Actions, including thinking, phantasy, and emotions and feelings, if they are to occur within self-awareness, must conform to the characteristics of the self. Otherwise they are "disassociated" or "selectively inattended."

The self may be said to be made up of or at least circumscribed by *reflected appraisals*. The child lacks the equipment and experience necessary for a careful and unclouded evaluation of himself. The only guide he has is that of the significant adults who take care of him, and who treat and regard him in accordance with the way in which they have developed from their own life experience. Hence, the child experiences himself and appraises himself in terms of what the parents and others close to him manifest. By empathy, facial expression, gestures, words, deeds they convey to him the attitudes they hold toward him and their regard or lack of it for him.

These he "naturally" accepts because he is not yet a questioning, evaluating being. If the significant people express a respecting, loving attitude toward him, he acquires a respecting, loving attitude toward himself. If they are derogatory and hateful, then he will acquire a derogatory and hateful attitude toward himself. Throughout life, save perhaps for the intervention of extraordinary circumstances and allowing for some modification through later experience, he will carry the attitudes toward himself he learned in early life around with him just as surely as he will carry his skin.

Sullivan suggests, however, that the controlling limiting function of the self is not absolute. Certain impelling needs, such as the need of sexual satisfaction, if thwarted, may prove too powerful even for the self system. Fortunately children retain a capacity for change. A loving teacher may undo somewhat the effects of a destructive parent, but a hateful destructive teacher may limit or slow up the effects of the loving care of tender parents.

To the extent to which limitations and peculiarities of the self interfere with biologically necessary satisfactions and security, then to that extent a person is mentally ill.

The self-dynamism is not synonymous with momentary self-awareness. It is a more or less stable organization or configuration of interpersonal processes, past, present, and of the prospective future. The self has a before and after. Since it merges with other processes occurring outside discriminating awareness, it has "background," it shades imperceptibly into marginal processes of awareness. These marginal processes of awareness may often be noted just before one "drops off" to sleep. Because the self also manifests itself in focal awareness, it has a "foreground."

SELECTIVE INATTENTION AND DISASSOCIATION

It does not seem necessary to emphasize the fact that much of human experience and behavior occurs outside self-awareness. Freud formulated phenomena occurring outside self-awareness in terms of the "preconscious" and "unconscious." But for Freud these concepts have "topographical" and other features which are foreign to Sullivan's thought. Hence the latter usually avoids the use of such terms because they are "loaded" with meaning to which he does not subscribe.

The concepts by which he tries to formulate his thoughts on such matters are labeled "selective inattention" and "disassociation." The difference between the two is one of degree, measured by the difficulty of access to discriminating awareness.

The child gradually learns to pay close attention to behavior which is approved and disapproved. He must in order to maintain security and avoid anxiety. His attention becomes focused on these performances. This process is analogous to what goes on when, say, a music lover is present at a thrilling concert. Such a person becomes absorbed in the music, "wrapped up" in it. His attention will be entirely focused on the performance and enjoyment of it. To everything else he will pay little heed. In fact, he will not be conscious of anything else, such as the people around him, the passage of time, and so on. For the child his security is at issue, which of course is vitally important, and he will pay close attention to what goes on when approval or disapproval is involved. Certain other experiences either of himself or others will not be so clearly noticed because they entail no particular approval and tenderness or disapproval. Hence, his attention and inattention become selective. To some of his experience and behavior he will be inattentive, and this will then not be carefully discriminated. It will go on outside of discriminated awareness.

Some of these processes can more easily become the object of careful awareness than others. Thus, a friend may call attention to some of them, point them out, and in this case they then become subject to the person's awareness. Such processes are said to be selectively inattended. They can be accepted by the self.

But there are other processes which, when pointed out, do not get careful attention and scrutiny. In spite of the friend's efforts, they will not be clearly noticed. On the contrary, the person will not be able to become consciously aware of them. He will deny their existence, perhaps becoming tense and angry at the efforts of his friend. Nor will he, usually, be able to recall any experience of them. Such experiences are said to be disassociated. The self refuses to grant them awareness.

Motivational systems or dynamisms existing in disassociation are not necessarily "abnormal." And they may find expression in an interpersonal situation without those who participate becoming consciously aware of what is going on. In general, disassociated tendencies are expressed in dreams, phantasies and in unnoticed everyday behavior. In fact, if this were not so, the self system of "normal" people would disintegrate. In other words, the disassociated tendencies would prove too powerful for the inhibitions of the self, thus causing unbearable anxiety, and the person would "go to pieces."

THE MEANING OF INTERPERSONAL

There is a final point to be mentioned. The term "interpersonal" refers not only to real people existing in space and time but also to "fantastic personifications" or to people who exist physically but who serve rather as "potent representations" of other people once significant in a person's past, say, one's mother or father. In general, any frame of reference, whether constituted by real people, imaginary people existing only in story books, illusory personifications of real people (eidetic persons), or any idea or object given traits or characteristics possessed by human beings, along with one other real person, can serve to make up an interpersonal situation. We can personify and become "integrated" with almost anything, including cultural entities like the government, the church, the school who "have their being and their manifestation so far as any particular person is concerned in other people who are significant for one reason or another to him . . ."[14]

THE STAGES OF PERSONALITY DEVELOPMENT

For the sake of greater clarity, we shall sketch in the briefest fashion some of Sullivan's ideas on the various "epochs" or "eras" of personality development. These are:

1. *Infancy* to the maturation of the capacity for language behavior.
2. *Childhood* to the maturation of the capacity for living with compeers.
3. *Juvenile Era* to the maturation of the capacity for isophilic intimacy.
4. *Preadolescence* to the maturation of the genital lust dynamism.
5. *Early Adolescence* to the patterning of lustful behavior.
6. *Late Adolescence* to maturity.[15]

Infancy

Since the new-born is completely helpless if unaided by people, he is modified by the human element in his environment from the earliest stages outside the womb. Because of the empathic linkage, certain attitudes of the mother are communicated to him resulting in a loss of euphoria, a state

which is presumed to be constituted by the most severe form
of anxiety experienced by man. The unrestricted expression
of the power motive becomes gradually checked because of
frustration. The infant learns, for example, that he cannot
touch the moon. Thus, by attending to outer objects and
by exploring the possibilities and limits of his own body,
he gradually learns to mark off the limits of his own private
world. Everything ceases to be part of the infant's own
cosmic world. He gradually, so to speak, shrinks to life size.

In infancy, the first pair of personifications is said to
develop: the *good mother*, a shadowy and vague personification associated with the experience of the relaxation of
tensions due to recurrent needs, and the *bad mother*, associated
with the undergoing of anxiety. Subsequently they are blended
to conform more or less to the actual mother as she "really"
is. But throughout life in periods of stress people are said
to manifest characteristics of the original bifurcation of
experience into good and bad or evil mother. All later "eidetic
people," a complement of which each of us is said to carry
and live with, are founded on the original experiences of
these two fantastic personifications.

The self begins to evolve in late infancy. During the
first twelve months, many *covert* as well as overt processes,
it is inferred, develop. To put this another way, needs manifest a certain hierarchical order. Sometimes hunger will interrupt something else going on. When the hunger has been
appeased, the interrupted behavior continues, but with some
change. The *inference* is that something has been going on
while the other activity, hunger and its satisfaction, was
manifested. The inference that the interrupted behavior somehow continued unobtrusively all the time is the basis for the
theory of covert processes. Many covert processes of infancy
later arouse anxiety because of some connection with the
disapproval of the parents and are kept out of awareness.
They become disassociated.

Childhood

Deliberate training and acculturation in the folkways of the culture are said to begin as the infant passes into the epoch of childhood, carried on mainly by rewards (approval and tenderness) and punishments (disapproval and the withholding of tenderness). In this period the development of the self system proceeds rapidly.

"Childhood includes a rapid acculturation, but not alone in the basic acquisition of language, which is itself an enormous cultural entity. By this I mean that in childhood the peculiar mindlessness of the infant which seems to be assumed by most parents passes off and they begin to regard the little one as in need of training, as being justifiably an object of education; and what they train the child in consists of select excerpts from the cultural heritage, from that surviving of past people, incorporated in the personality of the parent. This includes such things as habits of cleanliness . . . and a great many other things. And along with all this acculturation, toilet habits, eating habits, and so on and so forth, there proceeds the learning of language as a tool of communication."[16]

A need for an audience response is said to appear. In this way, of course, a child learns a great deal. He learns, for example, ways of manipulating people. Such techniques, which occur in the parataxic mode, do not help the development of an adequate self.

In childhood, also, the youngster's capacity to feel disgust comes to be felt with words, acts, and so on, due to acculturation. Hence, certain impulses become sublimated. Sublimation is said to make up a large part of learning. The integration of experience in such a way that impulses which collide with the self system (provoke anxiety) are unwittingly combined with socially approved patterns of performance so that the basic impulse is partially satisfied without provoking anxiety is called sublimation. An attempt at a syntaxic formulation would make it impossible because that would tend to bring the impulse into clear awareness. The unsatisfied components of the basic impulse will be discharged in sleep (dreaming) or in deep reverie or in other unnoticed behavior. Needless to say, this is not an ideal way of expressing impulses.

When sublimatory reformulations fail, when in other words, a motivational system disintegrates, there has to be (1) refinement of the old integration, or (2) a reintegration into quite new patterns of behavior, or (3) a re-activation of the original pattern (regression). In the case of (3), experience then *looks* as if it had been destroyed. Regression is not rare. When the child is tired, before sleep, regression often appears.

However, experience grows by integration. When the need for tenderness is frequently rebuffed due to "parental vicissitudes," a "malevolent transformation" of personality may occur. The awareness of the need for tenderness then becomes associated with rebuff. In other words, when he feels a need for tenderness, he is manifesting "bad-me." His behavior is disapproved. The experience of the need for tenderness becomes associated with felt anxiety. Needless to say, this leads to unpleasant behavior. He feels he is surrounded by enemies. Later paranoid developments are related to this experience.

In childhood anger comes to be of great aid as a complex process for minimizing anxiety. Although there is no escape from anxiety, it can be neutralized, so to speak, by anger. In other words, at the threat of anxiety one gets angry at someone or something and no longer feels anxious. The anxiety becomes concealed because then attention is diverted. Because of this misuse of anger few people know when they are anxious.

More and more pressure is brought to bear as the

youngster progresses through childhood. If possible he is made obedient. In the place of expressing frustration, he develops a complication of anger, anxiety, etc. When his resentment, which he is at first apt to perceive, is disapproved, it is carried to greater lengths. Then the self excludes it from awareness, at least in part. Something else appears. One feels tired or preoccupied.

In childhood, also, revery processes develop and grow.

The elements of frequency and consistency of experience in learning have a great deal to do with acquiring complex patterns of behavior. In fact, there is perhaps nothing which impresses one so much as to the validity of an idea or an event than its frequency and consistency of occurrence. The infant is said to learn by pantomime. The parental response to the youngster's efforts to use words begins to be most important. He learns the tremendous prestige of words, and he gradually acquires the use of speech. With the development of skill at language behavior, which can refer to events more precisely, thought begins to appear.

The Juvenile Era

As the need for compeers—people significantly like one— matures, the juvenile era begins. "The child manifests a shift from contentment in an environment of authoritarian adults and the more or less personalized pets, toys and other objects, towards an environment of persons significantly *like* him. If playmates are available, his integrations with them show new meaningfulness. If there are no playmates, the child's revery processes create imaginary playmates. In brief, the child proceeds into the *juvenile era* of personality development by virtue of a new tendency towards cooperation, to doing things in accommodation to the personality of others. Along with this budding ability to play with other children, there goes a learning of those performances which we call competition and compromise."[17]

In our culture, schooling begins at this time, an experience, of course, fraught with great consequences. If the youngster has been reared in a home with eccentric parents, schooling may have very great consequences for good. "The child, at first—because novel experience is very difficult to get within the focus of the self—may feel that the teacher is some queer kind of dangerous inferior creature, the sort of person with whom one's parents would not associate. Still gradually, gradually, because other children who are now important put up with this, take it for granted, seem to think that it is perfectly natural; because of this powerful support or validation of the novelty, the self may expand somewhat. This is always a difficult achievement; but the self may come as it were to doubt certain of the harsh puritanical restrictions which have been incorporated in it, and while perhaps they do not disappear and in times of stress throughout life may manifest themselves clearly, still the experience of the school may head the self dynamism in another direction which will make for much greater opportunity for contented living, for mental health."[18]

School teaching facilitates some experience in the syntaxic mode. But a great deal has to be sublimated.

Education calls out "supervisory patterns" in the self. An internal auditor or "writing critic" is said to appear. This internal critic is a sub-organization in the self system.

Alertness as to what may happen in interpersonal relations increases. While the need for contact and for an audience appears in the era of childhood, it increases to the point of vulnerability during the juvenile era. If such contacts are made difficult for one reason or another, loneliness appears. A fear of ostracism, having its roots in the teaching by *indifference*, which parents often use as a weapon in educating the child, or a fear of depreciative evaluation, also arise. Juvenile society is said to contribute greatly to the personification of the self in the shape of *reputation*. Reputation begins in this era: one is popular, average, or unpopular.

Eventually, unless a person is very unfortunate, some *one* begins to be remarkably desirable, the *chum*, who is conducive to the satisfaction of needs and the avoidance of anxiety. This phenomenon ushers in the era of preadolescence.

Before turning to preadolescence, there is another point to be mentioned here. During the juvenile era there is a growth of personal stereotypes, abstract personifications. If one is psychologically warped, this phenomenon can be very serious and take a malevolent turn. These abstract personifications are used as attempts to avoid anxiety. Examples are: "the girls," "the boys," "the Catholics," "the Jews," "the Masons." Life is often said to be taken up with a struggle to escape from such abstractions.

Preadolescence

Between the ages of eight and one-half and twelve years the period of preadolescence is said to begin. In this era the capacity to love matures. In Sullivan's formulation, love exists *if and only if* the satisfactions and security of the loved one are as significant to one as one's own satisfactions and security. According to Sullivan love exists under no other conditions, regardless of popular use of the word. There is said to be as yet no real understanding of lust.

"This state of affectional rapport—generically love—ordinarily occurs under restricted circumstances. In the beginning many factors must be present. Some of these may be called obvious likeness, parallel impulse, parallel physical development. These make for situations in which boys feel at ease with boys rather than with girls. This feeling of species identity or identification influences the feeling involved in the preadolescent change. The appearance of the capacity to love ordinarily first involves a member of one's own sex. The boy finds a chum who is a boy, the girl finds a chum who is a girl. When this has happened, there follows in its wake a great increase in the consensual validation of symbols, of symbol operations, and of information, data about life and the world."[19]

The preadolescent learns to see himself through the other's eyes. Hence there is "consensual validation" of one's personal worth.

"In this period there begins the illumination of a real world community. As soon as one finds that all this vast autistic and somewhat validated structure to which one refers as one's mind, one's thoughts, one's personality, is really open to some comparing of notes, to some checking and counter-checking, one begins to feel human in a sense in which one has not previously felt human. One becomes more fully human in that one begins to appreciate the common humanity of people—there comes a new sympathy for the other fellow, whether he be present to the senses or mediated by rumors in the geography, or the like. In other words, the feeling of humanity is one of the aspects of the expansion of personality which comes in preadolescence. Learning at this stage begins to assume its true aspect of implementing the person in securing satisfactions and maintaining his security in interpersonal relations through the rest of life."[20]

During preadolescence "the great controlling power of the cultural, social, forces is finally inescapably written into the human personality."[21]

There is a linkage of interpersonal relations. Thus A is a chum of B, but B has a relation to C, C to D, and so on.

According to Sullivan, "isophilic" does *not* mean homosexual. The "genital lust dynamism" has not yet matured. But the time comes when it does mature, adolescence, and then what is usually called homosexuality often represents desperate measures against failure to make a heterosexual change.

Adolescence

Personality, as we have indicated, evolves gradually stage by stage. Each step in the developmental process is predicated on the successful realization of the previous steps. The successful realization of any period depends likewise on the maturation of capacities appropriate to that period. Maturation occurs in due time when the proper kind of environment exists. "When, and only when, maturation of capacities has occurred, experience of a valuable kind can occur: *If it does not occur*, if experience is definitely unsuited to providing competence for living with others at this particular level of development, the probabilities of future adequate and appropriate interpersonal relations are definitely and *specifically* reduced. The reduction of probability is specifically related to the forms of competence which are customarily developed under favorable circumstances in the course of this particular stage.

"Seen from this viewpoint, not the earlier stages only but each and every stage is equally important in its own right, in the unfolding of possibilities for interpersonal relations, in the progression from birth towards mature competence for life in a fully human world."[22]

If adolescence is "successfully negotiated, the person comes forth with self-respect adequate to almost any situation, with the respect for others that this competent self-respect entails, with the dignity that befits the high achievement of competent personality, and with the freedom of personal initiative that represents a comfortable adaptation of one's personal situation to the circumstances that characterize the social order of which one is a part."[23] Although it may seem that most people "successfully negotiate" adolescence, appearances in this case are deceptive. According to Sullivan, preadolescence for most people in this culture is the nearest they ever come to untroubled human life; the stresses and problems of life from then on distort them to "inferior caricatures of what they might have been."[24]

One of the necessary conditions for successful satisfaction of the "genital lust dynamism" is intimacy. People are said to have an intimacy need for the adequate performance of sexual satisfaction, and, if intimacy is lacking, a precautionary need to hide such a lack. By intimacy Sullivan means a feeling of closeness and tenderness with the sexual partner. Many people are not able to satisfy this intimacy need in sexual performances but they may hide this fact from themselves and others with, for example, eloquent protestations of love and devotion. The vicissitudes of life, especially in the periods before adolescence, for a variety of reasons, have warped them to such a degree that never will they feel intimate with the sexual partner—or perhaps in any situation. Sullivan once in a lecture characterized sexual performances of this sort as "instrumental masturbation."

The patterning of genital behavior takes various forms. Besides the usual "proper" forms there are numerous others popularly known as "perversions." But those considered perverse in one culture may be considered proper in another.

Sullivan does not consider sex to be a "nuclear explanatory concept" of personality or of personality disorder. And he adds the "lurid twilight which invests sex in our culture is primarily a function of two factors. We still try to discourage pre-marital sexual performances; hold that abstinence is the moral course before marriage. And we discourage early marriage; in fact progressively widen the gap between the adolescent awakening of lust and the proper circumstances for marriage. These two factors work through many cultural conventions to make us the most sex-ridden people of whom I have any knowledge."[25]

It is however, not easy to disassociate lust or to "sublimate" it. Sublimation sometimes works, and "works beautifully"—but not always. "Under certain circumstances, the self is able to dissociate lust and the impulses to genital behavior. This can be achieved only by the development of new and elaborate 'apparatus' in living . . . The point I wish to emphasize now is that, late as it is in maturing, the genital lust dynamism is something that can be dissociated only at grave risk to effective living, and that in most people it cannot be dissociated at all. It will again and again, at whatever great expense to security, whatever suffering from anxiety, manifest itself."26

Sublimation is of course not the same thing as disassociation. In the latter case, impulses are expressed and activities carried on without fundamental alteration outside discriminated awareness. Sublimated processes are part of the self and represent a compromise partial satisfaction of conflict-provoking tendencies. Except for basic biological needs, like food and drink, any motivational system can sometimes be disassociated or sublimated.

THE CONCEPT OF SITUATION

We shall round out our exposition of Sullivan with a brief discussion of his concept of *situation*. One talks about impulses, tendencies, goals because, as Sullivan would say, that is the way we conceive behavior. If we are very psychologically naive, we tend to think almost that impulses and feelings are things which float around inside of us, like casks in the sea. Of course, it would be absurd to accuse Freud of such naiveté; nevertheless, he speaks of the "id" as "a cauldron of seething excitement." This is very picturesque and has considerable literary power—but it is a very poor way of conceiving psychology. In any case, we may occasionally picture impulses as inwardly pressing against us, forcing us to act. Although we may not often resort to such imagery, we sometimes forget that we always think, feel and act as a unit, as an organism, in spite of the fact that the notion of

conflict complicates matters. If we do not act as a unit, as
a complete being—we do not act at all. Our habits of thought
and of speech, which themselves have a long history, are such
that it is not easy to conceive behavior without resorting to
ideas of instinctual drives, impulses, strivings, and the rest.
But if we are empiricists, what do we actually *observe?*

We observe a situation in which two or more people are
acting in a certain way. They act in a certain way together
and this is ostensibly and *prima facie* what an interpersonal
situation is. This is what we originally encounter. This is,
apparently, the "raw material" or "crude data" of empirical
psychology. Because of our habits of thought and speech
and the structure of the language, we say that "A is striving
toward so and so from B." But all we observe originally is
certain modes of action going on by the two people: talking,
laughing, etc. As Sullivan puts it:

"When we speak of impulse to such and such action, of
tendency toward such and such goal, or use any of these
words which sound as if you, as a unit, have these things in
you and as if they can be studied by and for themselves, we
are talking, according to the structure of our language and
the habits of common speech, about something which is ob-
servably manifested as action in a situation. The situation
is not any old thing, it is you and someone else integrated
in a particular fashion which can be converted in the alembic
of speech into a statement that 'A is striving toward so and
so from B.'

"As soon as I say this, you realize that B is a very
highly significant element in the situation. Many situations
are integrated in which A wants deference from B, and B,
mirabile dictu, wants deference from A. It looks as if there
were something in A and something in B that happened to
collide. But when one studies the situation in which A and B
pursue, respectively, the aim of getting from the other person
what he himself needs and what the other person needs, we

find that it is not as simple as it looks. The *situation* is still the valid object of study, or rather that which we can observe; namely, the action which indicates the situation and the character of its integration."[27]

As our skill in observation of ourselves and others improves, we learn to note other things. But ultimately all anyone can observe are *tensions* and *energy transformations*, many of the latter being manifested as *actions*. Except for the tension of anxiety, tensions themselves may be regarded as needs for particular energy transformations which will dissipate the tension, "often with an accompanying change of awareness, to which we can apply the general term, *satisfaction*."[28] The tension of anxiety calls for energy transformations which Sullivan calls "security operations" to terminate or diminish anxiety and to protect or enhance "self-esteem."

The reader will recall that at the outset we distinguished two closely related categories of human behavior characterized by the pursuit of satisfactions and the pursuit of security. These categories represent fundamental guiding principles in understanding an interpersonal situation. In other words, they are presumed to be the "integrating tendencies" which bring people together in an interpersonal situation. These assumptions make behavior intelligible. Their validity and usefulness are tested in the on-going, never ending, process of psychiatric inquiry. This process will determine whether they are to be accepted, modified, or rejected.

The traits which characterize interpersonal situations, in the long run and on the whole, which one "integrates," prescribe what one is, what one's personality is. The interpersonal situations in which one is involved, in the long run furnish the acid test as to what sort of person one is— regardless of what one would like to think of oneself. A loving person is one who integrates situations with another person in which the satisfactions and security of the loved one are as important as one's own. What one does in situations with the loved person provide the acid test.

In interpersonal situations "some dynamic component," such as the need for companionship or sexual satisfaction, is fulfilled or expressed, and then the situation is at least temporarily adjourned. It becomes a memory and a possibility for similar situations in the future. Because some dynamic processes occur outside awareness, in many situations both a witting impulse, a known impulse, that is, and an unrecognized impulse, a disassociated impulse, for example, are discharged.

Of course, when the frame of reference with which one is "integrated" is an "illusory personification" or an inhabitant of dreamland, the theory of interpersonal relations gets pretty complicated.

Since human behavior with others is always an interaction, the psychiatrist who treats patients is always a "participant observer." As he observes and studies the patient's problems, he is at the same time participating in an interpersonal situation with the patient. And the psychiatrist's alertness in the therapeutic situation in which he participates as to what role he is playing fixes the limits as to what he observes. And his alertness will be determined by his own self system.

The reader, if he was not already well cognizant of the fact, can now see that the state of psychiatric theory is still in an early stage of development. More refined observational methods and techniques of inquiry—"operational methods"— are needed. As Sullivan characteristically phrases it:

"Psychiatry as it is—the preoccupation of extant psychiatric specialists—is not science nor art but confusion. In defining it as the study of interpersonal relations, I sought to segregate from everything else a disciplinary field in which operational methods could be applied with great practical benefits. This made psychiatry the probable locus of another evolving discipline, one of the social sciences, namely *social psychology*. Both seek an adequate statement of living, including every instance of relative success or failure that is open to participant observation. The scientific psychiatrist would know wherein and wherefore his patient fails and whether his remedial efforts could reasonably be expected to lead to improved facility for living."[29]

THE OEDIPUS COMPLEX

As we have seen Sullivan attaches fundamental importance to the role of the parents, especially the mother or her surrogate in infancy and childhood. But this role is not a sexual one, even in the wide sense in which Freud conceives sexuality. The feeling of familiarity which a parent has toward his or her child of the same sex is said to lead to an authoritarian attitude, which, of course, produces resentment and hostility in the child. On the other hand, because of the difference in sex, leading to a sense of strangeness, the parent treats his or her child of the opposite sex with more consideration. Why? In the first case, the parent thinks that he is justified in dictating to someone who seems to be like himself, while in the latter case the feeling of strangeness deprives him of the notion that he is peculiarly fitted to run the child's life. Hence parents tend to treat their children of the opposite sex, so to speak, "with kid gloves." In this case, the freedom or relative freedom from pressure by the parent of the other sex results, at least often, in a feeling of greater affection and attraction by the child for him.[30]

CONCLUSION

Because Sullivan has not yet published any work which would give a systematic account of his ideas, we have been able to present in this chapter only a summary of his more fundamental views. What he has thus far published is a very inadequate outline of his present theories.

II. CONCLUSION -
A BRIEF CRITICISM AND APPRECIATION

FREUD

By founding and developing psychoanalysis Sigmund Freud inaugurated a movement which has penetrated and enriched so many fields of thought and endeavor that it would be difficult to list them all. Some of those fields are, besides psychology and psychiatry, sociology, anthropology, mythology, the various fine arts, religion, philosophy, education. His influence already approaches that of Darwin or Marx. And this influence is growing.

There is another point to be made here. All post-Freudians, if we may use a hackneyed phrase, are standing on his shoulders. If they—or at least some of them—can see farther than Freud, it is because he first pointed out the way.

After mentioning such an achievement, to acknowledge the fact that Freud was a genius is almost trivial. To say also that he was not perfect seems equally banal—were it not for the fact that some people refuse to recognize his imperfections and limitations.[1] Yet we must insist that perfection is God's exclusive privilege. As certain contemporary psychoanalysts and others have pointed out, Freud could not surmount certain limitations of his culture and of his own nature. This was inevitable. Even a genius can do only so much.

Therefore, the work of criticism, revision, elaboration and emendation of Freudian theory goes on and of course will go on. In this connection a remark of Sullivan is so felicitously phrased that we shall quote it. "The great debt that psychiatry owes to Sigmund Freud does not require us to try to stop our thinking at the points at which his thinking ceased. If anyone thinks that Freud, or any post-Freudian psychiatrist, has reached or approached the Truth, well and good; but that one is not a scientist. All scientific hypotheses must undergo change as man's grasp on the Universe continues to develop. This cannot but be strikingly the case in the traditionally neglected fields of psychiatry and the social sciences."[2]

It is not easy to criticize fairly a man whose terminology and concepts are as vague as are some of Freud's. Freud was a great literary stylist. His writing flows smoothly, vividly. It abounds in picturesque imagery. At first blush it seems as if his thoughts are expressed with crystal clarity. However, as soon as one begins to analyze some of his fundamental concepts such as libido, instinct, affect, psychic energy, one becomes bogged down in a maze of elusive or analogical notions, few of which are defined with any clarity. While we attempted in our exposition, wherever possible, to give some kind of definition which would be both faithful to Freud and at least superficially meaningful, we must now point out some of the vagueness and contradictions in Freudian theory.

The concept of instinct is one of the most obscure of all his ideas. From one point of view an instinct is pictured as a certain sum or quantity of energy forcing its way in a certain direction. From a biological point of view it is a "borderland concept" between the mental and the physical (or somatic). It is the mental representative of the stimuli emanating from within the organism, and at the same time it is a measure of the demand made upon the energy of the

mind because of the mind's connection with the body. Now
if an instinct is a sum or quantity of energy, how can it be
at the same time a "borderland concept" or occupy an intermediate position between the physical and mental, a mental
representative of physical (somatic) stimuli, and also simul-
tanously be a measure of the demand made upon the energy
of the mind? In other words, what does Freud mean by mind
and mental energy, so that an instinct can be both a mental
representative and a measure of energy?

There is another point to be made in connection with
instincts. Freud pointed out that in mental life we know an
instinct only by its aims. But how are we to know its aims?
Instincts do not announce their aims. People do. This in
other words means we "know" instincts only from the way
people act and strive for goals. In effect, to say we know
instincts only from their aims is an admission that we do
not know instincts at all. We experience needs, desires, and
so on, and we strive toward goals. Instincts in Freud's sense
are an elaborate—and unnecessary—intellectual construction
built up in order to account for certain observed facts. Did
not Freud say that instincts are "our mythology?"

Another point is the concept of libido. One definition
holds that it is the energy of all those instincts which refer
to all that may be comprised under the word love. Another
is that it is the force by which the sexual instinct is represented in the mind. Most generally, we think, it is a pleasure
striving force of a certain qualitative character. The libido
can get dammed up, flow backwards, and so on, like a fluid
current. Sexual impulse excitations, which, we assume, are
libidinal impulse excitations, he says, resemble a network of
communicating canals filled with liquid. This is another example of Freud's inveterate practice of reifying his concepts,
i. e., representing them as a substance.

Let us consider an early formulation of Freud's, one
which, so far as we know, he never abandoned. There is

"something," an amount of affect, a sum of excitation, having all the attributes of a quantity, capable of increase, displacement, and discharge, which extends itself over the memory-traces of an idea like an electric charge over the surface of the body. Anything which has all the attributes of a non-numerical quantity must, so it seems to us, be a physical entity. Apparently this "something" is the source of sexual excitement or constitutes sexual impulse excitations. It is this "something," apparently, which generates the excitations which are related to one another like a network of communicating canals.

We should like now to take up the pleasure-pain principle. Relief from the pressure of internal stimuli or stimulus-tension or the pressure of impulse-excitations constitutes pleasure. An increase beyond a certain point causes pain. In other words there is, as Freud says, a quantitative alteration of stimulus-tension. He later admitted there was a qualitative factor which he could not explain. The fact that Freud cannot explain qualitative factors is not surprising; he has no theoretical basis for understanding qualitative factors.

Affects comprise both motor discharges and sensations, including the perceptions of the motor actions which have been performed.[3] In accordance with his notions of the quantitative character of what we ordinarily call feelings, he seems to think of internal stimuli as existing physical pressure on the organism, somewhat like water against a dam. This pressure sometimes gets too great and eventually, after a devious underground passage, bursts forth in the symptoms of mental illness—an idea that is self-contradictory.

The concept of sublimation—one of the key Freudian concepts—is formulated in physical terms, or at least on a physical analogy. It is not always possible to tell what is literal and what is metaphor. In sublimation energy is diverted from its sexual goal and directed to other ends. Here again Freud is conceiving energy as flowing, as being diverted from its path. But at best this is sheer metaphor and neither explains nor proves anything.

To conclude these illustrations, nearly everything is conceived or explained in physical quantitative terms, except when a qualitative aspect is noted but which Freud cannot explain. This brings us to a point we have been leading up to, namely, that Freud's intellectual framework, his whole orientation, despite his preoccupation with the mind, is a mechanistic-materialistic one. And from a logical point of view, as we shall show in more detail, it vitiated some of his most fundamental discoveries. Freud grew up in the second half of the nineteenth century when scientific men generally espoused a philosophy of mechanistic-materialism—at least on weekdays. The whole universe was conceived in terms of mechanics, although a few men were already working toward a different view. Fundamentally there was one science—physics.

In striving to be as scientific as possible, Freud formulates his theories as well as he can substantively and quantitatively. Nearly everything is conceived and formulated as physical entities or as quasi-physical or as an analogy with mechanical behavior, which, of course, proves nothing about the mind. If one assumes that human nature is to be understood according to the principles of classical mechanics, of masses in motion, of forces acting in certain directions, or of any limited number of physical laws, how can one explain *purpose, consciousness*, what we loosely call *will*, not to mention the *unconscious*, which are qualities and modes of experience and behavior, not physical entities?

In order to avoid misunderstanding, we must point out that one can be a determinist, that is, one can assume that events have causes, without being a mechanist. One can be a determinist and be a supernaturalist, idealist, or naturalist.

We are also not forgetful of the fact that Freud constructed many of his ideas in order to devise a workable scheme for understanding mental illness. But we do mean to suggest that in the light of our present knowledge, several of his formulations should be abandoned and replaced by more adequate ones.

Freud's mechanistic outlook led him to think of the personality and personality development likewise in a somewhat mechanical, materialistic fashion. Consider his concept of personality organization. The personality for Freud is divided into id, ego, and superego. To be sure, he says that the superego is a part of the ego, and that the ego in turn is part of the id. Yet he almost constantly speaks of them as if they were separate entities. They are three "psychic regions" having, as he puts it, topographical features, or as he also says, they are separate psychical systems. Furthermore, they also have, or at least the id has, "economic" features, namely quantities of stimulation at their disposal, quantities of that "something" which we mentioned above. Or to put this in a different way, Freud hypostasizes the id, ego, and superego. They become substantial entities.

Furthermore, the relations between these "provinces" is also mechanical and external. They do not interact in any dynamic sense. The ego, having no energy of its own, gets pushed around by the id and the superego. However, Freud does preserve the notion of dynamic processes within these "provinces."

No wonder then that Freud conceives of the relation of the person to his environment as external and also mechanical. Essentially the organism is conceived as separate and isolated. Its contact with the world is based in part on reflex mechanisms and in part on instinctual activity, which essentially consists of mechanical contact with objects in order to remove the internal stimulus by which need is defined.

Critics of Freud have pointed out that, according to him, the role of culture is essentially a negative one: to suppress, to inhibit, and to forbid. Now suppression is itself conceived mechanically as a *forcing back* of that "something." From a theoretical point of view, there is no interaction between the organism and its environment, only physical contact. Hence, the environment cannot be understood, logically speaking, as playing a creative role in the development and experience of the person.

Healy, Bronner and Bowers seem to give tacit recognition to the point we have been making here, although they do not explicitly commit themselves concerning Freud. In any case, even if they wish to imply that Freud is not a mechanist, they offer no proof. They strongly urge the use of the term "dynamism" instead of "mechanism." "We have long felt," they say, "certain incongruities in the employment of the latter term and one of us, at an academic meeting of scientific people, heard some forceful criticisms and even amusement expressed concerning the taking over of the term 'mechanism,' as in 'mental mechanisms,' by psychiatrists . . . An equation might be set up—Mechanics: Mechanisms:: Dynamics: Dynamisms. It is perfectly clear that mechanics cannot be under consideration in discussing mental life, while as for mechanism, that, properly speaking, is the arrangement of the parts of a machine—a combination of objects not necessarily doing anything. To be sure, a mechanism is sometimes spoken of as a mechanical operation or action. Now psychiatry, and especially psychoanalysis, is particularly interested in the dynamics of mental life, in 'moving forces and the laws which relate to them.' Then, as a physicist might formulate it, a dynamism is a specific force operating in a specific manner or direction. This exactly fits the conception of displacement, repression, sublimation and the other specific processes by means of which the Ucs [the unconscious as a 'psychical system'] operates."[4]

We pass over their definition of mechanism to note that one cannot solve this problem by a verbal reshuffle. Even under the new terminology the authors are thinking in terms of mechanics—in terms of forces operating in a specific manner or direction.

We believe that if they offered a definition of dynamism in terms of processes, they would be on firmer ground. Force is a shorthand reference to complicated interrelated processes. Dynamism would then signify a structure or ordered arrangement of processes and their relations, not forces. There is, of course, much more to be said on this matter, but that would lead us into an involved philosophic discussion.[5]

Another questionable concept is the death instinct theory. This theory has no empirical proof at all. No competent contemporary biologist we know of has ever claimed that living matter has an inherent tendency to die, in Freud's sense. The theory is purely speculative, put forth in order to "explain" the enormous amount of aggressiveness and destructiveness which he actually observed. This theory has an unfortunate consequence in that it gives an ostensible rationale for the pessimistic, ultimately hopeless outlook of Freud's theories when taken literally.

The speculations of Freud concerning man's archaic heritage are among the most controversial of all his theories. This archaic heritage is said to occur not through social transmission but biologically. The individual at birth brings with him not only "dispositions" but ideational contents and memory traces of the experiences of former generations. This notion of Freud is not generally accepted by biologists nor by psychoanalysts; while accepting his factual discoveries, they reject the complicated theories adduced to explain them.

His speculations concerning the primal horde, related as they are to the idea of a phylogenetic heritage, are no less doubtful. No contemporary anthropologist of recognized standing, with the possible exception of a few men like Geza Roheim who are committed in advance to Freudian theory, as far as we know, has ever offered any confirmation of Freud's speculations concerning a primal horde.[6] Westermarck, after submitting Freud's notions about the Oedipus complex to a long searching examination, concludes that the "facts which have been adduced in support of the supposed prehistoric events to which Freud has attributed the inhibition of incest have thus in each case been found to be worthless as evidence."[7] Westermarck seems to be equally skeptical concerning the universality of the Oedipus complex.

After these somewhat cursory remarks on a subject which, to do it justice, requires a book in itself, we wish to conclude our criticism of Freud with a reminder that it is not meant to nor does it invalidate his factual discoveries, observations, and therapeutic techniques. In our judgment the process of rectification already proceeds apace in the work of people like Fromm, Horney, Sullivan and others. To slight the importance of Freud or his genuinely great contributions because of certain limitations would be an egregious mistake.

ADLER

Alfred Adler has sometimes been criticized for his superficiality. Even though superficiality is a relative term, one may recognize the justness of the criticism without ignoring his importance. At the very least he called attention to an aspect of psychology which Freud seems to have underestimated: the striving for power and domination in Western society. It remained for subsequent writers like Horney and especially Fromm to find deeper significance in the striving for power. Unfortunately Adler apparently was too much taken in by the feelings of inferiority and powerlessness he observed in his patients. He assumed that feelings of inferiority and powerlessness are of primary significance in all children without seeing that children brought up in a healthy environment are not overwhelmed or burdened by such feelings.

Furthermore, he did not see clearly the difference between the striving for irrational power—the striving for power over people—and the sense of adequacy, competence, and power which comes from self-respect and respect for others—a rational feeling of power. Hence, he was not able to see that it is the manner in which human potentialities are given a chance to develop or are thwarted or distorted which is the essential point.

He did see, however, through not very deeply, that one's "style of life" is of primary significance. Adler also understood, though again not very profoundly, that one's attitude toward one's fellow men—social feeling, as he put it—and love are of the greatest significance for human well-being and happiness. His emphasis on the unity of personality as it is achieved by the person's guiding fiction or guiding image anticipates later writers. Finally, he was the first of all the writers we have discussed to abandon a mechanistic biological psychology and elaborate a dynamic theory of personality.[8]

JUNG

In spite of the fact that Jung has committed certain intellectual excesses and indulged in some very dubious speculations, we think his achievements are at present underrated. Very early he saw with considerable clarity what contemporary post-Freudians have driven home, that it is the emotional interplay between parents and children which is primary, not the sexual attraction between children and parents. His application of psychoanalysis to the more severe mental disorders was pioneering. Jung also saw with no little clarity that the struggle to achieve a "real individual line of life" is of the utmost importance for understanding "neuroses."[9] Nor was he unaware of the fear of and the struggle to escape individuality in general. His theory of introverted and extraverted personalities, whatever its virtues or defects, is now well known to all psychologists. His "association experiments" have been assimilated into academic psychology. He saw the prospective, that is, auto-therapeutic, aspect of dreams and neuroses. Finally, he put his finger on one of Freud's most fundamental errors, his reductive fallacy. His influence on people like Rank and Horney is obvious; and Freud, too, has admitted some indebtedness.

Unfortunately, he does not seem able to assimilate contemporary empirical anthropology. Instead he resorts to a very dubious explanation of the real or alleged similarity of myths and symbols: the collective unconscious. The alleged vehicle of the unconscious historical background is engrams. These engrams, we suspect, are products of Jung's imagination, for we know of no one who has encountered them. The collective unconscious seems to us a crude and artificial construction. The alleged striking similarity of myths is no proof of the existence of a collective unconscious. If myths show certain similarities throughout the world, it is logically possible that similar conditions of life generate the similarities. There are, of course, other logically possible explanations, but we must leave it to the anthropologists to pass on such matters. Similar arguments hold concerning the theory of archetypes.

In short, we think that Jung, like Freud, has an insufficient understanding of the process of acculturation and the modes of social communication.

Jung also slights or disparages reason apparently because of the shortcomings of rationalism and because of a certain animus against science. Instead he leans toward "spirit." As far as we can make out, spirit, for Jung, is an immaterial substance. It "is characterized first of all by the principle of spontaneous movement and activity, secondly by the property of free creation of images outside of sense perception, thirdly by the autonomous and absolute manipulation of these images."[10] Since such a notion cannot be put to any kind of empirical scientific test, it cannot make any claim to scientific standing.

However, these excesses need not blind us to Jung's other contributions.

RANK

Our discussion of Rank ended on a negative criticism of his theory of truth. We wish now to add that his, to us, mistaken theory of truth, of course, does not in itself invalidate his other theories. They have to be judged on their own merits.

Rank, beyond all other writers we discuss, is vague, and only by prolonged and intense labor can one elicit an approximate summary of his ideas. For this reason alone, if not for others, his work has suffered. Yet he is one of the most gifted of post-Freudians, and he has anticipated several of the ideas of contemporary psychoanalysts, of Horney, Fromm and Sullivan. His influence on literary writers on matters of aesthetics has been considerable. And there is a contemporary "school" of social workers who are greatly influenced by his theories and teachings.

His theory of the birth trauma, phantastic as it may sound when taken literally, appears in a different light when viewed from the angle of his later theories. With the knowledge of his later work, we can see that he was groping toward his most important ideas on the birth of individuality. His own work is a living example of the struggle if not the pain of the birth of individuality and creative achievement.

Since Rank's writings are characterized by long brilliant passages interspersed with ideas that are highly speculative, obscure, or even contradictory, it is impossible to express a precise appreciation of his contributions in a short space. However, we believe we are on safe ground when we say that, by and large, his notions concerning individuality, the stages of the development of individuality and "autonomous will" are sound and of lasting importance. In this connection his ideas on love and hate are noteworthy. He also saw with considerable clarity how the will of the child is moulded by the parents and how it is weakened or broken by them; how also some children are able to put up a fight for their own integrity. Rank also saw something of the conflict of the son and the father in what is called a patriarchal society, a fact which later Fromm was to elucidate with much greater clarity and depth. Finally, Rank was one of the first to claim that analysis is concerned, not with the past, but the present situation.

These are some but by no means all of Rank's contributions. However, Rank, like many others, not infrequently allowed his versatile mind to speculate and express ideas for which little if any empirical evidence exists. His speculations on anthropology and sociology contain much that is highly dubious and which perhaps only a confirmed Rankian would take seriously. His main contributions seem to lie, not unnaturally, in the realm of psychology.

HORNEY

Karen Horney was among the first psychoanalysts in this country to abandon the artificial and cumbersome libido theory; she thereby paved the way for an understanding of people primarily in terms of the social environment and the problems which it generates. Personality is no longer divided into regional organizations. The genetic method of analysis is superseded by a functional method in trying to understand the neuroses. For such reasons her work on the neurotic personality is widely acknowledged to be a great improvement over that of Freud. Culture is no longer conceived as playing a mechanical role by frustrating libidinal or other drives but as providing the framework within which personality develops and operates. In other words, specific cultural conditions engender specific qualities and faculties in people.

But, some one may object, is not the biological make-up of man a factor to be taken into account? Of course it is, but the answer requires elaboration. First of all, from one point of view or for certain purposes, the biological make-up of man may be considered as pretty much the same all over the world. We all have similar basic organic structures and needs. We all have essentially equal human powers. Hence, the fundamental problem is to discover how the biological conditions of human nature interact with the social conditions under which men live. These social conditions, in other words, mold the individual, by and large, into a certain kind of personality, having a certain basic personality structure. The differences which men manifest may be accounted for by the differences in their experiences, in their social environment, and perhaps—though it has not been proved in any scientific fashion—differences in constitutional make-up. But as others have pointed out, we are all essentially alike. In other words, for many purposes we may assume the biological conditions of man as a constant.

The second point to be made is that we never observe the full-blown biological make-up of human beings in isolation. We always observe them as acculturated beings, as social beings. Hence, it is misleading and confusing to set up an opposition between the person and his environment. And this is precisely what Freud and others have done. The error which Freud committed is a product of nineteenth century individualism. The mechanistic-materialistic framework in which he thought and formulated his ideas is the scientific version of the pervasive social patterns of his time. Further, not a little of what passes for biology in Freud is pseudo-biology. The death instinct theory is a good example.

Horney, like most psychoanalysts, often makes no distinction between a temporal and a logical order. For example, she says that the basic conflict is born of the three incompatible attitudes. This means, if we take the statement literally, that the three incompatible attitudes are logically prior to the basic conflict; the basic conflict presupposes the existence of the three attitudes. Yet the three attitudes enter in as, or contribute toward, major attempts at solution of the basic conflict. This, then, implies that the basic conflict is prior to the incompatible attitudes. Formally, at any rate, this is a contradiction.[11]

Actually, Horney seems to mean that there is a relation of interaction between the incompatible attitudes and the basic conflict. The incompatible attitudes are "conflicting." Furthermore, she implies, that the incompatible attitudes become exaggerated in the course of time by the effort to escape anxiety and conversely. We could, following popular usage, put this in another way by saying that the incompatible attitudes are both cause and effect of the basic anxiety.

But every situation has an indefinite number of complex relations and qualities. We can, if we wish, restrict ourselves to noting and describing a uniform conjunction of traits repeatedly observed to exist with no understanding of why the conjunction occurs. In that case we are empiricists in the bad sense of the word. We have no theory which states the rationale of why such a conjunction of traits occurs. We are like an automobile mechanic who knows that an engine operates in a certain way without knowing the physical principles involved. We may say that the basic conflict is associated with the incompatible attitudes in a relation of both cause and effect—if that strictly is meaningful—or that they interact, but we do not then tell *why*. We must go further. We may redefine our concepts and we may search for a more fundamental ground or frame of reference from which the explanation of observable phenomena may be logically derived.

All of this in no way denies the fact that events are constantly interacting. But if we are to explain in the logical sense, not merely describe what happens, we must elucidate the logical structure of what occurs.

In any case, we think that Horney has not yet sufficiently clarified her fundamental concepts.

FROMM

In the opinion of many people, Erich Fromm's *Escape From Freedom* is a contemporary classic piece of sociological and psychological analysis, although critics have not infrequently shown a curious lack of understanding of what that work actually is about. His second book attempts to establish a logico-philosophical foundation for an explanation of man's nature and behavior. As Fromm has pointed out, Freud and most of his disciples have shown a singular lack of sociological sophistication, although they are not unique in this respect.

Fromm brings to his work a wide knowledge of sociology, anthropology, and history. For this reason, if not for others, his writings have a profundity which those of most psychoanalysts lack. Fromm does not suffer from the illusion that all psychological knowledge began with Freud—or with Fromm. An Aristotle, a Spinoza, a Meister Eckhardt, a Kafka may not have known much about the so-called libido, but they knew a great deal about other matters—perhaps ultimately much more important matters—concerning what has been traditionally called man's spirit. Among contemporary major psychoanalysts, Fromm alone has availed himself freely of the rich literary and philosophical tradition of the West.[12] Not that philosophers, as they themselves well know, have not written much nonsense—a phenomenon incidentally that is not confined to philosophers. But it is a mark of intellectual maturity to recognize and to be able to separate the chaff from the wheat.

This does not mean that we agree on all points with Fromm's philosophy, but we are not here concerned with technical philosophical problems. The chief disagreement with Fromm which we wish to mention is based on the belief that, as we understand him, he is not sufficiently an "interactionist" in his description of social and psychological processes. For example, we think he has slighted the role of science and technology in the history of Western civilization in recent centuries. As we understand it, science has played a causal role in the development of modern capitalism and in general in various sectors of modern life. At least Fromm uses the categories, socio-economic, psychological, and ideological so broadly that it is difficult to know how he thinks science and technology have operated. Were they an effect of socio-economic conditions, or are they included in the concept of socio-economic conditions, or do they play a causal role in the creation of socio-economic conditions? This point is not clear to us.

An analogous problem exists in Fromm's concept of character. In his first book he states that character determines the thinking, feeling, and acting of individuals.[13] We doubt if this is to be taken literally because the combined modes of thinking, feeling and acting constitute character. Recently Fromm has stated that ideas, judgments, and actions result from a person's character.[14] But ideas, judgments, and actions, we believe, are constituent elements of character, not a result of character. This is not a mere matter of phraseology. It is a factual, not merely a formal, question. In Fromm's formulation, something else, character, is given a primary causal function, and ideas, judgments, and actions are said to be an effect or result of character. Fromm like most, if not all, psychoanalysts apparently wants to make the emotional attitude of a person primary. But no one has shown more eloquently than Fromm the role of ideas, of reason, in human life. Hence, we suspect that ideas and judgments, for example, instead of being a result of character, are as efficacious in the constitution of character as anything else.

SULLIVAN

Sullivan first became known for his spectacular success with young schizophrenic patients. And while more recently he has attempted to work out a theory of personality and personality development, his ideas always retain a therapy-oriented formulation. For good or ill they retain, as someone said, something of "the odor of the clinic." His main contribution, however, is his theory of interpersonal relations. This theory attempts to show *how* the patterns of the culture come to make up the warp and woof of mind and personality. Whatever may be the virtues or defects of Sullivan's theories in detail, this is a great step in advance of the mere *assertion* that they do. Furthermore, he has succeeded to a considerable degree, we believe, in showing *how* mind and personality always operate in an interpersonal reference, not as an isolated and more or less self-contained entity. In other words, he has attempted to demonstrate *how* and *why* psychiatry is ultimately the locus of social psychology. In theory, psychiatry as the specialized professional preoccupation of doctors with the mentally ill is replaced by a conception of psychiatry as the study of processes that involve or go on between people. Therefore, a theory of interpersonal relations becomes a nuclear explanatory concept for social psychologists and sociologists.

Partly because of his preoccupation with interpersonal processes, Sullivan in recent years has developed a curious animus against the concept of individuality. This, we believe, is a mistake. Individuality in no way contradicts the fact that personality develops and has its being in interpersonal relations. Furthermore, we know of no contemporary concept of individuality which answers to the character that Sullivan's repeated attacks would imply it has. In fact we think that Sullivan is attacking a straw man—a nineteenth century notion of individuality.

Another point we wish to mention refers to the concept of power. We believe that, in theory, Sullivan has not yet adequately distinguished between power as ability, which goes with respect for oneself and others and the achievement of satisfactions and security; and power in the sense of gaining domination and control over others. While, of course, he does recognize the malicious effects of a domineering mother, for example, the theoretical explanation of the irrational craving for power over people remains in part to be worked out.

Until Sullivan's ideas have been worked out and elaborated in a more comprehensive fashion, it is difficult to know whether the charge that he is a cultural relativist, for which he has been criticized, is correct. There seems to be some justification for the charge in view of the fact that he seems to have given little attention to the qualitative differences in acculturation. What significance do the differences in culture and acculturation between us and the Chinese, for example, have for personality development? Is there any trans-cultural criterion for appraising such differences? Or is each culture and each set of values so unique that the last question is illegitimate?

Because the *meaning* of native capacities is not native but acquired in a cultural context, it does not seem to us to follow that some cultures may not develop a richer meaning in terms of human happiness of such capacities.

In other words, are there any values which are so intrinsically important for the well-being of the person that any culture which slights them is self-defeating? Are morality and ethics unique to a given culture, which no outsider can legitimately criticize; or has mankind in the course of its history discovered certain values which serve as a criterion in judging the success or failure of a given culture in its function of providing the materials of humanness to its members?

FINAL REMARKS

By and large, psychoanalytic theory has made magnificent progress in the fifty or sixty years of its existence. Freud, of course, remains the most imposing individual figure, although, as is the fate of all great innovators, much of his work has to be superseded by more refined formulations. For some time psychoanalysis has been more than a technique of therapy. It is a system of psychology; when the newer contributions are granted in addition, by far the most comprehensive and powerful psychological system in existence.

We believe that it is fitting to give a Greek title to a work on psychology. Although it is fashionable these days for writers on the social sciences to disparage the Greeks— usually without much detailed knowledge of Greek culture— the Greeks may fairly be given credit for establishing a science of psychology. The very word "psyche," which has been a favorite term among European psychoanalysts, is Greek. But it is far more than a matter of terminology. The philosophers, Socrates, Plato and Aristotle, and the dramatists, especially Aeschylus, Sophocles and Euripides, possessed a profound knowledge and understanding of the human psyche. Who but a Socrates would have said that the unexamined life is not worth living? Twenty-three hundred years ago Aristotle held that a friend is another self. And Greek naturalism is summed up beautifully by the saying of Sophocles that among the many wonders of the world the greatest of these is man.

Certain writings of Aristotle, we believe, may fairly be said to be the first scientific work on bio-social psychology.

Except for some professional students of philosophy, his work is practically unknown to students of human nature and behavior. Yet a careful study of his work will reveal the fundamentals of several of our advanced psychoanalytical theories. You will find, for example, "contextualism" or what others call "situationism." You will find determinism, which has been vaunted by psychoanalysts as one of the glories of Freudian theory. You will find behaviorism—but not a crude Watsonian behaviorism. You will find the notion also that man is naturally a social being. And, for those who are interested, you will find the life of reason commended.

While the Greeks had little interest in control over nature, they were supremely interested in understanding, and they recorded in "winged words" some of the most profound truths of human life. They were also supremely interested in the "good life": the life that is good for man here and now. As one scholar put it, their ideal was a beautiful soul (psyche) in a beautiful body. They had no sense of sin in the Christian sense and no need of salvation. The good of man is his own happiness, to be achieved, according to the Aristotelian formulation, by the realization or actualization of man's powers, especially the power of reason, for reason is most divine, and in so far as man has a divine element in him he will pursue the life of reason.

The trilogy of Sophocles embodies the wisdom of the Greeks at their best—a wisdom that has not been surpassed. Perhaps it is no accident that different writers find a different interpretation. Passion, sexual and otherwise, was no stranger to the Greeks. Nor was the longing for immortality, as the writings of Plato testify. And Greek history has many bloody pages which tell of the struggle for democracy against authoritarianism. In any case, whether the trilogy is susceptible to a manifold interpretation, these facts of Greek life and history are well established.

At last, twenty-three hundred years later, we rediscover the insights of the great Greeks and something of their wisdom. We can still learn from them.

THE OEDIPUS TRILOGY

By

SOPHOCLES

OEDIPUS REX

CHARACTERS IN THE PLAY

OEDIPUS, *King of Thebes*
PRIEST OF ZEUS
CREON, *brother of* JOCASTA
TEIRESIAS, *the blind prophet*
JOCASTA
FIRST MESSENGER, *a shepherd from Corinth*
A SHEPHERD, *formerly in the service of Laius*
SECOND MESSENGER, *from the house*
CHORUS OF THEBAN ELDERS

Mute Persons

A train of Suppliants (old men, youths, and children).
The children ANTIGONE *and* ISMENE, *daughters of*
OEDIPUS *and* JOCASTA.

OEDIPUS REX

(SCENE:—*Before the royal palace of Oedipus at Thebes. In front of the large central doors there is an altar; a smaller altar stands also near each of the two side-doors. Suppliants—old men, youths, and young children—are seated on the steps of the altars. They are dressed in white tunics and cloaks,—their hair bound with white fillets. On the altars they have laid down olive-branches wreathed with fillets of wool. The* Priest of Zeus, *a venerable man, is alone standing, facing the central doors of the palace. These are now thrown open. Followed by two attendants, who place themselves on either side of the doors,* Oedipus *enters, in the robes of a king. For a moment he gazes silently on the groups at the altars, and then speaks.*)

Oedipus

My children, latest-born to Cadmus who was of old, why are ye set before me thus with wreathed branches of suppliants, while the city reeks with incense, rings with prayers for health and cries of woe? I deemed it unmeet, my children, to hear these things at the mouth of others, and have come hither myself, I, Oedipus renowned of all.

Tell me, then, thou venerable man—since it is thy natural part to speak for these—in what mood are ye placed here, with what dread or what desire? Be sure that I would gladly give all aid; hard of heart were I, did I not pity such suppliants as these.

Priest of Zeus

Nay, Oedipus, ruler of my land, thou seest of what years we are who beset thy altars,—some, nestlings still too tender for far flights,—some, bowed with age, priests, as I of Zeus,— and these, the chosen youth; while the rest of the folk sit with wreathed branches in the market-places, and before the two shrines of Pallas, and Ismenus gives answer by fire.

For the city, as thou thyself seest, is now too sorely vexed, and can no more lift her head from beneath the angry waves of death; a blight is on her in the fruitful blossoms of the land, in the herds among the pastures, in the barren pangs of women; and withal the flaming god, the malign plague, hath swooped on us, and ravages the town; by whom the house of Cadmus is made waste, but dark Hades rich in groans and tears.

It is not as deeming thee ranked with gods that I and these children are suppliants at thy hearth, but as deeming thee first of men, both in life's common chances, and when mortals have to do with more than man: seeing that thou camest to the town of Cadmus, and didst quit us of the tax that we rendered to the hard songstress; and this, though thou knewest nothing from us that could avail thee, nor hadst been schooled; no, by a god's aid, 'tis said and believed, didst thou uplift our life.

And now, Oedipus, king glorious in all eyes, we beseech thee, all we suppliants, to find for us some succour, whether by the whisper of a god thou knowest it, or haply as in the power of man; for I see that, when men have been proved in deeds past, the issues of their counsels, too, most often have effect.

On, best of mortals, again uplift our State! On, guard thy fame,—since now this land calls thee saviour for thy former zeal; and never be it our memory of thy reign that we were first restored and afterward cast down: nay, lift up this State in such wise that it fall no more!

With good omen didst thou give us that past happiness; now also show thyself the same. For if thou art to rule this land, even as thou art now its lord, 'tis better to be lord of men than of a waste: since neither walled town nor ship is anything, if it is void and no men dwell with thee therein.

OEDIPUS

Oh my piteous children, known, well known to me are the desires wherewith ye have come: well wot I that ye suffer all; yet, sufferers as ye are, there is not one of you whose suffering is as mine. Your pain comes on each one of you for himself alone, and for no other; but my soul mourns at once for the city, and for myself, and for thee.

So that ye rouse me not, truly, as one sunk in sleep: no, be sure that I have wept full many tears, gone many ways in wanderings of thought. And the sole remedy which, well pondering, I could find, this I have put into act. I have sent the son of

Menoeceus, Creon, mine own wife's brother, to the Pythian house of Phoebus, to learn by what deed or word I might deliver this town. And already, when the lapse of days is reckoned, it troubles me what he doth; for he tarries strangely, beyond the fitting space. But when he comes, then shall I be no true man if I do not all that the god shows.

PRIEST

Nay, in season hast thou spoken; at this moment these sign to me that Creon draws near.

OEDIPUS

O king Apollo, may he come to us in the brightness of saving fortune, even as his face is bright!

PRIEST

Nay, to all seeming, he brings comfort; else would he not be coming crowned thus quickly with berry-laden bay.

OEDIPUS

We shall know soon: he is at range to hear.—(*Enter* CREON) Prince, my kinsman, son of Menoeceus, what news hast thou brought us from the god?

CREON

Good news: I tell thee that even troubles hard to bear,—if haply they find the right issue,—will end in perfect peace.

OEDIPUS

But what is the oracle? So far, thy words make me neither bold nor yet afraid.

CREON

If thou wouldest hear while these are nigh, I am ready to speak; or else to go within.

OEDIPUS

Speak before all: the sorrow which I bear is for these more than for mine own life.

CREON

With thy leave, I will tell what I heard from the god. Phoebus our lord bids us plainly to drive out a defiling thing, which (he saith) hath been harboured in this land, and not to harbour it, so that it cannot be healed.

OEDIPUS

By what rite shall we cleanse us? What is the manner of the misfortune?

CREON

By banishing a man, or by bloodshed in quittance of bloodshed, since it is that blood which brings the tempest on our city.

OEDIPUS

And who is the man whose fate he thus reveals?

CREON

Laius, king, was lord of our land before thou wast pilot of this State.

OEDIPUS

I know it well—by hearsay, for I saw him never.

CREON

He was slain; and the god now bids us plainly to wreak vengeance on his murderers—whosoever they be.

OEDIPUS

And where are they upon the earth? Where shall the dim track of this old crime be found?

CREON

In this land,—said the god. What is sought for can be caught; only that which is not watched escapes.

OEDIPUS

And was it in the house, or in the field, or on strange soil that Laius met this bloody end?

CREON

'Twas on a visit to Delphi, as he said, that he had left our land; and he came home no more, after he had once set forth.

OEDIPUS

And was there none to tell? Was there no comrade of his journey who saw the deed, from whom tidings might have been gained, and used?

CREON

All perished, save one who fled in fear, and could tell for certain but one thing of all that he saw.

OEDIPUS

And what was that? One thing might show the clue to many, could we get but a small beginning for hope.

CREON

He said that robbers met and fell on them, not in one man's might, but with full many hands.

OEDIPUS

How, then, unless there was some trafficking in bribes from here, should the robber have dared thus far?

CREON

Such things were surmised; but, Laius once slain, amid our troubles no avenger arose.

OEDIPUS

But, when royalty had fallen thus, what trouble in your path can have hindered a full search?

CREON

The riddling Sphinx had made us let dark things go, and was inviting us to think of what lay at our doors.

OEDIPUS

Nay, I will start afresh, and once more make dark things plain. Right worthily hath Phoebus, and worthily hast thou, bestowed this care on the cause of the dead; and so, as is meet, ye shall find me too leagued with you in seeking vengeance for this land, and for the god besides. On behalf of no far-off friend, no, but in mine own cause, shall I dispel this taint. For whoever was the slayer of Laius might wish to take vengeance on me also with a hand as fierce. Therefore, in doing right to Laius, I serve myself.

Come, haste ye, my children, rise from the altar-steps, and lift these suppliant boughs; and let some other summon hither the folk of Cadmus, warned that I mean to leave nought untried; for our health (with the god's help) shall be made certain—or our ruin.

PRIEST

My children, let us rise; we came at first to seek what this man promises of himself. And may Phoebus, who sent these oracles, come to us therewith, our saviour and deliverer from the pest.

(*Exeunt* OEDIPUS *and* PRIEST. *Enter* CHORUS OF THEBAN ELDERS.)

CHORUS (*singing*)

strophe 1

O sweetly-speaking message of Zeus, in what spirit hast thou come from golden Pytho unto glorious Thebes? I am on the rack, terror shakes my soul, O thou Delian healer to whom wild cries rise, in holy fear of thee, what thing thou wilt work for me, perchance unknown before, perchance renewed with the revolving years: tell me, thou immortal Voice, born of Golden Hope!

antistrophe 1

First call I on thee, daughter of Zeus, divine Athena, and on thy sister, guardian of our land, Artemis, who sits on her throne of fame, above the circle of our Agora, and on Phoebus the far-darter: O shine forth on me, my three-fold help against death! If ever aforetime, in arrest of ruin hurrying on the city, ye drove a fiery pest beyond our borders, come now also!

strophe 2

Woe is me, countless are the sorrows that I bear; a plague is on all our host, and thought can find no weapon for defence. The fruits of the glorious earth grow not; by no birth of children do women surmount the pangs in which they shriek; and life on life mayest thou see sped, like bird on nimble wing, aye, swifter than resistless fire, to the shore of the western god.

antistrophe 2

By such deaths, past numbering, the city perishes: unpitied, her children lie on the ground, spreading pestilence, with none to mourn: and meanwhile young wives, and grey-haired mothers with them, uplift a wail at the steps of the altars, some here, some there, entreating for

OEDIPUS REX

349

their weary woes. The prayer to the Healer rings clear, and, blent therewith, the voice of lamentation: for these things, golden daughter of Zeus, send us the bright face of comfort.

strophe 3

And grant that the fierce god of death, who now with no brazen shields, yet amid cries as of battle, wraps me in the flame of his onset, may turn his back in speedy flight from our land, borne by a fair wind to the great deep of Amphitrite, or to those waters in which none find haven, even to the Thracian wave; for if night leave aught undone, day follows to accomplish this. O thou who wieldest the powers of the fire-fraught lightning, O Zeus our father, slay him beneath thy thunderbolt!

antistrophe 3

Lycean King, fain were I that thy shafts also, from thy bent bow's string of woven gold, should go abroad in their might, our champions in the face of the foe; yea, and the flashing fires of Artemis wherewith she glances through the Lycian hills. And I call him whose locks are bound with gold, who is named with the name of this land, ruddy Bacchus to whom Bacchants cry, the comrade of the Maenads, to draw near with the blaze of his blithe torch, our ally against the god unhonoured among gods. (OEDIPUS *enters during the closing strains of the choral song.*)

OEDIPUS

Thou prayest: and in answer to thy prayer,—if thou wilt give a loyal welcome to my words and minister to thine own disease,—thou mayest hope to find succour and relief from woes. These words will I speak publicly, as one who has been a stranger to this report, a stranger to the deed; for I should not be far on the track, if I were tracing it alone, without a clue. But as it is,— since it was only after the time of the deed that I was numbered a Theban among Thebans,—to you, the Cadmeans all, I do thus proclaim.

Whosoever of you knows by whom Laius son of Laddacus was slain, I bid him to declare all to me. And if he is afraid, I tell him to remove the danger of the charge from his path by denouncing himself; for he shall suffer nothing else unlovely, but only leave the land, unhurt. Or if any one knows an alien, from another land, as the assassin, let him not keep silence; for I will pay his guerdon, and my thanks shall rest with him besides.

But if ye keep silence—if any one, through fear, shall seek to screen friend or self from my behest—hear ye what I then shall do. I charge you that no one of this land, whereof I hold the empire and the throne, give shelter or speak word unto that murderer, whosoever he be,—make him partner of his prayer or sacrifice, or serve him with the lustral rite; but that all ban him their homes, knowing that *this* is our defiling thing, as the oracle of the Pythian god hath newly shown me. I then am on this wise the ally of the god and of the slain. And I pray solemnly that the slayer, whoso he be, whether his hidden guilt is lonely or hath partners, evilly, as he is evil, may wear out his unblest life. And for myself I pray that if, with my privity, he should become an inmate of my house, I may suffer the same things which even now I called down upon others. And on you I lay it to make all these words good, for my sake, and for the sake of the god, and for our land's, thus blasted with barrenness by angry heaven.

For even if the matter had not been urged on us by a god, it was not meet that ye should leave the guilt thus unpurged, when one so noble, and he your king, had perished; rather were ye bound to search it out. And now, since 'tis I who hold the powers which once he held, who possess his bed and the wife who bare seed to him; and since, had his hope of issue not been frustrate, children born of one mother would have made ties betwixt him and me—but, as it was, fate swooped upon his head; by reason of these things will I uphold this cause, even as the cause of mine own sire, and will leave nought untried in seeking to find him whose hand shed that blood, for the honour of the son of Labdacus and of Polydorus and elder Cadmus and Agenor who was of old.

And for those who obey me not, I pray that the gods send them neither harvest of the earth nor fruit of the womb, but that they be wasted by their lot that now is, or by one yet more dire. But for all you, the loyal folk of Cadmus to whom these things seem good, may Justice, our ally, and all the gods be with you graciously for ever.

LEADER OF THE CHORUS

As thou hast put me on my oath, on my oath, O king, I will speak. I am not the slayer, nor can I point to him who slew. As for the question, it was for Phoebus, who sent it, to tell us this thing—who can have wrought the deed.

OEDIPUS

Justly said; but no man on the earth can force the gods to what they will not.

LEADER

I would fain say what seems to me next best after this.

OEDIPUS

If there is yet a third course, spare not to show it.

LEADER

I know that our lord Teiresias is the seer most like to our lord Phoebus; from whom, O king, a searcher of these things might learn them most clearly.

OEDIPUS

Not even this have I left out of my cares. On the hint of Creon, I have twice sent a man to bring him; and this long while I marvel why he is not here.

LEADER

Indeed (his skill apart) the rumours are but faint and old.

OEDIPUS

What rumours are they? I look to every story.

LEADER

Certain wayfarers were said to have killed him.

OEDIPUS

I, too, have heard it, but none sees him who saw it.

LEADER

Nay, if he knows what fear is, he will not stay when he hears thy curses, so dire as they are.

OEDIPUS

When a man shrinks not from a deed, neither is he scared by a word.

LEADER

But there is one to convict him. For here they bring at last the godlike prophet, in whom alone of men doth live the truth.

(*Enter* TEIRESIAS, *led by a boy.*)

OEDIPUS

Teiresias, whose soul grasps all things, the lore that may be told and the unspeakable, the secrets of heaven and the low things of earth,—thou feelest, though thou canst not see, what a plague doth haunt our State,—from which, great prophet, we find in thee our protector and only saviour. Now, Phoebus—if indeed thou knowest it not from the messengers—sent answer to our question that the only riddance from this pest which could come was if we should learn aright the slayers of Laius, and slay them, or send them into exile from our land. Do thou, then, grudge neither voice of birds nor any other way of seer-lore that thou hast, but rescue thyself and the State, rescue me, rescue all that is defiled by the dead. For we are in thy hand; and man's noblest task is to help others by his best means and powers.

TEIRESIAS

Alas, how dreadful to have wisdom where it profits not the wise! Aye, I knew this well, but let it slip out of mind; else would I never have come here.

OEDIPUS

What now? How sad thou hast come in!

TEIRESIAS

Let me go home; most easily wilt thou bear thine own burden to the end, and I mine, if thou wilt consent.

OEDIPUS

Thy words are strange, nor kindly to this State which nurtured thee, when thou withholdest this response.

TEIRESIAS

Nay, I see that thou, on thy part, openest not thy lips in season: therefore I speak not, that neither may I have thy mishap.

OEDIPUS

For the love of the gods, turn not away, if thou hast knowledge: all we suppliants implore thee on our knees.

TEIRESIAS

Aye, for ye are all without knowledge; but never will I reveal my griefs—that I say not thine.

OEDIPUS

How sayest thou? Thou knowest the secret, and wilt not tell it, but art minded to betray us and to destroy the State?

TEIRESIAS

I will pain neither myself nor thee. Why vainly ask these things? Thou wilt not learn them from me.

OEDIPUS

What, basest of the base,—for thou wouldest anger a very stone,—wilt thou never speak out? Can nothing touch thee? Wilt thou never make an end?

TEIRESIAS

Thou blamest my temper, but seest not that to which thou thyself art wedded: no, thou findest fault with me.

OEDIPUS

And who would not be angry to hear the words with which thou now dost slight this city?

TEIRESIAS

The future will come of itself, though I shroud it in silence.

OEDIPUS

Then, seeing that it must come, thou on thy part shouldst tell me thereof.

TEIRESIAS

I will speak no further; rage, then, if thou wilt, with the fiercest wrath thy heart doth know.

OEDIPUS

Aye, verily, I will not spare—so wroth I am—to speak all my thought. Know that thou seemest to me e'en to have helped in plotting the deed, and to have done it, short of slaying with thy hands. Hadst thou eyesight, I would have said that the doing, also, of this thing was thine alone.

TEIRESIAS

In sooth?—I charge thee that thou abide by the decree of thine own mouth, and from this day speak neither to these nor to me: *thou* art the accursed defiler of this land.

OEDIPUS

So brazen with thy blustering taunt? And wherein dost thou trust to escape thy due?

TEIRESIAS

I have escaped: in my truth is my strength.

OEDIPUS

Who taught thee this? It was not, at least, thine art.

TEIRESIAS

Thou: for thou didst spur me into speech against my will.

OEDIPUS

What speech? Speak again that I may learn it better.

TEIRESIAS

Didst thou not take my sense before? Or art thou tempting me in talk?

OEDIPUS

No, I took it not so that I can call it known:—speak again.

TEIRESIAS

I say that thou art the slayer of the man whose slayer thou seekest.

OEDIPUS

Now thou shalt rue that thou hast twice said words so dire.

TEIRESIAS

Wouldst thou have me say more, that thou mayest be more wroth?

OEDIPUS

What thou wilt; it will be said in vain.

TEIRESIAS

I say that thou hast been living in unguessed shame with thy nearest kin, and seest not to what woe thou hast come.

OEDIPUS

Dost thou indeed think that thou shalt always speak thus without smarting?

TEIRESIAS

Yes, if there is any strength in truth.

OEDIPUS

Nay, there is,—for all save thee; for thee that strength is not, since thou art maimed in ear, and in wit, and in eye.

TEIRESIAS

Aye, and thou art a poor wretch to utter taunts which every man here will soon hurl at thee.

OEDIPUS

Night, endless night hath thee in her keeping, so that thou canst never hurt me, or any man who sees the sun.

TEIRESIAS

No, thy doom is not to fall by *me*: Apollo is enough, whose care it is to work that out.

OEDIPUS

Are these Creon's devices, or thine?

TEIRESIAS

Nay, Creon is no plague to thee; thou art thine own.

OEDIPUS

O wealth, and empire, and skill surpassing skill in life's keen rivalries, how great is the envy that cleaves to you, if for the sake, yea, of this power which the city hath put into my hands, a gift unsought, Creon the trusty, Creon mine old friend, hath crept on me by stealth, yearning to thrust me out of it, and hath suborned such a scheming juggler as this, a tricky quack, who hath eyes only for his gains, but in his art is blind!

Come, now, tell me, where hast thou proved thyself a seer? Why, when the Watcher was here who wove dark song, didst thou

say nothing that could free this folk? Yet the riddle, at least, was
not for the first comer to read; there was need of a seer's skill;
and none such thou wast found to have either by help of birds,
or as known from any god: no, I came, I, Oedipus the ignorant,
and made her mute, when I had seized the answer by my wit,
untaught of birds. And it is I whom thou art trying to oust,
thinking to stand close to Creon's throne. Methinks thou and the
plotter of these things will rue your zeal to purge the land. Nay,
didst thou not seem to be an old man, thou shouldst have learned
to thy cost how bold thou art.

LEADER

To our thinking, both this man's words and thine, Oedipus,
have been said in anger. Not for such words is our need, but to
seek how we shall best discharge the mandates of the god.

TEIRESIAS

King though thou art, the right of reply, at least, must be
deemed the same for both; of that I too am lord. Not to thee do
I live servant, but to Loxias; and so I shall not stand enrolled
under Creon for my patron. And I tell thee—since thou hast
taunted me even with blindness—that thou hast sight, yet seest not
in what misery thou art, nor where thou dwellest, nor with whom.
Dost thou know of what stock thou art? And thou hast been an
unwitting foe to thine own kin, in the shades, and on the earth
above; and the double lash of thy mother's and thy father's curse
shall one day drive thee from this land in dreadful haste, with
darkness then on the eyes that now see true.

And what place shall not be harbour to thy shriek, what of all
Cithaeron shall not ring with it soon, when thou hast learnt the
meaning of the nuptials in which, within that house, thou didst find
a fatal haven, after a voyage so fair? And a throng of other ills
thou guessest not, which shall make thee level with thy true self
and with thine own brood.

Therefore heap thy scorns on Creon and on my message: for
no one among men shall ever be crushed more miserably than thou.

OEDIPUS

Are these taunts to be indeed borne from *him?*—Hence, ruin
take thee! Hence, this instant! Back!—away!—avaunt thee from
these doors!

TEIRESIAS

I had never come, not I, hadst thou not called me.

OEDIPUS

I knew not that thou wast about to speak folly, or it had been long ere I had sent for thee to my house.

TEIRESIAS

Such am I,—as thou thinkest, a fool; but for the parents who begat thee, sane.

OEDIPUS

What parents? Stay . . . and who of men is my sire?

TEIRESIAS

This day shall show thy birth and shall bring thy ruin.

OEDIPUS

What riddles, what dark words thou always speakest!

TEIRESIAS

Nay, art not thou most skilled to unravel dark speech?

OEDIPUS

Make that my reproach in which thou shalt find me great.

TEIRESIAS

Yet 'twas just that fortune that undid thee.

OEDIPUS

Nay, if I delivered this town, I care not.

TEIRESIAS

Then I will go: so do thou, boy, take me hence.

OEDIPUS

Aye, let him take thee: while here, thou art a hindrance, thou, a trouble: when thou hast vanished, thou wilt not vex me more.

TEIRESIAS

I will go when I have done mine errand, fearless of thy frown: for thou canst never destroy me. And I tell thee—the man of whom thou hast this long while been in quest, uttering threats, and proclaiming a search into the murder of Laius—that man is here,—in seeming, an alien sojourner, but anon he shall be found

a native Theban, and shall not be glad of his fortune. A blind
man, he who now hath sight, a beggar, who now is rich, he shall
make his way to a strange land, feeling the ground before him
with his staff. And he shall be found at once brother and father
of the children with whom he consorts; son and husband of the
woman who bore him; heir to his father's bed, shedder of his
father's blood.

So go thou in and think on that; and if thou find that I have
been at fault, say thenceforth that I have no wit in prophecy.

(TEIRESIAS *is led out by the boy.* OEDIPUS *enters the palace.*)

CHORUS (*singing*)

strophe 1

Who is he of whom the divine voice from the Delphian rock hath spoken, as having wrought with red hands
horrors that no tongue can tell?

It is time that he ply in flights a foot stronger than
the feet of storm-swift steeds: for the son of Zeus is
springing on him, all armed with fiery lightnings, and
with him come the dread, unerring Fates.

antistrophe 1

Yea, newly given from snowy Parnassus, the message
hath flashed forth to make all search for the unknown
man. Into the wild wood's covert, among caves and rocks
he is roaming, fierce as a bull, wretched and forlorn on
his joyless path, still seeking to put from him the doom
spoken at Earth's central shrine: but that doom ever
lives, ever flits around him.

strophe 2

Dreadly, in sooth, dreadly doth the wise augur move
me, who approve not, nor am able to deny. How to speak,
I know not; I am fluttered with forebodings; neither in
the present have I clear vision, nor of the future. Never
in past days, nor in these, have I heard how the house of
Labdacus or the son of Polybus had, either against other,
any grief that I could bring as proof in assailing the
public fame of Oedipus, and seeking to avenge the line of
Labdacus for the undiscovered murder.

antistrophe 2

Nay, Zeus indeed and Apollo are keen of thought,
and know the things of earth; but that mortal seer wins

knowledge above mine, of this there can be no sure test;
though man may surpass man in lore. Yet, until I see the
word made good, never will I assent when men blame
Oedipus. Before all eyes, the winged maiden came against
him of old, and he was seen to be wise; he bore the test,
in welcome service to our State; never, therefore, by the
verdict of my heart shall he be adjudged guilty of crime.

(Enter CREON*)*

CREON

Fellow-citizens, having learned that Oedipus the king lays
dire charges against me, I am here, indignant. If, in the present
troubles, he thinks that he has suffered from *me,* by word or deed,
aught that tends to harm, in truth I crave not my full term of
years, when I must bear such blame as this. The wrong of this
rumour touches me not in one point alone, but has the largest
scope, if I am to be called a traitor in the city, a traitor too by
thee and by my friends.

LEADER OF THE CHORUS

Nay, but this taunt came under stress, perchance, of anger,
rather than from the purpose of the heart.

CREON

And the saying was uttered, that *my* counsels won the seer
to utter his falsehoods?

LEADER

Such things were said—I know not with what meaning.

CREON

And was this charge laid against me with steady eyes and
steady mind?

LEADER

I know not; I see not what my masters do: but here comes
our lord forth from the house.

(Enter OEDIPUS*)*

OEDIPUS

Sirrah, how camest thou here? Hast thou a front so bold
that thou hast come to my house, who are the proved assassin of
its master,—the palpable robber of my crown? Come, tell me, in

the name of the gods, was it cowardice or folly that thou sawest in me, that thou didst plot to do this thing? Didst thou think that I would not note this deed of thine creeping on me by stealth, or, aware, would not ward it off? Now is not thine attempt foolish,— to seek, without followers or friends, a throne,—a prize which followers and wealth must win?

CREON

Mark me now,—in answer to thy words, hear a fair reply, and then judge for thyself on knowledge.

OEDIPUS

Thou art apt in speech, but I have a poor wit for thy lessons, since I have found thee my malignant foe.

CREON

Now first hear how I will explain this very thing—

OEDIPUS

Explain me not one thing—that thou art not false.

CREON

If thou deemest that stubbornness without sense is a good gift, thou art not wise.

OEDIPUS

If thou deemest that thou canst wrong a kinsman and escape the penalty, thou art not sane.

CREON

Justly said, I grant thee: but tell me what is the wrong that thou sayest thou hast suffered from me.

OEDIPUS

Didst thou advise, or didst thou not, that I should send for that reverend seer?

CREON

And now I am still of the same mind.

OEDIPUS

How long is it, then, since Laius—

CREON

Since Laius . . .? I take not thy drift . . .

OEDIPUS

—was swept from men's sight by a deadly violence?

CREON

The count of years would run far into the past?

OEDIPUS

Was this seer, then, of the craft in those days?

CREON

Yea, skilled as now, and in equal honour.

OEDIPUS

Made he, then, any mention of me at that time?

CREON

Never, certainly, when I was within hearing.

OEDIPUS

But held ye not a search touching the murder?

CREON

Due search we held, of course—and learned nothing.

OEDIPUS

And how was it that this sage did not tell his story *then?*

CREON

I know not; where I lack light, 'tis my wont to be silent.

OEDIPUS

Thus much, at least, thou knowest, and couldst declare with light enough.

CREON

What is that? If I know it, I will not deny.

OEDIPUS

That, if he had not conferred with thee, he would never have named *my* slaying of Laius.

CREON

If so he speaks, thou best knowest; but I claim to learn from thee as much as thou hast now from me.

OEDIPUS

Learn thy fill: I shall never be found guilty of the blood.

CREON

Say, then—thou hast married my sister?

OEDIPUS

The question allows not of denial.

CREON

And thou rulest the land as she doth, with like sway?

OEDIPUS

She obtains from me all her desire.

CREON

And rank not I as a third peer of you twain?

OEDIPUS

Aye, 'tis just therein that thou art seen a false friend.

CREON

Not so, if thou wouldst reason with thine own heart as I with mine. And first weigh this,—whether you thinkest that any one would choose to rule amid terrors rather than in unruffled peace,— granting that he is to have the same powers. Now I, for one, have no yearning in my nature to be a king rather than to do kingly deeds, no, nor hath any man who knows how to keep a sober mind. For now I win all boons from thee without fear; but, were I ruler myself, I should be doing much e'en against mine own pleasure.

How, then, could royalty be sweeter for me to have than painless rule and influence? Not yet am I so misguided as to desire other honours than those which profit. Now, all wish me joy; now, every man has a greeting for me; now, those who have a suit to thee crave speech with me, since therein is all their hope of success. Then why should I resign these things, and take those? No mind will become false, while it is wise. Nay, I am no lover of such policy, and, if another put it into deed, never could I bear to act with him.

And, in proof of this, first, go to Pytho, and ask if I brought thee true word of the oracle; then next, if thou find that I have planned aught in concert with the soothsayer, take and slay me, by the sentence not of one mouth, but of twain—by mine own, no less than thine. But make me not guilty in a corner, on unproved surmise. It is not right to adjudge bad men good at random, or good men bad. I count it a like thing for a man to cast off a true friend as to cast away the life in his own bosom, which most he loves. Nay, thou wilt learn these things with sureness in time, for time alone shows a just man; but thou couldst discern a knave even in one day.

LEADER

Well hath he spoken, O king, for one who giveth heed not to fall: the quick in counsel are not sure.

OEDIPUS

When the stealthy plotter is moving on me in quick sort, I, too, must be quick with my counterplot. If I await him in repose, his ends will have been gained, and mine missed.

CREON

What wouldst thou, then? Cast me out of the land?

OEDIPUS

Not so: I desire thy death—not thy banishment—that thou mayest show forth what manner of thing is envy.

CREON

Thou speakest as resolved not to yield or to believe?

OEDIPUS

No; for thou persuadest me not that thou art worthy of belief.

CREON

No, for I find thee not sane.

OEDIPUS

Sane, at least, in mine own interest.

CREON

Nay, thou shouldst be so in mine also.

OEDIPUS

Nay, thou art false.

CREON

But if thou understandest nought?

OEDIPUS

Yet must I rule.

CREON

Not if thou rule ill.

OEDIPUS

Hear him, O Thebes!

CREON

Thebes is for me also—not for thee alone.

(JOCASTA *enters from the palace.*)

LEADER

Cease, princes; and in good time for you I see Jocasta coming yonder from the house, with whose help ye should compose your present feud.

JOCASTA

Misguided men, why have ye raised such foolish strife of tongues? Are ye not ashamed, while the land is thus sick, to stir up troubles of your own? Come, go thou into the house,—and thou, Creon, to thy home,—and forbear to make much of a petty grief.

CREON

Kinswoman, Oedipus thy lord claims to do dread things unto me, even one or other of two ills,—to thrust me from the land of my fathers, or to slay me amain.

OEDIPUS

Yea; for I have caught him, lady, working evil, by ill arts, against my person.

CREON

Now may I see no good, but perish accursed, if I have done aught to thee of that wherewith thou chargest me!

JOCASTA

O, for the gods' love, believe it, Oedipus—first, for the awful sake of this oath unto the gods,—then for my sake and for theirs who stand before thee!

(*The following lines between the* CHORUS *and* OEDIPUS *and between the* CHORUS, JOCASTA, *and* OEDIPUS *are chanted responsively.*)

CHORUS

strophe 1

Consent, reflect, hearken, O my king, I pray thee!

OEDIPUS

What grace, then wouldest thou have me grant thee?

CHORUS

Respect him who aforetime was not foolish, and who now is strong in his oath.

OEDIPUS

Now dost thou know what thou cravest?

CHORUS

Yea.

OEDIPUS

Declare, then, what thou meanest

CHORUS

That thou shouldest never use an unproved rumour to cast a dishonouring charge on the friend who has bound himself with a curse.

OEDIPUS

Then be very sure that, when thou seekest this, for me thou art seeking destruction, or exile from this land.

CHORUS

strophe 2

No, by him who stands in the front of all the heavenly host, no, by the Sun! Unblest, unfriended, may I die by the uttermost doom, if I have that thought! But my unhappy soul is worn by the withering of the land, and again by the thought that our old sorrows should be crowned by sorrows springing from you twain.

OEDIPUS

Then let him go, though I am surely doomed to death, or to be thrust dishonoured from the land. Thy lips, not his, move my compassion by their plaint; but he, where'er he be, shall be hated.

CREON

Sullen in yielding art thou seen, even as vehement in the excesses of thy wrath; but such natures are justly sorest for themselves to bear.

OEDIPUS

Then wilt thou not leave me in peace, and get thee gone?

CREON

I will go my way; I have found thee undiscerning, but in the sight of these I am just.

(*Exit* CREON.)

CHORUS

antistrophe 1

Lady, why dost thou delay to take yon man into the house?

JOCASTA

I will do so, when I have learned what hath chanced.

CHORUS

Blind suspicion, bred of talk, arose; and, on the other part, injustice wounds.

JOCASTA

It was on both sides?

CHORUS

Aye.

JOCASTA

And what was the story?

CHORUS

Enough, methinks, enough—when our land is already vexed—that the matter should rest where it ceased.

OEDIPUS

Seest thou to what thou hast come, for all thy honest purpose, in seeking to slack and blunt my zeal?

CHORUS

antistrophe 2

King, I have said it not once alone—be sure that I should have been shown a madman, bankrupt in sane counsel, if I put thee away—thee, who gavest a true course to my beloved country when distraught by troubles —thee, who now also art like to prove our prospering guide.

JOCASTA

In the name of the gods, tell me also, O king, on what account thou hast conceived this steadfast wrath.

OEDIPUS

That will I; for I honour thee, lady, above yonder men:— the cause is Creon, and the plots that he hath laid against me.

JOCASTA

Speak on—if thou canst tell clearly how the feud began.

OEDIPUS

He says that I stand guilty of the blood of Laius.

JOCASTA

As on his own knowledge? Or on hearsay from another?

OEDIPUS

Nay, he hath made a rascal seer his mouthpiece; as for himself, he keeps his lips wholly pure.

JOCASTA

Then absolve thyself of the things whereof thou speakest; hearken to me, and learn for thy comfort that nought of mortal birth is a sharer in the science of the seer. I will give thee pithy proof of that.

An oracle came to Laius once—I will not say from Phoebus himself, but from his ministers—that the doom should overtake him to die by the hand of his child, who should spring from him and me.

Now Laius,—as, at least, the rumour saith,—was murdered one day by foreign robbers at a place where three highways meet. And the child's birth was not three days past, when Laius pinned its ankles together, and had it thrown, by others' hands, on a trackless mountain.

So, in that case, Apollo brought it not to pass that the babe should become the slayer of his sire, or that Laius should die— the dread thing which he feared—by his child's hand. Thus did the messages of seer-craft map out the future. Regard them, thou, not at all. Whatsoever needful things the god seeks, he himself will easily bring to light.

OEDIPUS

What restlessness of soul, lady, what tumult of the mind hath just come upon me since I heard thee speak!

JOCASTA

What anxiety hath startled thee, that thou sayest this?

OEDIPUS

Methought I heard this from thee,—that Laius was slain where three highways meet.

JOCASTA

Yea, that was the story; nor hath it ceased yet.

OEDIPUS

And where is the place where this befell?

JOCASTA

The land is called Phocis; and branching roads lead to the same spot from Delphi and from Daulia.

OEDIPUS

And what is the time that hath passed since these things were?

JOCASTA

The news was published to the town shortly before thou wast first seen in power over this land.

OEDIPUS

O Zeus, what hast thou decreed to do unto me?

JOCASTA

And wherefore, Oedipus, doth this thing weigh upon thy soul?

OEDIPUS

Ask me not yet; but say what was the stature of Laius, and how ripe his manhood.

JOCASTA

He was tall,—the silver just lightly strewn among his hair; and his form was not greatly unlike to thine.

OEDIPUS

Unhappy that I am! Methinks I have been laying myself even now under a dread curse, and knew it not.

JOCASTA

How sayest thou? I tremble when I look on thee, my king.

OEDIPUS

Dread misgivings have I that the seer can see. But thou wilt show better if thou wilt tell me one thing more.

JOCASTA

Indeed—though I tremble—I will answer all thou askest, when I hear it.

OEDIPUS

Went he in small force, or with many armed followers, like a chieftain?

JOCASTA

Five they were in all,—a herald one of them; and there was one carriage, which bore Laius.

OEDIPUS

Alas! 'Tis now clear indeed.—Who was he who gave you these tidings lady?

JOCASTA

A servant—the sole survivor who came home.

OEDIPUS

Is he haply at hand in the house now?

JOCASTA

No, truly; so soon as he came thence, and found thee reigning in the stead of Laius, he supplicated me, with hand laid on mine, that I would send him to the fields, to the pastures of the flocks, that he might be far from the sight of this town. And I sent him; he was worthy, for a slave, to win e'en a larger boon than that.

OEDIPUS

Would, then, that he could return to us without delay!

JOCASTA

It is easy: but wherefore dost thou enjoin this?

OEDIPUS

I fear, lady, that mine own lips have been unguarded; and therefore am I fain to behold him.

JOCASTA

Nay, he shall come. But I too, methinks, have a claim to learn what lies heavy on thy heart, my king.

OEDIPUS

Yea, and it shall not be kept from thee, now that my forebodings have advanced so far. Who, indeed, is more to me than thou, to whom I should speak in passing through such a fortune as this?

My father was Polybus of Corinth,—my mother, the Dorian Merope; and I was held the first of all the folk in that town, until a chance befell me, worthy, indeed, of wonder, though not worthy of mine own heat concerning it. At a banquet, a man full of wine cast it at me in his cups that I was not the true son of my sire. And I, vexed, restrained myself for that day as best I might; but on the next I went to my mother and father, and questioned them; and they were wroth for the taunt with him who had let that word fly. So on their part I had comfort; yet was this thing ever rankling in my heart; for it still crept abroad with strong rumour. And, unknown to mother or father, I went to Delphi; and Phoebus sent me forth disappointed of that knowledge for which I came, but in his response set forth other things, full of sorrow and terror and woe; even that I was fated to defile my mother's bed; and that I should show unto men a brood which they could not endure to behold; and that I should be the slayer of the sire who begat me.

And I, when I had listened to this, turned to flight from the land of Corinth, thenceforth wotting of its region by the stars alone, to some spot where I should never see fulfilment of the infamies foretold in mine evil doom. And on my way I came to the regions in which thou sayest that this prince perished. Now, lady, I will tell thee the truth. When in my journey I was near to those three roads, there met me a herald, and a man seated in a carriage drawn by colts, as thou hast described; and he who was in front, and the old man himself, were for thrusting me rudely

from the path. Then, in anger, I struck him who pushed me aside—
the driver; and the old man, seeing it, watched the moment when
I was passing, and, from the carriage, brought his goad with two
teeth down full upon my head. Yet was he paid with interest; by
one swift blow from the staff in this hand he was rolled right out
of the carriage, on his back; and I slew every man of them.

But if this stranger had any tie of kinship with Laius, who
is now more wretched than the man before thee? What mortal
could prove more hated of heaven? Whom no stranger, no citizen,
is allowed to receive in his house; whom it is unlawful that any
one accost; whom all must repel from their homes! And this—
this curse—was laid on me by no mouth but mine own! And I
pollute the bed of the slain man with the hands by which he
perished. Say, am I vile? Oh, am I not utterly unclean?—seeing
that I must be banished, and in banishment see not mine own
people, nor set foot in mine own land, or else be joined in wedlock
to my mother, and slay my sire, even Polybus, who begat and
reared me.

Then would not he speak aright of Oedipus, who judged
these things sent by some cruel power above man? Forbid, forbid,
ye pure and awful gods, that I should see that day! No, may I
be swept from among men, ere I behold myself visited with the
brand of such a doom!

LEADER OF THE CHORUS

To us, indeed, these things, O king, are fraught with fear;
yet have hope, until at least thou hast gained full knowledge from
him who saw the deed.

OEDIPUS

Hope, in truth, rests with me thus far alone; I can await the
man summoned from the pastures.

JOCASTA

And when he has appeared—what wouldst thou have of him?

OEDIPUS

I will tell. If his story be found to tally with thine, I, at
least, shall stand clear of disaster.

JOCASTA

And what of special note didst thou hear from me?

OEDIPUS

Thou wast saying that he spoke of Laius as slain by robbers. If, then, he still speaks, as before, of several, I was not the slayer: a solitary man could not be held the same with that band. But if he names one lonely wayfarer, then beyond doubt this guilt leans to me.

JOCASTA

Nay, be assured that thus, at least, the tale was first told; he cannot revoke that, for the city heard it, not I alone. But even if he should diverge somewhat from his former story, never, king, can he show that the murder of Laius, at least, is truly square to prophecy; of whom Loxias plainly said that he must die by the hand of my child. Howbeit that poor innocent never slew him, but perished first itself. So henceforth, for what touches divination, I would not look to my right hand or my left.

OEDIPUS

Thou judgest well. But nevertheless send some one to fetch the peasant, and neglect not this matter.

JOCASTA

(OEDIPUS and JOCASTA go into the palace.)

CHORUS (singing)

strophe 1

May destiny still find me winning the praise of reverent purity in all words and deeds sanctioned by those laws of range sublime, called into life throughout the high clear heaven, whose father is Olympus alone; their parent was no race of mortal men, no, nor shall oblivion ever lay them to sleep; the god is mighty in them and he grows not old.

antistrophe 1

Insolence breeds the tyrant; Insolence, once vainly surfeited on wealth that is not meet nor good for it, when it hath scaled the topmost ramparts, is hurled to a dire doom, wherein no service of the feet can serve. But I pray that the god never quell such rivalry as benefits the State; the god will I ever hold for our protector.

strophe 2

But if any man walks haughtily in deed or word, with no fear of Justice, no reverence for the images of gods, may an evil doom seize him for his ill-starred pride, if he will not win his vantage fairly, nor keep him from unholy deeds, but must lay profaning hands on sanctities.

Where such things are, what mortal shall boast any more that he can ward the arrows of the gods from his life? Nay, if such deeds are in honour, wherefore should we join in the sacred dance?

antistrophe 2

No more will I go reverently to earth's central and inviolate shrine, no more to Abae's temple or Olympia, if these oracles fit not the issue, so that all men shall point at them with the finger. Nay, king,—if thou art rightly called,—Zeus all-ruling, may it not escape thee and thine ever-deathless power!

The old prophecies concerning Laius are fading; already men are setting them at nought, and nowhere is Apollo glorified with honours; the worship of the gods is perishing.

(JOCASTA *comes forth, bearing a branch, wreathed with festoons of wool, which, as a suppliant, she is about to lay on the altar of the household god, Lycean, Apollo, in front of the palace.*)

JOCASTA

Princes of the land, the thought has come to me to visit the shrines of the gods, with this wreathed branch in my hands, and these gifts of incense. For Oedipus excites his soul overmuch with all manner of alarms, nor, like a man of sense, judges the new things by the old, but is at the will of the speaker, if he speak terrors.

Since, then, by counsel I can do no good, to thee, Lycean Apollo, for thou art nearest, I have come, a suppliant with these symbols of prayer, that thou mayest find us some riddance from uncleanness. For now we are all afraid, seeing *him* affrighted, even as they who see fear in the helmsman of their ship.

(*While* JOCASTA *is offering her prayers to the god, a* MESSENGER, *evidently a stranger, enters and addresses the Elders of the* CHORUS.)

MESSENGER

Might I learn from you, strangers, where is the house of the king Oedipus? Or, better still, tell me where he himself is—if ye know.

LEADER OF THE CHORUS

This is his dwelling, and he himself, stranger, is within; and this lady is the mother of his children.

MESSENGER

Then may she be ever happy in a happy home, since she is his heaven blest queen.

JOCASTA

Happiness to thee also, stranger! 'tis the due of thy fair greeting.—But say what thou hast come to seek or to tell.

MESSENGER

Good tidings, lady, for thy house and for thy husband.

JOCASTA

What are they? And from whom hast thou come?

MESSENGER

From Corinth: and at the message which I will speak anon thou wilt rejoice—doubtless; yet haply grieve.

JOCASTA

And what is it? How hath it thus a double potency?

MESSENGER

The people will make him king of the Isthmian land, as 'twas said there.

JOCASTA

How then? Is the aged Polybus no more in power?

MESSENGER

No, verily: for death holds him in the tomb.

JOCASTA

How sayest thou? Is Polybus dead, old man?

Messenger

If I speak not the truth, I am content to die.

Jocasta

O handmaid, away with all speed, and tell this to thy master! O ye oracles of the gods, where stand ye now! This is the man whom Oedipus long feared and shunned, lest he should slay him; and now this man hath died in the course of destiny, not by his hand.

(OEDIPUS *enters from the palace.*)

Oedipus

Jocasta, dearest wife, why hast thou summoned me forth from these doors?

Jocasta

Hear this man, and judge, as thou listenest, to what the awful oracles of the gods have come.

Oedipus

And he—who may he be, and what news hath he for me?

Jocasta

He is from Corinth, to tell that thy father Polybus lives no longer, but hath perished.

Oedipus

How, stranger? Let me have it from thine own mouth.

Messenger

If I must first make these tidings plain, know indeed that he is dead and gone.

Oedipus

By treachery, or by visit of disease?

Messenger

A light thing in the scale brings the aged to their rest.

Oedipus

Ah, he died, it seems, of sickness?

Messenger

Yea, and of the long years that he had told.

OEDIPUS

Alas, alas! Why, indeed, my wife, should one look to the hearth of the Pythian seer, or to the birds that scream above our heads, on whose showing I was doomed to slay my sire? But he is dead, and hid already beneath the earth; and here am I, who have not put hand to spear.—Unless, perchance, he was killed by longing for me: thus, indeed, I should be the cause of his death. But the oracles as they stand, at least, Polybus hath swept with him to his rest in Hades: they are worth nought.

JOCASTA

Nay, did I not so foretell to thee long since?

OEDIPUS

Thou didst: but I was misled by my fear.

JOCASTA

Now no more lay aught of those things to heart.

OEDIPUS

But surely I must needs fear my mother's bed?

JOCASTA

Nay, what should mortal fear, for whom the decrees of Fortune are supreme, and who hath clear foresight of nothing? 'Tis best to live at random, as one may. But fear not thou touching wedlock with thy mother. Many men ere now have so fared in dreams also: but he to whom these things are as nought bears his life most easily.

OEDIPUS

All these bold words of thine would have been well, were not my mother living; but as it is, since she lives, I must needs fear— though thou sayest well.

JOCASTA

Howbeit thy father's death is a great sign to cheer us.

OEDIPUS

Great, I know; but my fear is of her who lives.

MESSENGER

And who is the woman about whom ye fear?

OEDIPUS

Merope, old man, the consort of Polybus.

MESSENGER

And what is it in her that moves your fear?

OEDIPUS

A heaven-sent oracle of dread import, stranger.

MESSENGER

Lawful, or unlawful, for another to know?

OEDIPUS

Lawful, surely. Loxias once said that I was doomed to espouse mine own mother, and to shed with mine own hands my father's blood. Wherefore my home in Corinth was long kept by me afar; with happy event, indeed,—yet still 'tis sweet to see the face of parents.

MESSENGER

Was it indeed for fear of this that thou wast an exile from that city?

OEDIPUS

And because I wished not, old man, to be the slayer of my sire.

MESSENGER

Then why have I not freed thee, king, from this fear, seeing that I came with friendly purpose?

OEDIPUS

Indeed thou shouldst have guerdon due from me.

MESSENGER

Indeed 'twas chiefly for this that I came—that, on thy return home, I might reap some good.

OEDIPUS

Nay, I will never go near my parents.

MESSENGER

Ah my son, 'tis plain enough that thou knowest not what thou doest.

OEDIPUS

How, old man? For the gods' love, tell me.

MESSENGER

If for these reasons thou shrinkest from going home.

OEDIPUS

Aye, I dread lest Phoebus prove himself true for me.

MESSENGER

Thou dreadest to be stained with guilt through thy parents?

OEDIPUS

Even so, old man—this is it that ever affrights me.

MESSENGER

Dost thou know, then, that thy fears are wholly vain?

OEDIPUS

How so, if I was born of those parents?

MESSENGER

Because Polybus was nothing to thee in blood.

OEDIPUS

What sayest thou? Was Polybus not my sire?

MESSENGER

No more than he who speaks to thee, but just so much.

OEDIPUS

And how can my sire be level with him who is as nought to me?

MESSENGER

Nay, he begat thee not, any more than I.

OEDIPUS

Nay, wherefore, then, called he me his son?

MESSENGER

Know that he had received thee as a gift from my hands of yore.

OEDIPUS

And yet he loved me so dearly, who came another's hand?

MESSENGER

Yea, his former childlessness won him thereto.

Oedipus

And thou—hadst thou bought me or found me by chance, when thou gavest me to him?

Messenger

Found thee in Cithaeron's winding glens.

Oedipus

And wherefore wast thou roaming in those regions?

Messenger

I was there in charge of mountain flocks.

Oedipus

What, thou wast a shepherd—a vagrant hireling?

Messenger

But thy perserver, my son, in that hour.

Oedipus

And what pain was mine when thou didst take me in thine arms?

Messenger

The ankles of thy feet might witness.

Oedipus

Ah me, why dost thou speak of that old trouble?

Messenger

I freed thee when thou hadst thine ankles pinned together.

Oedipus

Aye, 'twas a dread brand of shame that I took from my cradle.

Messenger

Such, that from that fortune thou wast called by the name which still is thine.

Oedipus

Oh, for the gods' love—was the deed my mother's or father's? Speak!

Messenger

I know not; he who gave thee to me wots better of than than I.

OEDIPUS

What, thou hadst me from another? Thou didst not light on me thyself?

MESSENGER

No: another shepherd gave thee up to me.

OEDIPUS

Who was he? Art thou in case to tell clearly?

MESSENGER

I think he was called one of the household of Laius.

OEDIPUS

The king who ruled this country long ago?

MESSENGER

The same: 'twas in his service that the man was a herd.

OEDIPUS

Is he still alive, that I might see him?

MESSENGER

Nay, ye folk of the country should know best.

OEDIPUS

Is there any of you here present that knows the herd of whom he speaks—that hath seen him in the pastures or the town? Answer! The hour hath come that these things should be finally revealed.

LEADER OF THE CHORUS

Methinks he speaks of no other than the peasant whom thou wast already fain to see; but our lady Jocasta might best tell that.

OEDIPUS

Lady, wottest thou of him whom we lately summoned? Is it of him that this man speaks?

JOCASTA

Why ask of whom he spoke? Regard it not . . . waste not a thought on what he said . . . 'twas idle.

OEDIPUS

It must not be that, with such clues in my grasp, I should fail to bring my birth to light.

JOCASTA

For the god's sake, if thou hast any care for thine own life, forbear this search! My anguish is enough.

OEDIPUS

Be of good courage; though I be found the son of servile mother,—aye, a slave by three descents,—*thou* wilt not be proved base-born.

JOCASTA

Yet hear me, I implore thee: do not thus.

OEDIPUS

I must not hear of not discovering the whole truth.

JOCASTA

Yet I wish thee well—I counsel thee for the best.

OEDIPUS

These best counsels, then, vex my patience.

JOCASTA

Ill-fated one! Mayst thou never come to know who thou art!

OEDIPUS

Go, some one, fetch me the herdsman hither,—and leave yon woman to glory in her princely stock.

JOCASTA

Alas, alas, miserable!—that word alone can I say unto thee, and no other word henceforth for ever.

(She rushes into the palace.)

LEADER

Why hath the lady gone, Oedipus, in a transport of wild grief? I misdoubt, a storm of sorrow will break forth from this silence.

OEDIPUS

Break forth what will! Be my race never so lowly, I must crave to learn it. Yon woman, perchance,—for she is proud with more than a woman's pride—thinks shame of my base source. But I, who hold myself son of Fortune that gives good, will not be dishonoured. She is the mother from whom I spring; and the months, my kinsmen, have marked me sometimes lowly, sometimes great. Such being my lineage, never more can I prove false to it, or spare to search out the secret of my birth.

CHORUS (*singing*)

strophe

If I am a seer or a wise of heart, O Cithaeron, thou shalt not fail—by yon heaven, thou shalt not!—to know at tomorrow's full moon that Oedipus honours thee as native to him, as his nurse, and his mother, and that thou art celebrated in our dance and song, because thou art well-pleasing to our prince. O Phoebus to whom we cry, may these things find favour in thy sight!

antistrophe

Who was it, my son, who of the race whose years are many that bore thee in wedlock with Pan, the mountain-roaming father? Or was it a bride of Loxias that bore thee? For dear to him are all the upland pastures. Or perchance 'twas Cyllene's lord, or the Bacchants' god, dweller on the hill-tops, that received thee, a new-born joy, from one of the Nymphs of Helicon, with whom he most doth sport.

OEDIPUS

Elders, if 'tis for me to guess, who have never met with him, I think I see the herdsman of whom we have long been in quest; for in his venerable age he tallies with yon stranger's years, and withal I know those who bring him, methinks, as servants of mine own. But perchance thou mayest have the advantage of me in knowledge, if thou hast seen the herdsman before.

LEADER

Aye, I know him, be sure; he was in the service of Laius—trusty as any man, in his shepherd's place.

(*The* HERDSMAN *is brought in.*)

OEDIPUS

I ask thee first, Corinthian stranger, is this he whom thou meanest?

MESSENGER

This man whom thou beholdest.

OEDIPUS

Ho thou, old man—I would have thee look this way, and answer all that I ask thee. Thou wast once in the service of Laius?

HERDSMAN

I was—a slave not bought, but reared in his house.

OEDIPUS

Employed in what labour, or what way of life?

HERDSMAN

For the best part of my life I tended flocks.

OEDIPUS

And what the regions that thou didst chiefly haunt?

HERDSMAN

Sometimes it was Cithaeron, sometimes the neighbouring ground.

OEDIPUS

Then wottest thou of having noted yon man in these parts—

HERDSMAN

Doing what? . . . What man dost thou mean? . . .

OEDIPUS

This man here—or of having ever met him before?

HERDSMAN

Not so that I could speak at once from memory.

MESSENGER

And no wonder, master. But I will bring clear recollection to his ignorance. I am sure that he well wots of the time when we abode in the region of Cithaeron,—he with two flocks, I, his comrade, with one,—three full half-years, from spring to Arcturus; and then for the winter I used to drive my flock to mine own fold, and he took to the fold of Laius. Did aught of this happen as I tell, or did it not?

HERDSMAN

Thou speakest the truth—though 'tis long ago.

MESSENGER

Come, tell me now—wottest thou of having given me a boy in those days, to be reared as mine own foster-son?

HERDSMAN

What now? Why dost thou ask the question?

MESSENGER

Yonder man, my friend, is he who when was young.

HERDSMAN

Plague seize thee—be silent once for all!

OEDIPUS

Ha! chide him not, old man—thy words need chiding more than his.

HERDSMAN

And wherein, most noble master, do I offend?

OEDIPUS

In not telling of the boy concerning whom he asks.

HERDSMAN

He speaks without knowledge—he is busy to no purpose.

OEDIPUS

Thou wilt not speak with a good grace, but thou shalt on pain.

HERDSMAN

Nay, for the god's love, misuse not an old man!

OEDIPUS

Ho, some one—pinion him this instant!

HERDSMAN

Alas, wherefore? what more wouldst thou learn?

OEDIPUS

Didst thou give this man the child of whom he asks?

HERDSMAN

I did,—and would I have had perished that day!

OEDIPUS

Well, thou wilt come to that, unless thou tell the honest truth.

HERDSMAN

Nay, much more am I lost, if I speak.

OEDIPUS

The fellow is bent, methinks, on more delays . . .

HERDSMAN

No, no!—I said before that I gave it to him.

OEDIPUS

Whence hadst thou got it? In thine own house, or from another?

HERDSMAN

Mine own it was not—I had received it from a man.

OEDIPUS

From whom of the citizens here? from what home?

HERDSMAN

Forbear, for the god's love, master, forbear to ask more!

OEDIPUS

Thou art lost if I have to question thee again.

HERDSMAN

It was a child then, of the house of Laius.

OEDIPUS

A slave? or one born of his own race?

HERDSMAN

Ah me—I am on the dreaded brink of speech.

OEDIPUS

And I of hearing; yet must I hear.

HERDSMAN

Thou must know, then, that 'twas said to be his own child— but thy lady within could best say how these things are.

OEDIPUS

How? She gave it to thee?

HERDSMAN

Yea, O king.

OEDIPUS

For what end?

HERDSMAN

That I should make away with it.

OEDIPUS

Her own child, the wretch?

HERDSMAN

Aye, from fear of evil prophecies.

OEDIPUS

What were they?

HERDSMAN

The tale ran that he must slay his sire.

OEDIPUS

Why, then, didst thou give him up to this old man?

HERDSMAN

Through pity, master, as deeming that he would bear him away to another land, whence he himself came; but he saved him for the direst woe. For if thou art what this man saith, know that thou wast born to misery.

OEDIPUS

Oh, oh! All brought to pass—all true! Thou light, may I now look my last on thee—I who have been found accursed in birth, accursed in wedlock, accursed in the shedding of blood!

(He rushes into the palace.)

CHORUS (*singing*)

strophe I

Alas, ye generations of men, how mere a shadow do I count your life! Where, where is the mortal who wins more of happiness than just the seeming, and, after the semblance, a falling away? Thine is a fate that warns me,—thine, thine, unhappy Oedipus—to call no earthly creature blest.

antistrophe 1

For he, O Zeus, sped his shaft with peerless skill, and won the prize of an all-prosperous fortune; he slew the maiden with crooked talons who sang darkly; he arose for our land as a tower against death. And from that time, Oedipus, thou hast been called our king, and hast been honoured supremely, bearing sway in great Thebes.

strophe 2

But now whose story is more grievous in men's ears? Who is a more wretched captive to fierce plagues and troubles, with all his life reversed?

Alas, renowned Oedipus! The same bounteous place of rest sufficed thee, as child and as sire also, that thou shouldst make theron thy nuptial couch. Oh, how can the soil wherein thy father sowed, unhappy one, have suffered thee in silence so long?

antistrophe 2

Time the all-seeing hath found thee out in thy despite: he judgeth the monstrous marriage wherein begetter and begotten have long been one.

Alas, thou child of Laius, would, would that I had never seen thee! I wail as one who pours a dirge from his lips; sooth to speak, 'twas thou that gavest me new life, and through thee darkness hath fallen upon mine eyes.

(*Enter* SECOND MESSENGER *from the palace.*)

SECOND MESSENGER

Ye who are ever most honoured in this land, what deeds shall ye hear, what deeds behold, what burden of sorrow shall be yours, if, true to your race, ye still care for the house of Labdacus! For I ween that not Ister nor Phasis could wash this house clean, so many are the ills that it shrouds, or will soon bring to light,— ills wrought not unwittingly, but of purpose. And those griefs smart most which are seen to be of our own choice.

LEADER

Indeed those which we knew before fall not short of claiming sore lamentation: besides them, what dost thou announce?

SECOND MESSENGER

This is the shortest tale to tell and to hear: our royal lady Jocasta is dead.

LEADER

Alas, hapless one! From what cause?

SECOND MESSENGER

By her own hand. The worst pain in what hath chanced is not for you, for yours it is not to behold. Nevertheless, so far as mine own memory serves, ye shall learn that unhappy woman's fate.

When, frantic, she had passed within the vestibule, she rushed straight towards her nuptial couch, clutching her hair with the fingers of both hands; once within the chamber, she dashed the doors together at her back; then called on the name of Laius, long since a corpse, mindful of that son, begotten long ago, by whom the sire was slain, leaving the mother to breed accursed offspring with his own.

And she bewailed the wedlock wherein, wretched, she had borne a twofold brood, husband by husband, children by her child. And how thereafter she perished, is more than I know. For with a shriek Oedipus burst in, and suffered us not to watch her woe unto the end; on him, as he rushed around, our eyes were set. To and fro he went, asking us to give him a sword,—asking where he should find the wife who was no wife, but a mother whose womb had borne alike himself and his children. And, in his frenzy, a power above man was his guide; for 'twas none of us mortals who were nigh. And with a dread shriek, as though some one beckoned him on, he sprang at the double doors, and from their sockets forced the bending bolts, and rushed into the room.

There beheld we the woman hanging by the neck in a twisted noose of swinging cords. But he, when he saw her, with a dread, deep cry of misery, loosed the halter whereby she hung. And when the hapless woman was stretched upon the ground, then was the sequel dread to see. For he tore from her raiment the golden brooches wherewith she was decked, and lifted them, and smote full on his own eye-balls, uttering words like these: 'No more shall ye behold such horrors as I was suffering and working! long enough have ye looked on those whom ye ought never to have seen, failed in knowledge of those whom I yearned to know—henceforth ye shall be dark!'

To such dire refrain, not once alone but oft struck he his

eyes with lifted hand; and at each blow the ensanguined eye-balls bedewed his beard, nor sent forth sluggish drops of gore, but all at once a dark shower of blood came down like hail.

From the deeds of twain such ills have broken forth, not on one alone, but with mingled woe for man and wife. The old happiness of their ancestral fortune was aforetime happiness indeed; but to-day—lamentation, ruin, death, shame, all earthly ills can be named—all, all are theirs.

LEADER

And hath the sufferer now any respite from pain?

SECOND MESSENGER

He cries for some one to unbar the gates and show to all the Cadmeans his father's slayer, his mother's—the unholy word must not pass my lips,—as purposing to cast himself out of the land, and abide no more, to make the house accursed under his own curse. Howbeit he lacks strength, and one to guide his steps; for the anguish is more than man may bear. And he will show this to thee also; for lo, the bars of the gates are withdrawn, and soon thou shalt behold a sight which even he who abhors it must pity.

(*The central door of the palace is now opened.* OEDIPUS *comes forth, leaning on attendants; the bloody stains are still upon his face. The following lines between* OEDIPUS *and the* CHORUS *are chanted responsively.*)

CHORUS

O dread fate for men to see, O most dreadful of all that have met mine eyes! Unhappy one, what madness hath come on thee? Who is the unearthly foe that, with a bound of more than mortal range, hath made thine ill-starred life his prey?

Alas, alas, thou hapless one! Nay, I cannot e'en look on thee, though there is much that I would fain ask, fain learn, much that draws my wistful gaze,—with such a shuddering dost thou fill me!

OEDIPUS

Woe is me! Alas, alas, wretched that I am! Whither, whither am I borne in my misery? How is my voice swept abroad on the wings of the air? Oh my Fate, how far hast thou sprung!

CHORUS

To a dread place, dire in men's ears, dire in their sight.

OEDIPUS

strophe 1

O thou horror of darkness that enfoldest me, visitant unspeakable, resistless, sped by a wind too fair!

Ay me! and once again ay me!

How is my soul pierced by the stab of these goads, and withal by the memory of sorrows!

CHORUS

Yea, amid woes so many a twofold pain may well be thine to mourn and to bear.

OEDIPUS

antistrophe 1

Ah, friend, thou still art steadfast in thy tendence of me,—thou still hast patience to care for the blind man! Ah me! Thy presence is not hid from me—no, dark though I am, yet know I thy voice full well.

CHORUS

Man of dread deeds, how couldst thou in such wise quench thy vision? What more than human power urged thee?

OEDIPUS

strophe 2

Apollo, friends, Apollo was he that brought these my woes to pass, these my sore, sore woes: but the hand that struck the eyes was none save mine, wretched that I am! Why was I to see, when sight could show me nothing sweet?

CHORUS

These things were even as thou sayest.

OEDIPUS

Say, friends, what can I more behold, what can I love, what greeting can touch mine ear with joy? Haste, lead me from the land, friends, lead me hence, the utterly lost, the thrice accursed, yea, the mortal most abhorred of heaven!

CHORUS

Wretched alike for thy fortune and for thy sense
thereof, would that I had never so much as known thee!

OEDIPUS

antistrophe 2

Perish the man, whoe'er he was, that freed me in the
pastures from the cruel shackle on my feet, and saved
me from death, and gave me back to life,—a thankless
deed! Had I died then, to my friends and to thine own
soul I had not been so sore a grief.

CHORUS

I also would have had it thus.

OEDIPUS

So had I not come to shed my father's blood, nor
been called among men the spouse of her from whom I
sprang: but now am I forsaken of the gods, son of a
defiled mother, successor to his bed who gave me mine
own wretched being: and if there be yet a woe surpassing
woes, it hath become the portion of Oedipus.

CHORUS

I know not how I can say that thou hast counselled
well: for thou wart better dead than living and blind.

OEDIPUS

Show me not at large that these things are not best done
thus: give me counsel no more. For, had I sight, I know not with
what eyes I could e'en have looked on my father, when I came
to the place of the dead, aye, or on my miserable mother, since
against both I have sinned such sins as strangling could not
punish. But deem ye that the sight of children, born as mine
were born, was lovely for me to look upon? No, no, not lovely
to mine eyes for ever! No, nor was this town with its towered
walls, nor the sacred statues of the gods, since I, thrice wretched
that I am,—I, noblest of the sons of Thebes,—have doomed myself
to know these no more, by mine own command that all should
thrust away the impious one,—even him whom gods have shown
to be unholy—and of the race of Laius!

After bearing such a stain upon me, was I to look with

392

steady eyes on this folk? No, verily: no, were there yet a way to choke the fount of hearing, I had not spared to make a fast prison of this wretched frame, that so I should have known nor sight nor sound; for 'tis sweet that our thought should dwell beyond the sphere of griefs.

Alas, Cithaeron, why hadst thou a shelter for me? When I was given to thee, why didst thou not slay me straightway, that so I might never have revealed my source to men? Ah, Polybus,— ah, Corinth, and thou that wast called the ancient house of my fathers, how seeming-fair was I your nurseling, and what ills were festering beneath! For now I am found evil, and of evil birth. O ye three roads, and thou secret glen,—thou coppice, and narrow way where three paths met—ye who drank from my hands that father's blood which was mine own,—remember ye, perchance, what deeds I wrought for you to see,—and then, when I came hither, what fresh deeds I went on to do?

O marriage-rites, ye gave me birth, and when ye had brought me forth, again ye bore children to your child, ye created an incestuous kinship of fathers, brothers, sons,—brides, wives, mothers,—yea, all the foulest shame that is wrought among men! Nay, but 'tis unmeet to name what 'tis unmeet to do:—haste ye, for the gods' love, hide me somewhere beyond the land, or slay me, or cast me into the sea, where ye shall never behold me more! Approach,—deign to lay your hands on a wretched man;—harken, fear not,—my plague can rest on no mortal beside.

(Enter CREON*)*

LEADER

Nay, here is Creon, in meet season for thy requests, crave they act or counsel; for he alone is left to guard the land in thy stead.

OEDIPUS

Ah me, indeed shall I accost him? What claim to credence can be shown on my part? For in the past I have been found wholly false to him.

CREON

I have not come in mockery, Oedipus, nor to reproach thee with any bygone fault. (*To the attendants.*) But ye, if ye respect the children of men no more, revere at least the all-nurturing flame of our lord the Sun,—spare to show thus nakedly a pollution such as this,—one which neither earth can welcome, nor the holy rain, nor the light. Nay, take him into the house as quickly as ye may; for it best accords with piety that kinsfolk alone should see and hear a kinsmans' woes.

OEDIPUS

For the gods' love—since thou hast done a gentle violence to my presage, who hast come in a spirit so noble to me, a man most vile—grant me a boon:—for thy good I will speak, not for mine own.

CREON

And what wish art thou so fain to have of me?

OEDIPUS

Cast me out of this land with all speed, to a place where no mortal shall be found to greet me more.

CREON

This would I have done, be thou sure, but that I craved first to learn all my duty from the god.

OEDIPUS

Nay, his behest hath been set forth in full,—to let me perish, the parricide, the unholy one, that I am.

CREON

Such was the purport; yet, seeing to what a pass we have come, 'tis better to learn clearly what should be done.

OEDIPUS

Will ye, then, seek a response on behalf of such a wretch as I am?

CREON

Aye, for thou thyself wilt now surely put faith in the god.

OEDIPUS

Yea; and on thee lay I this charge, to thee will I make this entreaty:—give to her who is within such burial as thou thyself wouldest; for thou wilt meetly render the last rites to thine own. But for me—never let this city of my sire be condemned to have me dwelling therin, while I live: no, suffer me to abide on the hills, where yonder is Cithaeron, famed as mine,—which my mother and sire, while they lived, set for my appointed tomb,—that so I may die by their decree who sought to slay me. Howbeit of thus much am

I sure,—that neither sickness nor aught else can destroy me; for never had I been snatched from death, but in reserve for some strange doom.

Nay, let *my* fate go whither it will: but as touching my children,—I pray thee, Creon, take no care on thee for my sons; they are men, so that, be they where they may, they can never lack the means to live. But my two girls, poor hapless ones,—who never knew my table spread apart, or lacked their father's presence, but ever in all things shared my daily bread,—I pray thee, care for *them;* and—if thou canst—suffer me to touch them with my hands, and to indulge my grief. Grant it, prince, grant it, thou noble heart! Ah, could I but once touch them with my hands, I should think that they were with me, even as when I had sight. . .

(CREON's *attendants lead in the children* ANTIGONE *and* ISMENE.)

Ha? O ye gods, can it be my loved ones that I hear sobbing,— can Creon have taken pity on me and sent me my children—my darlings? Am I right?

CREON

Yea: 'tis of my contriving, for I knew thy joy in them of old, —the joy that now is thine.

OEDIPUS

Then blessed be thou, and, for guerdon of this errand, may heaven prove to thee a kinder guardian than it hath to me! My children, where are ye? hither,—hither to the hands of him whose mother was your own, the hands whose offices have wrought that your sire's once bright eyes should be such orbs as these,—his, who seeing nought, knowing nought, became your father by her from whom he sprang! For you also do I weep—behold you I cannot— when I think of the bitter life in days to come which men will make you live. To what company of the citizens will ye go, to what festival, from which ye shall not return home in tears, instead of sharing in the holiday? But when ye are now come to years ripe for marriage, who shall he be, who shall be the man, my daughters, that will hazard taking unto him such reproaches as must be baneful alike to my offspring and to yours? For what misery is wanting? Your sire slew his sire, he had seed of her who bare him, and begat you at the sources of his own being!

Such are the taunts that will be cast at you; and who then will wed? The man lives not, no, it cannot be, my children, but ye must wither in barren maidenhood.

Ah, son of Menoeceus, hear me—since thou art the only father left to them, for we, their parents, are lost, both of us,—allow them not to wander poor and unwed, who are thy kinswomen, nor abase them to the level of my woes. Nay, pity them, when thou seest them at this tender age so utterly forlorn, save for thee. Signify thy promise, generous man, by the touch of thy hand! To you, my children, I would have given much counsel, were your minds mature; but now I would have this to be your prayer—that ye live where occasion suffers, and that the life which is your portion may be happier than your sire's.

CREON

Thy grief hath had large scope enough: nay, pass into the house.

OEDIPUS

I must obey, though 'tis in no wise sweet.

CREON

Yea: for it is in season that all things are good.

OEDIPUS

Knowest thou, then, on what conditions I will go?

CREON

Thou shalt name them; so shall I know them when I hear.

OEDIPUS

See that thou send me to dwell beyond this land.

CREON

Thou askest me for what the god must give.

OEDIPUS

Nay, to the gods I have become most hateful.

CREON

Then shalt thou have thy wish anon.

OEDIPUS

So thou consentest?

CREON

'Tis not my wont to speak idly what I do not mean.

OEDIPUS

Then 'tis time to lead me hence

CREON

Come, then,—but let thy children go.

OEDIPUS

Nay, take not these from me!

CREON

Crave not to be master in all things: for the mastery which thou didst win hath not followed thee through life.

CHORUS (*singing*)

Dwellers in our native Thebes, behold, this is Oedipus, who knew the famed riddle, and was a man most mighty; on whose fortunes what citizen did not gaze with envy? Behold unto what a stormy sea of dread trouble he hath come!

Therefore, while our eyes wait to see the destined final day, we must call no one happy who is of mortal race, until he hath crossed life's border, free from pain.

OEDIPUS AT COLONUS

CHARACTERS IN THE PLAY

OEDIPUS
ANTIGONE ⎱ *his daughters*
ISMENE ⎰
A MAN OF COLONUS
THESEUS, *King of Athens*
CREON, *of Thebes*
POLYNEICES, *the elder son of* OEDIPUS
A MESSENGER
CHORUS OF ELDERS OF COLONUS

OEDIPUS AT COLONUS

(SCENE:—*At Colonus in Attica, a little more than a mile north-west of the Acropolis at Athens. The back-scene shows the grove sacred to the Erinyes or Furies, there worshipped under the propitiatory name of the Eumenides, or Kindly Powers. The grove is luxuriant with laurel, olive, and vine. Near the middle of the stage is seen a rock, affording a seat which is supposed to be just within the bounds of the grove. The hero Colonus is perhaps represented by a statue on the stage.*

The blind OEDIPUS, *who is conceived as coming into Attica from the west or north-west, enters on the spectators' left, led by* ANTIGONE. *He is old and way-worn, his haggard face bearing the traces of the self-inflicted wounds. The garb of both the wanderers betokens indigence and hardship. After replying to his first questions, his daughter leads him to the rocky seat.*)

OEDIPUS

DAUGHTER of the blind old man, to what region have we come, Antigone, or what city of men? Who will entertain the wandering Oedipus to-day with scanty gifts? Little crave I, and win yet less than that little, and therewith am content; for patience is the lesson of suffering, and of the years in our long fellowship, and lastly of a noble mind.—My child, if thou seest any resting-place, whether on profane ground or by groves of the gods, stay me and set me down, that we may inquire where we are: for we stand in need to learn as strangers of denizens, and to perform their bidding.

ANTIGONE

Father, toil-worn Oedipus, the towers that guard the city, to judge by sight, are far off; and this place is sacred, to all seeming, —thick-set with laurel, olive, vine; and in its heart a feathered choir of nightingales makes music. So sit thee here on this unhewn stone; thou hast travelled a long way for an old man.

OEDIPUS

Seat me, then, and watch over the blind.

ANTIGONE

If time can teach, I need not to learn that.

OEDIPUS

Canst thou tell me, now, where we have arrived?

ANTIGONE

Athens I know, but not this place.

OEDIPUS

Aye, so much every wayfarer told us.

ANTIGONE

Well, shall I go and learn how the spot is called?

OEDIPUS

Yes, child,—if indeed 'tis habitable.

ANTIGONE

Nay, inhabited it surely is;—but I think there is no need;—
yonder I see a man near us.

OEDIPUS

Hitherward moving and setting forth?

ANTIGONE

Nay, he is at our side already. Speak as the moment prompts
thee, for the man is here.

(*A* STRANGER, *a man of Colonus, enters.*)

OEDIPUS

Strange (hearing from this maiden, who hath sight for herself and for me, that thou hast drawn nigh with timely quest for
the solving of our doubts—

STRANGER

Now, ere thou question me at large, quit this seat; for thou
art on ground which 'tis not lawful to tread.

OEDIPUS

And what is this ground? To what deity sacred?

STRANGER

Ground inviolable, whereon none may dwell: for the dread goddesses hold it, the daughters of Earth and Darkness.

OEDIPUS

Who may they be, whose awful name I am to hear and invoke?

STRANGER

The all-seeing Eumenides the folk here would call them: but other names please otherwhere.

OEDIPUS

Then graciously may they receive their suppliant! for nevermore will I depart from my rest in this land.

STRANGER

What means this?

OEDIPUS

'Tis the watchword of my fate.

STRANGER

Nay, for my part, I dare not remove thee without warrant from the city, ere I report what I am doing.

OEDIPUS

Now for the gods' love, stranger, refuse me not, hapless wanderer that I am, the knowledge for which I sue to thee.

STRANGER

Speak, and from me thou shalt find no refusal.

OEDIPUS

What, then, is the place that we have entered?

STRANGER

All that *I* know, thou shalt learn from my mouth. This whole place is sacred; awful Poseidon holds it, and therein is the fire-fraught god, the Titan Prometheus; but as for the spot whereon thou treadest, 'tis called the Brazen Threshold of this land, the stay of Athens; and the neighbouring fields claim yon knight Colonus for their primal lord, and all the people bear his name in common for their own. Such, thou mayest know, stranger, are these haunts, not honoured in story, but rather in the life that loves them.

OEDIPUS

Are there indeed dwellers in this region?

STRANGER

Yea, surely, the namesakes of yonder god.

OEDIPUS

Have they a king? Or doth speech rest with the folk?

STRANGER

These parts are ruled by the king in the city.

OEDIPUS

And who is thus sovereign in counsel and in might?

STRANGER

Theseus he is called, son of Aegeus who was before him.

OEDIPUS

Could a messenger go for him from among you?

STRANGER

With what aim to speak, or to prepare his coming?

OEDIPUS

That by small service he may find a great gain.

STRANGER

And what help can be from one who sees not?

OEDIPUS

In all that I speak there shall be sight.

STRANGER

Mark me now, friend—I would not have thee come to harm,—
for thou art noble, if one may judge by thy looks, leaving thy
fortune aside;—stay here, e'en where I found thee, till I go and
tell these things to the folk on this spot,—not in the town: they
will decide for thee whether thou shalt abide or retire.

(*The* STRANGER *departs.*)

OEDIPUS

My child, say, is the stranger gone?

ANTIGONE

He is gone, and so thou canst utter what thou wilt, father, in quietness, as knowing that I alone am near.

OEDIPUS

Queens of dread aspect, since your seat is the first in this land whereat I have bent the knee, show not yourselves ungracious to Phoebus or to myself; who, when he proclaimed that doom of many woes, spake of *this* as a rest for me after long years,—on reaching my goal in a land where I should find a seat of the Awful Goddesses, and a hospitable shelter,—even that there I should close my weary life, with benefits, through my having dwelt therein, for mine hosts, but ruin for those who sent me forth— who drove me away. And he went on to warn me that signs of these things should come, in earthquake, or in thunder, haply, or in the lightning of Zeus.

Now I perceive that in this journey some faithful omen from you hath surely led me home to this grove: never else could I have met with you, first of all, in my wanderings,—I, the austere, with you who delight not in wine,—or taken this solemn seat not shaped by man.

Then, goddesses, according to the word of Apollo, give me at last some way to accomplish and close my course,—unless, perchance, I seem beneath your grace, thrall that I am evermore to woes the sorest on the earth. Hear, sweet daughters of primeval Darkness! Hear, thou that art called the city of great Pallas,— Athens, of all cities most honoured! Pity this poor wraith of Oedipus,—for verily 'tis the man of old no more.

ANTIGONE

Hush! Here come some aged men, I wot, to spy out thy resting-place.

OEDIPUS

I will be mute,—and do thou hide me in the grove, apart from the road, till I learn how these men will speak; for in knowledge is the safeguard of our course.

(OEDIPUS and ANTIGONE *withdraw into the grove. The* CHORUS OF ELDERS OF COLONUS *enter the orchestra, from the right of the spectators, as if in eager search.*)

CHORUS (*singing*)

strophe 1

Give heed—who was he, then? Where lodges he?—
whither hath he rushed from this place, insolent, he, above
all who can live? Scan the ground, look well, urge the
quest in every part.

A wanderer that old man must have been,—a wanderer, not a dweller in the land; else never would he
have advanced into this untrodden grove of the maidens
with whom none may strive, whose name we tremble to
speak, by whom we pass with eyes turned away, moving
our lips, without sound or word, in still devotion.

But now 'tis rumoured that one hath come who in no
wise reveres them; and him I cannot yet discern, though
I look round all the holy place, nor wot I where to find
his lodging.

(OEDIPUS *steps forward, with* ANTIGONE, *from his place
of concealment in the grove.*)

OEDIPUS

systema 1

Behold the man whom ye seek! for in sound is my
sight, as the saying hath it.

CHORUS

O! O!
Dread to see, and dread to hear!

OEDIPUS

Regard me not, I entreat you, as a lawless one.

CHORUS

Zeus defend us! who may the old man be?

OEDIPUS

Not wholly of the best fortune, that ye should envy
him, O guardians of this land!—'Tis plain: else would I
not be walking thus by the eyes of others, and buoying
my strength upon weakness.

CHORUS

antistrophe 1

Alas! wast thou sightless e'en from thy birth? Evil
have been thy days, and many, to all seeming; but at least,
if I can help, thou shalt not add this curse to thy doom.
Too far thou goest—too far! But, lest thy rash steps
intrude on the sward of yonder voiceless glade, where
the bowl of water blends its stream with the flow of
honied offerings (be thou well ware of such trespass,
unhappy stranger) retire,—withdraw!—A wide space
parts us: hearest thou, toil-worn wanderer? If thou hast
aught to say in converse with us, leave forbidden ground,
and speak where 'tis lawful for all; but, till then, refrain.

OEDIPUS

systema 2

Daughter, to what counsel shall we incline?

ANTIGONE

My father, we must conform us to the customs of
the land, yielding, where 'tis meet, and hearkening.

OEDIPUS

Then give me thy hand.

ANTIGONE

'Tis laid in thine.

OEDIPUS

Strangers, oh let me not suffer wrong when I have
trusted in you, and have passed from my refuge!

CHORUS

strophe 2

Never, old man, never shall any one remove thee from
this place of rest against thy will.

(OEDIPUS now begins to move forward.)

OEDIPUS (pausing in his gradual advance)
Further, then?

CHORUS

Come still further.

OEDIPUS (*having advanced another step*)
Further?

ANTIGONE

Lead him onward, maiden, for thou understandest.
[*A verse for* ANTIGONE, *a verse for* OEDIPUS, *and
then another verse for* ANTIGONE, *seem to have
been lost here.*]

ANTIGONE

Come, follow me this way with thy dark steps,
father, as I lead thee.

[*Here has been lost a verse for* OEDIPUS.]

CHORUS

A stranger in a strange land, ah, hapless one, incline
thy heart to abhor that which the city holds in settled
hate, and to reverence what she loves!

OEDIPUS

systema 3

Lead me thou, then, child, to a spot where I may
speak and listen within piety's domain, and let us not
wage war with necessity.

(*Moving forward, he now sets foot on a platform of rock
at the verge of the grove.*)

CHORUS

antistrophe 2

There!—bend not thy steps beyond that floor of
native rock.

OEDIPUS

Thus far?

CHORUS

Enough, I tell thee.

OEDIPUS

Shall I sit down?

CHORUS

Yea, move sideways and crouch low on the edge of
the rock.

ANTIGONE

Father, this is my task: to quiet step.

OEDIPUS

Ah me! ah me!

ANTIGONE

Knit step, and lean thy aged frame upon my loving arm.

OEDIPUS

Woe for the doom of a dark soul!

(ANTIGONE *seats him on the rock.*)

CHORUS

Ah, hapless one, since now thou hast ease, speak,—whence art thou sprung? In what name art thou led on thy weary way? What is the fatherland whereof thou to tell us?

OEDIPUS

Strangers, I am an exile—but forbear . . .

CHORUS

What is this that thou forbiddest, old man?

OEDIPUS

—forbear, forbear to ask me who I am;—seek—probe—no further!

CHORUS

What means this?

OEDIPUS

Dread the birth . . .

CHORUS

Speak!

OEDIPUS (*to* ANTIGONE)

My child—alas!—what shall I say?

CHORUS

What is thy lineage, stranger,—speak!—and who thy sire?

OEDIPUS

Woe is me!—What will become of me, my child?

ANTIGONE

Speak,—for thou art driven to the verge.

OEDIPUS

Then speak I will—I have no way to hide it.

CHORUS

Ye twain make a long delay—come, haste thee!

OEDIPUS

Know ye a son of Laius . . . (*The* CHORUS *utter a cry*) . . . and the race of the Labdacidae? . . .

CHORUS

O Zeus! . . .

OEDIPUS

The hapless Oedipus? . . .

CHORUS

THOU art he?

OEDIPUS

Have no fear of any words that I speak—

The CHORUS *drown his voice with a great shout of execration, half turning away, and holding their mantels before their eyes.*)

OEDIPUS

Unhappy that I am! . . . (*The clamour of the* CHORUS *continues*) . . . Daughter, what is about to befall?

CHORUS

Out with you! forth from the land!

OEDIPUS

And thy promise—to what fulfillment wilt thou bring it?

CHORUS

No man is visited by fate if he requites deeds which were first done to himself; deceit on the one part matches deceits on the other, and gives pain, instead of benefit, for reward. And thou—back with thee! out from these seats! avaunt! away from my land with all speed, lest thou fasten some heavier burden on my city!

ANTIGONE

Strangers of reverent soul, since ye have not borne with mine aged father,—knowing, as ye do, the rumour of his unpurposed deeds,—pity, at least, my hapless self, I implore you, who supplicate you for my sire alone,— supplicate you with eyes that can still look on your own, even as though I were sprung from your own blood, that the sufferer may find compassion.

On you, as on a god, we depend in our misery. Nay, hear us! grant the boon for which we scarce dare hope! By everything sprung from you that ye hold dear, I implore you, yea, by child—by wife, or treasure, or god! Look well and thou wilt not find the mortal who, if a god should lead him on, could escape.

LEADER OF THE CHORUS

Nay, be thou sure, daughter of Oedipus, we pity thee and him alike for your fortune; but, dreading the judgment of the gods, we could not say aught beyond what hath now been said to thee.

OEDIPUS

What good comes, then, of repute or fair fame, if it ends in idle breath; seeing that Athens, as men say, has the perfect fear of Heaven, and the power, above all cities, to shelter the vexed stranger, and the power, above all, to succour him?

And where find I these things, when, after making me rise up from these rocky seats, ye then drive me from the land, afraid of my name alone? Not, surely, afraid of my person or of mine acts; since mine acts, at least, have been in suffering rather than doing— were it seemly that I should tell you the story of my mother or my sire, by reason whereof ye dread me—that know I full well.

And yet in *nature* how was I evil? I, who was but requiting a wrong, so that, had I been acting with knowledge, even then I could not be accounted wicked; but, as it was, all unknowing went I—whither I went—while they who wronged me knowingly sought my ruin.

Wherefore, strangers, I beseech you by the gods, even as ye made me leave my seat, so protect me, and do not, while ye honour the gods, refuse to give those gods their due; but rather deem that they look on the god-fearing among men, and on the godless, and that never yet hath escape been found for an impious mortal on the earth.

With the help of those gods, spare to cloud the bright fame of Athens by ministering to unholy deeds; but, as yet have received the suppliant under your pledge, rescue me and guard me to the end; nor scorn me when ye look on this face unlovely to behold: for I have come to you as one sacred, and pious, and fraught with comfort for this people. But when the master is come, whosoever he be that is your chief, then shall ye hear and know all; meanwhile in no wise show yourself false.

LEADER

The thoughts urged on thy part, old man, must needs move awe; they have been set forth in words not light; but I am content that the rulers of our country should judge in this cause.

OEDIPUS

And where, strangers, is the lord of this realm?

LEADER

He is at the city of his father in our land; and the messenger who sent us hither hath gone to fetch him.

OEDIPUS

Think ye that he will have any regard or care for the blind man, so as to come hither himself?

LEADER

Yea, surely, so soon as he learns thy name.

OEDIPUS

Who is there to bring him that message?

LEADER

The way is long, and many rumours from wayfarers are wont to go abroad; when he hears them, he will soon be with us, fear not. For thy name, old man, hath been mightily noised through all lands; so that, even if he is taking his ease, and slow to move, when he hears of *thee* he will arrive with speed.

OEDIPUS

Well, may he come with a blessing to his own city, as to me!—
What good man is not his own friend?

ANTIGONE

O Zeus! what shall I say, what shall I think, my father?

OEDIPUS

What is it, Antigone, my child?

ANTIGONE

I see a woman coming towards us, mounted on a colt of
Etna; she wears a Thessalian bonnet to screen her face from the
sun. What shall I say? Is it she, or is it not? Doth fancy cheat
me? Yes—no—I cannot tell—ah me! It is no other—yes!—she
greets me with bright glances as she draws nigh, and shows that
Ismene, and no other, is before me.

OEDIPUS

What sayest thou, my child?

ANTIGONE

That I see thy daughter and my sister;—thou canst know her
straightway by her voice.

(ISMENE *enters, attended by one servant.*)

ISMENE

Father and sister, names most sweet to me! How hardly have
I found you! and now I scarce can see you for my tears.

OEDIPUS

My child, thou hast come?

ISMENE

Ah, father, sad is thy fate to see!

OEDIPUS

Thou art with us, my child!

ISMENE

And it hath cost me toil.

OEDIPUS

Touch me, my daughter!

ISMENE

I give a hand to each.

OEDIPUS

Ah, children—ah, ye sisters!

ISMENE

Alas, twice-wretched life!

OEDIPUS

Her life and mine?

ISMENE

And mine, hapless, with you twain.

OEDIPUS

Child, and why hast thou come?

ISMENE

Through care, father, for thee.

OEDIPUS

Through longing to see me?

ISMENE

Yes, and to bring thee tidings by mine own mouth,—with the only faithful servant that I had.

OEDIPUS

And where are the young men thy brothers at our need?

ISMENE

They are—where they are: 'tis their dark hour.

OEDIPUS

O, true image of the ways of Egypt that they show in their spirit and their life! For there the men sit weaving in the house, but the wives go forth to win the daily bread. And in your case, my daughters, those to whom these toils belonged keep the house at home like girls, while ye, in their stead, bear your hapless father's burdens.

One, from the time when her tender age was past and she came to a woman's strength, hath ever been the old man's guide in weary wanderings, oft roaming, hungry and barefoot, through the wild wood, oft sore-vexed by rains and scorching heat,—but regarding not the comforts of home, if so her father should have tendance.

And thou, my child, in former days camest forth, bringing thy father, unknown of the Cadmeans, all the oracles that had been given touching Oedipus; and thou didst take on thee the office of a faithful watcher in my behalf, when I was being driven from the land. And now what new tidings hast thou brought thy father, Ismene? On what mission hast thou set forth from home? For thou comest not empty-handed, well I wot, or without some word of fear for me.

ISMENE

The sufferings that I bore, father, in seeking where thou wast living, I will pass by; I would not renew the pain in the recital. But the ills that now beset thine ill-fated sons,—'tis of these that I have come to tell thee.

At first it was their desire that the throne should be left to Creon, and the city spared pollution, when they thought calmly on the blight of the race from of old, and how it hath clung to thine ill-starred house. But now, moved by some god and by a sinful mind, an evil rivalry hath seized them, thrice infatuate!—to grasp at rule and kingly power.

And the hot-brained youth, the younger born, hath deprived the elder, Polyneices, of the throne, and hath driven him from his fatherland. But he, as the general rumour saith among us, hath gone, an exile, to the hill-girt Argos, and is taking unto him a new kinship, and warriors for his friends,—as deeming that Argos shall soon possess the Cadmean land in honour, or lift that land's praise to the stars.

These are no vain words, my father, but deeds terrible; and where the gods will have pity on thy griefs, I cannot tell.

OEDIPUS

What, hadst thou come to hope that the gods would ever look on me for my deliverance?

ISMENE

Yea, mine is that hope, father, from the present oracles.

OEDIPUS

What are they? What hath been prophesied, my child?

ISMENE

That thou shalt yet be desired, alive and dead, by the men of that land, for their welfare's sake.

OEDIPUS

And who could have good of such an one as I?

ISMENE

Their power, 'tis said, comes to be in *thy* hand.

OEDIPUS

When I am nought, in that hour, then, I am a man?

ISMENE

Yea, for the gods lift thee now, but before they were working thy ruin.

OEDIPUS

'Tis little to lift age, when youth was ruined.

ISMENE

Well, know, at least, that Creon will come to thee in this cause —and rather soon than late.

OEDIPUS

With what purpose, daughter? Expound to me.

ISMENE

To plant thee near the Cadmean land, so that they may have thee in their grasp, but thou mayest not set foot on their borders.

OEDIPUS

And how can I advantage them while I rest beyond their gates?

ISMENE

Thy tomb hath a curse for them, if all be not well with it.

OEDIPUS

It needs no god to help our wit so far.

ISMENE

Well, therefore they would fain acquire thee as a neighbour, in a place where thou shalt not be thine own master.

OEDIPUS

Will they also shroud me in Theban dust?

ISMENE

Nay, the guilt of a kinsman's blood debars thee, father.

OEDIPUS

Then never shall they become my masters.

ISMENE

Some day, then, this shall be a grief for the Cadmeans.

OEDIPUS

In what conjuncture of events, my child?

ISMENE

By force of thy wrath, when they take their stand at thy tomb.

OEDIPUS

And who hath told thee what thou tellest, my child?

ISMENE

Sacred envoys, from the Delphian hearth.

OEDIPUS

And Phoebus hath indeed spoken thus concerning me?

ISMENE

So say the men who have come back to Thebes.

OEDIPUS

Hath either of my sons, then, heard this?

ISMENE

Yea, both have heard, and know it well.

OEDIPUS

And then those base ones, aware of this, held the kingship dearer than the wish to recall me?

ISMENE

It grieves me to hear that,—but I must bear it.
Then may the gods quench not their fated strife, and may it become mine to decide this warfare whereto they are now setting their hands, spear against spear! For then neither should he abide

who now holds the sceptre and the throne, nor should the banished one ever return; seeing that when I, their sire, was being thrust so shamefully from my country, they hindered not, nor defended me; no, they saw me sent forth homeless, they heard my doom of exile cried aloud.

Thou wilt say that it was mine own wish then, and that the city meetly granted me that boon. No, verily: for in that first day, when my soul was seething, and my darling wish for death, aye, death by stoning, no one was found to help me in that desire: but after a time, when all my anguish was now assuaged, and when I began to feel that my wrath had run too far in punishing those past errors,—then it was that the city, on her part, went about to drive me perforce from the land—after all that time; and my sons, when they might have brought help—the sons to the sire—would not do it: no—for lack of one little word from them, I was left to wander, an outcast and a beggar evermore.

'Tis to these sisters, girls as they are, that, so far as nature enables them, I owe my daily food, and a shelter in the land, and the offices of kinship; the brothers have bartered their sire for a throne, and sceptred sway, and rule of the realm. Nay, never shall they win Oedipus for an ally, nor shall good ever come to them from this reign at Thebes; that know I, when I hear this maiden's oracles, and meditate on the old prophecies stored in mine own mind, which Phoebus hath fulfilled for me at last.

Therefore let them send Creon to seek me, and whoso beside is mighty in Thebes. For if ye, strangers,—with the championship of the dread goddesses who dwell among your folk,—are willing to succour, ye shall procure a great deliverer for this State, and troubles for my foes.

LEADER

Right worthy art thou of compassion, Oedipus, thou, and these maidens; and since to this plea thou addest thy power to save our land, I fain would advise thee for thy weal.

OEDIPUS

Kind sir, be sure, then, that I will obey in all,—stand thou my friend.

LEADER

Now make atonement to these deities, to whom thou hast first come, and on whose ground thou hast trespassed.

OEDIPUS

With what rites? instruct me, strangers.

LEADER

First, from a perennial spring fetch holy drink-offerings, borne in clean hands.

OEDIPUS

And when I have gotten this pure draught?

LEADER

Bowls there are, the work of a cunning craftsman: crown their edges and the handles at either brim.

OEDIPUS

With branches, or woollen cloths, or in what wise?

LEADER

Take the freshly-shorn wool of an ewe-lamb.

OEDIPUS

Good; and then,—to what last rite shall I proceed?

LEADER

Pour thy drink-offerings, with thy face to the dawn.

OEDIPUS

With these vessels whereof thou speakest shall I pour them?

LEADER

Yea, in three streams; but empty the last vessel wholly.

OEDIPUS

Wherewith shall I fill this, ere I set it? Tell me this also.

LEADER

With water and honey; but bring no wine thereto.

OEDIPUS

And when the ground under the dark shade hath drunk of these?

LEADER

Lay on it thrice nine sprays of olive with both thine hands, and make this prayer the while.

OEDIPUS

The prayer I fain would hear—'tis of chief moment.

LEADER

That, as we call them Benign Powers, with hearts benign they may receive the suppliant for saving: be this the prayer,—thine own, or his who prays for thee; speak inaudibly, and lift not up thy voice; then retire, without looking behind. Thus do, and I would be bold to stand by thee; but otherwise, stranger. I would fear for thee.

OEDIPUS

Daughters, hear ye these strangers, who dwell near?

ANTIGONE

We have listened; and do thou bid us what to do.

OEDIPUS

I cannot go; for I am disabled by lack of strength and lack of sight, evils twain. But let one of you two go and do these things. For I think that one soul suffices to pay this debt for ten thousand, if it come with good will to the shrine. Act, then, with speed; yet leave me not solitary; for the strength would fail me to move without help or guiding hand.

ISMENE

Then I will go to perform the rite; but where I am to find the spot—this I fain would learn.

LEADER

On the further side of this grove, maiden. And if thou hast need of aught, there is a guardian of the place, who will direct thee.

ISMENE

So to my task:—but thou, Antigone, watch our father here. In parents' cause, if toil there be, we must not reck of toil.

(ISMENE *departs*.)

CHORUS (*chanting*)

strophe 1

Dread is it, stranger, to arouse the old grief that hath so long been laid to rest: and yet I yearn to hear . . .

OEDIPUS

What now? . . .

CHORUS

—of that grievous anguish, found cureless, wherewith thou hast wrestled.

OEDIPUS

By thy kindness for a guest, bare not the shame that I have suffered!

CHORUS

Seeing, in sooth, that the tale is wide-spread, and in no wise wanes, I am fain, friend, to hear it aright.

OEDIPUS

Woe is me!

CHORUS

Be content, I pray thee!

OEDIPUS

Alas, alas!

CHORUS

Grant my wish, as I have granted thine in its fulness.

antistrophe 1

OEDIPUS

I have suffered misery, strangers, — suffered it through unwitting deeds, and of those acts—be Heaven my witness!—no part was of mine own choice.

CHORUS

But in what regard?

OEDIPUS

By an evil wedlock, Thebes bound me, all unknowing, to the bride that was my curse. . . .

CHORUS

Can it be, as I hear, that thou madest thy mother the partner of thy bed, for its infamy?

OEDIPUS

Woe is me! Cruel as death, strangers, are these words in mine ears;—but those maidens, begotten of me—

CHORUS

What wilt thou say?—

OEDIPUS

—two daughters—two curses—

CHORUS

O Zeus!

OEDIPUS

—sprang from the travail of the womb that bore me.

CHORUS

strophe 2

These, then, are at once thine offspring, and . . .

OEDIPUS

—yea, very sisters of their sire.

CHORUS

Oh, horror!

OEDIPUS

Horror indeed—yea, horrors untold sweep back upon my soul.

CHORUS

Thou hast suffered—

OEDIPUS

Suffered woes dread to bear.—

CHORUS

Thou hast sinned—

OEDIPUS

No wilful sin—

CHORUS

How?—

OEDIPUS

A gift was given to me—O, broken-hearted that I am, would I had never won from Thebes that meed for having served her!

Chorus

antistrophe 2

Wretch! How then? . . . thine hand shed blood? . . .

Oedipus

Wherefore this? What wouldst thou learn?

Chorus

A father's blood?

Oedipus

Oh! oh! a second stab—wound on wound!

Chorus

Slayer!

Oedipus

Aye, slayer—yet have I a plea—

Chorus

What canst thou plead?—

Oedipus

—a plea in justice. . . .

Chorus

What? . . .

Ye shall hear it; they whom I slew would have taken
mine own life: stainless before the law, void of malice,
have I come unto this pass!

Leader of the Chorus

Lo, yonder cometh our prince, Theseus son of Aegeus, at thy
voice, to do the part whereunto he was summoned.

(Theseus *enters from the right of the spectators.*)

Theseus

Hearing from many in time past concerning the cruel marring
of thy sight, I have recognised thee, son of Laius; and now, through
hearsay in this my coming, I have the fuller certainty. For thy
garb, and that hapless face, alike assure me of thy name; and in
all compassion would I ask thee, ill-fated Oedipus, what is thy suit
to Athens or to me that thou hast taken thy place here, thou and
the hapless maiden at thy side. Declare it; dire indeed must be

the fortune told by thee, from which I should stand aloof; who know that I myself also was reared in exile, like to thine, and in strange lands wrestled with perils to my life, as no man beside. Never, then, would I turn aside from a stranger, such as thou art now, or refuse to aid in his deliverance; for well know I that I am a man, and that in the morrow my portion is no greater than thine.

OEDIPUS

Theseus, thy nobleness hath in brief words shown such grace that for me there is need to say but little. Thou hast rightly said who I am, from what sire I spring, from what land I have come; and so nought else remains for me but to speak my desire,—and the tale is told.

THESEUS

Even so—speak that—I fain would hear.

OEDIPUS

I come to offer thee my woe-worn body as a gift,—not goodly to look upon; but the gains from it are better than beauty.

THESEUS

And what gain dost thou claim to have brought?

OEDIPUS

Hereafter thou shalt learn; not yet, I think.

THESEUS

At what time, then, will thy benefit be shown?

OEDIPUS

When I am dead, and thou hast given me burial

THESEUS

Thou cravest life's last boon; for all between thou hast no memory,—or no care.

OEDIPUS

Yea, for by that boon I reap all the rest.

THESEUS

Nay, then, this grace which thou cravest from me hath small compass.

OEDIPUS

Yet give heed; this issue is no light one,—no, verily.

THESEUS

Meanest thou, as between thy sons and me?

OEDIPUS

King, they would fain convey me to Thebes.

THESEUS

But if to thy content, then for thee exile is not seemly.

OEDIPUS

Nay, when *I* was willing, *they* refused.

THESEUS

But, foolish man, temper in misfortune is not meet.

OEDIPUS

When thou hast heard my story, chide; till then, forbear.

THESEUS

Say on: I must not pronounce without knowledge.

OEDIPUS

I have suffered, Theseus, cruel wrong on wrong.

THESEUS

Wilt thou speak of the ancient trouble of thy race?

OEDIPUS

No, verily: *that* is noised throughout Hellas.

THESEUS

What, then, is thy grief that passeth the griefs of man?

OEDIPUS

Thus it is with me. From my country I have been driven by mine own offspring; and my doom is to return no more, as guilty of a father's blood.

THESEUS

How, then, should they fetch thee to them, if ye must dwell apart?

OEDIPUS

The mouth of the god will constrain them.

THESEUS

In fear of what woe foreshown?

OEDIPUS

That they must be smitten in this land.

THESEUS

And how should bitterness come between them and me?

OEDIPUS

Kind son of Aegeus, to the gods alone comes never old age or death, but all else is confounded by all-mastering time. Earth's strength decays, and the strength of the body; faith dies, distrust is born; and the same spirit is never steadfast among friends, or betwixt city and city; for, be it soon or be it late, men find sweet turn to bitter, and then once more to love.

And if now all is sunshine between Thebes and thee, yet time, in his untold course, gives birth to days and nights untold, wherein for a small cause they shall sunder with the spear that plighted concord of to-day; when my slumbering and buried corpse, cold in death, shall one day drink their warm blood, if Zeus is still Zeus, and Phoebus, the son of Zeus, speaks true.

But, since I would not break silence touching mysteries, suffer me to cease where I began; only make thine own word good, and never shalt thou say that in vain didst thou welcome Oedipus to dwell in this realm,—unless the gods cheat my hope.

LEADER

King, from the first yon man hath shown the mind to perform these promises, or the like, for our land.

THESEUS

Who, then, would reject the friendship of such an one?—to whom, first, the hearth of an ally is ever open, by mutual right, among us; and then he hath come as a suppliant to our gods, fraught with no light recompense for this land and for me. In reverence for these claims, I will never spurn his grace, but will establish him as a citizen in the land. And if it is the stranger's pleasure

to abide here, I will charge you to guard him; or if to come with
me be more pleasing,—this choice, or that, Oedipus, thou canst
take; thy will shall be mine.

OEDIPUS

O Zeus, mayest thou be good unto such men!

THESEUS

What wouldst thou, then? wouldst thou come to my house?

OEDIPUS

Yea, were it lawful;—but *this* is the place—

THESEUS

What art thou to do here? I will not thwart thee . . .

OEDIPUS

—where I shall vanquish those who cast me forth.

THESEUS

Great were this promised boon from thy presence.

OEDIPUS

It shall be—if thy pledge is kept with me indeed.

THESEUS

Fear not touching me; never will I fail thee.

OEDIPUS

I will not bind thee with an oath, as one untrue.

THESEUS

Well, thou wouldst win nought more than by my word.

OEDIPUS

How wilt thou act, then?

THESEUS

What may be thy fear?

OEDIPUS

Men will come—

THESEUS

Nay, these will look to that.

OEDIPUS

Beware lest, if thou leave me—

THESEUS

Teach me not my part.

OEDIPUS

Fear constrains—

THESEUS

My heart feels not fear.

OEDIPUS

Thou knowest not the threats—

THESEUS

I know that none shall take thee hence in my despite. Oft
have threats blustered, in men's wrath, with threatenings loud and
vain; but when the mind is lord of himself once more, the threats
are gone. And for yon men, haply,—aye, though they have waxed
bold to speak dread things of bringing thee back,—the sundering
waters will prove wide, and hard to sail. Now I would have thee
be of a good courage, apart from any resolve of mine, if indeed
Phoebus hath sent thee on thy way; still, though I be not here, my
name, I wot, will shield thee from harm.

(THESEUS departs.)

CHORUS (singing)

strophe 1

Stranger, in this land of goodly steeds thou hast come
to earth's fairest home, even to our white Colonus; where
the nightingale, a constant guest, trills her clear note in
covert of green glades, dwelling amid the wine-dark ivy
and the god's inviolate bowers, rich in berries and fruit,
unvisited by sun, unvexed by wind of any storm; where the
reveller Dionysus ever walks the ground, companion of the
nymphs that nursed him.

antistrophe 1

And, fed of heavenly dew, the narcissus blooms morn
by morn with fair clusters, crown of the Great Goddesses
from of yore; and the crocus blooms with golden beam.
Nor fail the sleepless founts whence the waters of

Cephisus wander, but each day with stainless tide he moveth over the plains of the land's swelling bosom, for the giving of quick increase; nor hath the Muses' quire abhorred this place, nor Aphrodite of the golden rein.

strophe 2

And a thing there is such as I know not by fame on Asian ground, or as ever born in the great Dorian isle of Pelops,—a growth unconquered, self-renewing, a terror to the spears of the foemen, a growth which mightily flourishes in this land,—the grey-leafed olive, nurturer of children. Youth shall not mar it by the ravage of his hand, nor any who dwells with old age; for the sleepless eye of the Morian Zeus beholds it, and the grey-eyed Athena.

antistrophe 2

And another praise have I to tell for this the city our mother, the gift of a great god, a glory of the land most high; the might of horses, the might of young horses, the might of the sea.

For thou, son of Cronus, our lord Poseidon, hast throned her in this pride, since in these roads first thou didst show forth the curb that cures the rage of steeds. And the shapely oar, apt to men's hands, hath a wondrous speed on the brine, following the hundred-footed Nereids.

ANTIGONE

O land that art praised above all lands, now is it for thee to make those bright praises seen in deeds!

OEDIPUS

What new thing hath chanced, my daughter?

ANTIGONE

Yonder Creon draws near us,—not without followers, father.

OEDIPUS

Ah, kind elders, now give me, I pray you, the final proof of my safety!

LEADER OF THE CHORUS

Fear not-it shall be thine. If *I* am aged, this country's strength hath not grown old.

(CREON *enters with a train of attendants.*)

CREON

Sirs, noble dwellers in this land, I see that a sudden fear hath troubled your eyes at my coming; but shrink not from me, and let no ungentle word escape you.

I am here with no thought of force;—I am old, and I know that the city whereunto I have come is mighty, if any in Hellas hath might;—no,—I have been sent, in these my years, to plead with yonder man that he return with me to the land of Cadmus;—not one man's envoy am I, but with charge from our people all; since 'twas mine, by kinship, to mourn his woes as no Theban beside.

Nay, unhappy Oedipus, hear us, and come home! Rightfully art thou called by the Cadmean folk, and in chief by me, even as I —unless I am the basest of all men born—chiefly sorrow for thine ills, old man, when I see thee, hapless one, a stranger and a wanderer evermore, roaming in beggary, with one handmaid for thy stay. Alas, I had not thought that she could fall to such a depth of misery as that whereunto she hath fallen—yon hapless girl!—while she ever tends thy dark life amid penury,—in ripe youth, but unwed,—a prize for the first rude hand.

Is it not a cruel reproach—alas!—that I have cast thee, and me, and all our race? But indeed an open shame cannot be hid; in the name of thy fathers' gods, harken to me, Oedipus!—hide it *thou,* by consenting to return to the city and the house of thy fathers, after a kindly farewell to this State,—for she is worthy: yet thine own hath the first claim on thy piety, since 'twas she that nurtured thee of old.

OEDIPUS

All-daring, who from any plea of right wouldst draw a crafty device, why dost thou attempt me thus, and seek once more to take me in the toils where capture would be sorest? In the old days— when, distempered by my self-wrought woes, I yearned to be cast out of the land—thy will went not with mine to grant the boon. But when my fierce grief had spent its force, and the seclusion of the house was sweet, *then* wast thou for thrusting me from the house and from the land—nor had this kinship any dearness for thee then; and now, again—when thou seest that I have kindly welcome from this city and from all her sons, thou seekest to pluck me away, wrapping hard thoughts in soft words. And yet what joy is there here,—in kindness shown to us against our will? As if a man should give thee no gift, bring thee no aid, when thou wast fain of the boon; but after thy soul's desire was sated, should grant it then, when the grace could be gracious no more: wouldst thou not find that pleasure vain? Yet such are thine own offers unto me,—good in name, but in their substance evil.

And I will declare it to these also, that I may show thee false. Thou hast come to fetch me, not that thou mayest take me home, but that thou mayest plant me near thy borders, and so thy city may escape unscathed by troubles from this land. *That* portion is not for thee, but *this,*—my curse upon the country, ever abiding therein; —and for my sons, this heritage—room enough in my realm wherein—to die.

Am I not wiser than thou in the fortunes of Thebes? Yea, wiser far, as truer are the sources of my knowledge, even Phoebus, and his father, Zeus most high. But thou hast come hither with fraud on thy lips, yea, with a tongue keener than the edge of the sword; yet by thy pleading thou art like to reap more woe than weal. Howbeit, I know that I persuade thee not of this,—go!— and suffer us to live here; for even in this plight our life would not be evil, so were we content therewith.

CREON

Which, thinkest thou, most suffers in this parley,—I by thy course, or thou by thine own?

OEDIPUS

For me, 'tis enough if thy pleading fails, as with me, so with yon men who are nigh.

CREON

Unhappy man, shall it be seen that not even thy years have brought thee wit? Must thou live to be the reproach of age?

OEDIPUS

Thou hast a ready tongue, but I know not the honest man who hath fair words for every cause.

CREON

Words may be many, and yet may miss their aim.

OEDIPUS

As if thine, forsooth, were few, but aimed aright.

CREON

No, truly, for one whose wit is such as thine.

OEDIPUS

Depart—for I will say it in the name of yon men also!—and beset me not with jealous watch in the place where I am destined to abide.

CREON

These men—not thee—call I to witness: but, as for the strain of thine answer to thy kindred, if ever I take thee—

OEDIPUS

And who could take me in despite of these allies?

CREON

I promise thee, thou soon shalt smart without that.

OEDIPUS

Where is the deed which warrants that blustering word?

CREON

One of thy two daughters hath just been seized by me, and sent hence,—the other I will remove forthwith.

OEDIPUS

Woe is me!

CREON

More woeful thou wilt find it soon.

OEDIPUS

Thou hast my child?

CREON

And will have this one ere long.

OEDIPUS

Alas! friends, what will ye do? Will ye forsake me? will ye not drive the godless man from this land?

LEADER

Hence, stranger, hence—begone! Unrighteous is thy present deed—unrighteous the deed which thou hast done.

CREON (*to his attendants*)
'Twere time for you to lead off yon girl perforce, if she will not go of her free will.

ANTIGONE
Wretched that I am! whither shall I fly?—where find help from gods or men?

LEADER (*threateningly, to* CREON)
What wouldst thou, stranger?

CREON
I will not touch yon man, but her who is mine.

OEDIPUS
O, elders of the land!

LEADER
Stranger,—thy deed is not just.

CREON
'Tis just.

LEADER
How just?

CREON
I take mine own.

(*He lays his hand on* ANTIGONE.)

OEDIPUS
strophe
Hear, O Athens!

CHORUS
What wouldst thou, stranger? Release her! Thy strength, and ours, will soon be proved.

(*They approach him with threatening gestures.*)

CREON
Stand back!

CHORUS
Not from thee, while this is thy purpose.

CREON

Nay, 'twill be war with Thebes for thee, if thou harm me.

OEDIPUS

Said I not so?

CHORUS

Unhand the maid at once!

CREON

Command not where thou art not master.

CHORUS

Leave hold, I tell thee!

CREON

(*to one of his guards, who at a signal seizes* ANTIGONE)
And I tell thee—begone!

CHORUS

To the rescue, men of Colonus—to the rescue! Athens —yea, Athens—is outraged with the strong hand! Hither, hither to our help!

ANTIGONE

They drag me hence—ah me!—friends, friends!

OEDIPUS (*blindly seeking for her*)

Where art thou, my child?

ANTIGONE

I am taken by force—

OEDIPUS

Thy hands, my child!—

ANTIGONE

Nay, I am helpless.

CREON (*to his guards*)

Away with you!

OEDIPUS

Ah me, ah me!

(*The guards lead* ANTIGONE *off.*)

CREON

So *those* two crutches shall never more prop thy steps. But since 'tis thy will to worst thy country and thy friends—whose mandate, though a prince, I here discharge—then be that victory thine. For hereafter, I wot, thou wilt come to know all this,— that now, as in time past, thou hast done thyself no good, when, in despite of friends, thou hast indulged anger, which is ever thy bane.

(He turns to follow his guards.)

LEADER

Hold, stranger!

CREON

Hands off, I say!

LEADER

I will not let thee go, unless thou give back the maidens.

CREON

Then wilt thou soon give Thebes a still dearer prize:—I will seize more than those two girls.

LEADER

What—whither wilt thou turn?

CREON

Yon man shall be my captive.

LEADER

A valiant threat!

CREON

'Twill fortwith be a deed.

LEADER

Aye, unless the ruler of this realm hinder thee.

OEDIPUS

Shameless voice! Wilt thou indeed touch me?

CREON

Be silent!

OEDIPUS

Nay, may the powers of this place suffer me to utter yet this curse! Wretch, who, when these eyes were dark, hast reft from me by force the helpless one who was mine eyesight! Therefore to thee and to thy race may the Sun-god, the god who sees all things, yet grant an old age such as mine!

CREON

See ye this, people of the land?

OEDIPUS

They see both me and thee; they know that my wrongs are deeds, and my revenge—but breath.

CREON

I will not curb my wrath—nay, alone though I am, and slow with age, I'll take yon man by force.

(*He approaches* OEDIPUS *as if to seize him.*)

OEDIPUS

antistrophe

Woe is me!

CHORUS

'Tis a bold spirit that thou hast brought with thee, stranger, if thou thinkest to achieve this.

CREON

I do.

CHORUS

Then will I deem Athens a city no more.

CREON

In a just cause the weak vanquishes the strong.

OEDIPUS

Hear ye his words?

CHORUS

Yea, words which he shall not turn to deeds. Zeus knows!

CREON

Zeus haply knows—thou dost not.

CHORUS

Insolence!

CREON

Insolence which thou must bear.

CHORUS

What ho, people, rulers of the land, ho, hither with all speed, hither! These men are on their way to cross our borders!

(THESEUS *enters with his attendants in haste.*)

THESEUS

What means this shout? What is the trouble? What fear can have moved you to stay my sacrifice at the altar unto the sea-god, the lord of your Colonus? Speak, that I may know all, since therefore have I sped hither with more than easeful speed of foot.

OEDIPUS

Ah, friend,—I know thy voice,—yon man, but now, hath done me foul wrong.

THESEUS

What is that wrong? And who hath wrought it? Speak!

OEDIPUS

Creon, whom thou seest there, hath torn away from me my two children,—mine all.

THESEUS

What dost thou tell me?

OEDIPUS

Thou hast heard my wrong.

THESEUS (*to his attendants*)

Haste, one of you, to the altars yonder,—constrain the folk to leave the sacrifice and to speed—footmen,—horsemen all, with slack rein,—to the region where the two highways meet, lest the maidens pass, and I become a mockery to this stranger, as one spoiled by force. Away, I tell thee—quick!—(*Some guards go out. Turning towards* CREON) As for yon man—if my wrath went as far as he deserves—I would not have suffered him to go scatheless from my hand. But now such law as he himself hath brought, and no other, shall be the rule for his correction.—(*Addressing* CREON) Thou shalt not quit this land until thou bring those maidens, and produce them in my sight; for thy deed is a disgrace to me, and to thine own race, and to thy country. Thou hast come unto a city that observes justice, and sanctions nothing without law,—yet thou hast put her lawful powers aside,—thou hast made this rude inroad,—thou art taking captives at thy pleasure, and snatching prizes by violence, as in the belief that my city was void of men, or manned by slaves, and I—a thing of nought.

Yet 'tis not by Theban training that thou art base; Thebes is not want to rear unrighteous sons; nor would she praise thee, if she learned that thou art spoiling me,—yea, spoiling the gods, when by force thou leadest off their hapless suppliants. Now, were my foot upon thy soil, never would I wrest or plunder, without licence from the ruler of the land, whoso he might be—no, though my claim were of all claims most just: I should know how an alien ought to live among citizens. But thou art shaming a city that deserves it not, even thine own; and the fulness of thy years brings thee an old age bereft of wit.

I have said, then, and I say it once again—let the maidens be brought hither with all speed, unless thou wouldst sojourn in this land by no free choice;—and this I tell thee from my soul, as with my lips.

LEADER OF THE CHORUS
Seest thou thy plight, O stranger? Thou art deemed to come of a just race; but thy deeds are found evil.

CREON
Not counting this city void of manhood, son of Aegeus, nor of counsel,—as thou sayest,—have I wrought this deed; but because I judged that its folk could never be so enamoured of my kinsfolk as to foster them against my will. And I knew that this people would not receive a patricide,—a polluted man,—a man with whom had been found the unholy bride of her son. Such the wisdom, I knew, that dwells on the Mount of Ares in their land; which suffers not such wanderers to dwell within this realm. In that faith, I sought to take this prize. Nor had I done so, but that he was calling down bitter curses on me, and on my race; when, being so wronged, I deemed that I had warrant for this requital. For anger knows no old age, till death come; the dead alone feel no smart.

Therefore thou shalt act as seems to thee good; for, though my cause is just, the lack of aid makes me weak: yet, old though I am, I will endeavour to met deed with deed.

OEDIPUS

O shameless soul, where thinkest thou, falls this thy taunt,—
on my age, or on thine own? Bloodshed—incest—misery—all this
thy lips have launched against me,—all this I have borne, woe is
me! by no choice of mine: for such was the pleasure of the gods,
wroth, haply, with the race from of old. Take me alone, and thou
couldst find no sin to upbraid me withal, in quittance whereof I
was driven to sin thus against myself and against my kin. Tell
me, now,—if, by voice of oracle, some divine doom was coming
on my sire, that he should die by a son's hand, how couldst thou
justly reproach me therewith, who was then unborn,—whom no sire
had yet begotten, no mother's womb conceived? And if, when born
to woe—as I was born—I met my sire in strife, and slew him, all
ignorant what I was doing, and to whom,—how couldst thou justly
blame the unknowing deed?

And my mother—wretch, hast thou no shame in forcing me
to speak of her nuptials, when she was thy sister, and they such
as I will now tell—for verily I will not be silent, when thou hast
gone so far in impious speech. Yea, she was my mother,—oh,
misery!—my mother,—I knew it not, nor she—and, for her shame,
bare children to the son whom she had borne. But one thing, at
least, I know,—that thy will consents thus to revile her and me;
but not of my free will did I wed her, and not of free will do I
speak now.

Nay, not in this marriage shall I be called guilty, nor in that
slaying of my sire which thou ever urgest against me with bitter
reviling. Answer me but one thing that I ask thee. If, here and
now, one should come up and seek to slay thee—thee, the righteous
—wouldst thou ask if the murderer was thy father, or wouldst
thou reckon with him straightway? I think, as thou lovest thy life,
thou wouldst requite the culprit, nor look around thee for thy
warrant. But such the plight into which *I* came, led by gods; and
in this, could my sire come back to life, methinks he would not
gainsay me.

Yet *thou,*—for thou art not a just man, but one who holds all
things meet to utter, knowing no barrier betwixt speech and silence
—*thou* tauntest me in such wise, before yon men. And thou findest
it timely to flatter the renowned Theseus, and Athens, saying how
well her State hath been ordered: yet, while giving such large
praise, thou forgettest this,—that if any land knows how to worship
the gods with due rites, this land excels therein; whence thou hadst

planned to steal me, the suppliant, the old man, and didst seek to
seize me, and hast already carried off my daughters. Wherefore
I now call on yon goddesses, I supplicate them, I adjure them with
prayers, to bring me help and to fight in my cause, that thou mayest
learn well by what manner of men this realm is guarded.

LEADER

The stranger is a good man, O king; his fate hath been accurst;
but 'tis worthy of our succour.

THESEUS

Enough of words:—the doers of the deed are in flight, while
we, the sufferers, stand still.

CREON

What, then, wouldst thou have a helpless man to do?

THESEUS

Show the way in their track,—while I escort thee, that, if
in these regions thou hast the maidens of our quest, thou thyself
mayest discover them to me; but if thy men are fleeing with the
spoil in their grasp, we may spare our trouble; the chase is for
others, from whom they will never escape out of this land, to thank
their gods.

Come,—forward! The spoiler hath been spoiled, I tell thee—
Fate hath taken the hunter in the toils; gains got by wrongful arts
are soon lost. And thou shalt have no ally in thine aim, for well
wot I that not without accomplice or resource hast thou gone to
such a length of violence in the daring mood which hath inspired
thee here: no,—there was some one in whom thou wast trusting
when thou didst essay these deeds. And to this I must look, nor
make this city weaker than one man. Dost thou take my drift? Or
seem these words as vain as seemed the warnings when thy deed
was still a-planning?

CREON

Say what thou wilt while thou art here,—I will not cavil: but
at home I, too, will know how to act.

THESEUS

For the present, threaten, but go forward.—Do thou, Oedipus,
stay here in peace, I pray thee,—with my pledge that, unless I die
before, I will not cease till I put thee in possession of thy children.

OEDIPUS

Heaven reward thee, Theseus, for thy nobleness, and thy loyal care in my behalf!

(THESEUS *and attendants, with* CREON, *go out on spectators' left.*)

CHORUS (*singing*)

strophe 1

Oh, to be where the foeman, turned to bay, will soon join in the brazen clangour of battle, haply by the shores loved of Apollo, haply by that torch-lit strand where the Great Goddesses cherish dread rites for mortals, on whose lips the ministrant Eumolpidae have laid the precious seal of silence; where, methinks, the war-waking Theseus and the captives twain, the sister maids, will soon meet within our borders, amid a war-cry of men strong to save!

antistrophe 1

Or perchance they will soon draw night to the pastures on the west of Oea's snowy rock, borne on horses in their flight, or in chariots racing at speed.

Creon will be worsted! Terrible are the warriors of Colonus, and the followers of Theseus are terrible in their might. Yea, the steel of every bridle flashes,—with slack bridle-rein all the knighthood rides apace that worships our Queen of Chivalry, Athena, and the earth-girdling Sea-god, the son of Rhea's love.

strophe 2

Is the battle now, or yet to be? For somehow my soul woos me to the hope that soon I shall be face to face with the maidens thus sorely tried, thus sorely visited by the hand of a kinsman.

To-day, to-day, Zeus will work some great thing: I have presage of victory in the strife. O to be a dove with swift strength as of the storm, that I might reach an airy cloud, with gaze lifted above the fray!

antistrophe 2

Hear, all-ruling lord of heaven, all-seeing Zeus! Enable the guardians of this land, in might triumphant, to achieve the capture that gives the prize to their hands! So grant thy daughter also, our dread Lady, Pallas

Athena! And Apollo, the hunter, and his sister, who follows the dappled, swift-footed deer—fain am I that they should come, a twofold strength, to this land and to her people.

LEADER OF THE CHORUS

Ah, wanderer friend, thou wilt not have to tax thy watcher with false augury,—for yonder I see the maidens drawing near with an escort.

OEDIPUS

Where—where? How? What sayest thou?

(ANTIGONE and ISMENE enter, with THESEUS and his attendants, on the spectators' left.)

ANTIGONE

O father, father, that some god would suffer thine eyes to see this noble man, who hath brought us here to thee!

OEDIPUS

My child!—ye are here indeed?

ANTIGONE

Yea, for these strong arms have saved us—Theseus, and his trusty followers.

OEDIPUS

Come ye hither, my child,—let me embrace you—restored beyond all hope!

ANTIGONE

Thy wish shall be granted—we crave what we bestow.

OEDIPUS

Where, then, where are ye?

ANTIGONE

Here approaching thee together.

OEDIPUS

My darlings!

ANTIGONE

A father loves his own.

OEDIPUS AT COLONUS ... 441

OEDIPUS

Props of mine age!

ANTIGONE

And sharers of thy sorrow.

OEDIPUS

I hold my dear ones; and now, should I die, I were not wholly wretched, since ye have come to me. Press close to me on either side, children, cleave to your sire, and repose from this late roaming, so forlorn, so grievous! And tell me what hath passed as shortly as ye may; brief speech sufficeth for young maidens.

ANTIGONE

Here is our deliverer: from him thou shouldst hear the story, father, since his is the deed; so shall my part be brief.

OEDIPUS

Sir, marvel not, if with such yearning I prolong my words unto my children, found again beyond my hope. For well I wot that this joy in respect of them hath come to me from thee, and thee alone: thou hast rescued them, and no man beside. And may the gods deal with thee after my wish,—with thee, and with this land; for among you, above all human kind, have I found the fear of heaven, and the spirit of fairness, and the lips that lie not. I know these things, which with these words I requite; for what I have, I have through thee, and no man else.

Stretch forth thy right hand, O king, I pray thee, that I may touch it and, if 'tis lawful, kiss thy cheek.—But what am I saying? Unhappy as I have become, how could I wish thee to touch one with whom all stain of sin hath made its dwelling? No, not I,— nor allow thee, if thou wouldst. They alone can share this burden, to whom it hath come home.—Receive my greeting where thou standest; and in the future still give me thy royal care, as thou hast given it to this hour.

THESEUS

No marvel is it to me, if thou hast shown some mind to large discourse, for joy in these thy children, and if thy first care hath been for their words, rather than for me; indeed, there is nought to vex me in that. Not in words so much as deeds would I make the lustre of my life. Thou hast the proof; I have failed in nothing of my sworn faith to thee, old man; here am I, with the maidens living,—yea, scatheless of those threats. And how the fight was won, what need that I should idly boast, when thou wilt learn it from these maidens in converse?

But there is a matter that hath newly chanced to me, as I came hither; lend me thy counsel thereon, for, small though it be, 'tis food for wonder and mortal man should deem nothing beneath his care.

OEDIPUS

What is it, son of Aegeus? Tell me;—I myself know nought of that whereof thou askest.

THESEUS

A man, they say,—not thy countryman, yet thy kinsman,— hath somehow cast himself, a suppliant, at our altar of Poseidon, where I was sacrificing when I first set out hither.

OEDIPUS

Of what land is he? What craves he by the supplication?

THESEUS

I know one thing only; they say, he asks brief speech with thee, which shall not irk thee much.

OEDIPUS

On what theme? That suppliant posture is not trivial.

THESEUS

He asks, they say, no more than that he may confer with thee, and return unharmed from his journey hither.

OEDIPUS

Who can he be who thus implores the god?

THESEUS

Look if ye have any kinsman at Argos, who might crave this boon of thee.

OEDIPUS

O friend! Say no word more!

THESEUS

What ails thee?

OEDIPUS

Ask it not of me—

THESEUS

Ask what?—Speak!

OEDIPUS

By those words I know who is the suppliant.

THESEUS

And who can he be, against whom I should have a grief?

OEDIPUS

My son, O king,—the hated son whose words would vex mine ear as the words of no man beside.

THESEUS

What? Canst thou not listen, without doing what thou wouldst not? Why should it pain thee to hear him?

OEDIPUS

Most hateful, king, hath that voice become to his sire:—lay me not under constraint to yield in this.

THESEUS

But think whether his suppliant state constrains thee: what if thou hast a duty of respect for the god?

ANTIGONE

Father, hearken to me, though I be young who counsel. Allow the king to gratify his own heart, and to gratify the god as he wishes; and, for thy daughter's sake, allow our brother to come. For he will not pluck thee perforce from thy resolve,—never fear, —by such words as shall not be spoken for thy good. But to hear him speak,—what harm can be in that? Ill-devised deeds, thou knowest, are bewrayed by speech. Thou art his sire; so that, e'en if he were to wrong thee with the most impious of foul wrongs, my father, it is not lawful for thee to wrong him again.

Oh, let him come: other men, also, have evil offspring, and are swift to wrath; but they hear advice, and are charmed from their mood by the gentle spells of friends.

Look thou to the past, not to the present,—think on all that thou hast borne through sire and mother; and if thou considerest those things, well I wot, thou wilt discern how evil is the end that waits on evil wrath; not slight are thy reasons to think thereon, bereft, as thou art, of the sight that returns no more.

Nay, yield to us! It is not seemly for just suitors to sue long; it is not seemly that a man should receive good, and thereafter lack the mind to requite it.

OEDIPUS

My child, 'tis sore for me, this pleasure that ye win from me by your pleading;—but be it as ye will. Only, if that man is to come hither,—friend, let no one ever become master of my life!

THESEUS

I need not to hear such words more than once, old man:—I would not boast; but be sure that thy life is safe, while any god saves mine.

(THESEUS *goes out, to the right of the spectators.*)

CHORUS (*singing*)

strophe

Whoso craves the ampler length of life, not content to desire a modest span, him will I judge with no uncertain voice; he cleaves to folly.

For the long days lay up full many things nearer unto grief than joy; but as for thy delights, their place shall know them no more, when a man's life hath lapsed beyond the fitting term; and the Deliverer comes at the last to all alike,—when the doom of Hades is suddenly revealed, without marriage-song, or lyre, or dance,— even Death at the last.

antistrophe

Not to be born is, past all prizing, best; but, when a man hath seen the light, this is next best by far, that with all speed he should go thither, whence he hath come.

For when he hath seen youth go by, with its light follies, what troublous affliction is strange to his lot, what suffering is not therein?—envy, factions, strife, battles and slaughters; and, last of all, age claims him for her own,—age, dispraised, infirm, unsociable, unfriended, with whom all woe of woe abides.

epode

In such years is yon hapless one, not I alone: and as some cape that fronts the North is lashed on every side by the wave of winter, so he also is fiercely lashed ever-more by the dread troubles that break on him like billows, some from the setting of the sun, some from the rising, some in the region of the noon-tide beam, some from the gloom-wrapped hills of the North.

ANTIGONE

Lo, yonder, methinks, I see the stranger coming hither,—yea, without attendants, my father,—the tears streaming from his eyes.

OEDIPUS

Who is he?

ANTIGONE

The same who was in our thoughts from the first;—Polyneices hath come to us.

(POLYNEICES *enters, on the spectators' left.*)

POLYNEICES

Ah me, what shall I do? Whether shall I weep first for mine own sorrows, sisters, or for mine aged sire's, as I see them yonder? Whom I have found in a strange land, an exile here with you twain, clad in such raiment, whereof the foul squalor hath dwelt with that aged form so long, a very blight upon his flesh,—while above the sightless eyes the unkempt hair flutters in the breeze; and matching with these things, meseems, is the food that he carries, hapless one, against hunger's pinch.

Wretch that I am! I learn all this too late: and I bear witness that I am proved the vilest of men in all that touches care for thee: —from mine own lips hear what I am. But, seeing that Zeus himself, in all that he doeth, hath Mercy for the sharer of his throne, may she come to thy side also, my father; for the faults can be healed, but can never more be made worse.

(*A pause*)

Why art thou silent? . . . Speak, father:—turn not away from me. Hast thou not even an answer for me? Wilt thou dismiss me in mute scorn, without telling wherefore thou art wroth?

O ye, his daughters, sisters mine, strive ye, at least, to move our sire's implacable, inexorable silence, that he send me not away dishonoured,—who am the suppliant of the god,—in such wise as this, with no word of response.

ANTIGONE

Tell him thyself, unhappy one, what thou hast come to seek. As words flow, perchance they touch to joy, perchance they glow with anger, or with tenderness, and so they somehow give a voice to the dumb.

POLYNEICES

Then will I speak boldly,—for thou dost admonish me well,— first claiming the help of the god himself, from whose altar the king of this land raised me, that I might come hither, with warranty to speak and hear, and go my way unharmed. And I will crave, strangers, that these pledges be kept with me by you, and by my sisters here, and by my sire.—But now I would fain tell thee, father, why I came.

I have been driven, an exile, from my fatherland, because, as eldest-born, I claimed to sit in thy sovereign seat. Wherefore Eteocles, though the younger, thrust me from the land, when he had neither worsted me in argument, nor come to trial of might and deed,—no, but won the city over. And of this I deem it most likely that the curse on thy house is the cause; then from sooth-sayers also I so hear. For when I came to Dorian Argos, I took the daughter of Adratus to wife; and I bound to me by oath all of the Apian land who are foremost in renown of war, that with them I might levy the sevenfold host of spearmen against Thebes, and die in my just cause, or cast the doers of this wrong from the realm.

Well, and wherefore have I come hither now? With suppliant prayers, my father, unto thee—mine own, and the prayers of mine allies, who now, with seven hosts behind their seven spears, have set their leaguer round the plain of Thebes; of whom is swift-speared Amphiaraus, matchless warrior, matchless augur; then the son of Oeneus, Aetolian Tydeus; Eteoclus third, of Argive birth; the fourth, Hippomedon, sent by Talaos, his sire; while Capaneus, the fifth, vaunts that he will burn Thebes with fire, unto the ground; and sixth, Arcadian Parthenopaeus rushes to the war, named from that virgin of other days whose marriage in after-time gave him birth, trusty son of Atalanta. Last, I, thy son,—or if not thine, but offspring of an evil fate, yet thine at least in name,—lead the fearless host of Argos unto Thebes.

And we, by these thy children and by thy life, my father, implore thee all, praying thee to remit thy stern wrath against me, as I go forth to chastise my brother, who hath thrust me out and robbed me of my fatherland. For if aught of truth is told by oracles, they said that victory should be with those whom thou shouldst join.

Then, by our fountains and by the gods of our race, I ask thee to hearken and to yield; a beggar and an exile am I, an exile thou; by court to others we have a home, both thou and I, sharers of one doom; while *he,* king in the house—woe is me!—mocks in his pride at thee and me alike. But, if thou assist my purpose, small toil or time, and I will scatter his strength to the winds: and so will I bring thee and stablish thee in thine own house, and stablish myself, when I have cast him out by force. Be thy will with me, and that boast may be mine: without thee, I cannot e'en return alive.

LEADER OF THE CHORUS

For his sake who hath sent him, Oedipus, speak, as seems thee good, ere thou send the man away.

OEDIPUS

Nay, then, my friends, guardians of this land, were not Theseus he who had sent him hither to me, desiring that he should have my response, never should he have heard this voice. But now he shall be graced with it, ere he go,—yea, and hear from me such words as shall never gladden his life:—villain, who when thou hadst the sceptre and the throne, which now thy brother hath in Thebes, dravest me, thine own father, into exile, and madest me citiless, and madest me to wear this garb which now thou weepest to behold, when thou hast come unto the same stress of misery as I. The time for tears is past: no, *I* must bear this burden while I live, ever thinking of thee as a murderer; for 'tis thou that hast brought my days to this anguish, 'tis thou that hast thrust me out; to thee I owe it that I wander, begging my daily bread from strangers. And, had these daughters not been born to be my comfort, verily I had been dead, for aught of help from thee. Now, these girls preserve me, these my nurses, these who are men, not women, in true service: but ye are aliens, and no sons of mine.

Therefore the eyes of Fate look upon thee—not yet as they

will look anon, if indeed those hosts are moving against Thebes. Never canst thou overthrow that city; no, first shalt thou fall stained with bloodshed, and thy brother likewise. Such the curses that my soul sent forth before against you twain, and such do I now invoke to fight for me, that ye may deem it meet to revere parents, nor scorn your father utterly, because he is sightless who begat such sons; for these maidens did not thus. So my curses have control of thy 'supplication' and thy 'throne,'—if indeed Justice, revealed from of old, sits with Zeus in the might of the eternal laws.

And thou—begone, abhorred of me, and unfathered!—begone, thou vilest of the vile, and with thee take these curses which I call down on thee—never to vanquish the land of thy race, no, nor ever return to hillgirt Argos, but by a kindred hand to die, and slay him by whom thou hast been driven out. Such is my prayer; and I call the paternal darkness of dread Tartarus to take thee unto another home,—I call the spirits of this place,—I call the Destroying God, who hath set that dreadful hatred in you twain. Go, with these words in thine ears—go, and publish it to the Cadmeans all, yea, and to thine own staunch allies, that Oedipus hath divided such honours to his sons.

LEADER

Polyneices, in thy past goings I take no joy; and now go thy way with speed.

POLYNEICES

Alas, for my journey and my baffled hope: alas, for my comrades! What an end was that march to have, whereon we sallied forth from Argos: woe is me!—aye, such an end, that I may not even utter it to any of my companions, or turn them back, but must go in silence to meet this doom.

Ah ye, his daughters and my sisters,—since ye hear these hard prayers of your sire,—if this father's curses be fulfilled, and some way of return to Thebes be found for you, oh, as ye fear the gods, do not, for your part, dishonour me,—nay, give me burial, and due funeral rites. And so the praise which ye now win from yonder man, for your service, shall be increased by another praise not less, by reason of the office wrought for me.

ANTIGONE

Polyneices, I entreat thee, hear me in one thing!

POLYNEICES

What is it, dearest Antigone? Speak!

ANTIGONE

Turn thy host back to Argos,—aye, with all speed,—and destroy not thyself and Thebes.

POLYNEICES

Nay, it cannot be: for how again could I lead the same host, when once I had blenched?

ANTIGONE

But why, my brother, should thine anger rise again? What gain is promised thee in destroying thy native city?

POLYNEICES

'Tis shame to be an exile, and, eldest born as I am, to be thus mocked on my brother's part.

ANTIGONE

Seest thou, then, to what sure fulfilment thou art bringing his prophecies, who bodes mutual slaying for you twain?

POLYNEICES

Aye, for he wishes it:—but I must not yield.

ANTIGONE

Ah me unhappy!—But who will dare to follow thee, hearing what prophecies yon man hath uttered?

POLYNEICES

I will not e'en report ill tidings: 'tis a good leader's part to tell the better news, and not the worse.

ANTIGONE

Brother! Thy resolve, then, is thus fixed?

POLYNEICES

Yea,—and detain me not. For mine it now shall be to tread yon path, with evil doom and omen from this my sire and from his Furies; but for you twain, may Zeus make your path bright, if ye do my wishes when I am dead,—since in my life ye can do

them no more.—(*He gently disengages himself from their embrace.*)
Now, release me,—and farewell; for nevermore shall ye behold me
living.

ANTIGONE

Woe is me!

POLYNEICES

Mourn not for me.

ANTIGONE

And who would not bewail thee, brother, who thus art hurrying
to death foreseen?

POLYNEICES

If 'tis fate, I must die.

ANTIGONE

Nay, nay,—hear my pleading!

POLYNEICES

Plead not amiss.

ANTIGONE

Then woe is me, indeed, if I must lose thee!

POLYNEICES

Nay, that rests with Fortune,—that end or another.—For you
twain, at least, I pray the gods that ye never meet with ill; for
in all men's eyes ye are unworthy to suffer.

(*He goes out on the spectators' left.*)

CHORUS (*chanting*)

strophe 1

Behold, new ills have newly come, in our hearing,
from the sightless stranger,—ills fraught with a heavy
doom; unless, perchance, Fate is finding its goal. For 'tis
not mine to say that a decree of Heaven is ever vain:
watchful, aye watchful of those decrees is Time overthrowing some fortunes, and on the morrow lifting others,
again, to honour.—Hark that sound in the sky!—Zeus
defend us!

(*Thunder is heard.*)

OEDIPUS

My children, my children! If there be any man to send, would
that some one would fetch hither the peerless Theseus!

ANTIGONE

And what, father, is the aim of thy summons?

OEDIPUS

This winged thunder of Zeus will lead me anon to Hades:
nay, send, and tarry not.

(A second peal is heard.)

CHORUS (*chanting*)

antistrophe 1

Hark! With louder noise it crashes down, unutter-
able, hurled by Zeus! The hair of my head stands up for
fear, my soul is sore dismayed; for again the lightning
flashes in the sky. Oh, to what event will it give birth? I
am afraid, for never in vain doth it rush forth, or without
grave issue. O thou dread sky! O Zeus!

OEDIPUS

Daughters, his destined end hath come upon your sire; he can
turn his face from it no more.

ANTIGONE

How knowest thou? What sign hath told thee this?

OEDIPUS

I know it well.—But let some one go, I pray you, with all
speed, and bring hither the lord of this realm.

(Another peal is heard.)

CHORUS (*chanting*)

strophe 2

Ha! Listen! Once again that piercing thunder-voice
is around us! Be merciful, O thou god, be merciful, if
thou art bringing aught of gloom for the land our mother!
Gracious may I find thee, nor, because I have looked on a
man accurst, have some meed, not of blessing for my
portion! O Zeus our lord, to thee I cry!

OEDIPUS

Is the man near? Will he find me still alive, children, and master of my mind?

ANTIGONE

And what is the pledge which thou wouldst have fixed in thy mind?

OEDIPUS

In return for his benefits, I would duly give him the requital promised when I received them.

CHORUS (*chanting*)

antistrophe 2

What ho, my son, hither, come hither! Or if in the glade's inmost recess, for the honour of the sea-god Poseidon, thou art hallowing his altar with sacrifice,—come thence! Worthy art thou in the stranger's sight, worthy are thy city and thy folk, that he should render a just recompense for benefits. Haste, come quickly, O king!

(THESEUS *enters, on the spectators' right.*)

THESEUS

Wherefore once more rings forth a summons from you all,—from my people as clearly as from our guest? Can a thunderbolt from Zeus be the cause, or rushing hail in its fierce onset? All forebodings may find place, when the god send such a storm.

OEDIPUS

King, welcome is thy presence; and 'tis some god that hath made for thee the good fortune of this coming.

THESEUS

And what new thing hath now befallen, son of Laius?

OEDIPUS

My life hangs in the scale: and I fain would die guiltless of bad faith to thee and to this city, in respect of my pledges.

THESEUS

And what sign of thy fate holds thee in suspense?

OEDIPUS

The gods, their own heralds, bring me the tidings, with no failure in the signs appointed of old.

THESEUS

What sayest thou are the signs of these things, old man?

OEDIPUS

The thunder, peal on peal,—the lightning, flash on flash, hurled from the unconquered land.

THESEUS

Thou winnest my belief, for in much I find thee a prophet whose voice is not false;—then speak what must be done.

OEDIPUS

Son of Aegeus, I will unfold that which shall be a treasure for this city, such as age can never mar. Anon, unaided, and with no hand to guide me, I will show the way to the place where I must die. But that place reveal thou never unto mortal man,— tell not where it is hidden, nor in what region it lies; that so it may ever make for thee a defence, better than many shields, better than the succouring spear of neighbours.

But, for mysteries which speech may not profane, thou shalt mark them for thyself, when thou comest to that place alone: since neither to any of this people can I utter them, nor to mine own children, dear though they are. No, guard them thou alone; and when thou art coming to the end of life, disclose them to thy heir alone; let him teach his heir, and so thenceforth.

And thus shalt thou hold this city unscathed from the side of the Dragon's brood;—full many States lightly enter on offence, e'en though their neighbour lives aright. For the gods are slow, though they are sure, in visitation, when men scorn godliness, and in turn to frenzy. Not such be thy fate, son of Aegeus.— Nay, thou knowest such things, without my precepts.

But to that place—for the divine summons urges me—let us now set forth, and hesitate no more.—(*As if suddenly inspired, he moves with slow but firm steps towards the left of the scene, beckoning the others onward.*) My children, follow me,—thus,— for I now have in strange wise been made your guide, as ye were your sire's. On,—touch me not,—nay, suffer me unaided to find

out that sacred tomb where 'tis my portion to be buried in this
land.

This way,—hither,—this way!—for this way doth Guiding
Hermes lead me, and the goddess of the dead!

O light,—no light to me,—mine once thou wast, I ween,—
but now my body feels thee for the last time! For now go I to
hide the close of my life with Hades.—Truest of friends! blessed
be thou, and this land, and thy lieges; and, when your days are
blest, think on me the dead, for your welfare evermore.

(*He passes from the stage on the spectators' left, followed by his
daughters,* THESEUS, *and attendants.*)

CHORUS (*singing*)

strophe

If with prayer I may adore the Unseen Goddess, and
thee, lord of the children of night, O hear me, Aidoneous,
Aidoneus! Not in pain, not by a doom that wakes sore
lament, may the stranger pass to the fields of the dead
below, the all-enshrouding, and to the Stygian house.
Many were the sorrows that came to him without cause;
but in requital a just god will lift him up.

antistrophe

Goddesses Infernal! And thou, dread form of the
unconquered hound, thou who hast thy lair in those gates
of many guests, thou untameable Watcher of Hell,
gnarling from the cavern's jaws, as rumour from the
beginning tells of thee!

Hear me, O Death, son of Earth and Tartarus!
May that Watcher leave a clear path for the stranger on
his way to the nether fields of the dead! To thee I call,
giver of the eternal sleep.

(*A* MESSENGER *enters from the left.*)

MESSENGER

Countrymen, my tidings might most shortly be summed thus:
Oedipus is gone. But the story of the hap may not be told in brief
words, as the deeds yonder were not briefly done.

LEADER OF THE CHORUS

He is gone, hapless one?

MESSENGER

Be sure that he hath passed from life.

LEADER

Ah, how? by a god-sent doom, and painless?

MESSENGER

There thou touchest on what is indeed worthy of wonder. How he moved hence, thou thyself must know, since thou wast here,—with no friend to show the way, but guide himself unto us all.

Now, when he had come to the sheer Threshold, bound by brazen steps to earth's deep roots, he paused in one of many branching paths, near the basin in the rock, where the inviolate covenant of Theseus and Peirithous hath its memorial. He stood midway between that basin and the Thorician stone,—the hollow pear-tree and the marble tomb; then sate him down, and loosed his sordid raiment.

And then he called his daughters, and bade them fetch water from some fount, that he should wash, and make a drink-offering. And they went to the hill which was in view, Demeter's hill who guards the tender plants, and in short space brought that which their father had enjoined; then they ministered to him with washing, and dressed him, as use ordains.

But when he had content of doing all, and no part of his desire was now unheeded, then was thunder from the Zeus of the Shades: and the maidens shuddered as they heard; they fell at their father's knees, and wept, nor ceased from beating the breast, and wailing very sore.

And when he heard their sudden bitter cry, he put his arms around them, and said: 'My children, this day ends your father's life. For now all hath perished that was mine, and no more shall ye bear the burden of tending me,—no light one, well I know, my children; yet one little word makes all those toils as nought; *love* had ye from me, as from none beside; and now ye shall have me with you no more, through all your days to come.'

On such wise, close-clinging to each other, sire and daughters sobbed and wept. But when they had made an end of wailing, and the sound went up no more, there was a stillness; and suddenly a voice of one who cried aloud to him, so that the hair of all stood up on their heads for sudden fear, and they were afraid. For the god called him with many callings and manifold: *'Oedipus, Oedipus, why delay we to go? Thou tarriest too long.'*

But when he perceived that he was called of the god, he craved that the king Theseus should draw near; and when he came near, said: 'O my friend, give, I pray thee, the solemn pledge of thy right hand to my children, and ye, daughters, to him; and promise thou never to forsake them of thy free will, but to do all things for their good, as thy friendship and the time may prompt.' And he, like a man of noble spirit, without making lament, sware to keep that promise to his friend.

But when Theseus had so promised, straightway, Oedipus felt for his children with blind hands, and said: 'O my children, ye must be nobly brave of heart, and depart from this place, nor ask to behold unlawful sights, or to hear such speech as may not be heard. Nay, go with all haste; only let Theseus be present, as is his right, a witness of those things which are to be.'

So spake he, and we all heard; and with streaming tears and with lamentation we followed the maidens away. But when we had gone apart, after no long time we looked back, and Oedipus we saw nowhere any more, but the king alone, holding his hand before his face to screen his eyes, as if some dread sight had been seen, and such as none might endure to behold. And then, after a short space, we saw him salute the earth and the home of the gods above, both at once, in one prayer.

But by what doom Oedipus perished, no man can tell, save Theseus alone. No fiery thunderbolt of the god removed him in that hour, nor any rising of storm from the sea; but either a messenger from the gods, or the world of the dead, the nether adamant, riven for him in love, without pain; for the passing of the man was not with lamentation, or in sickness and suffering, but, above mortal's, wonderful. And if to any I seem to speak folly, I would not woo their belief, who count me foolish.

LEADER

And where are the maidens, and their escort?

MESSENGER

Not far hence; for the sounds of mourning tell plainly that they approach.

(ANTIGONE *and* ISMENE *enter, chanting their song of lamentation.*)

ANTIGONE

strophe 1

Woe, woe! Now, indeed, is it for us, unhappy sisters, in all fulness to bewail the curse on the blood that is ours from our sire! For him, while he lived, we bore that long pain without pause; and at the last a sight and a loss that baffle thought are ours to tell.

CHORUS

And how is it with you?

ANTIGONE

We can but conjecture, friends.

CHORUS

He is gone?

ANTIGONE

Even as thou mightest wish: yea, surely, when death met him not in war, or on the deep, but he was snatched to the viewless fields by some swift, strange doom. Ah me! and a night as of death hath come on the eyes of us twain: for how shall we find our bitter livelihood, roaming to some far land, or on the waves of the sea?

ISMENE

I know not. Oh that deadly Hades would join me in death unto mine aged sire! Woe is me! I cannot live the life that must be mine.

CHORUS

Best of daughters, sisters twain, Heaven's doom must be borne: be no more fired with too much grief: ye have so fared that ye should not repine.

ANTIGONE

antistrophe 1

Ah, so care past can seem lost joy! For that which was no way sweet had sweetness, while therewith I held *him* in mine embrace. Ah, father, dear one, ah thou who hast put on the darkness of the under-world for ever, not even there shalt thou ever lack our love,—her love and mine.

CHORUS

He hath fared—

ANTIGONE

He hath fared as he would.

CHORUS

In what wise?

ANTIGONE

On foreign ground, the ground of his choice, he hath died; in the shadow of the grave he hath his bed for ever; he hath left mourning behind him, not barren of tears. For with these streaming eyes, father, I bewail thee; nor know I, ah me, how to quell my sorrow for thee, my sorrow that is so great.—Ah me! 'twas thy wish to die in a strange land; but now thou hast died without gifts at my hand.

ISMENE

Woe is me! What new fate, think'st thou, awaits thee and me, my sister, thus orphaned of our sire?

CHORUS

Nay, since he hath found a blessed end, my children, cease from this lament; no mortal is hard for evil fortune to capture.

ANTIGONE

strophe 2

Sister, let us hasten back.

ISMENE

Unto what deed?

ANTIGONE

A longing fills my soul.

ISMENE

Whereof?

ANTIGONE

To see the dark home—

ISMENE

Of whom?

ANTIGONE

Ah me! of our sire.

ISMENE

And how can this thing be lawful? Hast thou no understanding?

ANTIGONE

Why this reproof?

ISMENE

And knowest thou not this also—

ANTIGONE

What wouldst thou tell me more?—

ISMENE

That he was perishing without tomb, apart from all?

ANTIGONE

Lead me thither, and then slay me also.

ISMENE

Ah me unhappy! Friendless and helpless, where am I now to live my hapless life?

CHORUS

antistrophe 2

My children, fear not.

ANTIGONE

But whither am I to flee?

CHORUS

Already a refuge hath been found—

ANTIGONE

How meanest thou?—

CHORUS

—for your fortunes, that no harm should touch them.

ANTIGONE

I know it well.

CHORUS

What, then, is thy thought?

ANTIGONE

How we are to go home, I cannot tell.

CHORUS

And do not seek to go.

ANTIGONE

Trouble besets us.

CHORUS

And erstwhile bore hardly on you.

ANTIGONE

Desperate then, and now more cruel than despair.

CHORUS

Great, verily, is the sea of your troubles.

ANTIGONE

Alas, alas! O Zeus, whither shall we turn? To what last hope doth fate now urge us?

(THESEUS *enters.*)

THESEUS

systema

Weep no more, maidens; for where the kindness of the Dark Powers is an abiding grace to the quick and to the dead, there is no room for mourning; divine anger would follow.

ANTIGONE

Son of Aegeus, we supplicate thee!

THESEUS

For the obtaining of what desire, my children?

ANTIGONE

We fain would look with our own eyes upon our father's tomb.

THESEUS

Nay, it is not lawful.

ANTIGONE

How sayest thou, king, lord of Athens?

THESEUS

My children, he gave me charge that no one should draw night unto that place, or greet with voice the sacred tomb wherein he sleeps. And he said that, while I duly kept that word, I should always hold the land unharmed. These pledges, therefore, were heard from my lips by the god, and by the all-seeing Watcher of oaths, the servant of Zeus.

ANTIGONE

Nay, then, if this is pleasing to the dead, with this we must content us. But send us to Thebes the ancient, if haply we may hinder the bloodshed that is threatened to our brothers.

THESEUS

So will I do; and if in aught beside I can profit you, and pleasure the dead who hath lately gone from us, I am bound to spare no pains.

CHORUS

Come, cease lamentation, lift it up no more; for verily these things stand fast.

ANTIGONE

CHARACTERS IN THE PLAY

ANTIGONE ⎫ *daughters of Oedipus*
ISMENE ⎬
CREON, *King of Thebes*
EURYDICE, *his wife*
HAEMON, *his son*
TEIRESIAS, *the blind prophet*
GUARD, *set to watch the corpse of Polyneices*
FIRST MESSENGER
SECOND MESSENGER, *from the house*
CHORUS OF THEBAN ELDERS

ANTIGONE

(SCENE:—*The same as in the Oedipus the King, an open space before the royal palace, once that of Oedipus, at Thebes. The backscene represents the front of the palace, with three doors, of which the central and largest is the principal entrance into the house. The time is at daybreak on the morning after the fall of the two brothers, Eteocles and Polyneices, and the flight of the defeated Argives.* ANTIGONE *calls* ISMENE *forth from the palace, in order to speak to her alone.*)

ANTIGONE

ISMENE, sister, mine own dear sister, knowest thou what ill there is, of all bequeathed by Oedipus, that Zeus fulfills not for us twain while we live? Nothing painful is there, nothing fraught with ruin, no shame, no dishonour, that I have not seen in thy woes and mine.

And now what new edict is this of which they tell, that our Captain hath just published to all Thebes? knowest thou aught? Hast thou heard? Or is it hidden from thee that our friends are threatened with the doom of our foes?

ISMENE

No word of friends, Antigone, gladsome or painful, hath come to me, since we two sisters were bereft of brothers twain, killed in one day by a twofold blow; and since in this last night the Argive host hath fled, I know no more, whether my fortune be brighter, or more grievous.

ANTIGONE

I knew it well, and therefore sought to bring thee beyond the gates of the court, that thou mightest hear alone.

ISMENE

What is it? 'Tis plain that thou art brooding on some dark tidings.

ANTIGONE

What, hath not Creon destined our brothers, the one to honoured burial, the other to unburied shame? Eteocles, they say, with due observance of right and custom, he hath laid in the earth, for his honour among the dead below. But the hapless corpse of Polyneices—as rumour saith, it hath been published to the town that none shall entomb him or mourn, but leave unwept, unsepulchred, a welcome store for the birds, as they espy him, to feast on at will.

Such, 'tis said, is the edict that the good Creon hath set forth for thee and for me,—yes, for *me*,—and is coming hither to proclaim it clearly to those who know it not; nor counts the matter light, but, whoso disobeys in aught, his doom is death by stoning before all the folk. Thou knowest it now; and thou wilt soon show whether thou art nobly bred, or the base daughter of a noble line.

ISMENE

Poor sister,—and if things stand thus, what could I help to do or undo?

ANTIGONE

Consider if thou wilt share the toil and the deed.

ISMENE

In what venture? What can be thy meaning?

ANTIGONE

Wilt thou aid this hand to lift the dead?

ISMENE

Thou wouldst bury him,—when 'tis forbidden to Thebes?

ANTIGONE

I will do my part,—and thine, if thou wilt not,—to a brother. False to him will I never be found.

ISMENE

Ah, over-bold! when Creon hath forbidden?

ANTIGONE

Nay, he hath no right to keep me from mine own.

ISMENE

Ah me! think, sister, how our father perished, amid hate and scorn, when sins bared by his own search had moved him to strike both eyes with self-blinding hand; then the mother wife, two names in one, with twisted noose did despite unto her life; and last, our two brothers in one day,—each shedding, hapless one, a kinsman's blood,—wrought out with mutual hands their common doom. And now *we* in turn—we two left all alone—think how we shall perish, more miserably than all the rest, if, in defiance of the law, we brave a king's decree or his powers. Nay, we must remember, first, that we were born women, as who should not strive with men; next, that we are ruled of the stronger, so that we must obey in these things, and in things yet sorer. I, therefore, asking the Spirits Infernal to pardon, seeing that force is put on me herein, will hearken to our rulers; for 'tis witless to be over busy.

ANTIGONE

I will not urge thee,—no, nor, if thou yet shouldst have the mind, wouldst thou be welcome as a worker with *me*. Nay, be what thou wilt; but I will bury him: well for me to die in doing that. I shall rest, a loved one with him whom I have loved, sinless in my crime; for I owe a longer allegiance to the dead than to the living: in that world I shall abide for ever. But if *thou* wilt, be guilty of dishonouring laws which the gods have stablished in honour.

ISMENE

I do them no dishonour; but to defy the State,—I have no strength for that.

ANTIGONE

Such be thy plea:—I, then, will go to heap the earth above the brother whom I love.

ISMENE

Alas, unhappy one! How I fear for thee!

ANTIGONE

Fear not for me: guide thine own fate aright.

ISMENE

At least, then, disclose this plan to none, but hide it closely, —and so, too, will I.

ANTIGONE

Oh, denounce it! Thou wilt be far more hateful for thy silence, if thou proclaim not these things to all.

ISMENE

Thou hast a hot heart for chilling deeds.

ANTIGONE

I know that I please where I am most bound to please.

ISMENE

Aye, if thou canst; but thou wouldst what thou canst not.

ANTIGONE

Why, then, when my strength fails, I shall have done.

ISMENE

A hopeless quest should not be made at all.

ANTIGONE

If thus thou speakest, thou wilt have hatred from me, and will justly be subject to the lasting hatred of the dead. But leave me, and the folly that is mine alone, to suffer this dread thing; for I shall not suffer aught so dreadful as an ignoble death.

ISMENE

Go, then, if thou must; and of this be sure,—that, though thine errand is foolish, to thy dear ones thou art truly dear.

(*Exit* ANTIGONE *on the spectators' left.* ISMENE *retires into the palace by one of the two side-doors. When they have departed, the* CHORUS OF THEBAN ELDERS *enters.*)

CHORUS (*singing*)

strophe 1

Beam of the sun, fairest light that ever dawned on Thebe of the seven gates, thou hast shone forth at last, eye of golden day, arisen above Dirce's streams! The warrior of the white shield, who came from Argos in his panoply, hath been stirred by thee to headlong flight, in swifter career;

LEADER OF THE CHORUS

systema 1

who set forth against our land by reason of the vexed claims of Polyneices; and, like shrill-screaming eagle, he flew over into our land, in snow-white pinion sheathed, with an armed throng, and with plumage of helms.

CHORUS

antistrophe 1

He paused above our dwellings; he ravened around our sevenfold portals with spears athirst for blood; but he went hence, or ever his jaws were glutted with our gore, or the Fire-god's pine-fed flame had seized our crown of towers. So fierce was the noise of battle raised behind him, a thing too hard for him to conquer, as he wrestled with his dragon foe.

LEADER

systema 2

For Zeus utterly abhors the boasts of a proud tongue; and when he beheld them coming on in a great stream, in the haughty pride of clanging gold, he smote with brandished fire one who was now hasting to shout victory at his goal upon our ramparts.

CHORUS

strophe 2

Swung down, he fell on the earth with a crash, torch in hand, he who so lately, in the frenzy of the mad onset, was raging against us with the blasts of his tempestuous hate. But those threats fared not as he hoped; and to other foes the mighty War-god dispensed their several dooms, dealing havoc around, a mighty helper at our need.

LEADER

systema 3

For seven captains at seven gates, matched against seven, left the tribute of their panoplies to Zeus who turns the battle; save those two of cruel fate, who, born of one sire and one mother, set against each other their twain conquering spears, and are sharers in a common death.

CHORUS

antistrophe 2

But since Victory of glorious name hath come to us, with joy responsive to the joy of Thebe whose chariots are many, let us enjoy forgetfulness after the late wars, and visit all the temples of the gods with night-long dance and song; and may Bacchus be our leader, whose dancing shakes the land of Thebe.

LEADER

systema 4

But lo, the king of the land comes yonder, Creon, son of Menoeceus, our new ruler by the new fortunes that the gods have given; what counsel is he pondering, that he hath proposed this special conference of elders, summoned by his general mandate?

(*Enter* CREON, *from the central doors of the palace, in the garb of king, with two attendants.*)

CREON

Sirs, the vessel of our State, after being tossed on wild waves, hath once more been safely steadied by the gods: and ye, out of all the folk, have been called apart by my summons, because I knew, first of all, how true and constant was your reverence for the royal power of Laius; how, again, when Oedipus was ruler of our land, and when he had perished, your steadfast loyalty still upheld their children. Since, then, his sons have fallen in one day by a twofold doom,—each smitten by the other, each stained with a brother's blood,—I now possess the throne and all its powers, by nearness of kinship to the dead.

No man can be fully known, in soul and spirit and mind, until he hath been seen versed in rule and law-giving. For if any, being supreme guide of the State, cleaves not to the best counsels, but, through some fear, keeps his lips locked, I hold, and have ever held, him most base; and if any makes a friend of more account than his fatherland, that man hath no place in my regard. For I— be Zeus my witness, who sees all things always—would not be silent if I saw ruin, instead of safety, coming to the citizens; nor would I ever deem the country's foe a friend to myself; remembering this, that our country is the ship that bears us safe, and that only while she prospers in our voyage can we make true friends.

Such are the rules by which I guard this city's greatness. And in accord with them is the edict which I have now published to the folk touching the sons of Oedipus;—that Eteocles, who hath fallen fighting for our city, in all renown of arms, shall be entombed, and crowned with every rite that follows the noblest dead to their rest. But for his brother, Polyneices,—who came back from exile, and sought to consume utterly with fire the city of his fathers and the shrines of his fathers' gods,—sought to taste of kindred blood, and to lead the remnant into slavery;—touching this man, it hath been proclaimed to our people that none shall grace him with sepulture or lament, but leave him unburied, a corpse for birds and dogs to eat, a ghastly sight of shame.

Such the spirit of my dealing; and never, by deed of mine, shall the wicked stand in honour before the just; but whoso hath good will to Thebes, he shall be honoured of me, in his life and in his death.

LEADER OF THE CHORUS
Such is thy pleasure, Creon, son of Menoeceus, touching this city's foe, and its friend; and thou hast power, I ween, to take what order thou wilt, both for the dead, and for all us who live.

CREON
See, then, that ye be guardians of the mandate.

LEADER
Lay the burden of this task on some younger man.

CREON
Nay, watchers of the corpse have been found.

LEADER
What, then, is this further charge that thou wouldst give?

CREON
That ye side not with the breakers of these commands.

LEADER
No man is so foolish that he is enamoured of death.
In sooth, that is the meed; yet lucre hath oft ruined men through their hopes.

(*A* GUARD *enters from the spectators' left.*)

GUARD

My liege, I will not say that I come breathless from speed, or that I have plied a nimble foot; for often did my thoughts make me pause, and wheel round in my path, to return. My mind was holding large discourse with me; 'Fool why goest thou to thy certain doom?' wretch, tarrying again? And if Creon hears this from another, must not thou smart for it?' So debating, I went on my way with lagging steps, and thus a short road was made long. At last, however, it carried the day that I should come hither—to thee; and, though my tale be nought, yet will I tell it; for I come with a good grip on one hope,—that I can suffer nothing but what is my fate.

CREON

And what is it that disquiets thee thus?

GUARD

I wish to tell thee first about myself—I did not do the deed— I did not see the doer—it were not right that I should come to any harm.

CREON

Thou hast a shrewd eye for thy mark; well dost thou fence thyself round against the blame; clearly thou hast some strange things to tell.

GUARD

Aye, truly; dread news makes one pause long.

CREON

Then tell it, wilt thou, and so get thee gone?

GUARD

Well, this is it.—The corpse—some one hath just given it burial, and gone away,—after sprinkling thirsty dust on the flesh, with such other rites as piety enjoins.

CREON

What sayest thou? What living man hath dared this deed?

GUARD

I know not; no stroke of pickaxe was seen there, no earth thrown up by mattock; the ground was hard and dry, unbroken, without track of wheels; the doer was one who had left no trace. And when the first day-watchman showed it to us, sore wonder fell

on all. The dead man was veiled from us; not shut within a tomb,
but lightly strewn with dust, as by the hand of one who shunned a
curse. And no sign met the eye as though any beast of prey or any
dog had come nigh to him, or torn him.

Then evil words flew fast and loud among us, guard accusing
guard; and it would e'en have come to blows at last, nor was there
any to hinder. Every man was the culprit, and no one was convicted,
but all disclaimed knowledge of the deed. And we were ready to
take red-hot iron in our hands;—to walk through fire;—to make
oath by the gods that we had not done the deed,—that we were not
privy to the planning or the doing.

At last, when all our searching was fruitless, one spake, who
made us all bend our faces on the earth in fear; for we saw not
how we could gainsay him, or escape mischance if we obeyed. His
counsel was that this deed must be reported to thee, and not hidden.
And this seemed best; and the lot doomed my hapless self to win
this prize. So here I stand,—as unwelcome as unwilling, well I
wot; for no man delights in the bearer of bad news.

LEADER

O king, my thoughts have long been whispering, can this deed,
perchance, be e'en the work of gods?

CREON

Cease, ere thy words fill me utterly with wrath, lest thou be
found at once an old man and foolish. For thou sayest what is not
to be borne, in saying that the gods have care for this corpse. Was
it for high reward of trusty service that they sought to hide his
nakedness, who came to burn their pillared shrines and sacred
treasures, to burn their land, and scatter its laws to the winds?
Or dost thou behold the gods honouring the wicked? It cannot be.
No! From the first there were certain in the town that muttered
against me, chafing at this edict, wagging their heads in secret; and
kept not their neck duly under the yoke, like men contented with
my sway.

'Tis by them, well I know, that these have been beguiled and
bribed to do this deed. Nothing so evil as money ever grew to be
current among men. This lays cities low, this drives men from
their homes, this trains and warps honest souls till they set themselves to works of shame; this still teaches folk to practise villainies,
and to know every godless deed.

But all the men who wrought this thing for hire have made

it sure that, soon or late, they shall pay the price. Now, as Zeus still hath my reverence, know this—I tell it thee on my oath:— If ye find not the very author of this burial, and produce him before mine eyes, death alone shall not be enough for you, till first, hung up alive, ye have revealed this outrage,—that henceforth ye may thieve with better knowledge whence lucre should be won, and learn that it is not well to love gain from every source. For thou wilt find that ill-gotten pelf brings more men to ruin than to weal.

GUARD

May I speak? Or shall I just turn and go?

CREON

Knowest thou not that even now thy voice offends?

GUARD

Is thy smart in the ears, or in the soul?

CREON

And why wouldst thou define the seat of my pain?

GUARD

The doer vexes thy mind, but I, thine ears.

CREON

Ah, thou art a born babbler, 'tis well seen.

GUARD

May be, but never the doer of this deed.

CREON

Yea, and more,—the seller of thy life for silver.

GUARD

Alas! 'Tis sad, truly, that he who judges should misjudge.

CREON

Let thy fancy play with 'judgment' as it will;—but, if ye show me not the doers of these things, ye shall avow that dastardly gains work sorrows.

(CREON *goes into the palace.*)

GUARD

Well, may he be found! so 'twere best. But, be he caught or
be he not—fortune must settle that—truly thou wilt not see me
here again. Saved, even now, beyond hope and thought, I owe the
gods great thanks.

(The GUARD *goes out on the spectators' left.)*

CHORUS *(singing)*

Wonders are many, and none is more wonderful than
man; the power that crosses the white sea, driven by the
stormy south-wind, making a path under surges that
threaten to engulf him; and Earth, the eldest of the gods,
the immortal, the unwearied, doth he wear, turning the
soil with the offspring of horses, as the ploughs go to and
fro from year to year.

antistrophe 1

And the light-hearted race of birds, and the tribes of
savage beasts, and the sea-brood of the deep, he snares in
the meshes of his woven toils, he leads captive, man excellent in wit. And he masters by his arts the beast whose
lair is in the wilds, who roams the hills; he tames the
horse of shaggy mane, he puts the yoke upon its neck,
he tames the tireless mountain bull.

strophe 2

And speech, and wind-swift thought, and all the
moods that mould a state, hath he taught himself; and
how to flee the arrows of the frost, when 'tis hard lodging
under the clear sky, and the arrows of the rushing rain;
yea, he hath resource for all; without resource he meets
nothing that must come: only against Death shall he call
for aid in vain; but from baffling maladies he hath devised
escapes.

antistrophe 2

Cunning beyond fancy's dream is the fertile skill
which brings him, now to evil, now to good. When he
honours the laws of the land, and that justice which he
hath sworn by the gods to uphold, proudly stands his
city: no city hath he who, for his rashness, dwells with

sin. Never may he share my hearth, never think my thoughts, who doth these things!

(*Enter the* GUARD *on the spectators' left, leading in* ANTIGONE.)

LEADER OF THE CHORUS

What portent from the gods is this?—my soul is amazed. I know her—how can I deny that yon maiden is Antigone?

O hapless, and child of hapless sire,—of Oedipus! What means this? Thou brought a prisoner?—thou, disloyal to the king's laws, and taken in folly?

GUARD

Here she is, the doer of the deed:—we caught this girl burying him:—but where is Creon?

(CREON *enters hurriedly from the palace.*)

LEADER

Lo, he comes forth again from the house, at our need.

CREON

What is it? What hath chanced, that makes my coming timely?

GUARD

O king, against nothing should men pledge their word; for the afterthought belies the first intent. I could have vowed that I should not soon be here again,—scared by thy threats, with which I had just been lashed: but,—since the joy that surprises and transcends our hopes is like in fulness to no other pleasure,—I have come, though 'tis in breach of my sworn oath, bringing this maid; who was taken showing grace to the dead. This time there was no casting of lots; no, this luck hath fallen to me, and to none else. And now, sire, take her thyself, question her, examine her, as thou wilt; but I have a right to free and final quittance of this trouble.

CREON

And thy prisoner here—how and whence hast thou taken her?

GUARD

She was burying the man; thou knowest all.

CREON

Dost thou mean what thou sayest? Dost thou speak aright?

GUARD

I saw her burying the corpse that thou hadst forbidden to bury. Is that plain and clear?

CREON

And how was she seen? how taken in the act?

GUARD

It befell on this wise. When we had come to the palace,— with those dread menaces of thine upon us,—we swept away all the dust that covered the corpse, and bared the dank body well; and then sat us down on the brow of the hill, to windward, heedful that the smell from him should not strike us; every man was wide awake, and kept his neighbour alert with torrents of threats, if anyone should be careless of this task.

So went it, until the sun's bright orb stood in mid heaven, and the heat began to burn: and then suddenly a whirlwind lifted from the earth a storm of dust, a trouble in the sky, and filled the plain, marring all the leafage of its woods; and the wide air was choked therewith: we closed our eyes, and bore the plague from the gods.

And when, after a long while, this storm had passed, the maid was seen; and she cried aloud with the sharp cry of a bird in its bitterness,—even as when, within the empty nest, it sees the bed stripped of its nestlings. So she also, when she saw the corpse bare, lifted up a voice of wailing, and called down curses on the doers of that deed. And straightway she brought thirsty dust in her hands; and from a shapely ewer of bronze, held high, with thrice-poured drink-offering she crowned the dead.

We rushed forward when we saw it, and at once closed upon our quarry, who was in no wise dismayed. Then we taxed her with her past and present doings; and she stood not on denial of aught, —at once to my joy and to my pain. To have escaped from ills one's self is a great joy; but 'tis painful to bring friends to ill. Howbeit, all such things are of less account to me than mine own safety.

CREON

Thou—thou whose face is bent to earth—dost thou avow, or disavow, this deed?

ANTIGONE

I avow it; I make no denial.

CREON (*to* GUARD)

Thou canst betake thee whither thou wilt, free and clear of a grave charge.

(*Exit* GUARD)

(*To* ANTIGONE) Now, tell me thou—not in many words, but briefly—knewest thou that an edict had forbidden this?

ANTIGONE

I knew it: could I help it? It was public.

CREON

And thou didst indeed dare to transgress that law?

ANTIGONE

Yes; for it was not Zeus that had published me that edict; not such are the laws set among men by the Justice who dwells with the gods below; nor deemed I that thy decrees were of such force, that a mortal could override the unwritten and unfailing statutes of heaven. For their life is not of to-day or yesterday, but from all time, and no man knows when they were first put forth.

Not through dread of any human pride could I answer to the gods for breaking *these*. Die I must,—I knew that well (how should I not?)—even without thy edicts. But if I am to die before my time, I count that a gain: for when any one lives, as I do, encompassed about with evils, can such an one find aught but gain in death?

So for me to meet this doom is trifling grief; but if I had suffered my mother's son to lie in death an unburied corpse, that would have grieved me; for this, I am not grieved. And if my present deeds are foolish in thy sight, it may be that a foolish judge arraigns my folly.

LEADER OF THE CHORUS

The maid shows herself passionate child of passionate sire, and knows not how to bend before troubles.

CREON

Yet I would have thee know that o'er-stubborn spirits are most often humbled; 'tis the stiffest iron, baked to hardness in the fire, that thou shalt oftenest see snapped and shivered; and I have known horses that show temper brought to order by a little curb; there is no room for pride when thou art thy neighbour's slave.—This girl was already versed in insolence when she transgressed the laws that had been set forth; and, that done, lo, a second insult,— to vaunt of this, and exult in her deed.

Now verily I am no man, she is the man, if this victory shall rest with her, and bring no penalty. No! be she sister's child, or nearer to me in blood than any that worships Zeus at the altar of our house,—she and her kinsfolk shall not avoid a doom most dire; for indeed I charge that other with a like share in the plotting of this burial.

And summon her—for I saw her e'en now within,—raving, and not mistress of her wits. So oft, before the deed, the mind stands self-convicted in its treason, when folks are plotting mischief in the dark. But verily this, too, is hateful,—when one who hath been caught in wickedness then seeks to make the crime a glory.

ANTIGONE

Wouldst thou do more than take, and slay me?

CREON

No more, indeed; having that, I have all.

ANTIGONE

Why then dost thou delay? In thy discourse there is nought that pleases me,—never may there be!—and so my words must needs be unpleasing to thee. And yet, for glory—whence could I have won a nobler, than by giving burial to mine own brother? All here would own that they thought it well were not their lips sealed by fear. But royalty, blest in so much besides, hath the power to do and say what it will.

CREON

Thou differest from all these Thebans in that view.

ANTIGONE

These also share it; but they curb their tongues for thee.

CREON

And art thou not ashamed to act apart from them?

ANTIGONE

No; there is nothing shameful in piety to a brother.

CREON

Was it not a brother, too, that died in the opposite cause?

ANTIGONE

Brother by the same mother and the same sire.

CREON

Why, then, dost thou render a grace that is impious in his sight?

ANTIGONE

The dead man will not say that he so deems it.

CREON

Yea, if thou makest him but equal in honour with the wicked.

ANTIGONE

It was his brother, not his slave, that perished.

CREON

Wasting this land; while *he* fell as its champion.

ANTIGONE

Nevertheless, Hades desires these rites.

CREON

But the good desires not a like portion with the evil.

ANTIGONE

Who knows but this seems blameless in the world below?

CREON

A foe is never a friend—not even in death.

ANTIGONE

'Tis not my nature to join in hating, but in loving.

CREON

Pass, then, to the world of the dead, and, if thou must needs love, love them. While I live, no woman shall rule me.

(*Enter* ISMENE *from the house, led in by two attendants.*)

CHORUS (*chanting*)

Lo, yonder Ismene comes forth, shedding such tears as fond sisters weep; a cloud upon her brow casts its shadow over her darkly-flushing face, and breaks in rain on her fair cheek.

CREON

And thou, who, lurking like a viper in my house, wast secretly draining my life-blood, while I knew not that I was nurturing two pests, to rise against my throne—come, tell me now, wilt thou also confess thy part in this burial, or wilt thou forswear all knowledge of it?

ISMENE

I have done the deed,—if she allows my claim,—and share the burden of the charge.

ANTIGONE

Nay, justice will not suffer thee to do that: thou didst not consent to the deed, nor did I give thee part in it.

ISMENE

But, now that ills beset thee, I am not ashamed to sail the sea of trouble at thy side.

ANTIGONE

Whose was the deed, Hades and the dead are witnesses: a friend in words is not the friend that I love.

ISMENE

Nay, sister, reject me not, but let me die with thee, and duly honour the dead.

ANTIGONE

Share not thou my death, nor claim deeds to which thou hast not put thy hand: my death will suffice.

ISMENE

And what life is dear to me, bereft of thee?

ANTIGONE

Ask Creon; all thy care is for him.

ISMENE

Why vex me thus, when it avails thee nought?

ANTIGONE
Indeed, if I mock, 'tis with pain that I mock thee.

ISMENE
Tell me,—how can I serve thee, even now?

ANTIGONE
Save thyself: I grudge not thy escape.

ISMENE
Ah, woe is me! And shall I have no share in thy fate?

ANTIGONE
Thy choice was to live; mine, to die.

ISMENE
At least thy choice was not made without my protest.

ANTIGONE
One world approved thy wisdom; another, mine.

ISMENE
Howbeit, the offence is the same for both of us.

ANTIGONE
Be of good cheer; thou livest; but my life hath long been given to death, that so I might serve the dead.

CREON
Lo, one of these maidens hath newly shown herself foolish, as the other hath been since her life began.

ISMENE
Yea, O king, such reason as nature may have given abides not with the unfortunate, but goes astray.

CREON
Thine did, when thou chosest vile deeds with the vile.

ISMENE
What life could I endure, without her presence?

CREON
Nay, speak not of her 'presence'; she lives no more.

ISMENE
But wilt thou slay the betrothed of thine own son?

CREON
Nay, there are other fields for him to plough.

ISMENE
But there can never be such love as bound him to her.

CREON
I like not an evil wife for my son.

ANTIGONE
Haemon, beloved! How thy father wrongs thee!

CREON
Enough, enough of thee and of thy marriage!

LEADER OF THE CHORUS
Wilt thou indeed rob thy son of this maiden?

CREON
'Tis Death that shall stay these bridals for me.

LEADER
'Tis determined, it seems, that she shall die.

CREON
Determined, yes, for thee and for me.—(*To the two atten-dants*) No more delay—servants, take them within! Henceforth they must be women, and not range at large; for verily even the bold seek to fly, when they see Death now closing on their life.

(*Exeunt attendants, guarding* ANTIGONE *and* ISMENE.—CREON *remains.*)

CHORUS (*singing*)
strophe 1

Blest are they whose days have not tasted of evil. For when a house hath once been shaken from heaven, there the curse fails nevermore, passing from life to life of the race; even as, when the surge is driven over the darkness of the deep by the fierce breath of Thracian seawinds, it rolls up the black sand from the depths, and

there is a sullen roar from wind-vexed headlands that
front the blows of the storm.

antistrophe 1

I see that from olden time the sorrows in the house
of the Labdacidae are heaped upon the sorrows of the
dead; and generation is not freed by generation, but some
god strikes them down, and the race hath no deliverance.

For now that hope of which the light had been spread
above the last root of the house of Oedipus—that hope,
in turn, is brought low—by the blood-stained dust due
to the gods infernal, and by folly in speech, and frenzy
at the heart.

strophe 2

Thy power, O Zeus, what human trespass can limit?
That power which neither Sleep, the all-ensnaring, nor
the untiring months of the gods can master; but thou,
a ruler to whom time brings not old age, dwellest in
the dazzling splendour of Olympus.

And through the future, near and far, as through
the past, shall this law hold good: Nothing that is vast
enters into the life of mortals without a curse.

antistrophe 2

For that hope whose wanderings are so wide is to
many men a comfort, but to many a false lure of giddy
desires; and the disappointment comes on one who
knoweth nought till he burn his foot against the hot fire.

For with wisdom hath some one given forth the
famous saying, that evil seems good, soon or late, to him
whose mind the god draws to mischief; and but for the
briefest space doth he fare free of woe.

LEADER OF THE CHORUS

But lo, Haemon, the last of thy sons;—comes he
grieving for the doom of his promised bride, Antigone,
and bitter for the baffled hope of his marriage?

(*Enter* HAEMON)

CREON

We shall know soon, better than seers could tell us.—My
son, hearing the fixed doom of thy betrothed, art thou come in
rage against thy father? Or have I thy good will, act how I may?

HAEMON

Father, I am thine; and thou, in thy wisdom, tracest for me rules which I shall follow. No marriage shall be deemed by me a greater gain than thy good guidance.

CREON

Yea, this, my son, should be thy heart's fixed law,—in all things to obey thy father's will. 'Tis for this that men pray to see dutiful children grow up around them in their homes,—that such may requite their father's foe with evil, and honour, as their father doth, his friend. But he who begets unprofitable children— what shall we say that he hath sown, but troubles for himself, and much triumph for his foes? Then do not thou, my son, at pleasure's beck, dethrone thy reason for a woman's sake; knowing that this is a joy that soon grows cold in clasping arms,—an evil woman to share thy bed and thy home. For what wound could strike deeper than a false friend? Nay, with loathing, and as if she were thine enemy, let this girl go to find a husband in the house of Hades. For since I have taken her, alone of all the city, in open disobedience, I will not make myself a liar to my people— I will slay her.

So let her appeal as she will to the majesty of kindred blood. If I am to nurture mine own kindred in naughtiness, needs must I bear with it in aliens. He who does his duty in his own household will be found righteous in the State also. But if any one transgresses, and does violence to the laws, or thinks to dictate to his rulers, such an one can win no praise from me. No, whom-soever the city may appoint, that man must be obeyed, in little things and great, in just things and unjust; and I should feel sure that one who thus obeys would be a good ruler no less than a good subject, and in the storm of spears would stand his ground where he was set, loyal and dauntless at his comrade's side.

But disobedience is the worst of evils. This it is that ruins cities; this makes homes desolate; by this, the ranks of allies are broken into headlong rout; but, of the lies whose course is fair, the greater part owes safety to obedience. Therefore we must support the cause of order, and in no wise suffer a woman to worst us. Better to fall from power, if we must, by a man's hand; then we should not be called weaker than a woman.

LEADER

To us, unless our years have stolen our wit, thou seemest to say wisely what thou sayest.

HAEMON

Father, the gods implant reason in men, the highest of all things that we call our own. Not mine the skill—far from me be the quest!—to say wherein thou speakest not aright; and yet another man, too, might have some useful thought. At least, it is my natural office to watch, on thy behalf, all that men say, or do, or find to blame. For the dread of thy frown forbids the citizen to speak such words as would offend thine ear; but I can hear these murmurs in the dark, these moanings of the city for this maiden; 'no woman,' they say, 'ever merited her doom less,—none ever was to die so shamefully for deeds so glorious as hers; who, when her own brother had fallen in bloody strife, would not leave him unburied, to be devoured by carrion dogs, or by any bird:—deserves not *she* the meed of golden honour?'

Such is the darkling rumour that spreads in secret. For me, my father, no treasure is so precious as thy welfare. What, indeed, is a nobler ornament for children than a prospering sire's fair fame, or for sire than son's? Wear not, then, one mood only in thyself; think not that thy word, and thine alone, must be right. For if any man thinks that he alone is wise,—that in speech, or in mind, he hath no peer,—such a soul, when laid open, is ever found empty.

No, though a man be wise, 'tis no shame for him to learn many things, and to bend in season. Seest thou, beside the wintry torrent's course, how the trees that yield to it save every twig, while the stiff-necked perish root and branch? And even thus he who keeps the sheet of his sail taut, and never slackens it, upsets his boat, and finishes his voyage with keel uppermost.

Nay, forego thy wrath; permit thyself to change. For if I, a younger man, may offer my thought, it were far best, I ween, that men should be all-wise by nature; but, otherwise—and oft the scale inclines not so—'tis good also to learn from those who speak aright.

LEADER

Sire, 'tis meet that thou shouldest profit by his words, if he speaks aught in season, and thou, Haemon, by thy father's; for on both parts there hath been wise speech.

CREON

Men of my age—are we indeed to be schooled, then, by men of his?

HAEMON

In nothing that is not right; but if I am young, thou shouldest look to my merits, not to my years.

CREON

Is it a merit to honour the unruly?

HAEMON

I could wish no one to show respect for evil-doers.

CREON

Then is not she tainted with that malady?

HAEMON

Our Theban folk, with one voice, denies it.

CREON

Shall Thebes prescribe to me how I must rule?

HAEMON

See, there thou hast spoken like a youth indeed.

CREON

Am I to rule this land by other judgment than mine own?

HAEMON

That is no city which belongs to one man.

CREON

Is not the city held to be the ruler's?

HAEMON

Thou wouldst make a good monarch of a desert.

CREON

This boy, it seems, is the woman's champion.

HAEMON

If thou art a woman; indeed, my care is for thee.

CREON

Shameless, at open feud with thy father!

HAEMON

Nay, I see thee offending against justice.

CREON

Do I offend, when I respect mine own prerogatives?

HAEMON

Thou dost not respect them, when thou tramplest on the gods' honours.

CREON

O dastard nature, yielding place to woman!

HAEMON

Thou wilt never find me yield to baseness.

CREON

All thy words, at least, plead for that girl.

HAEMON

And for thee, and for me, and for the gods below.

CREON

Thou canst never marry her, on this side the grave.

HAEMON

Then she must die, and in death destroy another.

CREON

How! doth thy boldness run to open threats?

HAEMON

What threat is it, to combat vain resolves?

CREON

Thou shalt rue thy witless teaching of wisdom.

HAEMON

Wert thou not my father, I would have called thee unwise.

CREON

Thou woman's slave, use not wheedling speech with me.

HAEMON

Thou wouldest speak, and then hear no reply?

CREON

Sayest thou so? Now, by the heaven above us—be sure of it—thou shalt smart for taunting me in this opprobrious strain. Bring forth that hated thing, that she may die forthwith in his presence—before his eyes—at her bridegroom's side!

HAEMON

No, not at my side—never think it—shall she perish; nor shalt thou ever set eyes more upon my face:—rave, then, with such friends as can endure thee.

(*Exit* HAEMON)

LEADER

The man is gone, O king, in angry haste; a youthful mind, when stung, is fierce.

CREON

Let him do, or dream, more than man—good speed to him!— But he shall not save these two girls from their doom.

LEADER

Dost thou indeed purpose to slay both?

CREON

Not her whose hands are pure: thou sayest well.

LEADER

And by what doom mean'st thou to slay the other?

CREON

I will take her where the path is loneliest, and hide her, living, in a rocky vault, with so much food set forth as piety prescribes, that the city may avoid a public stain. And there, praying to Hades, the only god whom she worships, perchance she will obtain release from death; or else will learn, at last, though late, that it is lost labour to revere the dead.

(CREON *goes into the palace.*)

CHORUS (*singing*)

strophe

Love, unconquered in the fight, Love, who makest
havoc of wealth, who keepest thy vigil on the soft cheek
of a maiden; thou roamest over the sea, and among the
homes of dwellers in the wilds; no immortal can escape
thee, nor any among men whose life is for a day; and
he to whom thou hast come is mad.

antistrophe

The just themselves have their minds warped by thee
to wrong, for their ruin: 'tis thou that hast stirred up
this present strife of kinsmen; victorious is the love-
kindling light from the eyes of the fair bride; it is a
power enthroned in sway beside the eternal laws; for
there the goddess Aphrodite is working her unconquer-
able will.

(ANTIGONE *is led out of the palace by two of* CREON's
attendants who are about to conduct her to her doom.)

But now I also am carried beyond the bounds of
loyalty, and can no more keep back the streaming tears,
when I see Antigone thus passing to the bridal chamber
where all are laid to rest.

(*The following lines between* ANTIGONE *and the* CHORUS
are chanted responsively.)

ANTIGONE

strophe 1

See me, citizens of my fatherland, setting forth on
my last way, looking my last on the sunlight that is for
me no more; no, Hades who gives sleep to all leads me
living to Acheron's shore; who have had no portion in
the chant that brings the bride, nor hath any song been
mine for the crowning of bridals; whom the lord of the
Dark Lake shall wed.

CHORUS

systema 1

Glorious, therefore, and with praise, thou departest
to that deep place of the dead: wasting sickness hath not
smitten thee; thou hast not found the wages of the

sword; no, mistress of thine own fate, and still alive, thou shalt pass to Hades, as no other of mortal kind hath passed.

Antigone

antistrophe 1

I have heard in other days how dread a doom befell our Phrygian guest, the daughter of Tantalus, on the Sipylian heights, how, like clinging ivy, the growth of stone subdued her; and the rains fail not, as men tell, from her wasting form, nor fails the snow, while beneath her weeping lids the tears bedew her bosom; and most like hers is the fate that brings me to my rest.

Chorus

systema 2

Yet she was a goddess, thou knowest, and born of gods; we are mortals, and of mortal race. But 'tis great renown for a woman who hath perished that she should have shared the doom of the godlike, in her life, and afterward in death.

Antigone

strophe 2

Ah, I am mocked! In the name of our fathers' gods, can ye not wait till I am gone,—must ye taunt me to my face, O my city, and ye, her wealthy sons? Ah, fount of Dirce, and thou holy ground of Thebe whose chariots are many; ye, at least, will bear me witness, in what sort, unwept of friends, and by what laws I pass to the rock-closed prison of my strange tomb, ah me unhappy! who have no home on the earth or in the shades, no home with the living or with the dead.

Chorus

strophe 3

Thou hast rushed forward to the utmost verge of daring; and against that throne where Justice sits on high thou hast fallen, my daughter, with a grievous fall. But in this ordeal thou art paying, haply, for thy father's sin.

ANTIGONE

antistrophe 2

Thou hast touched on my bitterest thought,—awaking the ever-new lament for my sire and for all the doom given to us, the famed house of Labdacus. Alas for the horrors of the mother's bed! alas for the wretched mother's slumber at the side of her own son,—and my sire! From what manner of parents did I take my miserable being! And to them I go thus, accursed, unwed, to share their home. Alas, my brother, ill-starred in thy marriage, in thy death thou hast undone my life!

CHORUS

antistrophe 3

Reverent action claims a certain praise for reverence; but an offence against power cannot be brooked by him who hath power in his keeping. Thy self-willed temper hath wrought thy ruin.

ANTIGONE

epode

Unwept, unfriended, without marriage-song, I am led forth in my sorrow on this journey that can be delayed no more. No longer, hapless one, may I behold yon day-star's sacred eye; but for my fate no tear is shed, no friend makes moan.

(CREON *enters from the palace.*)

CREON

Know ye not that songs and wailings before death would never cease, if it profited to utter them? Away with her—away! And when ye have enclosed her, according to my word, in her vaulted grave, leave her alone, forlorn—whether she wishes to die, or to live a buried life in such a home. Our hands are clean as touching this maiden. But this is certain—she shall be deprived of her sojourn in the light.

ANTIGONE

Tomb, bridal-chamber, eternal prison in the caverned rock, whither I go to find mine own, those many who have perished, and whom Persephone hath received among the dead! Last of all shall I pass thither, and far most miserably of all, before the

term of my life is spent. But I cherish good hope that my coming
will be welcome to my father, and pleasant to thee, my mother,
and welcome, brother, to thee; for, when ye died, with mine own
hands I washed and dressed you, and poured drink-offerings at
your graves; and now, Polyneices, 'tis for tending thy corpse that
I win such recompense as this.

And yet I honoured thee, as the wise will deem, rightly.
Never, had I been a mother of children, or if a husband had
been mouldering in death, would I have taken this task upon me
in the city's despite. What law, ye ask, is my warrant for that
word? The husband lost, another might have been found, and
child from another, to replace the first-born; but, father and
mother hidden with Hades, no brother's life could ever bloom for
me again. Such was the law whereby I held thee first in honour;
but Creon deemed me guilty of error therein, and of outrage, ah
brother mine! And now he leads me thus, a captive in his hands;
no bridal bed, no bridal song hath been mine, no joy of marriage,
no portion in the nurture of children; but thus, forlorn of friends,
unhappy one, I go living to the vaults of death.

And what law of heaven have I transgressed? Why, hapless
one, should I look to the gods any more,—what ally should I
invoke,—when by piety I have earned the name of impious? Nay,
then, if these things are pleasing to the gods, when I have suffered
my doom, I shall come to know my sin; but if the sin is with
my judges, I could wish them no fuller measure of evil than
they, on their part, mete wrongfully to me.

CHORUS
Still the same tempest of the soul vexes this maiden
with the same fierce gusts.

CREON
Then for this shall her guards have cause to rue
their slowness.

ANTIGONE
Ah me! that word hath come very near to death.

CREON
I can cheer thee with no hope that this doom is not
thus to be fulfilled.

ANTIGONE

O city of my fathers in the land of Thebe! O ye gods, eldest of our race!—they lead me hence—now, now —they tarry not! Behold me, princes of Thebes, the last daughter of the house of your kings,—see what I suffer, and from whom, because I feared to cast away the fear of Heaven!

(ANTIGONE *is led away by the guards.*)

CHORUS (*singing*)

strophe 1

Even thus endured Danae in her beauty to change the light of day for brass-bound walls; and in that chamber, secret as the grave, she was held close prisoner; yet was she of a proud lineage, O my daughter, and charged with the keeping of the seed of Zeus, that fell in the golden rain.

But dreadful is the mysterious power of fate; there is no deliverance from it by wealth or by war, by fenced city, or dark, sea-beaten ships.

antistrophe 1

And bonds tamed the son of Dryas, swift to wrath, that king of the Edonians; so paid he for his frenzied taunts, when, by the will of Dionysus, he was pent in a rocky prison. There the fierce exuberance of his madness slowly passed away. That man learned to know the god, whom in his frenzy he had provoked with mockeries; for he had sought to quell the god-possessed women, and the Bacchanalian fire; and he angered the Muses that love the flute.

strophe 2

And by the waters of the Dark Rocks, the waters of the twofold sea, are the shores of Bosporus, and Thracian Salmydessus; where Ares, neighbour to the city, saw the accurst, blinding wound dealt to the two sons of Phineus by his fierce wife,—the wound that brought darkness to those vengeance-craving orbs, smitten with her bloody hands, smitten with her shuttle for a dagger.

antistrophe 2

Pining in their misery, they bewailed their cruel doom, those sons of a mother hapless in her marriage; but she traced her descent from the ancient line of the Erechtheidae; and in far-distance caves she was nursed amid her father's storms, that child of Boreas, swift as a steed over the steep hills, a daughter of gods; yet upon her also the gray Fates bore hard, my daughter.

(*Enter* TEIRESIAS, *led by a Boy, on the spectators' right.*)

TEIRESIAS

Prince of Thebes, we have come with linked steps, both served by the eyes of one; for thus, by a guide's help, the blind must walk.

CREON

And what, aged Teiresias, are thy tidings?

TEIRESIAS

I will tell thee; and do thou hearken to the seer.

CREON

Indeed, it has not been my wont to slight thy counsel.

TEIRESIAS

Therefore didst thou steer our city's course aright.

CREON

I have felt, and can attest, thy benefits.

TEIRESIAS

Mark that now, once more, thou standest on fate's fine edge.

CREON

What means this? How I shudder at thy message!

TEIRESIAS

Thou wilt learn, when thou hearest the warnings of mine art. As I took my place on mine old seat of augury, where all birds have been wont to gather within my ken, I heard a strange voice among them; they were screaming with dire, feverish rage, that drowned their language in a jargon; and I knew that they were rending each other with their talons, murderously; the whirr of wings told no doubtful tale.

Forthwith, in fear, I essayed burnt-sacrifice on a duly kindled altar: but from my offerings the Fire-god showed no flame; a dank moisture, oozing from the thigh-flesh, trickled forth upon the embers, and smoked, and sputtered; the gall was scattered to the air; and the streaming thighs lay bared of the fat that had been wrapped round them.

Such was the failure of the rites by which I vainly asked a sign, as from this boy I learned; for he is my guide, as I am guide to others. And 'tis thy counsel that hath brought this sickness on our State. For the altars of our city and of our hearths have been tainted, one and all, by birds and dogs, with carrion from the hapless corpse, the son of Oedipus: and therefore the gods no more accept prayer and sacrifice at our hands, or the flame of meat-offering; nor doth any bird give a clear sign by its shrill cry, for they have tasted the fatness of a slain man's blood.

Think, then, on these things, my son. All men are liable to err; but when an error hath been made, that man is no longer witless or unblest who heals the ill into which he hath fallen, and remains not stubborn.

Self-will, we know, incurs the charge of folly. Nay, allow the claim of the dead; stab not the fallen; what prowess is it to slay the slain anew? I have sought thy good, and for thy good I speak: and never is it sweeter to learn from a good counsellor than when he counsels for thine own gain.

CREON

Old man, ye all shoot your shafts at me, as archers at the butts;—ye must needs practise on me with seer-craft also;—aye, the seer-tribe hath long trafficked in me, and made me their merchandise. Gain your gains, drive your trade, if ye list, in the silver-gold of Sardis and the gold of India; but ye shall not hide that man in the grave,—no, though the eagles of Zeus should bear the carrion morsels to their Master's throne—no, not for dread of that defilement will I suffer his burial:—for well I know that no mortal can defile the gods.—But, aged Teiresias, the wisest fall with a shameful fall, when they clothe shameful thoughts in fair words, for lucre's sake.

TEIRESIAS

Alas! Doth any man know, doth any consider . . .

CREON

Whereof? What general truth dost thou announce?

TEIRESIAS

How precious, above all wealth, is good counsel.

CREON

As folly, I think, is the worst mischief.

TEIRESIAS

Yet thou art tainted with that distemper.

CREON

I would not answer the seer with a taunt.

TEIRESIAS

But thou dost, in saying that I prophesy falsely.

CREON

Well, the prophet-tribe was ever fond of money.

TEIRESIAS

And the race bred of tyrants loves base gain.

CREON

Knowest thou that thy speech is spoken of thy king?

TEIRESIAS

I know it; for through me thou hast saved Thebes.

CREON

Thou art a wise seer; but thou lovest evil deeds.

TEIRESIAS

Thou wilt rouse me to utter the dread secret in my soul.

CREON

Out with it!—Only speak it not for gain.

TEIRESIAS

Indeed, methinks, I shall not,—as touching thee.

CREON

Know that thou shalt not trade on my resolve.

TEIRESIAS

Then know thou—aye, know it well—that thou shalt not live through many more courses of the sun's swift chariot, ere one begotten of thine own loins shall have been given by thee, a corpse for corpses; because thou hast thrust children of the sunlight to the shades, and ruthlessly lodged a living soul in the grave; but keepest in this world one who belongs to the gods infernal, a corpse unburied, unhonoured, all unhallowed. In such thou hast no part, nor have the gods above, but this is a violence done to them by thee. Therefore the avenging destroyers lie in wait for thee, the Furies of Hades and of the gods, that thou mayest be taken in these same ills.

And mark well if I speak these things as a hireling. A time not long to be delayed shall awaken the wailing of men and of women in thy house. And a tumult of hatred against thee stirs all the cities whose mangled sons had the burial-rite from dogs, or from wild beasts, or from some winged bird that bore a polluting breath to each city that contains the hearths of the dead.

Such arrows for thy heart—since thou provokest me—have I launched at thee, archer-like, in my anger,—sure arrows, of which thou shalt not escape the smart.—Boy, lead me home, that he may spend his rage on younger men, and learn to keep a tongue more temperate, and to bear within his breast a better mind than now he bears.

(The Boy leads TEIRESIAS *out.)*

LEADER OF THE CHORUS

The man hath gone, O King, with dread prophecies. And, since the hair on this head, once dark, hath been white, I know that he hath never been a false prophet to our city.

CREON

I, too, know it well, and am troubled in soul. 'Tis dire to yield; but, by resistance, to smite my pride with ruin—this, too, is a dire choice.

LEADER

Son of Menoeceus, it behooves thee to take wise counsel.

CREON

What should I do, then? Speak, and I will obey.

LEADER

Go thou, and free the maiden from her rocky chamber, and make a tomb for the unburied dead.

CREON

And this is thy counsel? Thou wouldst have me yield?

LEADER

Yea, King, and with all speed; for swift harms from the gods cut short the folly of men.

CREON

Ah me, 'tis hard, but I resign my cherished resolve,—I obey. We must not wage a vain war with destiny.

LEADER

Go, thou, and do these things; leave them not to others.

CREON

Even as I am I'll go:—on, on, my servants, each and all of you,—take axes in your hands, and hasten to the ground that ye see yonder! Since our judgment hath taken this turn, I will be present to unloose her, as I myself bound her. My heart misgives me, 'tis best to keep the established laws, even to life's end.

(CREON *and his servants hasten out on the spectators' left.*)

CHORUS (*singing*)

strophe 1

O thou of many names, glory of the Cadmeian bride, offspring of loud-thundering Zeus! thou who watchest over famed Italia, and reignest, where all guests are welcomed, in the sheltered plain of Eleusinian Deo! O Bacchus, dweller in Thebe, mother-city of Bacchants, by the softly-gliding stream of Ismenus, on the soil where the fierce dragon's teeth were sown!

antistrophe 1

Thou hast been seen where torch-flames glare through smoke, above the crests of the twin peaks, where move the Corycian nymphs, the votaries, hard by Castalia's stream.

Thou comest from the ivy-mantled slopes of Nysa's hills, and from the shore green with many-clustered

500 OEDIPUS MYTH AND COMPLEX

vines, while thy name is lifted up on strains of more than mortal power, as thou visitest the ways of Thebe:

strophe 2

Thebe, of all cities, thou holdest first in honour, thou, and thy mother whom the lightning smote; and now, when all our people is captive to a violent plague, come thou with healing feet over the Parnassian height, or over the moaning strait!

antistrophe 2

O thou with whom the stars rejoice as they move, the stars whose breath is fire; O master of the voices of the night; son begotten of Zeus; appear, O king, with thine attendant Thyiads, who in night-long frenzy dance before thee, the giver of good gifts, Iacchus!

(*Enter* MESSENGER, *on the spectators' left.*)

MESSENGER

Dwellers by the house of Cadmus and of Amphion, there is no estate of mortal life that I would ever praise or blame as settled. Fortune raises and Fortune humbles the lucky or unlucky from day to day, and no one can prophesy to men concerning those things which are established. For Creon was blest once, as I count bliss; he had saved this land of Cadmus from its foes; he was clothed with sole dominion in the land; he reigned, the glorious sire of princely children. And now all hath been lost. For when a man hath forfeited his pleasures, I count him not as living,—I hold him but a breathing corpse. Heap up riches in thy house, if thou wilt; live in kingly state; yet, if there be no gladness therewith, I would not give the shadow of a vapour for all the rest, compared with joy.

LEADER OF THE CHORUS

And what is this new grief that thou hast to tell for our princes?

MESSENGER

Death; and the living are guilty for the dead.

LEADER

And who is the slayer? Who the stricken? Speak.

MESSENGER

Haemon hath perished; his blood hath been shed by no stranger.

LEADER

By his father's hand, or by his own?

MESSENGER

By his own, in wrath with his sire for the murder.

LEADER

O prophet, how true, then, hast thou proved thy word!

MESSENGER

These things stand thus; ye must consider of the rest.

LEADER

Lo, I see the hapless Eurydice, Creon's wife, approaching; she comes from the house by chance, haply,—or because she knows the tidings of her son.

(*Enter* EURYDICE *from the palace.*)

EURYDICE

People of Thebes, I heard your words as I was going forth, to salute the goddess Pallas with my prayers. Even as I was loosing the fastenings of the gate, to open it, the message of a household woe smote on mine ear: I sank back, terror-stricken, into the arms of handmaidens, and my senses fled. But say again what the tidings were; I shall hear them as one who is no stranger to sorrow.

MESSENGER

Dear lady, I will witness of what I saw, and will leave no word of the truth untold. Why, indeed, should I soothe thee with words in which I must presently be found false? Truth is ever best.—I attended thy lord as his guide to the furthest part of the plain, where the body of Polyneices, torn by dogs, still lay unpitied. We prayed the goddess of the roads, and Pluto, in mercy to restrain their wrath; we washed the dead with holy washing; and with freshly-plucked boughs we solemnly burned such relics as they were. We raised a high mound of his native earth; and then we turned away to enter the maiden's nuptial chamber with rocky couch, the caverned mansion of the bride of

Death. And, from afar off, one of us heard a voice of loud wailing at that bride's unhallowed bower; and came to tell our master Creon.

And as the king drew nearer, doubtful sounds of a bitter cry floated around him; he groaned, and said in accents of anguish, 'Wretched that I am, can my foreboding be true? Am I going on the wofullest way that ever I went? My son's voice greets me.— Go, my servants,—haste ye nearer, and when ye have reached the tomb, pass through the gap, where the stones have been wrenched away, to the cell's very mouth,—and look, and see if 'tis Haemon's voice that I know, or if mine ear is cheated by the gods.'

This search, at our despairing master's word, we went to make; and in the furthest part of the tomb we descried *her* hanging by the neck, slung by a thread-wrought halter of fine linen; while *he* was embracing her with arms thrown around her waist,— bewailing the loss of his bride who is with the dead, and his father's deeds, and his own ill-starred love.

But his father, when he saw him, cried aloud with a dread cry and went in, and called to him with a voice of wailing:— 'Unhappy, what a deed hast thou done! What thought hath come to thee? What manner of mischance hath marred thy reason? Come forth, my child! I pray thee—I implore!' But the boy glared at him with fierce eyes, spat in his face, and, without a word of answer, drew his cross-hilted sword:—as his father rushed forth in flight, he missed his aim;—then, hapless one, wroth with himself, he straightway leaned with all his weight against his sword, and drove it, half its length, into his side; and, while sense lingered, he clasped the maiden to his faint embrace, and, as he gasped, sent forth on her pale cheek the swift stream of the oozing blood.

Corpse enfolding corpse he lies; he hath won his nuptial rites, poor youth, not here, yet in the halls of Death; and he hath witnessed to mankind that, of all curses which cleave to man, ill counsel is the sovereign curse.

(EURYDICE *retires into the house.*)

LEADER

What wouldst thou augur from this? The lady hath turned back, and is gone, without a word, good or evil.

MESSENGER

I, too, am startled; yet I nourish the hope that, at these sore tidings of her son, she cannot deign to give her sorrow public vent, but in the privacy of the house will set her handmaids to mourn the household grief. For she is not untaught of discretion, that she should err.

LEADER

I know not; but to me, at least ,a strained silence seems to portend peril, no less than vain abundance of lament.

MESSENGER

Well, I will enter the house, and learn whether indeed she is not hiding some repressed purpose in the depths of a passionate heart. Yea, thou sayest well: excess of silence, too, may have a perilous meaning.

(The MESSENGER *goes into the palace. Enter* CREON, *on the spectators' left, with attendants, carrying the shrouded body of* HAEMON *on a bier. The following lines between* CREON *and the* CHORUS *are chanted responsively.)*

CHORUS

Lo, yonder the king himself draws near, bearing that which tells too clear a tale,—the work of no stranger's madness,—if we may say it,—but of his own misdeeds.

CREON

strophe 1

Woe for the sins of a darkened soul, stubborn sins, fraught with death! Ah, ye behold us, the sire who hath slain, the son who hath perished! Woe is me, for the wretched blindness of my counsels! Alas, my son, thou hast died in thy youth, by a timeless doom, woe is me!— thy spirit hath fled,—not by thy folly, but by mine own!

CHORUS

strophe 2

Ah me, how all too late thou seemest to see the right!

CREON

Ah me, I have learned the bitter lesson! But then, methinks, oh then, some god smote me from above with crushing weight, and hurled me into ways of cruelty,

woe is me,—overthrowing and trampling on my joy!
Woe, woe, for the troublous toils of men!

(*Enter* Messenger *from the house.*)

Messenger

Sire, thou hast come, methinks, as one whose hands are not
empty, but who hath store laid up besides; thou bearest yonder
burden with thee;; and thou art soon to look upon the woes within
thy house.

Creon

And what worse ill is yet to follow upon ills?

Messenger

Thy queen hath died, true mother of yon corpse—ah, hapless
lady!—by blows newly dealt.

Creon

antistrophe 1

Oh Hades, all-receiving, whom no sacrifice can
appease! Hast thou, then, no mercy for me? O thou
herald of evil, bitter tidings, what word dost thou utter?
Alas, I was already as dead, and thou hast smitten me
anew! What sayest thou, my son? What is this new
message that thou bringest—woe, woe is me!—of a wife's
doom,—of slaughter heaped on slaughter?

Chorus

Thou canst behold: 'tis no longer hidden within.
(*The doors of the palace are opened, and the corpse of*
Eurydice *is disclosed.*)

Creon

antistrophe 2

Ah me,—yonder I behold a new, a second woe! What
destiny, ah what, can yet await me? I have but now
raised my son in my arms,—and there, again, I see a
corpse before me! Alas, alas, unhappy mother! Alas,
my child!

Messenger

There, at the altar, self-stabbed with a keen knife, she
suffered her darkening eyes to close, when she had wailed for the

noble fate of Megareus who died before, and then for his fate
who lies there,—and when, with her last breath, she had invoked
evil fortunes upon thee, the slayer of thy sons.

CREON

strophe 3

Woe, woe! I thrill with dread. Is there none to strike
me to the heart with two-edged sword?—O miserable that
I am, and steeped in miserable anguish!

MESSENGER

Yea, both this son's doom, and that other's, were laid to thy
charge by her whose corpse thou seest.

CREON

And what was the manner of the violent deed by which she
passed away?

MESSENGER

Her own hand struck her to the heart, when she had learned
her son's sorely lamented fate.

CREON

strophe 4

Ah me, this guilt can never be fixed on any other
of mortal kind, for my acquittal! I, even I, was thy slayer,
wretched that I am—I own the truth. Lead me away, O
my servants, lead me hence with all speed, whose life is
but as death!

CHORUS

Thy counsels are good, if there can be good with ills; briefest
is best, when trouble is in our path.

CREON

antistrophe 3

Oh, let it come, let it appear, that fairest of fates
for me, that brings my last day,—aye, best fate of all!
Oh, let it come, that I may never look upon to-morrow's
light.

CHORUS

These things are in the future; present tasks claim our care:
the ordering of the future rests where it should rest.

CHORUS

All my desires, at least, were summed in that prayer.

CHORUS

Pray thou no more; for mortals have no escape from destined woe.

CREON

antistrophe 4

Lead me away, I pray you; a rash, foolish man; who have slain thee, ah my son, unwittingly, and thee, too, my wife—unhappy that I am! I know not which way I should bend my gaze, or where I should seek support; for all is amiss with that which is in my hands,—and yonder, again, a crushing fate hath leapt upon my head.

(*As* CREON *is being conducted into the palace, the* LEADER OF THE CHORUS *speaks the closing verses.*)

LEADER

Wisdom is the supreme part of happiness; and reverence towards the gods must be inviolate. Great words of prideful men are ever punished with great blows, and, in old age, teach the chastened to be wise.

FOOTNOTES

CHAPTER ONE

1 (Introductory Quotation to Chapter 1) "The Interpretation of Dreams" in *The Basic Writings of Sigmund Freud,* edited by A. A. Brill, The Modern Library, Random House, Inc., New York, 1938, p. 308.

2 For a brief account of the development of Freud's theories, see *An Autobiographical Study* by Sigmund Freud, authorized translation by James Strachey, The Hogarth Press, Ltd. and The Institute of Psycho-Analysis, London, 1936. For material on Freud's life and personality, see *Freud, Master and Friend* by Hanns Sachs, Harvard University Press, Cambridge, Mass., 1944; *From Thirty Years With Freud* by Theodor Reik, translated by Richard Winston, Farrar & Rinehart, Inc., New York, 1940; *Freud: His Life and His Mind* by Helen Walker Puner, Howell, Soskin & Company, Inc., New York, 1947.

3 *A General Introduction to Psychoanalysis* by Sigmund Freud, authorized English translation with a preface by Ernest Jones and G. Stanley Hall, Garden City Publishing Co., Garden City, New York, 1943, p. 311. This statement, however, has to be qualified in the case of masochism and sadism, which we discuss below.

4 *Beyond the Pleasure Principle* by Sigmund Freud, The Hogarth Press, Ltd. and The Institute of Psycho-Analysis, London, 1942, p. 1.

5 Op. cit., p. 3.

6 *Collected Papers,* Vol. II, by Sigmund Freud, The Hogarth Press, Ltd., and The Institute of Psycho-Analysis, London, 1924, p. 256.

7 Often in explaining his ideas Freud resorts to analogies or conceptions from the physical world. Another conception of his is "that among the psychic functions there is something which should be differentiated (an amount of affect, a sum of excitation), something having all the attributes of a quantity—although we possess no means of measuring it—a something which is capable of increase, displacement and discharge, and which extends itself over the memory-traces of an idea like an electric charge over the surface of the body . . . For the present it is justified by its utility in correlating and explaining diverse psychical conditions." *Collected Papers,* Vol. I, p. 75.

8 *Collected Papers,* Vol. IV, p. 61.

9 Op. cit., p. 64.

10 In mental life we know an instinct, according to Freud, only by its aims.

11 The primary function of education of children is "to inhibit, forbid and suppress, and it has at all times carried out this function to admiration." *New Introductory Lectures on Psychoanalysis* by Sigmund Freud, translated by J. H. Sprott, W. W. Norton & Company, Inc., New York, 1933, pp. 203-204. See also p. 151.

12 Inhibition is an expression of a functional limitation of the ego. It is not necessarily pathological. See *The Problem of Anxiety* by Sigmund Freud, The Psycho-Analytic Quarterly Press and W. W. Norton & Company, Inc., New York, 1936, Chapter I.

13 *Civilization and Its Discontents* by Sigmund Freud, translated by Joan Rivière, The Hogarth Press, Ltd. and The Institute of Psycho-Analysis, London, 1939, p. 13.

14 *Three Contributions to The Theory of Sex* by Sigmund Freud, authorized translation by A. A. Brill, with introduction by James J. Putnam, Nervous and Mental Disease Publishing Co., New York and Washington, 1920, p. 77. The energy of the libido is psychic energy but differs from the nutritional processes through a special chemism.

15 *A General Introduction*, p. 358.

16 *Civilization and Its Discontents*, p. 34 n.

17 *Collected Papers*, Vol. IV, p. 86.

18 The reader who is interested may study the gradual evolution of Freud's ideas on these matters in Volume I of *Collected Papers*.

19 "The Origin and Development of Psychoanalysis" by Sigmund Freud, *The American Journal of Psychology*, Vol. XXI, No. 2, April, 1910, pp. 193-194. In a beautiful passage Freud remarks: "He that has eyes to see and ears to hear may convince himself that no mortal can keep a secret. If his lips are silent, he chatters with his fingertips; betrayal oozes out of him at every pore. And thus the task of making conscious the most hidden recesses of the mind is one which it is quite possible to accomplish." *Collected Papers*, Vol III, p. 94.

20 See, for example, the two papers on "Repression" and "The Unconscious" in *Collected Papers*, Vol. IV, pp. 84-136.

21 Compare "Affects in Theory and Practice" by Marjorie Brierley, *The International Journal of Psycho-Analysis*, Vol. XVIII, Oct., 1937, pp. 256-267.

22 A "group of ideas which belong together and have a common emotive tone, according to the custom of the Zurich school (Bleuler, Jung and others) is a 'complex.'" "The Origin and Development of Psychoanalysis," p. 199.

23 Compare "Notes Upon A Case of Obsessional Neurosis," *Collected Papers,* Vol. III, pp. 293-383.

24 *Collected Papers,* Vol. IV, p. 87.

25 See, for example, "The Unconscious," *Collected Papers,* Vol. IV, pp. 98-136.

26 A similar distinction applies to the preconscious.

27 *Collected Papers,* Vol. IV, p. 27.

28 "The Origin and Development of Psychoanalysis," p. 207.

29 Freud makes no sharp distinction between infancy and childhood.

30 More accurately, he supplements the pleasure in sucking with other activities. Earlier and later phases of development may, so to speak, exist side by side.

31 For further details see, for example, "Character and Anal Eroticism," *Collected Papers,* Vol. II, p. 45, and "On the Transformation of Instincts," *Collected Papers,* Vol. II, p. 164.

32 *Collected Papers,* Vol. IV, p. 79.

33 Sadism is characterized by the impulse to master things and to inflict pain. Freud believes that aggressiveness and cruelty are intimately connected with the sexual impulse. Sadism always is accompanied by *masochism* in the same person. Masochism is said to comprise all passive attitudes to the sexual life and to the sexual object. In its most extreme form it involves gratification by suffering at the hands of the sexual agent. The person who enjoys causing pain to others in sexual relations can also feel the pain emanating from sexual relations as pleasure. *Three Contributions to The Theory of Sex,* p. 23. He goes on to say that a sadist is simultaneously a masochist.

34 The idea that childhood is a blissful period of life is summarily rejected by Freud as a distortion. Through childhood, children are "lashed" by the desire to be grown-up and to imitate the grown-ups. See *Leonardo da Vinci, A Study in Psychosexuality* by Sigmund Freud, authorized translation by A. A. Brill, Random House, New York, 1947, p. 107.

35 *A General Introduction,* p. 278.

36 Freud attaches great significance to this idea. See, for example, his paper "On the Sexual Theories of Children," *Collected Papers,* Vol. II, p. 59.

37 *A General Introduction,* p. 278.

38 Op. cit., p. 322. Bed-wetting, he says, is another important factor inducing the threat of castration.

39 Compare "Analysis of a Phobia in a Five-Year-Old Boy," *Collected Papers,* Vol. III, pp. 149-289.

40 *Collected Papers,* Vol. II, p. 246.

41 Op. cit., p. 248.

42 *A General Introduction,* p. 279.

43 Freud believes that "all the feelings of sympathy, friendship, trust and so forth which we expend in life are genetically connected with sexuality and have developed out of purely sexual desires by an enfeebling of their sexual aim, however pure and non-sensual they may appear in the forms they take on to our conscious perception." *Collected Papers,* Vol. II, p. 319. Love in the wider sense in which Freud sometimes uses it can occur only when sexual maturity is attained.

44 Compare "Certain Neurotic Mechanisms in Jealousy, Paranoia and Homosexuality," *Collected Papers,* Vol. II, p. 232.

45 *Collected Papers,* Vol. II, p. 272. See also the papers "A Child Is Being Beaten," Vol. II, p. 172, "Neurosis of Demoniacal Possession," Vol. IV, p. 436, "From the History of An Infantile Neurosis," Vol. III, pp. 473-605, all from *Collected Papers.*

46 *New Introductory Lectures,* p. 137. In general, ambivalence represents an attitude composed of two opposing elements such as love and hate. For Freud, love and hate are closely intertwined.

47 Final conviction of woman's lack of a penis is said to cause, at least to a considerable degree, depreciation of women, loathing, and a disposition toward homosexuality. *Collected Papers,* Vol. II, p. 247.

48 A reaction formation is said to be a development of a character trait which checks and conceals another one, usually of the opposite kind. *Moses and Monotheism* by Sigmund Freud, translated from the German by Katherine Jones, Alfred A. Knopf, Inc., New York, 1939, p. 218. Reaction formations are said to be marked in obsessional neurosis. See, for example, "The Predisposition to Obsessional Neurosis," *Collected Papers,* Vol. II, p. 122.

49 *Three Contributions to the Theory of Sex,* p. 81.

50 *Selected Papers on Psychoanalysis* by Karl Abraham, translated by Douglas Bryan and Alix Strachey, The International Psycho-Analytical Library, No. 13, p. 250.

51 For further details of family relationship from the Freudian point of view, see, for example *The Psycho-Analytic Study of the Family* by J. C. Flugel, The International Psycho-Analytical Library, No. 3, 1921, and *The Structure and Meaning of Psychoanalysis* by William Healy, Augusta F. Bronner, and Anna Mae Bowers, Alfred A. Knopf, Inc., New York, 1930, pp. 128-165.

CHAPTER TWO

1 *Selected Papers on Hysteria and Other Psychoneuroses* by Sigmund Freud, authorized translation by A. A. Brill, Nervous and Mental Disease Monograph Series, No. 4, 1920, p. 205.

2 *Collected Papers,* Vol. II, p. 395.

3 See "Analysis Terminable and Interminable" by Sigmund Freud, *The International Journal of Psycho-Analysis,* Vol. XVIII, October 1937, pp. 373-405.

4 *Beyond the Pleasure Principle,* pp. 20-25.

5 "Thoughts for the Times on War and Death (1915)," *Collected Papers,* Vol. IV, p. 288. However, there is as yet no clear indication of a theory of a "death instinct."

6 Freud, however, gives an ingenious explanation. See *New Introductory Lectures,* pp. 45-46.

7 Op. cit., p. 44.

8 *Beyond the Pleasure Principle,* pp. 44-45.

9 Compare *Man Against Himself* by Karl A. Menninger, Harcourt, Brace and Company, New York, 1938.

10 The reader who is interested in the details may consult *Beyond The Pleasure Principle* and *The Ego and the Id* by Sigmund Freud, The Hogarth Press, Ltd., and The Institute of Psycho-Analysis, London, 1935.

11 *New Introductory Lectures,* p. 147.

12 *Collected Papers,* Vol. IV, p. 138. Compare *A General Introduction,* pp. 361-362.

13 In Freud's final formulation, he would say of primary narcissism that all the libido is concentrated in the *id* since the ego is in process of formation. *The Ego and the Id,* p. 65. The ego, by taking over some of the energy from the "object cathexes," "desexualizes" it or transmutes it into a kind of sublimated energy.

14 *New Introductory Lectures,* p. 141.

15 *The Ego and the Id,* p. 56.

16 The reason given for this is highly speculative. See *Beyond the Pleasure Principle,* p. 63.

17 *The Ego and the Id,* p. 56.

18 *New Introductory Lectures,* pp. 144-145.

19 *The Ego and the Id,* p. 57.

20 *New Introductory Lectures,* p. 143.

21 For further implications of the theory of the death-instinct, see *Civilization and Its Discontents.*

22 *The Ego and the Id,* p. 33. Not "only what is lowest but also what is highest in the ego can be unconscious."

23 Op. cit., p. 30.

24 *New Introductory Lectures*, p. 104.

25 Op. cit., p. 84.

26 A part of the super-ego, like the ego, is unconscious without possessing the "primitive and irrational" quality of the id.

27 *The Ego and the Id*, pp. 39-40. Compare *New Introductory Lectures*, pp. 90-91.

28 *The Ego and the Id*, p. 41.

29 While we postpone discussion of the little girl's Oedipus complex, we may remark here that she normally identifies herself with the mother.

30 Op. cit., pp. 42-43. Compare "Psycho-Analytical Notes Upon an Auto-biographical Account of a Case of Paranoia," *Collected Papers*, Vol. III, p. 387-470.

31 *New Introductory Lectures*, p. 90.

32 *The Ego and the Id*, p. 36. But identification may also occur as a compensation or perhaps a disguise for hostility and jealousy, as in the case of an elder child who identifies himself with the younger siblings. Identification is usually, if not always, ambivalent.

33 For further details of the process of identification see *The Ego and the Id* and *Group Psychology and the Analysis of the Ego* by Sigmund Freud, authorized translation by James Strachey, Boni and Liveright, New York (no date), p. 60.

34 *The Ego and the Id*, pp. 44-45.

35 *New Introductory Lectures*, p. 95.

36 *Group Psychology and the Analysis of the Ego*, p. 80.

37 *Three Contributions to the Theory of Sex*, p. 79. See also *Civilization and Its Discontents*, pp. 77-78 n.

38 *New Introductory Lectures*, p. 158.

39 "The Economic Problem In Masochism," *Collected Papers*, Vol. II, p. 261.

40 Op. cit., p. 258.

41 Op. cit., p. 262.

42 Op. cit., p. 266.

43 See, for example, "Homosexuality in a Woman," *Collected Papers*, Vol. II, p. 202-231; and "Fragment of an Analysis of a Case of Hysteria," *Collected Papers*, Vol. III, pp. 13-146.

44 *New Introductory Lectures*, p. 161.

45 While we are not concerned at this point with an evaluation of Freud, we may observe that he seems to be, among other things, led astray by the Victorian milieu in which he lived the greater part of his life. See, for example, "Cultural Pressures in the Psychology of Women" by Clara Thompson, *Psychiatry,* Vol. V, No. 3, August, 1942.

46 Compare "Penis Envy in Women" by Clara Thompson, *Psychiatry,* Vol. VI, No. 2, May, 1943; and *New Ways in Psychoanalysis* by Karen Horney, W. W. Norton & Company, Inc., New York, 1939, Chapter VI.

47 *New Introductory Lectures,* p. 175.

48 "A husband is, so to speak, never anything but a proxy, never the right man; the first claim upon the love of a woman belongs to someone else, in typical cases to her father; the husband is at best a second." *Collected Papers,* Vol. IV, p. 229.

49 Analogous complications are of course manifested by the male.

CHAPTER THREE

1 The impulses are inhibited, denied a transformation into direct affective expression.

2 There are, of course, neuroses with no gross symptoms.

3 *A General Introduction,* p. 319. Freud also says that symptoms are formed for the purpose of escaping anxiety. Op. cit., p. 350. The notion that a symptom yields satisfaction is almost ignored in Freud's *New Introductory Lectures.*

4 *A General Introduction,* p. 326.

5 Freud's concept of anxiety is one of the most complicated and poorly articulated of all his ideas—or so it seems to us.

6 *Selected Papers on Psychoanalysis* by Karl Abraham, p. 408.

7 Op. cit., p. 397.

8 Op. cit., p. 395.

9 We borrow this formulation from Freud's exposition of the anal character.

10 Op. cit., p. 399.

11 *Collected Papers,* Vol. II, pp. 45-50.

12 Op. cit., p. 50. Compare "Libidinal Types" by Sigmund Freud, *The Psycho-Analytic Quarterly,* Vol. I, pp. 3-6.

13 *Selected Papers on Psychoanalysis* by Karl Abraham, p. 380.

14 Op. cit., pp. 410-411.

15 For further details see Chapter XXVI of the same work.

16 *New Introductory Lectures*, p. 126.

17 *Moses and Monotheism*, p. 157.

18 *Totem and Taboo* by Sigmund Freud, authorized translation with an introduction by A. A. Brill (copyright 1918 by Dodd, Mead & Co., Inc., New York), New Republic, Inc., New York, 1927, pp. 218-219.

19 Op. cit., pp. 246-247.

20 Freud does not attempt to work out further details of the theory in *Totem and Taboo*. Later, in *Group Psychology and the Analysis of the Ego*, p. 122, a few details are added. The women whom they desired were, of course, their mothers and sisters.

21 Freud had to confess (*Totem and Taboo*, p. 260) that he was at a loss to explain the evolution of maternal deities.

22 *Group Psychology and the Analysis of the Ego*, pp. 112-113.

23 In *Moses and Monotheism*, pp. 129-130, we learn that a good part of the power left vacant by the dead father passed to the women, and a matriarchate resulted. Hence, the first form of society following the death of the primal father was a matriarchy, only gradually evolving later into a patriarchal society, with a revolution in the existing state of the law, an echo of which can still be heard in the *Oresteia* of Aeschylus.

24 This does not mean, of course, that a tribe is aware of the origin of the totem or of its significance.

25 *Totem and Taboo*, pp. 254-255.

26 Compare *Three Essays on Sex and Marriage* by Edward Westermarck, Macmillan & Co., Limited, London, 1934.

27 Freud does not clarify this mechanism in *Totem and Taboo*. However, from *Group Psychology and the Analysis of the Ego*, we gather that this mechanism is *empathy* or is related to empathy.

28 *Totem and Taboo*, p. 276.

29 *Moses and Monotheism*, p. 173.

30 *Selected Papers on Hysteria and Other Psychoneuroses*, p. 211.

31 *Moses and Monotheism*, p. 185.

CHAPTER FOUR

1 *The Republic of Plato*, translated with introduction and notes by Francis Macdonald Cornford, Oxford University Press, New York, 1945, pp. 296-297.

2 There are sometimes, of course, stimuli of external origin such as the ringing of an alarm clock.

3 *A General Introduction,* pp. 127-128.

4 *The Basic Writings of Sigmund Freud,* p. 319.

5 *A General Introduction,* p. 152.

6 See *The Basic Writings of Sigmund Freud,* p. 320 ff.

7 Op. cit., p. 403.

8 An element of the manifest dream may refer to more than one of the latent thoughts and conversely.

9 However, the imagery need not be connected always with words.

10 *A General Introduction,* p. 109.

11 *The Basic Writings of Sigmund Freud,* pp. 346-349.

12 *A General Introduction,* p. 160.

13 It appears that more recently some orthodox psychoanalysts have altered their views about this, that they now incline toward the belief that "the meaning of the symbol cannot be known without the individual's associations called forth through analysis in the individual case." Healy, Bronner and Bowers, op. cit., p. 259.

14 *The Significance of Psychoanalysis for the Mental Sciences* by Otto Rank and Hanns Sachs, authorized English translation by Charles R. Payne, Nervous and Mental Disease Monograph Series, No. 23, 1916, p. 10.

15 Op. cit., pp. 13-20. Compare *Papers on Psychoanalysis* by Ernest Jones, Third Edition, William Ward and Company, 1923, Chapter VIII, "Symbolism."

16 Op. cit., p. 23.

17 Op. cit., pp.38-39.

18 Op. cit., pp. 52-55.

19 *The Myth of the Birth of the Hero* by Otto Rank, authorized translalation by Drs. F. Robbins and Smith Ely Jelliffe, Nervous and Mental Disease Monograph Series, No. 18, pp. 66-67.

20 *The Significance of Psychoanalysis for the Mental Sciences,* p. 29. Compare *Dreams and Myths* by Karl Abraham, translated by W. A. White, Nervous and Mental Disease Monograph Series, No. 15, New York, 1913; and *An Essay on Man: An Introduction to a Philosophy of Human Culture* by Ernst Cassirer, Yale University Press, New Haven, 1944, Chapter VII, "Myth and Religion."

21 Compare *Totem and Taboo,* Chapter III.

22 *The Significance of Psychoanalysis for the Mental Sciences,* pp. 67-68.

23 Op. cit., p. 69.

24 Freud, in *The Future of an Illusion,* The International Psycho-Analytical Library, No. 15, 1943, p. 9, avers that every person is virtually an enemy of culture.

25 *The Significance of Psychoanalysis for the Mental Sciences,* p. 69.

26 Op. cit., p. 74.

27 Op. cit., p. 75. Compare "Psychoanalytic Study of the Christian Creed" by Cavendish Maxon, *International Journal of Psychoanalysis,* Vol. II, pp. 54-64; and "A Psycho-Analytic Study of the Holy Ghost," Chapter XIII, by Ernest Jones, *Essays in Applied Psychoanalysis,* The International Psycho-Analytical Library, No. 5, 1923.

28 *The Significance of Psychoanalysis for the Mental Sciences,* pp. 76-78.

29 Compare *The Future of an Illusion* and *Moses and Monotheism* by Sigmund Freud, and *The Psychological Problems of Religion-Ritual* by Theodor Reik, with a preface by Sigmund Freud, translated from the second German edition by Douglas Bryan, Farrar, Straus and Company, Inc., New York, 1946.

30 *A General Introduction,* p. 327.

31 Hence, not only the material but also the creative force of art is chiefly sexual.

32 Op. cit., p. 328.

33 Compare *Freudianism and The Literary Mind* by Frederick F. Hoffman, Louisiana State University Press, Baton Rouge, La., 1945.

34 *The Significance of Psychoanalysis for the Mental Sciences,* p. 93.

35 Op. cit., p. 101.

36 Op. cit., pp. 102-103. A Freudian will perhaps find the following excerpts from Stendhal's memoirs concerning his relationship to his mother and father especially significant:
   " 'In loving her [Stendhal's mother] at the age of about six I had exactly the same character as when, in 1828, I loved Alberthe de Rubempré (his mistress) with mad passion—— I wanted to cover my mother with kisses, and for her to have no clothes on. She loved me passionately and kissed me often. I returned her kisses with such ardor that she was sometimes obliged to run away. I abhorred my father when he came to interrupt our kisses. I always wanted to kiss her bosom. You must remember that I lost my mother in childhood when I was barely seven.' "
   Stendhal also records in his memoirs that he loved his mother with a mad passion " 'as criminal as possible' with a jealousy of his father dimly formed in his mind." *Stendhal* by Matthew Josephson, Doubleday & Co., Inc., New York, 1946, pp. 6-7.

37 *The Significance of Psychoanalysis for the Mental Sciences,* p. 103.

38 "To A Very Young War Widow" by Carolyn Wilson Link, *The Saturday Evening Post,* March 11, 1944, taken from "A Study in Symbolism" by David B. Barron, M.D., *The Psychoanalytic Review,* Vol. XXXIV, No. 4, October, 1947, pp. 395-430.

39 Op. cit., pp. 396-400.

40 The "spirit" of the procreating power, as Barron would say, was projected into agriculture, while the "formal characteristics" of agriculture were "intrajected" into procreation.

41 Op. cit., p. 421. The same paper also contains an analysis of a story written by a seven-year-old child, which is said to contain a striking allegory of the Oedipus complex.

42 See, for example, "Psychoanalysis of Writers and of Literary Production" by Edmund Bergler, and "Psychoanalysis in Literature and Its Therapeutic Value" by Clarence P. Oberndorf in *Psychoanalysis and the Social Sciences,* An Annual, Vol. I, International Universities Press, New York, 1947, and "Psychoanalysis and Literature" by Fritz Wittels in *Psychoanalysis Today.*

43 The writer of the excerpt is obviously influenced by Jung and Rank.

44 Compare Fromm's interpretation of the Oedipus myth below.

45 Taken by courtesy of Mr. Nathan Halper, of New York City, from his forthcoming book on *Finnegan's Wake.* Adapted for publication here.

CHAPTER FIVE

1 *The Neurotic Constitution* by Alfred Adler, authorized English translation by Bernard Glueck, M.D. and John E. Lind, M.D., Moffatt, Yard and Company, New York, 1917, p. IX.

2 We do not discuss morphological inferiority since it is not essential for the purposes of this book.

3 *A Study of Organ Inferiority and Its Psychical Compensation* by Alfred Adler, authorized translation by Smith Ely Jelliffe, M.D., Nervous and Mental Disease Monograph Series, No. 24, 1917, p. 6.

4 Op. cit., p. 23. There is, of course, a third possible outcome of organ inferiority, namely, physical disease and degeneration.

5 For reasons such as this, Adler insists that a neurosis is a "creative act" and not a reversion to infantile and atavistic forms of life.

6 *Understanding Human Nature* by Alfred Adler, translated by Walter Beran Wolfe, Greenberg: Publisher, Inc., New York, 1927, p. 38.

7 *Social Interest: A Challenge to Mankind* by Alfred Adler, translated by John Linton, and Richard Vaughan, Faber and Faber, Ltd., London, 1938, p. 73.

8 Among classical psychoanalysts, Jones and Ferenczi have held that the difference between the normal and those with functional mental illness is one of degree. Freud likewise held that the healthy person is virtually a neurotic.

9 Op. cit., p. 99.

10 *Understanding Human Nature,* pp. 33-34.

11 The child tries to orient himself according to the following apperception of antithesis in Adler's scheme: Above-beneath, masculine-feminine.

12 Op. cit., p. 19.   ,

13 "The fundamental fact in human development is the dynamic and purposive striving of the psyche. A child, from its earliest infancy, is engaged in a constant struggle to develop, and this struggle is in accordance with an unconsciously formed but ever-present goal—a vision of greatness, perfection and superiority. This struggle, this goal-forming activity, reflects, of course the peculiarly human faculty of thinking and of imagining, and it dominates all our specific acts throughout life. It dominates even our thoughts, for we do not think objectively but in accordance with the goal and style of life we have formed." *The Education of Children* by Alfred Adler, George Allen & Unwin, Ltd., London, 1930, p. 5.

14 *Understanding Human Nature,* pp. 123-124.

15 *Problems of Neurosis* by Alfred Adler, with a prefatory essay by F. G. Crookshank, M.D., edited by P. Mainet, Cosmopolitan Book Corp., New York, 1930, p. 44.

16 *Social Interest,* p. 13.

17 *What Life Should Mean to You* by Alfred Adler, Grosset and Dunlap, New York, p. 8.

18 *Social Interest,* p. 45.

19 The pampering mother, or father, of course, is not alienated though even they will sooner or later find that their pampered and crippled child is quite a problem.

20 There are, of course, numerous variations and outcomes of such a line of development, for example, the possibility of withdrawal from others, "flight into illness," suicide, cultism, and so on, as fairly typical outcomes.

21 Op. cit., p. 51.

22 Op. cit., pp. 20-22.

CHAPTER SIX

1 Dr. A. A. Brill, among others, who knew Jung in Zurich in 1907, perhaps would have disagreed. See *The Basic Writings of Sigmund Freud,*

p. 26. Compare *Contributions to Analytical Psychology* by C. G. Jung, translated by H. G. and Cary F. Baynes, Harcourt, Brace and Company, New York, 1928, pp. 330-331.

2 *The Psychology of Dementia Praecox* by C. G. Jung, authorized translation with an introduction by A. A. Brill, Nervous and Mental Disease Monograph Series, No. 3, New York, 1936, Preface, p. iv.

3 "The Association Method" by Carl G. Jung, translated by A. A. Brill, *The American Journal of Psychology*, Vol. XXI, No. 2, April, 1910, pp. 246-247.

4 Compare *Modern Man In Search of a Soul* by C. G. Jung, translated by W. S. Dill and Cary F. Baynes, Harcourt, Brace and Company, New York, 1933, pp. 56-57: "Two primary factors come together in the treatment—that is, two persons, neither of whom is a fixed and determinable magnitude. Their fields of consciousness may be quite clearly defined, but they bring with them besides an indefinitely extended sphere of unconsciousness. For this reason the personalities of the doctor and patient have often more to do with the outcome of the treatment than what the doctor says or thinks—although we must not undervalue this latter factor as a disturbing or healing one. The meeting of two personalities is like the contact of two chemical substances: if there is any reaction, both are transformed."

5 *The Psychology of the Unconscious* by C. G. Jung, authorized translation with introduction by Beatrice M. Hinkle, Dodd, Mead and Company, New York, 1927, p. 145.

6 *The Theory of Psychoanalysis* by C. G. Jung, Nervous and Mental Disease Monograph Series, No. 19, New York, 1915, p. 40.

7 Op. cit., p. 35.

8 At first blush, Jung's theory of libido seems to be similar to Freud's Eros. Formally, it is. But there are important differences. The role of sexuality always is paramount. Furthermore, in Freud, Eros has to share the energy of life processes with that of the death instinct, while Jung has no death-instinct theory. However, Jung, somewhat vaguely, speaks of a primitive separation of the pairs of opposites which are hidden in all life: the will for life and for death.

9 Op. cit., p. 23.

10 Op. cit., p. 33.

11 In other words, "the libido returns to the mother-image [or to the father-image] in order to find there the memory associations by means of which further development can take place . . ." *Contributions to Analytical Psychology*, p. 24. It is a fundamental principle that symptoms represent at the same time a natural attempt at healing. Op. cit., pp. 106-107.

12 "On Psychological Understanding" by C. G. Jung, *Journal of Abnormal Psychology*, 1915, p. 391.

13 *Contributions to Analytical Psychology*, pp. 52-54.

14 "What is usually and generally called 'religion' is to such an amazing degree a substitute that I ask myself seriously whether this kind of 'religion,' which I prefer to call a creed, has not an important function in human society. The substitution has the obvious purpose of replacing immediate experience by a choice of suitable symbols invested in a solidly organized dogma and ritual. The Catholic Church maintains them by her indisputable authority, the Protestant Church (if this term is still applicable) by insistence upon faith and the evangelical message. As long as those two principles work, people are effectively defended and shielded against immediate religious experience." *Psychology and Religion* by C. G. Jung, Yale University Press, New Haven, 1938, pp. 52-53.

15 *Contributions to Analytical Psychology*, pp. 54-56.

16 Preface to First Edition, *Collected Papers on Analytical Psychology* by C. G. Jung, authorized translation, edited by Dr. Constance E. Long, Second Edition, Balliere, Tindall and Cox, London, 1920, pp. xiii-xiv.

17 Op. cit., pp. 385-395.

18 For Jung, the patient represents the "extraverted type" whose basic direction is toward the object. This type, he says, has ever symbolically expressed itself in sexuality. See *Psychological Types or The Psychology of Individuation* by C. G. Jung, translated by H. Godwin Baynes, Harcourt, Brace and Company, New York, 1926. For a good example of Jungian interpretation, unfortunately too long and involved to be discussed here, see *Collected Papers on Analytical Psychology*, p. 418 ff., and *The Integration of the Personality* by C. G. Jung, translated by Stanley M. Dell, Farrar & Rinehart, Inc., New York, 1939, Chapter IV.

19 Contrary to general opinion, Jung's notion of a "collective psyche" is in many respects quite close to Freud's "mass psyche." In fact, it is quite clear that Freud was influenced by Jung's ideas about the analogies of the phantasies of "neurotics" and primitive peoples. See Freud's *An Autobiographical Study*, p. 121.

20 Man, of course, also has an individual non-inherited psyche growing out of his own particular life experience.

21 The collective psyche is differentiated into collective mind and collective soul. The former represents collective thought, the latter, collective feeling.

22 Freud does not explicitly distinguish a "collective unconscious," but he tacitly assumes some such phenomenon.

23 *Collected Papers on Analytical Psychology*, p. 451.

24 His *Psychology of the Unconscious* is, among other things, an elaborate effort to demonstrate this point.

25 *Collected Papers on Analytical Psychology*, p. 435. Yet, of itself the unconscious is not "dangerous" nor "explosive"; it becomes so only with repression.

26 *Psychological Types*, p. 211.

27 *Collected Papers on Analytical Psychology*, p. 438.

28 *Contributions to Analytical Psychology*, p. 112.

29 Op. cit., p. 118.

30 *Contemporary Schools of Psychology* by Robert S. Woodworth, The Ronald Press Co., New York, 1931, pp. 177-178.

31 *Contributions to Analytical Psychology*, pp. 119-124.

32 "The overwhelming majority of men of the present cultural level do not advance beyond the maternal significance of women." Op. cit., p. 129.

33 *The Integration of the Personality*, p. 295.

34 *Contributions to Analytical Psychology*, p. 194.

35 "People will resort to any external means, even the most absurd, in order to escape from their own psyches. They practice Indian yoga of every denomination, observe rules of diet, learn theosophy by heart, pray according to mystic texts culled from the literature of the whole world—all this, because they are dissatisfied with themselves and lack every glimmer of faith that anything useful could come out of their own psyches. In this way the psyche has little by little become that Nazareth from which nothing good can come; and for this reason people seek it in the four corners of the world, the farther off and the more out of the way the better." *The Integration of the Personality*, pp. 128-129.

36 *Modern Man in Search of a Soul*, p. 278.

37 "Only a unified personality can experience life; an occurrence split up into partial aspects, though it likewise calls itself a human being, cannot do so." *The Integration of the Personality*, p. 120. The psyche is conceived by Jung as a self-regulating system which strives for equilibrium. But such a self-regulating system implies a nicely balanced play of elements or "forces," an opposition or tension among the psychic processes which keeps them in a dynamic equilibrium. Thus, for example, when the conscious life is impoverished or inadequate, say, emotionally, and there is an "over-exaggeration" of the intellectual function, the unconscious, as it were, comes to the rescue and strives to restore harmony by an increased unconscious emotional activity as manifested in dream, phantasy, vision. The symptoms of "neurotics" are danger-signals that there is an improper distribution of psychic energy.

38 "All that the human spirit has ever created has come from contents which, in the last analysis, existed once as unconscious seeds." *Contributions to Analytical Psychology,* pp. 147-148.

39 *Collected Papers on Analytical Psychology,* p. 442. But the images embody or represent not only "every great thought and feeling of humanity, but also every deed of shame and devilry of which human beings are capable." Op. cit., p. 414. Compare *Modern Man in Search of a Soul,* Chapter VIII.

40 *The Psychology of the Unconscious,* p. 446.

41 Op. cit., pp. 98-99.

42 Op. cit., pp. 260-267.

43 *Psychological Types,* p. 419.

44 *Modern Man in Search of a Soul,* p. 140.

45 *Two Essays on Analytical Psychology* by C. G. Jung, authorized translation by H. G. and C. F. Baynes, Dodd, Mead and Company, New York, 1928, p. 165.

46 *Collected Papers on Analytical Psychology,* p. 473.

47 *Modern Man in Search of a Soul,* p. 247. For a review of Jung, see *The Psychology of Jung* by Jolan Jacobi, translated by K. W. Bash, with a foreword by C. G. Jung, Yale University Press, New Haven, 1943. *The Inner World of Man* by Frances G. Wickes, Henry Holt and Co., New York, 1938, offers a good example of the practical application of Jung's theories.

CHAPTER SEVEN

1 *The Trauma of Birth* by Otto Rank, Harcourt, Brace and Company, New York, 1929, and Routledge and Kegan Paul, Ltd., London, pp. 187-188.

2 Op. cit., pp. 22-47.

3 Op. cit., pp. 44-45.

4 Op. cit., pp. 86-100.

5 Op. cit., pp. 112-113. Compare Freud, *Group Psychology and the Analysis of the Ego,* pp. 112-115.

6 *The Trauma of Birth,* pp. 90, 92.

7 Op. cit., p. 117.

8 Op. cit., p. 129.

9 Op. cit., pp. 156-159.

10 Ibid., pp. 144-145.

11 Op. cit., pp. 160-166.

12 Compare *Art and Artist* by Otto Rank, translated from the German by Charles Francis Atkinson, Alfred A. Knopf, Inc., New York, 1932.

13 *The Trauma of Birth,* pp. 150-151 and 152-153.

14 An early work of Rank.

15 *Will Therapy and Truth and Reality* by Otto Rank, authorized translation with a preface and introduction by Jessie Taft, Alfred A. Knopf, Inc., New York, 1945, pp. 209-210.

16 Op. cit., pp. 219-220.

17 Compare *Beyond Psychology* by Otto Rank, privately published, 1941, p. 50.

18 *Will Therapy and Truth and Reality,* pp. 111-112, footnote.

19 Op. cit., pp. 134-135.

20 Op. cit., p. 82.

21 A preponderance of fear of life is said to lead to neurotic repression, of death, to production, a perpetuation of oneself in work.

22 Op. cit., p. 134.

23 Ideal formation corresponds to Freud's super ego but differs in that it emphasizes the self-creating of ethical ideals and norms.

24 Op. cit., p. 265.

25 Compare *Art and Artist,* p. 27.
"The neurotic, no matter whether productive or obstructed, suffers fundamentally from the fact that he cannot or will not accept himself, his own individuality, his own personality. On [the] one hand he criticizes himself to excess, on the other he idealizes himself to excess, which means that he makes too great demands on himself and his completeness, so that failing to attain leads only to more self-criticism." The artist is in a sense the antithesis of the "neurotic." "Not that the artist does not criticize himself, but by accepting his personality he not only fulfills that for which the neurotic is striving in vain, but goes far beyond it."

26 *Will Therapy and Truth and Reality,* pp. 270-274. Compare *Modern Education* by Otto Rank, translated by Mabel E. Moxon, Alfred A. Knopf, Inc., New York, 1932, p. 76 ff.

27 Rank is not too clear on this point. The meaning seems to be that the "will" of the average man is so dependent on the judgments of society that he feels he is "good" or "bad" only as he lives in accordance with or in defiance of socially approved experience and behavior. The "neurotic" has a "will" which differs in that he does not think, feel and act in accordance with socially approved standards and

patterns, while at the same time, because of his experiences in life, he has never achieved a genuine conviction of his own worth and integrity.

28 Op. cit., p. 275. Even in the creative person, difference is inclined to be interpreted as inferiority unless one can prove, by achievement, that it implies superiority.

29 Op. cit., p. 95. In other words, he is the role he plays.

30 Op. cit., p. 212.

31 Op. cit., p. 242.

32 Op. cit., pp. 237-238.

33 There are, in fact, two types of "modern neurotic" but it exceeds our purpose to discuss them. See *Will Therapy and Truth and Reality,* pp. 54-56.

34 *Modern Education,* pp. 81-82.

35 Emotion also arises from the "moral ego," Rank also claims, in a somewhat unclear fashion, as well as from the "impulsive ego." "In the morally educated and ethically adjusted human being, not only are *individual* impulses operative as motives of action, feeling and thought, but the *collective* element also is operative as manifested religiously or socially." *Modern Education,* pp. 87-88. Here he seems to have in mind something like Adler's "social feeling," to which he refers.

36 *Modern Education,* pp. 80-84.

37 *Will Therapy and Truth and Reality,* p. 245. Compare *Modern Education,* pp. 84-85.

38 In *Beyond Psychology* Rank states a similar idea more clearly. Hating both oneself and others can be overcome "on the basis of self-love, which means self-acceptance. For only inasmuch as the individual accepts himself can he accept others as they are and in that sense 'love' them. The non-acceptance of the other, manifesting itself through assertion of difference in hatred, springs from the non-acceptance of the self, conceived of as being bad and therefore rejected. Thus self-hatred is the basis for hating others or the world at large. For self-hatred, being really unbearable, is easily justified by making the others and the world bad so they can become the object of hatred instead of the own self."

39 *Will Therapy and Truth and Reality,* p. 56. Compare *Beyond Psychology,* pp. 187-188.

40 *Will Therapy and Truth and Reality,* p. 276.

41 Compare *Art and Artist,* chapters XI-XIV.

42 *Modern Education,* p. 203.

43 Op. cit., p. 204.

44 *Beyond Psychology,* pp. 248-249.

45 Op. cit., p. 267.

46 *Modern Education,* pp. 182-184. Compare *Beyond Psychology,* pp. 120-121: "For centuries the social life of the primitives consisted of certain group activities divided chiefly according to sex and generation. The life of men and women was strictly separated and so, too, was the life of the younger generation from that of the matured and elders. Before maturity the children of any given clan were under the care of the women, a group of 'mothers' who formed the nucleus of the domestic life, just as the group of older men managed the community affairs. Those children belonging to the same clan were considered 'brothers' and 'sisters,' not in the sense of being blood relations but descendants from one and the same totem (spirit of the dead)."

47 *Modern Education,* p. 184.

48 *Beyond Psychology,* pp. 218-219.

49 *Modern Education,* pp. 192-194.

50 *Beyond Psychology,* p. 122.

51 *Modern Education,* p. 197. He recalls his own childhood in the "neurotic" sense as an expression of a wish to return to the mother.

52 *Modern Education,* p. 200. Compare *Beyond Psychology,* Chapter 3.

53 *Modern Education,* p. 201. No intermediate stage is mentioned.

54 *Will Therapy and Truth and Reality,* p. 247.

55 Op. cit., p. 250. Later Rank modified this view, though not fundamentally. Intelligence is assigned a more positive constructive function on behalf of the will. Op. cit., p. 177.

56 Op. cit., p. 250.

CHAPTER EIGHT

1 *New Ways in Psychoanalysis* by Karen Horney, W. W. Norton & Company, Inc., New York, 1939, pp. 12-13.

2 *The Neurotic Personality of Our Time* by Karen Horney, W. W. Norton & Company, Inc., New York, 1937, p. 15.

3 Op. cit., pp. 17-22.

4 Op. cit., p. 23.

5 Op. cit., pp. 28-29.

6 Here, too, however, the factor of preexisting psychological security is involved. The more secure a person is, the more he can "stand" the conflict and resolve it. Perhaps a better example is that of a persor

in a concentration camp in Nazi Germany, where even the strongest personality might disintegrate. Subsequently, Horney mentions the case of Elizabeth Barrett Browning as an example of a situation neurosis.

7 Op. cit., p. 31.

8 Op. cit., pp. 33-34.

9 See Freud's *New Introductory Lectures,* Chapter 4, and *The Problem of Anxiety.*

10 *The Neurotic Personality of Our Time,* p. 44. Compare Freud's *New Introductory Lectures,* pp. 113-130.

11 *The Neurotic Personality of Our Time,* p. 46.

12 Op. cit., p. 53.

13 Op. cit., p. 63.

14 Op. cit., pp. 70-74. Horney's concept of anxiety is discussed further in *New Ways in Psychoanalysis,* pp. 74-77, 193-206.

15 *The Neurotic Personality of Our Time,* pp. 80-81. However, Horney points out, a child (or an adult) can accept much deprivation if he feels it is just, fair, necessary or purposeful.

16 He may, for example, develop a pervasive masochistic attitude, which, according to Horney, is not essentially a sexual phenomenon but represents an attempt to gain safety and satisfaction in life through inconspicuousness and dependency. In general, masochism is said to be the result of conflicts in interpersonal relations.

17 Op. cit., pp. 89-92.

18 Op. cit., p. 96. Infantile and neurotic needs for affection are somewhat different. In a child the feeling of being wanted is vitally important for his harmonious development. A child needs more affection and help than the neurotic because the former is more helpless, but the expression of the need for affection in the normal child is also more spontaneous, while the neurotic's need for affection is compulsive.

19 Later Horney adopted a pluralistic theory of neurotic trends; there are not four such trends but several. In *Self Analysis,* W. W. Norton & Company, Inc., New York, 1942, pp. 54-60, she lists ten. Still later, in *Our Inner Conflicts,* W. W. Norton & Company, Inc., New York, 1945, a somewhat different formulation, which we discuss below, is worked out.

20 But he is himself incapable of love unless and until he frees himself from neurotic anxiety. "The difference between love and the neurotic need for affection lies in the fact that in love the feeling of affection is primary, whereas in the case of the neurotic the primary feeling is the need for reassurance, and the illusion of loving is only secondary." *The Neurotic Personality of Our Time, p.* 109.

21 Op. cit., p. 180.

22 Op. cit., p. 189.

23 Op. cit., p. 216.

24 Op. cit., p. 97.

25 *New Ways in Psychoanalysis,* p. 78.

26 In fact, does he not say that femininity is a "riddle"?

27 Op. cit., pp. 110-111.

28 Op. cit., pp. 107-108.

29 Compare the discussion below of Fromm's concept of selfishness and self-love.

30 *Our Inner Conflicts,* p. 116.

31 Compare our exposition of the neurotic need for affection above.

32 Compare our exposition of the need for power and control above.

33 Op. cit., p. 92.

34 Compare *Are You Considering Psychoanalysis?* edited by Karen Horney, W. W. Norton & Company, Inc., New York, 1946, p. 81.

35 *Our Inner Conflicts,* p. 116.

36 See, for example, *New Ways in Psychoanalysis,* p. 10.

37 *Our Inner Conflicts,* p. 19.

CHAPTER NINE

1 *The Individual and His Society* by Abram Kardiner, Columbia University Press, New York, 1939, and *The Psychological Frontiers of Society* by Abram Kardiner, Columbia University Press, New York, 1945. Others include *Our Age of Unreason* by Franz Alexander, Lippincott Co., New York, 1942; *Psychoanalytic Therapy: Principles and Application* by Franz Alexander and Thomas Morton French and Others, The Ronald Press Co., New York, 1946.

2 *Escape From Freedom* by Erich Fromm, Farrar & Rinehart, Inc., New York, 1941, p. 9.

3 Op. cit., pp. 10-11.

4 Op. cit., pp. 12-13.

5 *Man for Himself* by Erich Fromm, Rinehart & Company, Inc., New York, 1947, pp. 39-40.

6 Op. cit., p. 41.

7 Op. cit., p. 46.

8 *Escape from Freedom,* p. 33.

9 Op. cit., p. 35.

10 Op. cit., p. 26 n.

11 Op. cit., p. 29.

12 Op. cit., p. 144.

13 Op. cit., p. 179.

14 Op. cit., p. 180. Compare *Man for Himself,* pp. 214-217.

15 *Escape from Freedom,* p. 186.

16 For further details see *Escape from Freedom,* pp. 103-105, pp. 185-206, p. 240 ff.

17 *Man for Himself,* p. 58.

18 Op. cit., p. 59.

19 Op. cit., p. 129.

20 Op. cit., p. 139.

21 Op. cit., p. 84.

22 Op. cit., pp. 97-98.

23 See op. cit., pp. 112-117.

24 Op. cit., p. 144. This does not mean that conscience is necessarily of this kind. There is such a thing as a "humanistic conscience," which Fromm calls "the voice of our loving care for ourselves."

25 Whether or not a sado-masochistic person becomes neurotic largely depends on the task he fulfills in his society and the character of the society. It is the "normal" sado-masochist who is called authoritarian.

26 Op. cit., pp. 146-147. Compare *Escape from Freedom,* pp. 141-179.

27 See *Man for Himself,* pp. 67 ff., 136, 155 and *Escape from Freedom,* Chapter IV, Chapter VII, pp. 240-256, and the Appendix, pp. 277-299.

28 *Man for Himself,* p. 34.

29 Op. cit., pp. 172-197. For an excellent summary of Fromm's views on sex, see his "Sex and Character: The Kinsey Report Viewed from the Standpoint of Psychoanalysis" in *About the Kinsey Report,* The New American Library (Signet Books), New York, 1948, pp. 47-59.

30 Further discussed in *Man for Himself,* pp. 34-37.

31 Op. cit., p. viii.

32 Op. cit., p. 4.

33 The material on the Oedipus myth and complex is included by courtesy of Drs. Fromm and Anshen.

34 Quoted by permission of Dr. Ruth Nanda Anshen, Editor of *The Science of Culture Series;* from Volume V, "The Family: Its Function and Destiny"; Monograph by Erich Fromm: *The Oedipus Complex and the Oedipus Myth;* published, Autumn, 1948, Harper and Brothers.

35 Op. cit., quoted by permission of Dr. Anshen.

36 However, Fromm does not, like Rank, assume that matriarchy was a transitional development which succeeded a somewhat different form of society.

37 Op. cit., quoted by permission of Dr. Anshen.

38 Op. cit., quoted by permission of Dr. Anshen.

39 Op. cit., quoted by permission of Dr. Anshen.

40 Op. cit., quoted by permission of Dr. Anshen.

41 Op. cit., quoted by permission of Dr. Anshen.

42 Op. cit., quoted by permission of Dr. Anshen.

43 Compare *Man for Himself,* pp. 153-158.

CHAPTER TEN

1 Some of the material which we discuss in this chapter has never been published and is taken from lectures given by Sullivan at the William Alanson White Institute of Psychiatry in New York City during the academic year 1947-1948, and from conversations between Sullivan and the writer.

2 *Conceptions of Modern Psychiatry* by Harry Stack Sullivan, The William Alanson White Psychiatric Foundation, Washington, D. C., 1947, p. 6.

3 Op. cit., p. 43.

4 Op. cit., p. 44. Sullivan has changed his mind about empathizing comfort before the epoch of childhood, feeling that there is no certain evidence of its existence before then. (Personal communication to the writer)

5 Op. cit., p. 7.

6 Or "syntactic."

7 Op. cit., p. 16.

8 Op. cit., p. 16.

9 Anxiety is always *felt.* Contrary to previous formulations, Sullivan now is convinced it never occurs in the prototaxic mode but that it occurs mainly in the parataxic. (Personal communication to the writer)

10 "Introduction to the Study of Interpersonal Relations" by Harry Stack Sullivan, *Psychiatry*, Vol. I, 1938, p. 123, footnote.

11 *Conceptions of Modern Psychiatry*, pp. 9-10.

12 "The Meaning of Anxiety in Psychiatry and in Life" by Harry Stack Sullivan, *Psychiatry*, Vol. XI, No. 1, 1948, p. 4.

13 "A Theory of Interpersonal Relations and the Evolution of Personality" by Patrick Mullahy, *Psychiatry*, Vol. VIII, No. 2, 1945, p. 191.

14 *Conceptions of Modern Psychiatry*, p. 23.

15 "The Meaning of Anxiety in Psychiatry and in Life," p. 5.

16 *Conceptions of Modern Psychiatry*, p. 8.

17 Op. cit., p. 18.

18 Op. cit., pp. 18-19.

19 Op. cit., p. 20.

20 Op. cit., pp. 20-21.

21 Op. cit., p. 23.

22 "Towards a Psychiatry of Peoples" by Harry Stack Sullivan, *Psychiatry*, Vol. XI, pp. 105-116.

23 *Conceptions of Modern Psychiatry*, p. 28.

24 Op. cit., p. 27.

25 Op. cit., pp. 28-29.

26 Op. cit., p. 31.

27 Op. cit., p. 24.

28 "Towards a Psychiatry of Peoples," p. 107.

29 *Conceptions of Modern Psychiatry*, foreword, pp. v-vi.

30 Personal communication to the writer.

CHAPTER ELEVEN

1 Compare "Psychoanalysis Comes of Age" by Franz Alexander, *The Psychoanalytic Quarterly*, Vol. VII, 1938, pp. 299-306.

2 "Towards a Psychiatry of Peoples" by Harry Stack Sullivan.

3 *A General Introduction* by Sigmund Freud, p. 343.

4 *The Structure and Meaning of Psychoanalysis* by Healy, Bronner and Bowers, p. 193.

5 See, for example, "The Categories of Naturalism" by William R. Dennis in *Naturalism and the Human Spirit,* edited by Yervant H. Krikorian, Columbia University Press, New York, 1944.

6 Compare "Psycho-Analysis and Anthropology" by Geza Roheim in *Psycho-Analysis Today,* edited by Sandor Lorand, Covici-Friede, New York, 1933, as an example of Freudian psychoanalytic anthropology.

7 *Three Essays on Sex and Marriage* by Westermarck, p. 121. Freud, however, summarily dismisses ethnological findings which contradict his theories. See *Moses and Monotheism,* pp. 207-208. Compare *The Sexual Life of Savages* by Bronislaw Malinowski, Halcyon House, New York, 1929.

8 We owe this observation to Dr. Harry Bone of New York City.

9 "The psychoanalyst must never forget that *the final aim of psychoanalysis is the personal freedom and moral independence of the patient." The Theory of Psychoanalysis* by Jung, p. 109.

10 *The Psychology of the Spirit* by C. G. Jung, translated by Hildegard Nagel, published by The Analytical Psychology Club of New York, Incorporated, 1948, p. 7.

11 Compare the discussion of neuroses and anxiety in *The Neurotic Personality of Our Time* by Horney.

12 In his later years, we are told, Freud used to put a copy of Schopenhauer or Nietzsche in his pocket when he went on vacation. Jung, who calls himself an analytical psychologist rather than a psychoanalyst, of course has immense literary and philosophical erudition.

13 *Escape From Freedom* by Fromm, p. 278.

14 *Man For Himself* by Fromm, p. 60.

BIBLIOGRAPHY

SIGMUND FREUD

The Basic Writings of Sigmund Freud, edited by A. A. Brill, The Modern Library, Random House, Inc., New York, 1938.

An Autobiographical Study, authorized translation by James Strachey, The Hogarth Press, Ltd. and The Institute of Psycho-Analysis, London, 1936.

A General Introduction to Psychoanalysis, authorized English translation with a preface by Ernest Jones and G. Stanley Hall, Garden City Publishing Co., Garden City, New York, 1943.

Beyond The Pleasure Principle, The Hogarth Press, Ltd. and The Institute of Psycho-Analysis, London, 1942.

Collected Papers, The Hogarth Press, Ltd. and The Institute of Psycho-Analysis, London, 1924.

New Introductory Lectures on Psychoanalysis, translated by J. H. Sprott, W. W. Norton & Company, Inc., New York, 1933.

The Problem of Anxiety, The Psycho-Analytic Quarterly Press and W. W. Norton & Company, Inc., New York, 1936.

Civilization And Its Discontents, translated by Joan Riviere, The Hogarth Press, Ltd. and The Institute of Psycho-Analysis, London, 1939.

Three Contributions To The Theory of Sex, authorized translation by A. A. Brill with introduction by James J. Putnam, Nervous and Mental Disease Publishing Co., New York and Washington, D. C., 1920.

"The Origin and Development of Psychoanalysis," *The American Journal of Psychology,* Vol. XXI, No. 2, April, 1910.

Leonardo da Vinci, A Study in Psychosexuality, authorized translation by A. A. Brill, Random House, New York, 1947.

Moses and Monotheism, translated by Katherine Jones, Alfred A. Knopf, Inc., New York, 1939.

Selected Papers on Hysteria and Other Psychoneuroses, authorized translation by A. A. Brill, Nervous and Mental Disease Monograph Series, No. 4, 1920.

"Analysis Terminable and Interminable," *The International Journal of Psycho-Analysis,* Vol. XVIII, October, 1937.

The Ego and the Id, The Hogarth Press, Ltd. and The Institute of Psycho-Analysis, London, 1935.

Group Psychology and the Analysis of the Ego, authorized translation by James Strachey, Boni and Liveright, New York (no date).

"Libidinal Types," *The Psycho-Analytic Quarterly,* Vol. I, 1932.

Totem and Taboo, authorized translation with an introduction by A. A. Brill (copyright 1918 by Dodd, Mead & Co., Inc., New York), New Republic, Inc., New York, 1927.

The Future of an Illusion, The International Psycho-Analytical Library, No. 15, 1943.

ALFRED ADLER

The Neurotic Constitution, authorized English translation by Bernard Glueck, M.D. and John E. Lind, M.D., Moffatt, Yard and Company, New York, 1917.

A Study of Organ Inferiority and Its Psychical Compensation, authorized translation by Smith Ely Jelliffe, M.D., Nervous and Mental Disease Monograph Series, No. 24, New York, 1917.

Understanding Human Nature, translated by Walter Beran Wolfe, Greenberg: Publisher, Inc., New York, 1927.

Social Interest: A Challenge to Mankind, translated by John Linton and Richard Vaughan, Faber and Faber, Ltd., London, 1938.

The Education of Children, George Allen & Unwin, Ltd., London, 1930.

Problems of Neurosis, with a prefatory essay by F. G. Crookshank, M.D., edited by P. Mainet, Cosmopolitan Book Corp., New York, 1930.

What Life Should Mean To You, Grosset & Dunlap, New York.

CARL G. JUNG

Contributions to Analytical Psychology, translated by H. G. and Cary F. Baynes, Harcourt Brace and Company, New York, 1928.

The Psychology of Dementia Praecox, authorized translation with an introduction by A. A. Brill, Nervous and Mental Disease Monograph Series, No. 3, New York, 1936.

"The Association Method," translated by A. A. Brill, *The American Journal of Psychology,* Vol. XXI, No. 2, April, 1910.

Modern Man In Search Of A Soul, translated by W. S. Dill and Cary F. Baynes, Harcourt, Brace and Company, New York, 1933.

The Psychology of the Unconscious, authorized translation with introduction by Beatrice M. Hinkle, Dodd, Mead and Company, New York, 1927.

The Theory of Psychoanalysis, Nervous and Mental Disease Monograph Series, No. 19, New York, 1915.

"On Psychological Understanding," *Journal of Abnormal and Social Psychology,* 1915.

Psychology and Religion, Yale University Press, New Haven, 1938.

Collected Papers on Analytical Psychology, authorized translation, edited by Dr. Constance E. Long, Balliere, Tindall and Cox, London, 1920.

Psychological Types or the Psychology of Individuation, translated by H. Godwin Baynes, Harcourt, Brace and Company, New York, 1926.

The Integration of the Personality, translated by Stanley M. Dell, Farrar & Rinehart, Inc., New York, 1939.

Two Essays on Analytical Psychology, authorized translation by H. G. and C. F. Baynes, Dodd, Mead and Company, New York, 1928.

The Psychology of the Spirit, translated by Hildegard Nagel, The Analytical Psychology Club of New York Incorporated, 1948.

OTTO RANK

The Trauma of Birth, Harcourt, Brace and Company, New York, and Routledge and Kegan Paul, Ltd., London, 1929.

Art and Artist, translated by Charles Francis Atkinson, Alfred A. Knopf, Inc., New York, 1932.

Will Therapy and Truth and Reality, authorized translation with a preface and introduction by Jessie Taft, Alfred A. Knopf, Inc., New York, 1945.

Beyond Psychology, privately published, 1941.

Modern Education, translated by Mabel E. Moxon, Alfred A. Knopf, Inc., New York, 1932.

The Myth of the Birth of the Hero, authorized translation by Dr. F. Robbins and Dr. Smith Ely Jelliffe, Nervous and Mental Disease Monograph Series, No. 18.

OTTO RANK AND HANNS SACHS

The Significance of Psychoanalysis for the Mental Sciences, authorized English translation by Charles R. Payne, Nervous and Mental Disease Monograph Series, No. 23, 1916.

KAREN HORNEY

New Ways In Psychoanalysis, W. W. Norton & Company, Inc., New York, 1939.

The Neurotic Personality of Our Time, W. W. Norton & Company, Inc., New York, 1937.

Self Analysis, W. W. Norton & Company, Inc., New York, 1942.

Our Inner Conflicts, W. W. Norton & Company, Inc., New York, 1945.

EDITED BY KAREN HORNEY

Are You Considering Psychoanalysis? W. W. Norton & Company, Inc., New York, 1946.

ERICH FROMM

Escape From Freedom, Farrar & Rinehart, Inc., New York, 1941.

Man For Himself, Rinehart & Company, Inc., New York, 1947.

"Sex and Character; The Kinsey Report Viewed From The Standpoint of Psychoanalysis," *About The Kinsey Report,* The New American Library (Signet Books), New York, 1948.

"The Oedipus Complex and the Oedipus Myth," *The Family: Its Function and Destiny,* Vol. V, The Science of Culture Series, edited by Dr. Ruth Nanda Anshen, Harper & Brothers, New York, autumn, 1948.

HARRY STACK SULLIVAN

Conceptions of Modern Psychiatry, The William Alanson White
Psychiatric Foundation, Washington, D. C., 1947.
"Introduction to the Study of Interpersonal Relations," *Psychiatry,*
Vol. I, 1938.
"The Meaning of Anxiety in Psychiatry and in Life," *Psychiatry,*
Vol. XI, No. 1, 1948.
"Towards A Psychiatry of Peoples," *Psychiatry,* Vol. XI, 1948.

OTHER REFERENCES

KARL ABRAHAM
Selected Papers on Psychoanalysis, translated by Douglas Bryan
and Alix Strachey, The Hogarth Press and The Institute of
Psycho-Analysis, London.
Dreams and Myths, translated by W. A. White, Nervous and
Mental Disease Monograph Series, No. 15, New York, 1913.

FRANZ ALEXANDER
"Psychoanalysis Comes of Age," *The Psychoanalytic Quarterly,*
Vol. VII, 1938.
Our Age of Unreason, Lippincott Co., New York, 1942.

FRANZ ALEXANDER, THOMAS MORTON FRENCH, AND OTHERS
Psychoanalytic Therapy: Principles and Application, The Ronald
Press Co., New York, 1946.

DAVID B. BARRON
"A Study In Symbolism," *The Psychoanalytic Review,* Vol.
XXXIV, No. 4, October, 1947.

EDMUND BERGLER
"Psychoanalysis of Writers and of Literary Production," *Psycho-
analysis and the Social Sciences,* An Annual, Vol. I, International
Universities Press, New York, 1947.

MARJORIE BRIERLEY
"Affects in Theory and Practice," *The International Journal of
Psycho-Analysis,* Vol. XVIII, October, 1937.

ERNST CASSIRER
*An Essay on Man: An Introduction to a Philosophy of Human
Culture,* Yale University Press, New Haven, 1944.

WILLIAM R. DENNIS
"The Categories of Naturalism," *Naturalism and the Human*

Spirit, edited by Yervant H. Krikorian, Columbia University Press, New York, 1944.

J. C. FLUGEL
The Psycho-Analytic Study of the Family, The International Psycho-Analytical Library, No. 3, London, 1921.

WILLIAM HEALY, AUGUSTA F. BRONNER, AND ANNA MAY BOWERS
The Structure and Meaning of Psychoanalysis, Alfred A. Knopf, Inc., New York, 1930.

FREDERICK F. HOFFMAN
Freudianism and the Literary Mind, Louisiana State University Press, Baton Rouge, La., 1945.

JOLAN JACOBI
The Psychology of Jung, translated by K. W. Bash, with a foreword by C. G. Jung, Yale University Press, New Haven, 1943.

ERNEST JONES
Papers on Psychoanalysis, William Ward & Company, 1923.
Essays in Applied Psychoanalysis, The International Psycho-Analytical Library, No. 5, London, 1923.

MATTHEW JOSEPHSON
Stendhal, Doubleday & Co., Inc., New York, 1946.

ABRAM KARDINER
The Individual and his Society, Columbia University Press, New York, 1939.
The Psychological Frontiers of Society, Columbia University Press, New York, 1945.

BRONISLAW MALINOWSKI
The Sexual Life of Savages, Halcyon House, New York, 1929.

CAVENDISH MAXON
"Psychoanalytic Study of the Christian Creed," *International Journal of Psycho-Analysis,* Vol. II.

KARL A. MENNINGER
Man Against Himself, Harcourt, Brace and Company, New York, 1938.

PATRICK MULLAHY
"A Theory of Interpersonal Relations and the Evolution of Personality," *Psychiatry,* Vol. VIII, No. 2, 1945.

CLARENCE P. OBERNDORF
"Psychoanalysis in Literature and its Therapeutic Value," *Psycho-*

538 OEDIPUS MYTH AND COMPLEX

analysis and the Social Sciences, An Annual, Vol. I, International Universities Press, New York, 1947.

PLATO
The Republic, translated with introduction and notes by Francis Macdonald Cornford, Oxford University Press, New York, 1945.

HELEN WALKER PUNER
Freud, His Life and His Mind, Howell, Soskin & Company, Inc., New York, 1947.

THEODOR REIK
From Thirty Years With Freud, translated by Richard Winston, Farrar & Rinehart, Inc., New York, 1940.

The Psychological Problems of Religion-Ritual, translated by Douglas Bryan, with a preface by Sigmund Freud, Farrar, Straus and Company, Inc., New York, 1946.

GEZA ROHEIM
"Psycho-Analysis and Anthropology," *Psycho-Analysis Today,* edited by Sandor Lorand, Covici-Friede, New York, 1933.

HANNS SACHS
Freud, Master and Friend, Harvard University Press, Cambridge, Mass., 1944.

CLARA THOMPSON
"Cultural Pressures in the Psychology of Women," *Psychiatry,* Vol. V, No. 3, 1942.

"Penis Envy in Women," *Psychiatry,* Vol. VI, No. 2, 1943.

EDWARD WESTERMARCK
Three Essays on Sex and Marriage, Macmillan & Co., Ltd., London, 1934.

FRANCES WICKES
The Inner World of Man, Henry Holt & Co., New York, 1938.

FRITZ WITTELS
"Psychoanalysis and Literature," *Psychoanalysis Today,* edited by Sandor Lorand, Covici-Friede, New York, 1933.

ROBERT S. WOODWORTH
Contemporary Schools of Psychology, The Ronald Press Co., New York, 1931.